DATE DUE

JAN 2 5 1999	

James Monroe

GREAT DEBATES IN AMERICAN HISTORY

From the Debates in the British Parliament on the Colonial Stamp Act (1764–1765) to the Debates in Congress at the Close of the Taft Administration (1912–1913)

EDITED BY

MARION MILLS MILLER, Litt.D. (Princeton)

Editor of "The Life and Works of Abraham Lincoln," etc.

IN FOURTEEN VOLUMES

EACH DEALING WITH A SPECIFIC SUBJECT, AND CONTAINING A SPECIAL INTRODUC-
TION BY A DISTINGUISHED AMERICAN STATESMAN OR PUBLICIST

VOLUME TWO

FOREIGN RELATIONS: PART ONE

With an Introduction by WILLIAM JENNINGS BRYAN, LL.D.
Secretary of State

CURRENT LITERATURE PUBLISHING COMPANY
NEW YORK

49512

CONTENTS OF VOLUME TWO

ILLUSTRATIONS IN VOLUME TWO

INTRODUCTION

International Rivalry in Ideals[1]

William Jennings Bryan, LL. D.
Secretary of State

WE have reason to look with some degree of pride upon the achievement of the United States; we contemplate the present with satisfaction and look to the future with hope, and yet we may well remember that we are but building upon the foundations that have been laid for us. We did not create the fertile soil that is the basis of our agricultural greatness; the streams that drain and feed our valleys were not channeled by human hands. We did not fashion the climate that gives us the white cotton belt of the South, the yellow wheat belt of the North, and the central corn belt that joins the two and overlaps them both. We do not gather up the moisture and fix the date of the early and later rains; we did not hide away in the mountains the gold and the silver; we did not store in the earth the deposits of copper and of zinc; we did not create the measures of coal and the beds of iron. All these natural resources, which we have but commenced to develop, are the gift of Him before whom we bow in gratitude to-night.

Nor are we indebted to the Heavenly Father alone, for we have received much from those who are separated from us by the Atlantic. If we have great and flourishing industries we must not forget that every nation in

---

[1] Adapted from a speech delivered in London at the annual banquet of the American Society on Thanksgiving Day, November 26, 1903.

1

Europe has sent us its trained and skilled artisans. If we have made intellectual progress, we must remember that those who crossed the ocean as pioneers brought with them their intelligence and their desire for learning. Even our religion is not of American origin. We laid the foundations of our church in the Holy Land, and those who came in the *Mayflower* and in other ships brought a love of religious liberty. Free speech, which has been developed in our country, and which we prize so much, is not of American origin. I have been profoundly impressed with the part that Englishmen have taken in establishing the right of free speech. Passing through the Bank of England my attention was called to a protest that Admiral Cochrane wrote upon the bank note with which he paid the thousand pounds fine that had been assessed against him. I was interested in that protest because it showed a fearlessness that indicates the possibilities of the race. Let me read what he said: "My health having suffered by long and close confinement, and my oppressors having resolved to deprive me of property or life, I submit to robbery to protect myself from murder in the hope that I shall live to bring the delinquents to justice."

That is the spirit that moves the world! There was a man in prison. He must pay his fine in order to gain his liberty. He believed the action of the court unjust. He knew that if he stayed there he would lose his life and lose the chance for vindication, and yet, as he was going forth from the prison doors, he did not go with bowed head or cringing, but flung his protest in the face of his oppressors and told them he submitted to robbery to protect his life in the hope that, having escaped from their hands, he might bring them to justice. I like that in the Englishman, and during my short knowledge of public affairs I have looked across the ocean and admired the moral courage and the manliness of those Englishmen who have dared to stand out against overwhelming odds and assert their opinions before the world.

We sometimes feel that we have a sort of proprietary interest in the principles of government set forth in the Declaration of Independence. That is a document which we have given to the world, and yet the principles set forth therein were not invented by an American. Thomas Jefferson expressed them in felicitous language and put them into permanent form, but the principles had been known before. The doctrine that all men are created equal, that they are endowed with inalienable rights, that governments were instituted among men to secure these rights, and that they derived their just power from the consent of the governed—this doctrine which stands four square with all the world was not conceived in the United States, it did not spring from the American mind—ay, it did not come so much from any mind as it was an emanation from the heart, and it had been in the hearts of men for ages. Before Columbus turned the prow of his ship toward the west on that eventful voyage, before the Barons wrested Magna Charta from King John—yes, before the Roman legions landed on the shores of this island—ay, before Homer sang—that sentiment had nestled in the heart of man, and nerved him to resist the oppressor. That sentiment was not even of human origin. Our own great Lincoln declared that it was God himself who implanted in every human heart the love of liberty.

Yes, when God created man, He gave him life. He linked to life the love of liberty, and what God hath joined together let no man put asunder. We have received great blessings from God and from all the world, and what is our duty? We cannot make return to those from whom those gifts were received. It is not in our power to make return to the Father above. Nor can we make return to those who have sacrificed so much for our advancement. The child can never make full return to the mother whose life trembled in the balance at its birth, and whose kindness and care guarded it in all the years of infancy. The student cannot make full return to the teacher who awakened the mind and aroused an ambition for a broader intellectual life. The adult cannot make full return to the patriarch whose noble life gave inspiration and incentive. So a generation cannot make return to the generation gone; it must

make its return to the generations to come. Our nation
must discharge its debt not to the dead, but to the
living. How can our country discharge this great debt?
In but one way, and that is by giving to the world
something equal in value to that which it has received
from the world. And what is the greatest gift that
man can bestow upon man? Feed a man and he will
hunger again; give him clothing and his clothing will
wear out, but give him a noble ideal and that ideal
will be with him through every waking hour, lifting
him to a higher plane of life, and giving him a broader
conception of his relations to his fellows.

I know, therefore, of no greater service that my
country can render to the world than to furnish to the
world the highest ideal that the world has known. That
ideal must be so far above us that it will keep us looking
upward all our lives, and so far in advance of us that
we shall never overtake it. I know of no better illustration of an ideal life than the living spring, pouring forth
constantly of that which refreshes and invigorates—no
better illustration of a worthless life than the stagnant
pool which receives contribution from all the land around
and around and gives forth nothing. Our nation must
make a large contribution to the welfare of the world,
and it is no reflection upon those who have gone before
to say that we ought to do better than they have done.
We would not meet the responsibilities of to-day if we
did not build still higher the social structure to which
they devoted their lives.

I visited the Tower of London and saw upon the
wall a strange figure. It was made of swords, ramrods,
and bayonets, and was fashioned into the form of a
flower. Someone had put a card on it and aptly named
it the passion flower—and it has been too often the
international flower. But the world has made progress.
No longer do ambition and avarice furnish a sufficient
excuse for war. The world has made progress, and
to-day you cannot justify bloodshed except in defence
of a right already ascertained, and then only when all
peaceable means have been exhausted. The world has
made progress. We have reached a point where we re-

spect not the man who will die to secure some pecuniary advantages, but the man who will die in defence of his rights. We admire the courage of the man who is willing to die in defence of his rights, but there is yet before us a higher ground. Is he great who will die in defence of his rights? There is yet to come the greater man—the man who will die rather than trespass upon the rights of another. Hail to the nation whatever its name may be that leads the world toward the realization of this higher ideal. I am glad that we now recognize that there is something more powerful than physical force. No one has stated this better than Carlyle. He said that thought was stronger than artillery parks, and at last molded the world like soft clay; that behind thought was love, and that there never was a wise head that had not behind it a generous heart.

The world is coming to understand that armies and navies, however numerous and strong, are impotent to stop thought. Thought inspired by love will yet rule the world. I am glad that there is a national product more valuable than gold or silver, more valuable than cotton or wheat or corn or iron—an ideal. That is a merchandise—if I may call it such—that moves freely from country to country. You cannot vex it with an export tax or hinder it with an import tariff. It is greater than legislators, and rises triumphant over the machinery of government. In the rivalry to present the best ideal to the world, love, not hatred, will control; and I am glad that I can return thanks for what my country has received, thanks for the progress that the world has made, and that I can contemplate with joy the coming of that day when rivalry between nations will be, not to see which can injure the other most, but to show which can hold highest the light that guides the footsteps of the human race to higher ground.

W. J. Bryan

CHAPTER I

The French Alliance

Franco-British War—Opposing Views in Washington's Cabinet as to Proper Relations with France—Washington Issues Proclamation of Neutrality: Controversy Between "Pacificus" [Alexander Hamilton] and "Helvidius" [James Madison] as to Whether the President Encroached on the Powers of Congress.

THE essential object of the French-American treaty of 1778 was "to maintain the liberty, sovereignty, and independence of the United States as well in matters of government as of commerce." In the event of conquest Canada and Bermuda were to belong to the United States, and the West Indies to France. Each party was to fulfill its part of the treaty according to its own power and circumstances, and no after-claim of compensation was to be made on either side, whatever be the cost of the war.

As a result of this treaty events occurred in 1793 which inflamed partisanship to a degree hitherto not attained in the politics of America.

War had broken out between the new republic of France and Great Britain and Holland, and the American people in general were eager to support their former ally and present sister republic. Indeed, many individuals were ready to engage in privateering against the commerce of the enemies of France, regardless of consequences to the United States.

President Washington, however, from his high station, was called upon to view these great events as they might affect his own country, and he felt himself bound to consult the dictates of his judgment rather than the impulse of his feelings. He foresaw that the storm which was gathering in Europe must soon reach the United States, and he was satisfied that the best interests of his country dictated a state of neutrality, which, he was convinced, might be maintained without violation of national faith. Aware of the importance and delicacy of the crisis, he assembled his Cabinet in April for their advice. To them he submitted certain questions with respect to the existing and prospective relations with France.

THE PRESIDENT'S QUESTIONS

1. Shall a proclamation issue for the purpose of preventing interference of the citizens of the United States in the war between France and Great Britain, etc.? Shall it contain a declaration of neutrality or not? What shall it contain?

2. Shall a minister from the republic of France be received?

3. If received, shall it be absolutely or with qualifications; and, if with qualifications, of what kind?

4. Are the United States obliged by good faith to consider the treaties heretofore made with France as applying to the present situation of the parties? may they either renounce them or hold them suspended until the government of France shall be established?

5. If they have the right, is it expedient to do either? and which?

6. If they have an option, would it be a breach of neutrality to consider the treaties in operation?

7. If the treaties are to be considered as now in operation, is the guaranty in the treaty of alliance applicable to a defensive war only, or to a war, either offensive or defensive?

8. Does the war in which France is engaged appear to be offensive or defensive on her part? or of a mixed and equivocal character?

9. If of a mixed and equivocal character, does the guaranty in any event apply to such a war?

10. What is the effect of a guaranty, such as that to be found in the treaty of alliance between the United States and France?

11. Does any article in either of the treaties prevent ships of war, other than privateers, of the powers opposed to France, from coming into the ports of the United States to act as convoys to their own merchantmen? or does it lay any other restraints upon them more than would apply to the ships of war of France?

12. Should the future regent of France send a minister to the United States, ought he to be received?

13. Is it necessary or advisable to call together the two Houses of Congress with a view to the present posture of European affairs? if it is, what should be the particular objects of such call?

These questions were of course communicated confidentially, but they afterwards clandestinely found their way to the public.

The answers of the members of the Cabinet to these questions were requested in writing. On some of them the opinions of the members were unanimous; on others a difference prevailed. All were in favor of issuing a proclamation of neutrality, of receiving a minister from the existing French Government, and against convening Congress. Some of the Cabinet, however, were for receiving the minister with some degree of qualification, from a doubt whether the government of France could be considered as finally settled by the deliberate sense of the nation. The President, however, concluded to receive him in an unqualified manner. As to the clause of guaranty in the treaty of 1778 a difference of opinion also existed in the Cabinet. The Secretaries of the Treasury [Alexander Hamilton] and of War [Henry Knox] considered the cause as applicable only to a *defensive war,* and therefore not binding in a contest commenced by France herself, while the Secretary of State [Thomas Jefferson] and the Attorney-General [Edmund Randolph] thought it unnecessary at that time to decide the question. This divergence of views among the members of the Cabinet served to increase the divisions already existing among the people.

A proclamation was issued by the President on the 22nd of April, declaring it to be the duty and interest of the United States to pursue a conduct friendly and impartial toward the belligerent powers of Europe, and that it was their disposition to observe such conduct, warning the citizens to avoid all acts tending to contravene such a disposition, and declaring that those who might render themselves liable to punishment by committing, aiding, or abetting hostilities against any of the belligerents, or by carrying contraband of war, would not receive the protection of the United States.

"PACIFICUS" (*Hamilton*) vs. "HELVIDIUS" (*Madison*)

ON THE PRESIDENT'S PROCLAMATION OF NEUTRALITY

The proclamation created a heated debate in the press of the country. Alexander Hamilton wrote a series of articles in defence of the proclamation signed "Pacificus," which were replied to by James Madison in a series signed "Helvidius."

ARGUMENT OF HAMILTON

I

Hamilton first stated the objections to the proclamation:

1. That the proclamation was without authority.
2. That it was contrary to our treaties with France.
3. That it was contrary to the gratitude which is due from this to that country for the succors afforded to us in our own revolution.
4. That it was out of time and unnecessary.

Preliminary to answering the first objection, Hamilton stated the nature and design of a proclamation of neutrality. This, he said, was to announce to the belligerent powers that the country was at peace with both belligerents and without treaty obligations to become an *associate in the war* with either party, and therefore that it would remain strictly *neutral,* and to warn the citizens of the country where the proclamation issued to abstain from acts violating this neutrality under penalty of punishment by the law of the land of which the "law of nations" (*jus gentium*) is a part. Such a proclamation to the citizens is necessary to relieve the nation from responsibility for these acts (Vattel, Book III, Chapter 7, Section 113).

The first question was: Had the executive department a constitutional right to make this proclamation?

Hamilton affirmed that it had, the Constitution designating it as the treaty-making, and, under the general power of executing all laws, the treaty-executing power. He said that there were two and only two exceptions to the executive powers of the President as laid down in the Constitution: the Senate must coöperate with the President in treaty-making, and declarations of war and grants of letters of marque and reprisal must be made by Congress. A declaration of neutrality, he argued, did not, however, fall under either of these exceptions. It is the duty of the President to preserve peace until war is declared, and to exercise this duty he must necessarily construe treaty obligations.

Those who object to the proclamation will readily admit that it is the right and duty of the executive to interpret those articles of our treaties which give to France particular privileges, in order to the enforcement of them: but the necessary consequence of this is that the executive must judge what are their proper limits; what rights are given to other nations by our contracts with them; what rights the law of nature and nations gives and our treaties permit, in respect to those countries with which we have none; in fine, what are the reciprocal rights and obligations of the United States, and of all and each of the powers at war.

In the case of France, if there had been a treaty of alliance, *offensive* and defensive, between the United States and that country, the unqualified acknowledgment of the new government would have put the United States in a condition to become an associate in the war with France, and would have laid the legislature under an obligation, if required, and there was otherwise no valid excuse, of exercising its power of declaring war.

This serves as an example of the right of the executive, in certain cases, to determine the condition of the nation, though it may, in its consequences, affect the exercise of the power of the legislature to declare war. Nevertheless, the executive cannot thereby control the exercise of that power. The legislature is still free to perform its duties, according to its own sense of them; though the executive, in the exercise of its constitutional powers, may establish an antecedent state of things, which ought to weigh in the legislative decisions.

The division of the executive power in the Constitution creates a *concurrent* authority in the cases to which it relates.

Hence treaties can be made only by the President and Senate jointly; but their activity may be continued or suspended by the President alone.

No objection has been made to the President's having acknowledged the republic of France by the reception of its minister without having consulted the Senate; though that body is connected with him in the making of treaties, and though the consequence of his act of reception is to give operation to those heretofore made with that country. But he is censured for having declared the United States to be in a state of peace and neutrality, with regard to the powers at war; because the right of *changing* that state, and *declaring war,* belongs to the legislature.

It deserves to be remarked that, as the participation of the Senate in the making of treaties and the power of the legislature to declare war are exceptions out of the general "executive power" vested in the President, they are to be construed strictly, and ought to be extended no further than is essential to their execution.

While, therefore, the legislature can alone declare war, can alone actually transfer the nation from a state of peace to a state of hostility, it belongs to the "executive power" to do whatever *else* the law of nations, coöperating with the treaties of the country, enjoins in the intercourse of the United States with foreign powers.

In order to the observance of that conduct which the laws of nations, combined with our treaties, prescribed to this country, in reference to the present war in Europe, it was necessary for the President to judge for himself whether there was anything in our treaties incompatible with an adherence to neutrality. Having decided that there was not, he had a right, and, if in his opinion the interest of the nation required it, it was his duty, as executor of the laws, to proclaim the neutrality of the nation, to exhort all persons to observe it, and to warn them of the penalties which would attend its non-observance.

The proclamation has been represented as enacting some new law. This is a view of it entirely erroneous. It only proclaims a *fact,* with regard to the *existing state* of the nation; informs the citizens of what the laws previously established require of them in that state, and notifies them that these laws will be put in execution against the infractors of them.

II

The second and principal objection to the proclamation, namely, that it is inconsistent with the treaties between the United States and France, will now be examined.

Referring to Vattel, Book III, Chapter 6, Section 101, Hamilton said that those treaty obligations with a nation made prior to the existing quarrel between that nation and a third nation could be fulfilled without violating the law of neutrality, even though these were to furnish *determinate* succors of ships or troops in case of war, but that succors *not stipulated* in the treaty would be such a violation.

He conceded that execution of the clause of guaranty in the eleventh article of our treaty with France would engage us with our whole force as an *auxiliary* of France in the present war.

It becomes necessary, therefore, to examine whether the United States would have a valid justification for not complying with it in case of their being called upon for that purpose by France.

The alliance between the United States and France is of the defensive kind. The words of that article are as follows: "The essential and direct end of the present defensive alliance is to maintain effectually the liberty, sovereignty, and independence, absolute and unlimited, of the United States, as well in matters of government as of commerce."

The leading character then of our alliance with France being defensive, it will follow that the meaning, obligation, and force of every stipulation in the treaty must be tested by the principles of such an alliance; unless in any instance terms have been used which clearly and unequivocally denoted a different intent.

The principal question consequently is: what is the nature and effect of a defensive alliance? When does the *casus fœderis* (state of alliance) take place in relation to it?

Reason, the concurring opinions of writers, and the practice of nations will all answer: "When either of the allies is *attacked,* when war *is made upon him,* not when he *makes war upon another:*" in other words, the stipulated assistance is to be given "when our ally is engaged in a defensive, not when he is engaged in an offensive war." This obligation to assist only in a defensive war constitutes the essential difference between an alliance which is merely defensive, and one which is both offensive and defensive. In the latter case there is an obligation to coöperate as well when the war, on the part of our ally, is of the latter as when it is of the former description. To affirm, therefore, that the United States are bound to assist France in the war in which she is at present engaged will be to convert our treaty with her into an alliance offensive and defensive, contrary to the express declaration of the instrument itself.

Now the war in question is an *offensive* war on the part of France, in that she first declared and began the war.

Upon this point there is apt to be some incorrectness of ideas. Those who have not examined subjects of such a nature are led to imagine that the party which commits the first injury, or gives the first provocations, is on the offensive side, though hostilities are actually begun by the other party.

But the cause or the occasion of the war, and the war itself, are things entirely distinct. It is the commencement of the war itself which decides the question whether it be offensive or defensive. All writers on the laws of nations agree in this doctrine; but it is most accurately laid down in the following extracts from Burlemaqui (Vol. II, Book IV, Chap. III, Secs. 4, 5):

"Neither are we to believe (says he) that he who first injures another begins by that an offensive war, and that the other who demands the satisfaction for the injury received is always on the defensive. There are a great many unjust acts which may kindle a war, and which, however, are not the war itself."

We must therefore affirm, in general, that the first who takes up arms, whether justly or unjustly, commences an offensive war; and he who opposes him, whether with or without reason, begins a defensive war.

France, then, being on the offensive in the present war, and our alliance with her being defensive only, it follows that the *casus fœderis*, or condition of our guaranty, cannot take place; and that the United States are free to refuse a performance of that guaranty, if demanded.

III

A third objection to the proclamation is that it is inconsistent with the gratitude due to France for the services rendered to us in our revolution.

Those who make this objection disavow, at the same time, all intention to maintain the position that the United States ought to take part in the war. They profess to be friends to our remaining at peace. What, then, do they mean by the objection?

If it be no breach of gratitude to refrain from joining France in the war, how can it be a breach of gratitude to declare that such is our disposition and intention?

Faith and justice between nations are virtues of a nature the most necessary and sacred. They cannot be too strongly inculcated, nor too highly respected. Their obligations are absolute, their utility unquestionable; they relate to objects which, with probity and sincerity, generally admit of being brought within clear and intelligible rules.

But the same cannot be said of gratitude. It is not very often that between nations it can be pronounced with certainty that there exists a solid foundation for the sentiment; and how far it can justifiably be permitted to operate is always a question of still greater difficulty.

The basis of gratitude is a benefit received or intended, which there was no right to claim, originating in a regard to the interest or advantage of the party on whom the benefit is, or is meant to be, conferred. If a service is rendered from views relative to the immediate interest of the party who performs it, and is productive of reciprocal advantages, there seems scarcely in such a case to be an adequate basis for a sentiment like that of gratitude. The effect at least would be wholly disproportioned to the cause if such a service ought to beget more than a disposition to render in turn a correspondent good office, founded on mutual interest and reciprocal advantage. But gratitude would require much more than this; it would exact to a certain extent even a sacrifice of the interest of the party obliged to the service or benefit of the one by whom the obligation had been conferred.

Between individuals acts of gratitude not unfrequently occur. But among nations they perhaps never occur. It may be affirmed, as a general principle, that the predominant motive of good offices from one nation to another is the interest or advantage of the nation which performs them.

Indeed, the rule of morality in this respect is not precisely the same between nations as between individuals. The duty of making its own welfare the guide of its actions is much stronger upon the former than upon the latter; in proportion to the greater magnitude and importance of national compared with individual happiness, and to the greater permanency of the effect of national than of individual conduct. Existing millions, and for the most part future generations, are concerned in the present measures of a government; while the consequences of the private actions of an individual ordinarily terminate with himself or are circumscribed within a narrow compass. Rulers are only trustees for the happiness and interest of their nation, and cannot, consistently with their trust, follow the suggestions of kindness or humanity toward others to the prejudice of their constituents.

It is not here meant to recommend a policy absolutely selfish in nations; but to show that a policy regulated by their own interest, as far as justice and good faith permit, is and ought to be their prevailing one; and that either to ascribe to them a different principle of action or to deduce, from the supposition of it, arguments for a self-denying and self-sacrificing gratitude on the part of a nation, which may have received from another good offices, is to misrepresent or misconceive what usually are, and ought to be, the springs of national conduct.

Mr. Hamilton then examined the case of France's aid to the United States to see if it was *disinterested,* and therefore calling for gratitude on our part.

The dismemberment of this country from Great Britain was an obvious and a very important interest of France. It cannot be doubted that it was both the determining motive and an adequate compensation for the assistance afforded to us.

The inference from these facts is not obscure. Aid and co-operation, founded upon a great interest, pursued and obtained by a party rendering them, is not a proper stock upon which to engraft that enthusiastic gratitude which is claimed from us by those who love France more than the United States.

This view of the subject, extorted by the extravagancy of such a claim, is not meant to disparage the just pretensions of France to our good-will and acknowledgment of the favor.

But these sentiments are satisfied on the part of our nation when they produce a cordial disposition to render all good and friendly offices which can be rendered without prejudice to its own solid and permanent interests.

To ask of a nation so situated as we are to make a sacrifice of substantial interest; to expose itself to the jealousy, ill-will, or resentment of the rest of the world; to hazard, in an eminent degree, its own safety, would be to ask more than the nature of the case demands, more than the fundamental maxims of society authorize, more than the dictates of sound reason justify.

A question has arisen with regard to the proper object of that gratitude which is so much insisted upon: whether it be the unfortunate prince by whom the assistance received was given; or the nation of whom he was the chief or the organ? It is extremely interesting to the national justice to form right conceptions on this point.

The arguments which support the latter idea are as follows:

"Louis XVI was but the constitutional agent of the French people. He acted for and on behalf of the nation; it was with their money and their blood he supported our cause. It is to them, therefore, not to him, that our obligations are due.

Louis XVI, in taking our part, was no doubt actuated by state policy. An absolute prince could not love liberty. But the people of France patronized our cause with zeal, from sympathy in its object. The people, therefore, not its monarch, are entitled to our sympathy.''

This reasoning may be ingenious; but it is not founded in nature or fact.

Louis XVI, though no more than the constitutional agent of the nation, had at the time the sole power of managing its affairs, the legal right of directing its will and its force. It belonged to him to assist us, or not, without consulting the nation; and he did assist without such consultation. His will alone was active; that of the nation passive. If there was kindness in the decision, demanding a return of good-will, it was the kindness of Louis XVI—his heart was the depository of the sentiment.

But Louis XVI, it is said, acted from reasons of state, without regard to our cause; while the people of France patronized it with zeal and attachment.

With regard to the individual good wishes of the citizens of France, as they did not produce the services rendered to us as a nation, they can be no foundation for national gratitude. They can only call for a reciprocation of individual good wishes. They cannot form the basis of public obligation.

Our cause had also numerous friends in other countries; even in that with which we were at war. Conducted with prudence, moderation, justice, and humanity, it may be said to have been a popular cause among mankind, conciliating the countenance of princes and the affection of nations.

The dispositions of the individual citizens of France can therefore in no sense be urged as constituting a peculiar claim to our gratitude. As far as there is foundation for it it must be referred to the services rendered to us; and, in the first instance, to the unfortunate monarch that rendered them. This is the conclusion of nature and reason.

IV

The remaining objection to the proclamation of neutrality is that it was out of time and unnecessary.

To give color to this objection it is asked, why did not the proclamation appear when the war commenced with Austria and Prussia? Why was it forborne till Great Britain, Holland, and Spain became engaged? Why did not the Government wait till the arrival at Philadelphia of the minister of the French republic? Why did it volunteer a declaration not required of it by any of the belligerent parties?

Austria and Prussia are not maritime powers. Contraventions of neutrality as against them were not likely to take place to any extent, or in a shape that would attract their notice. It would therefore have been useless, if not ridiculous, to have made a formal declaration on the subject while they were the only parties opposed to France.

But the reverse of this is the case with regard to Spain, Holland, and England. These are all commercial and maritime nations. It was to be expected that their attentions would be immediately drawn toward the United States with sensibility, and even with jealousy. It was to be feared that some of our citizens might be tempted by the prospect of gain to go into measures which would injure them and hazard the peace of the country. Attacks by some of these powers upon the possessions of France in America were to be looked for as a matter of course. While the views of the United States, as to that particular, were problematical, they would naturally consider us as a power that might become their enemy. This they would have been the more apt to do on account of those public demonstrations of attachment to the cause of France of which there has been so prodigal a display.

It was therefore of great importance that our own citizens should understand as soon as possible the opinions which the Government entertained of the nature of our relations to the warring parties, and of the propriety or expediency of our taking a side or remaining neuter. The arrangements of our merchants could not but be very differently affected by the one hypothesis or the other; and it would necessarily have been very detrimental and perplexing to them to have been left in uncertainty.

The idea of its having been incumbent on the Government to delay the measure for the arrival of the minister of the French republic is as absurd as it is humiliating. Did the executive stand in need of the logic of a foreign agent to enlighten it as to the duties or interests of the nation? Or was it bound to ask his consent to a step which appeared to itself consistent with the former and conducive to the latter?

The sense of our treaties was to be learned from the instruments themselves. It was not difficult to pronounce beforehand that we had a greater interest in the preservation of peace than in any advantages with which France might tempt our participation in the war.

V

There has been an additional criticism, several times repeated, which may deserve a moment's attention. It has been urged that the proclamation ought to have contained some reference to our treaties; and that the generality of the promise to observe a conduct *friendly* and *impartial* toward the belligerent powers ought to have been qualified with expressions equivalent to these, *"as far as may consist with the treaties of the United States."*

The insertion of such a clause would have entirely defeated the object of a proclamation by rendering the intention of the Government equivocal. That object was to assure the powers at war and our own citizens that, in the opinion of the executive, it was consistent with the duty and interest of the nation to observe neutrality, and that it was intended to pursue a conduct corresponding with that opinion. Words equivalent to those contended for would have rendered the other part of the declaration nugatory, *by leaving it uncertain whether the executive did or did not believe a state of neutrality to be consistent with our treaties.* Neither foreign powers nor our own citizens would have been able to have drawn any conclusion from the proclamation; and both would have had a right to consider it as a mere equivocation.

By not inserting any such ambiguous expressions, the proclamation was susceptible of an intelligible and proper construction. While it denoted on the other hand that, in the judgment of the executive, there was nothing in our treaties obliging us *to become a party in the war;* it left it to be expected, on the other, that all stipulations compatible with neutrality, according to the laws and usages of nations, would be enforced. It follows that the proclamation was, in this particular, exactly what it ought to have been.

ARGUMENT OF MADISON

Madison began his reply by justifying his entrance into a controversy with one who was "despised by the steady friends" of "our republican Government and the French Revolution" on the ground that it was necessary to expose "Pacificus's" insidious presentation of "principles which strike at the vitals of the Constitution" under color of "vindicating an important public act of a chief magistrate who enjoys the confidence and love of his country."

For himself "Helvidius" declared that he was a

"friend of the Constitution," a lover of peace, and one who deeply respected the President.

Madison then proceeded to attack the arguments of "Pacificus."

The basis of his reasoning is the extraordinary doctrine that the powers of making war and treaties are in their nature *executive;* and therefore comprehended in the general grant of executive power, where not especially and strictly excepted out of the grant.

If there be any countenance to this position it must be found either, first, in the writers of authority on public law; or, 2d, in the quality and operation of the powers to make war and treaties; or, 3d, in the Constitution of the United States.

1. All writers on international law, particularly Wolsius, Burlemaqui, and Vattel, speak of the powers to declare war, to conclude peace, and to form alliances as among the highest acts of the sovereignty, of which the legislative power must at least be an integral and preëminent part.

2. The natural province of the executive magistrate is to execute laws, as that of the legislature is to make laws. All his acts, therefore, properly executive, must presuppose the existence of the laws to be executed. A treaty is not an execution of laws: it does not presuppose the existence of laws. It is, on the contrary, to have itself the force of a *law,* and to be carried into *execution,* like all *other laws,* by the *executive magistrate.* To say, then, that the power of making treaties, which are confessedly laws, belongs naturally to the department which is to execute laws is to say that the executive department naturally includes a legislative power. In theory this is an absurdity—in practice a tyranny.

The power to declare war is subject to similar reasoning. A declaration that there shall be war is not an execution of laws: it does not suppose preëxisting laws to be executed: it is not, in any respect, an act merely executive. It is, on the contrary, one of the most deliberate acts that can be performed; and when performed has the effect of *repealing* all the *laws* operating in a state of peace, so far as they are inconsistent with a state of war; and of *enacting, as a rule for the executive,* a *new code* adapted to the relation between the society and its foreign enemy. In like manner, a conclusion of peace *annuls* all the *laws* peculiar to a state of war, and *revives* the general *laws* incident to a state of peace.

These remarks will be strengthened by adding that treaties, particularly treaties of peace, have sometimes the effect of changing not only the external laws of the society, but operate also on the internal code, which is purely municipal, and to which the legislative authority of the country is of itself competent and complete.

From this view of the subject it must be evident that, although the executive may be a convenient organ of preliminary communications with foreign governments on the subjects of treaty or war: and the proper agent for carrying into execution the final determinations of the competent authority; yet it can have no pretensions, from the nature of the powers in question compared with the nature of the executive trust, to that essential agency which gives validity to such determinations.

It must be further evident that, if these powers be not in their nature purely legislative, they partake so much more of that than of any other quality that, under a constitution leaving them to result to their most natural department, the legislature would be without a rival in its claim.

Another important inference to be noted is that, the powers of making war and treaty being substantially of a legislative, not an executive, nature, the rule of interpreting exceptions strictly must *narrow*, instead of enlarging, executive pretensions on those subjects.

3. The Constitution does not explicitly give the President power to make war and peace. On the contrary this power is expressly lodged in Congress, and, since the Constitution was framed with the specific purpose of separating the three branches of government, the spirit of that instrument, as well as the letter, is against the use of such power by the executive.

The power of treaties is vested jointly in the President and in the Senate, which is a branch of the legislature. From this arrangement merely, there can be no inference that would necessarily exclude the power from the executive class, since the Senate is joined with the President in another power, that of appointing to offices, which, as far as relates to executive offices at least, is considered as of an executive nature. Yet, on the other hand, there are sufficient indications that the power of treaties is regarded by the Constitution as materially different from mere executive power, and as having more affinity to the legislative than to the executive character.

One circumstance indicating this is the constitutional regulation under which the Senate give their consent in the case of treaties. In all other cases the consent of the body is expressed by a majority of voices. In this particular case a concurrence of *two-thirds* at least is made necessary as a substitute or compensation for the other branch of the national legislature, which, on certain occasions, could not be conveniently a party to the transaction.

But the conclusive circumstance is that treaties, when formed according to the constitutional mode, are confessedly to have the force and operation of *laws,* and are to be a rule for the courts in controversies between man and man as much as any *other laws.* They are even emphatically declared by the Constitution to be "the supreme law of the land."

So far the argument from the Constitution is precisely in opposition to the doctrine. As little will be gained in its favor from a comparison of the two powers with those particularly vested in the President alone.

The President shall be commander-in-chief of the army and navy of the United States, and of the militia when called into the actual service of the United States.

There can be no relation worth examining between this power and the general power of making treaties. And instead of being analogous to the power of declaring war it affords a striking illustration of the incompatibility of the two powers in the same hands. Those who are to *conduct a war* cannot, in the nature of things, be proper or safe judges, whether a *war ought* to be *commenced, continued* or *concluded.* They are barred from the latter functions by a great principle in free government, analogous to that which separates the sword from the purse, or the power of executing from the power of enacting laws.

"He shall take care that the laws shall be faithfully executed, and shall commission all officers of the United States." To see the laws faithfully executed constitutes the essence of the executive authority. But what relation has it to the power of making treaties and war, that is, of determining what the *laws shall be* with regard to other nations? No other certainly than what subsists between the powers of executing and enacting laws, no other consequently than what forbids a coalition of the powers in the same department.

Thus it appears that by whatever standard we try this doctrine it must be condemned as no less vicious in theory than it would be dangerous in practice. It is countenanced neither by the writers on law, nor by the nature of the powers themselves,

nor by any general arrangement or particular expressions or
plausible analogies to be found in the Constitution.

Whence then can the writer have borrowed it?

There is but one answer to the question.

The power of making treaties and the power of declaring
war are *royal prerogatives* in the *British Government,* and are
accordingly treated as *executive prerogatives* by *British commentators.*

Madison then shrewdly quoted a passage from one
of Hamilton's letters in "The Federalist" (No. 75) as
contradictory of the position taken by "Pacificus." It
was a "secret of Punch" who "Pacificus" was, but
Madison, using an opportunity which is unique in the
annals of debate, assumed that "Pacificus" and Hamilton were different persons, and confuted the one by the
other.

This number of "The Federalist" (see Vol. I, page
401), expressly refuted the general idea that treaty-
making was an executive power, and showed that it was
a distinct department of government, the legislature
having part in it because of the operation of treaties as
laws, and the executive, because these treaties were to
be enforced.

"However true it may be" (says "Pacificus") "that the
right of the legislature to declare war *includes the right of judging* whether the legislature be under obligations to make war or
not, it will not follow that the executive is *in any case* excluded
from a *similar right* of judging in the execution of its own functions."

A material error of the writer in this application of his doctrine lies in his shrinking from its regular consequences. Had
he stuck to his principle in its full extent, and reasoned from it
without restraint, he would only have had to defend himself
against his opponents. By yielding the great point that the right
to declare war, *though to be taken strictly,* includes the right to
judge whether the nation be under obligations to make war or
not, he is compelled to defend his argument not only against
others, but against himself also. Observe how he struggles in his
own toils.

He had before admitted that the right to declare war is vested
in the legislature. He here admits that the right to declare war

includes the right to judge whether the United States be obliged to declare war or not. Can the inference be avoided that the executive, instead of having a similar right to judge, is as much excluded from the right to judge as from the right to declare?

Whatever difficulties may arise in defining the executive authority in particular cases there can be none in deciding on an authority clearly placed by the Constitution in another department. In this case the Constitution has decided what shall *not* be deemed an executive authority; though it may not have clearly decided in every case what shall be so deemed. The declaring of war is expressly made a legislative function. The judging of the obligations to make war is admitted to be included as a legislative function. Whenever, then, a question occurs whether war shall be declared or whether public stipulations require it, the question necessarily belongs to the department to which those functions belong—and no other department can be *in the execution of its proper functions* if it should undertake to decide such a question.

There can be no refuge against this conclusion, but in the pretext of a *concurrent* right in both departments to judge of the obligations to declare war; and this must be intended by the writer when he says, "It will not follow that the executive is excluded *in any case* from a *similar right* of judging," etc.

As this is the ground on which the ultimate defence is to be made, and which must either be maintained or the works erected on it demolished, it will be proper to give its strength a fair trial.

It has been seen that the idea of a *concurrent* right is at variance with other ideas advanced or admitted by the writer. Laying aside, for the present, that consideration, it seems impossible to avoid concluding that, if the executive, as such, has a concurrent right with the legislature to judge of obligations to declare war, and the right to judge be essentially included in the right to declare, it must have the same concurrent right to declare as it has to judge; and, by another analogy, the same right to judge of other causes of war as of the particular cause found in a public stipulation. So that, whenever the executive, *in the course of its functions*, shall meet with these cases, it must either infer an equal authority in all or acknowledge its want of authority in any.

A concurrent authority in two independent departments, to perform the same function with respect to the same thing, would be as awkward in practice as it is unnatural in theory.

If the legislature and executive have both a right to judge of the obligations to make war or not, it must sometimes happen, though not at present, that they will judge differently. The executive may proceed to consider the question to-day; may determine that the United States are not bound to take part in a war, and in the *execution of its functions* proclaim that determination to all the world. To-morrow the legislature may follow in the consideration of the same subject; may determine that the obligations impose war on the United States, and, *in the execution of its functions*, enter into a *constitutional declaration*, expressly contradicting the *constitutional proclamation*.

In what light does this present the Constitution to the people who established it? In what light would it present to the world a nation thus speaking, through two different organs, equally constitutional and authentic, two opposite languages, on the same subject, and under the same existing circumstances?

But it is not with the legislative rights alone that this doctrine interferes. The rights of the judiciary may be equally invaded. For it is clear that if a right declared by the Constitution to be legislative, and actually vested by it in the legislature, leaves, notwithstanding, a similar right in the executive, whenever a case for exercising it occurs, *in the course of its functions;* a right declared to be judiciary and vested in that department may, on the same principles, be assumed and exercised by the executive *in the course of its functions;* and it is evident that occasions and pretexts for the latter interference may be as frequent as for the former. So again the judiciary department may find equal occasions in the execution of *its* functions for usurping the authorities of the executive; and the legislature for stepping into the jurisdiction of both. And thus all the powers of government, of which a partition is so carefully made among the several branches, would be thrown into absolute hatchpot, and exposed to a general scramble.

It is certain that a faithful execution of the laws of neutrality may tend as much in some cases to incur war from one quarter as in others to avoid war from other quarters. The executive must nevertheless execute the laws of neutrality while in force, and leave it to the legislature to decide whether they ought to be altered or not. The executive has no other discretion than to convene and give information to the legislature on occasions that may demand it; and while this discretion is duly exercised the trust of the executive is satisfied, and that department is not responsible for the consequences. It could not be made responsible for them without vesting it with the legislative as well as with the executive trust.

In reply to the position of "Pacificus" that the right of the President to receive foreign ministers implies the right of recognizing, in the case of a revolution, the new government, "Helvidius" again quoted the "great constitutional authority," Hamilton, to the contrary. No. 69 of "The Federalist," written by Hamilton, says that this right is "more a matter of dignity than authority."

It is a circumstance, that will be *without consequence* in the administration of the Government, and it is far more convenient that it should be arranged in this manner than that there should be a necessity for convening the legislature or one of its branches upon every arrival of a foreign minister, though it were merely to take the place of a departed predecessor.

"Helvidius" comments on this as follows:

Had it been foretold in the year 1788, when this work was published, that, before the end of the year 1793, a writer, assuming the merit of being a friend to the Constitution, would appear and gravely maintain that this function, which was to be *without consequence* in the administration of the Government, might have the consequence of deciding on the validity of revolutions in favor of liberty, "of putting the United States in a condition to become an associate in war" . . . nay, "of laying the *legislature* under an *obligation* of *declaring* war," what would have been thought and said of so visionary a prophet?

Against "Pacificus's" inference that the executive has a right to give or refuse operation to preëxisting treaties, because of a change in the government of the foreign party, he quotes Burlamaqui, part IV, c. IX, § 16, ¶ 6, to show that a nation, by exercising the right of changing the organ of its will, even so far as from a monarchy to a republic, or *vice versa,* can neither disengage itself from the obligations, nor forfeit the benefits of its treaties.

"Helvidius" thus concludes the constitutional portion of his argument:

In no part of the Constitution is more wisdom to be found than in the clause which confides the question of war or peace to the legislature, and not to the executive department. Beside the

objection to such a mixture of heterogeneous powers, the trust
and the temptation would be too great for any one man; not
such as nature may offer as the prodigy of many centuries, but
such as may be expected in the ordinary successions of magistracy. War is in fact the true nurse of executive aggrandizement. In war a physical force is to be created; and it is the
executive will which is to direct it. In war the public treasures
are to be unlocked; and it is the executive hand which is to dispense them. In war the honors and emoluments of office are to
be multiplied; and it is the executive patronage under which
they are to be enjoyed. It is in war, finally, that laurels are to
be gathered; and it is the executive brow they are to encircle.
The strongest passions and most dangerous weaknesses of the
human breast: ambition, avarice, vanity, the honorable or venial
love of fame are all in conspiracy against the desire and duty of
peace.

Hence it has grown into an axiom that the executive is the department of power most distinguished by its propensity to war:
hence it is the practice of all states, in proportion as they are
free, to disarm this propensity of its influence.

Upon the specific instance of the executive's encroachment upon legislative and judicial powers in his
proclamation of neutrality ''Helvidius'' observes that
the President must have been ill-advised by some one
inimical to France, and regardless of the benefits which
were accruing to our young republic from the friendship
of that country, and were on the point of vastly increasing.

A greater error could not have been committed than in a
step that might have turned the present disposition of France to
open her commerce to us as far as a liberal calculation of her
interest would permit, and her friendship toward us, and confidence in our friendship toward her, could prompt, into a disposition to shut it as closely against us as the united motives of
interest, of distrust, and of ill will could urge her.

On the supposition that France might intend to claim the
guaranty, a hasty and harsh refusal before we were asked, on a
ground that accused her of being the aggressor in the war against
every power in the catalogue of her enemies, and in a crisis when
all her sensibility must be alive toward the United States, would
have given every possible irritation to a disappointment which
every motive that one nation could feel toward another and to-

ward itself required to be alleviated by all the circumspection and delicacy that could be applied to the occasion.

Notwithstanding Madison's arguments the proclamation of neutrality was approved by the American people as a whole, chiefly out of respect for Washington, and thus it became a strong precedent for similar action in similar cases by subsequent Presidents.

CHAPTER II

COMMERCIAL TREATY WITH GREAT BRITAIN (JAY'S TREATY)

John Jay's Treaty with Great Britain—Popular Opposition—Washington's
Reply—His Letter to Secretary Edmund Randolph—Objections of the
French Minister—Randolph's Reply—Resolution of Edward Livingston
[N. Y.] Calling on the President for the Correspondence Relating to the
Treaty—Debate: in Favor, James Madison [Va.] and Albert Gallatin
[Pa.]—Washington Refuses to Submit Correspondence—Resolution of
Theodore Sedgwick [Mass.] Calling for Action by the House to Carry
into Effect the Treaty—Debate: in Favor, William V. Murray, [Md.]
Fisher Ames [Mass.]; Opposed, William B. Giles [Va.]—Letters of
"Camillus" [Alexander Hamilton, Rufus King, and John Jay]—Treaty
Is Passed.

B EFORE the outbreak of the French Revolution
negotiations for a commercial treaty had been
proceeding between the United States and Great
Britain.

The British Government had promised to send a representative to America, but made evasive answers as
to the treaty, intimating that the British people were
offended by the Americans giving preference to their
own ships in tonnage dues, etc.

The war with France, which soon after arose, compelled an abandonment of these negotiations. Great
Britain and Holland, in order to compel the French to
submit to their terms, in June, 1793, went to the extreme
and extraordinary measure of ordering warships and
privateers to stop vessels bearing corn, flour, or meal to
French ports, and to sell the cargoes in British or
friendly ports. Notwithstanding remonstrances on the
part of the United States, the orders were rigidly enforced, and English ports were soon filled with American vessels, originally bound to France.

Jay's Mission to Great Britain

On April 16, during a discussion of non-intercourse with Great Britain, the President nominated John Jay as minister extraordinary to the British court. Jay's nomination was approved in the Senate.

The two great and primary objects of this mission were the cessation of the vexations and spoliations committed on American commerce under British orders and the adjustment of all differences concerning the treaty of peace. Should these points "be so accommodated as to promise the continuance of tranquility between the United States and Great Britain," "the subject of a commercial treaty," according to Mr. Jay's instructions, "might then be listened to, or even broken to the British Ministry."

Aware that the British Government might wish to detach the United States from France, and even make some overtures of that kind, Mr. Jay was specially instructed to say "that the Government of the United States would not derogate from their treaties and engagements with France."

On the 19th of November, 1794, Mr. Jay concluded and signed with Lord Grenville "a treaty of amity, commerce, and navigation between His Britannic Majesty and the United States." It was received by the President on the 7th of March, 1795, and on the 8th of June was submitted to the Senate, and on the 24th of the same month that body advised its ratification, with the exception of the 12th article, relating to the West India trade. This interesting subject occasioned violent debates in the Senate, and the treaty itself was finally sanctioned in that body (excluding the article relating to the West India trade) by a bare constitutional majority, twenty against ten.

Terms of the Treaty

The western military posts were to be surrendered to the United States on or before the first of June, 1796, but no compensation was made for negroes carried away

by the British commander after the peace of 1783. The
United States were to compensate British creditors for
losses occasioned by legal impediments to the collection
of debts, contracted before the Revolutionary War, to
be settled and adjusted by commissioners, and Great
Britain was to make compensation to American merchants for illegal captures of their property, to be adjusted also in the same mode. Provision was also made
for ascertaining more accurately the boundaries between the United States and the British North American
possessions.

British subjects holding lands in the territories of
the United States and American citizens holding lands
in the British dominions were to continue to hold them,
according to the nature and tenure of their respective
estates and titles therein, with power to sell, grant, or
devise the same, and by the tenth article it was expressly
provided that neither the debts due from individuals
of the one nation to individuals of the other, nor shares
or moneys in the public funds, or in the public or private
banks, should in any event of war or national differences
be sequestered or confiscated, "it being unjust and impolitic," as asserted in this article, "that debts and
engagements contracted and made by individuals having
confidence in each other and in their respective governments should ever be destroyed or impaired by national
authority on account of national differences and discontents."

Both parties had liberty to trade with the Indians
in their respective territories in America (with the exception of the country within the limits of the Hudson
Bay Company), and the river Mississippi was to be also
open to both nations.

The ten first articles principally embracing these important subjects were made permanent.

The other eighteen articles related to the future intercourse between the two countries, and in their duration were limited to twelve years, or two years after
the termination of the war in which the British nation
was then engaged. By the twelfth article a direct trade
was permitted between the United States and the British

West India Islands in American vessels not above the
burden of seventy tons, and in goods or merchandise
of the growth, manufacture, or produce of the States,
and in the productions of the islands, but the United
States were restrained from carrying molasses, sugar,
coffee, cocoa, or cotton either from the islands or from
the United States to any part of the world.

As a considerable quantity of cotton at that time
was produced in the Southern States, and had then begun
to be exported, and the quantity would probably increase, the twelfth article was excluded. The American
negotiator, it was said, was then ignorant that cotton
of the growth of the United States had or would become
an article of export.[1]

A reciprocal liberty of commerce and navigation
between the United States and the British dominions
in Europe was established, neither to be subject to
higher duties than other nations, the British Government reserving the right of countervailing the American
foreign duties. And American vessels were freely admitted into the ports of the British territories in the
East Indies, but not to carry on the coasting trade.

Timber for shipbuilding and material such as tar,
sails, copper, etc., for the equipment of vessels were
included in the list of contraband. With respect to provisions and other articles, not generally contraband, on
"account of the difficulty of agreeing on the precise
cases in which they should be regarded as such," and
for the purpose of providing against the inconveniences
and misunderstandings which might thence arise, it was
declared that whenever such articles should become contraband, according to the existing law of nations, the
same should not be confiscated, but the owners be completely indemnified by the captors or the Government.

---

[1] Eli Whitney (1765-1825), of Massachusetts, a Yale graduate, went to
Georgia to teach on the plantation of the widow of General Greene. At her
request he invented in 1793 the saw cotton gin for separating the seed from
the fiber. Within a year or so it had enormously increased the crop. Thus
in 1791 only 189,316 pounds were exported, and in 1800, 17,789,803 pounds.
It made the labor of slaves exceedingly profitable in the "cotton States,"
and so prevented that gradual emancipation which the Fathers of the country had hoped for.

Prizes made by ships of war and privateers of either party might enter and depart from the ports of each other without examination, and no shelter or refuge was allowed to such vessels as had made a prize upon the subjects or citizens of the parties. Nothing, however, in the treaty was to operate contrary to former and existing treaties with other nations.

Mr. Jay was unable to obtain a stipulation that free ships should make free goods. It was hardly to be expected that Great Britain in time of war would consent to any relaxation of the rigid rule of law on this subject.

These are the principal features of a treaty which gave such high offence to the rulers of France and created such divisions in the United States as to put in jeopardy the Government itself.

Unfortunately it left the important question with respect to provisions being contraband as it found it, resting on the existing law of nations, but Mr. Jay, to whom had been assigned a most difficult as well as most delicate task, in a private letter to the President on the subject of the treaty, said, "to do more was impossible." He also added, "I ought not to conceal from you that the confidence reposed in your personal character was visible and useful throughout the negotiations."

The treaty was approved by Thomas Pinckney, the resident Minister at the court of London. In his letter to the Secretary of State he observed, "although some points might have been arranged more beneficially for us, if the treaty had been dictated entirely by the United States, yet when it is considered as a composition of differences where mutual complaints had rendered mutual concessions necessary to establish a good understanding, I think it may fairly be said that as little has been conceded by Mr. Jay, and as much obtained for the United States as, under all circumstances considered, could be expected."

This treaty was the first with any foreign power under the new Government. Treaties had only been formed with the Indian tribes, and in these instances, as well as in the instance of an attempt to obtain the release of American prisoners by a treaty with the regency of Algiers, the President had in person attended the Senate and requested their advice as to the terms he was about to propose. In this mode of proceeding serious difficulties had arisen, and on reconsideration it had been deemed most consistent with the Constitution not to consult the Senate in a formal manner until a treaty had actually been made. The Senate, therefore, in this instance were not previously consulted by the President as to the terms of a treaty with Great Britain. This has ever since been considered the true construction of the Constitution, and the course then adopted has been invariably pursued.

POPULAR OPPOSITION TO TREATY

Although secrecy was enjoined, yet one member of the Senate, soon after that body had advised its ratification, caused the treaty to be published in one of the public newspapers in Philadelphia, and it immediately became a subject of discussion.

Many of the opponents of the administration were prepared to pronounce the treaty's condemnation. Meetings of the citizens were held on the subject, and such was the state of public feeling against Great Britain that the passions, rather than the understandings, of the people were addressed, and resolutions were passed and presented to the President condemning the treaty in the most unqualified manner, and requesting him to withhold his assent.

WASHINGTON'S REPLY

Washington's answer disclosed the course he intended to pursue—a course alike firm and dignified. After stating that in every act of his administration he had sought the happiness of his fellow citizens, and that to obtain this object, overlooking all local, partial, or personal considerations, he had contemplated the United States as one great whole, and trusting that sudden impressions, when erroneous, would yield to candid reflection, he had consulted only the substantial and permanent interests of his country, he said:

"Without a predilection for my own judgment I have
weighed with attention every argument which has, at any time,
been brought into view. But the Constitution is the guide
which I never can abandon. It has assigned to the President
the power of making treaties, with the advice and consent of the
Senate. It was doubtless supposed that these two branches of
government would combine without passion, and with the best
means of information, those facts and principles upon which the
success of our foreign relations will always depend; that they
ought not to substitute for their own conviction the opinions of
others; or to seek truth through any channel but that of a
temperate and well-informed investigation. Under this persuasion I have resolved on the manner of executing the duty before
me. To the high responsibility attached to it I freely submit;
and you, gentlemen, are at liberty to make these sentiments
known as the ground of my procedure. While I feel the most
lively gratitude for the many instances of approbation from my
country, I cannot otherwise deserve it than by obeying the dictates of my conscience."

In a letter to Edmund Randolph, who had succeeded
Thomas Jefferson as Secretary of State in 1794, Washington observes:

"To be wise and temperate, as well as firm, the crisis most
eminently calls for; for there is too much reason to believe, from
the pains which have been taken before, at, and since the advice
of the Senate respecting the treaty, that the prejudices against
it are more extensive than is generally imagined. This, from
men who are of no party, but well disposed to the Government,
I have lately learned is the case. How should it be otherwise?
when no stone has been left unturned that would impress the
people's minds with the most arrant misrepresentations of facts
—that their rights have not only been *neglected*, but absolutely
sold—that there are no reciprocal advantages in the treaty; that
the benefits are all on the side of Great Britain; and, what seems
to have more weight than all the rest, and has been most pressed,
is, that this treaty is made with a design to oppress the French,
in open violation of a treaty with that nation, and contrary, too,
to every principle of gratitude and sound policy. In time when
passion shall have yielded to sober reason the current may possibly turn; but, in the meanwhile, this Government, in relation
to France and England, may be compared to a ship between the
rocks of Scylla and Charybdis. If the treaty is ratified the

partizans of France (or rather of war and confusion) will excite them to hostile measures; or, at least, to unfriendly sentiments. If it is not, there is no foreseeing all the consequences that may follow, as it respects Great Britain. It is not to be inferred from this that I am, or shall be, disposed to quit the ground I have taken; unless circumstances, more imperious than have yet come to my knowledge, shall compel it; for there is but one straight course in these things, and that is to seek truth and pursue it steadily.''

OBJECTIONS OF THE FRENCH MINISTER

The treaty was ratified on August 14 on the terms proposed by the Senate.

In the negotiations with Great Britain perfect good faith was observed toward France. The French Minister, M. Adet, had been informed that Mr. Jay had instructions not to weaken the engagements with his nation. A copy of the treaty was also submitted to M. Adet by direction of the President with a request that he would state his objections. On the 30th of June he, in a note to the Secretary of the State, referred to such parts as appeared to him to destroy the effect of the treaty with France. The stipulations referred to were those which made contraband of war of naval stores excluded from that list in the French treaty, which subjected to seizure enemy's property in neutral bottoms, and admitted prizes in American ports. To the first and second the American secretary immediately answered that naval stores were contraband by the law of nations, that by the same law enemy's property in neutral bottoms was good prize, and that on these points Great Britain could not be prevailed upon to relax, and with respect to the admission of prizes into American ports this privilege did not extend to those made from the French during the present or any future war because contrary to the existing treaty with France.

PETITIONS AGAINST THE TREATY

On the first of March the President informed Congress by message that the treaty with Great Britain had been duly ratified, that he had directed it to be promulgated, and had transmitted a copy thereof for their information. This important subject in various ways occupied the attention of the House for a great part of the remainder of the session. Soon after its ratification by the President was known, petitions against it were circulated throughout the United States for signatures. These petitions, all couched in the same language, were addressed to the House of Representatives. The petitioners after stating that certain stipulations in the treaty tended to involve their country in the political intrigues of European nations, to infract the treaty of alliance with France, and to produce the sad spectacle of war between that magnanimous republic and the republic of the United States proceeded to declare that many of its stipulations were manifest encroachments on the constitutional powers of Congress. They presented the following instances of such encroachments:

1. The regulation of commerce with foreign nations.
2. The regulation of trade and intercourse with the Indian tribes.
3. Regulating the territory of the United States and of individual States.
4. Establishing duties and imposts.
5. Establishing a rule of naturalization.
6. Constituting a tribunal of appeal, paramount to the supreme judicial court of the United States.
7. Changing the terms of, and establishing a rule to hold, real estate.
8. Defining piracies committed on the high seas, and declaring the punishment thereof.
9. Depriving free citizens of the privilege of the writ of habeas corpus, in the case of piracy, as defined and punished by the said treaty; and,
10. Attempting, in various other instances, to restrain and limit the legislative authority of Congress.

The petitioners in conclusion said:

"Wherefore solemnly protesting against the exercise of power by the President and Senate, in any of the foregoing cases, without the concurrence of Congress, as manifestly tending to absorb all the powers of government in that department alone; to establish, as the sole rule of legislation over all the great foreign and domestic concerns of the United States, the mere will and absolute discretion of the President and Senate, in conjunction with a foreign power; and finally to overturn and effect a total change in the present happy Constitution of the United States— We most earnestly pray that the representatives of the people, in Congress assembled, will, in their wisdom, adopt such measures, touching the said treaty, as shall most effectually secure from encroachment the constitutional delegated powers of Congress, and the rights of the people, and preserve to our country an *uninterrupted continuance of the blessings of peace.*"

Many of these petitions were presented in the winter of 1796 from different parts of the Union, and laid the foundation of the proceedings of the House in relation to the treaty.

LIVINGSTON'S RESOLUTION

Before the merits of the treaty itself became a subject of debate an important preliminary question arose upon a resolution calling on the President for the instructions of Mr. Jay and the correspondence and documents relating to it. This resolution was offered by Edward Livingston (New York) on the 2nd of March, and was debated until the 24th of that month, when it passed, 62 to 37.

The principal question on this resolution was as to the constitutional power of the House in relation to treaties. Never since the adoption of the Constitution had so much talent been displayed or so much warmth manifested as in the debates on this preliminary question and on the merits of the treaty itself.

The speakers on both sides were numerous and a very wide range was taken in debate. Every article and every word in the Constitution having the least bearing on the question was critically examined and applied.

A sketch of the principal arguments is here presented.

POWER OF HOUSE OVER TREATIES

HOUSE OF REPRESENTATIVES, MARCH 2-24, 1796

In opposition to the call it was said that the Constitution in plain and explicit terms had declared that the
President should have power by and with the advice and
consent of the Senate to make treaties, and that all
treaties made, or which should be made, under the
authority of the United States should be the supreme
law of the land. That the power of making treaties
was an important act of sovereignty in every government, and in most countries was very properly intrusted
with the executive branch. That the American Constitution had vested this power with the President in concurrence with two-thirds of the Senate. That a treaty
fairly made and embracing those things which are the
proper objects of compact between nations when thus
assented to and duly ratified became a solemn compact
binding on the United States was the supreme law of
the land and ought to be carried into execution. That
legislative aid or assent was not necessary to give it
validity or *binding force,* though sometimes required
agreeably to the form of our Government to carry it
into complete effect. Where laws or appropriations of
money were requisite for this purpose it was in all
ordinary cases the duty of the legislative branch of the
Government to pass such laws and make such appropriations, and that a failure so to do would be a breach of
national faith, as much so as to refuse to make appropriations for the payment of a debt legally contracted.

Extraordinary cases, it was said, might occur in
which the legislature might be justified in refusing its aid
to carry a treaty into effect. The conduct of a nation
with which the compact was made might be such after
the completion of the treaty, or the stipulations in it
might be so ruinous to the State, as to render it proper
and even make it a duty for the legislative branch to
withhold its aid. These cases, however, it was said, were
not to be governed by ordinary rules, but when they

occurred would make a law for themselves not affecting the general rule.

The House of Representatives were not making a Constitution, but expounding one already made, and, while they should watch with a jealous eye every encroachment on their rights by another branch of the Government, they should be cautious not to usurp power constitutionally vested in others. That the treaties referred to in the Constitution included all those usually made—treaties of peace, alliance, and commerce, and that no precise limits to this power were fixed, and from the nature of the case could not be. The people of the United States who adopted the Constitution considered their interest and rights sufficiently secured by placing this necessary and important power in the hands of the President and one branch of the legislature, and that this necessarily excluded the other legislative branch. It was well known, it was also urged, that most of the treaties usually made must necessarily include regulations concerning many objects intrusted likewise by the Constitution to legislative regulations, and, if the treaty power could not operate on these, the power itself would be reduced to very narrow limits, and no treaty with a foreign nation could be made embracing these objects, as Congress, to whom all legislative power was given, had no authority to make treaties. It was necessary, also, it was said, to consider that the legislative power and treaty power operated differently and for different purposes. The former was limited to its own jurisdiction, and could not extend to a foreign jurisdiction and government. A legislature could indeed grant privileges to foreigners within its jurisdictional limits, but could not secure reciprocal privileges in a foreign country; this could only be done with the assent of a foreign government, and this assent was not usually given except by treaty.

Treaties, being the supreme law of the land, must also, it was said, be paramount to the laws of the United States as well as the Constitution and laws of the individual States. That Congress, under the Confederation, was invested with the power of "entering into

treaties and alliances'' on condition ''that no treaty of
commerce should be made, whereby the legislative power
of the respective States should be restrained from imposing such imposts and duties on foreigners as their
own people were subjected to, or from prohibiting the
exportation of any species of goods or commodities whatsoever.'' With these exceptions the power was general,
and treaties made in pursuance of it had been considered
paramount to State laws without the assent of the States
themselves. When some of the State laws were supposed
to contravene the treaty of peace with Great Britain,
Congress, in their address to the States on the subject,
declared that ''when a treaty was constitutionally made,
ratified, and published it immediately became binding on
the whole nation and superadded to the laws of the
land without the intervention of State legislatures.
That treaties derived their obligations from being compacts between the sovereigns of this and of another
nation, whereas laws or statutes derived their force
from being the acts of the legislature competent to the
passing them.'' They therefore unanimously ''resolved
that the legislatures of the several States cannot of
right pass any act or acts for interpreting, explaining,
or construing a national treaty, or any part or clause
of it, nor for restraining, limiting, or in any manner
impeding, retarding, or countervailing the operation or
execution of the same, for that, on being constitutionally
made, ratified, and published they become in virtue of
the Confederation part of the laws of the land and are
not only independent of the will and power of such legislatures, but also binding and obligatory on them.'' To
remove all ground of complaint, however, on the part
of Great Britain, Congress recommended to the States
to pass general acts repealing all laws repugnant to
that treaty. That afterwards in a discussion with the
British minister on this subject, Mr. Jefferson, then
Secretary of State, speaking of the repealing acts of the
States, said, ''indeed all this was supererogation. It
resulted from the instrument of confederation among the
States that treaties made by Congress according to the
Confederation were superior to the laws of the States.''

The opponents of the resolution also contended that the Constitution was so understood not only in the general convention, but in the State conventions which ratified that instrument, and in some of the latter this was made a strong ground of objection, particularly those of Virginia and North Carolina. One of the amendments proposed by the Virginia convention was "that no commercial treaty should be ratified without the concurrence of two-thirds of the whole number of Senators, and no treaty ceding, restraining, or suspending the territorial rights or claims of the United States, or any of their rights or claims to fishing in the American seas or navigating the American rivers, shall be, but in case of the most urgent and extreme necessity, nor shall any such treaty be ratified without the concurrence of three-fourths of the whole number of the members of both Houses respectively." The convention of North Carolina proposed an amendment "that no treaties which shall be directly opposed to the existing laws of the United States in Congress assembled shall be valid until such laws shall be repealed or made conformable to such treaty, nor shall any treaty be valid which is contradictory to the Constitution of the United States."

The same construction, it was said, had uniformly been given to this part of the Constitution by the House of Representatives; that various treaties had been made with the Indian tribes embracing a surrender of lands, settlement of boundaries, grants of money, etc., and when made and ratified by the President and Senate had been considered as laws of the land without the sanction of the House, and money, when necessary, had been appropriated as a matter of course; that the Constitution made no distinction between treaties with foreign nations and with Indian tribes, the same clause applying to both. And that the House, in June, 1790, declared by a resolution "that all treaties made, or which should be made and *promulgated* under the authority of the United States, should from time to time be published and annexed to *the code of laws* by the Secretary of State." That the secretaries had accordingly always annexed treaties to the laws as soon as ratified by the President and Senate and promulgated by the former.

The resolution was not only supported by the mover and others, but had the aid of all the ingenuity and talents of James Madison (Virginia) and Albert Gallatin (Pennsylvania).

MR. GALLATIN, alluding to the great constitutional question made by the opponents of the resolution, said he had hoped in that stage of the business this would have been avoided; but, as gentlemen in opposition "had come forward on that ground, he had no objection to follow them in it, and rest the decision of the constitutional powers of Congress on the fate of the present question. He would, therefore," he said, "state his opinion that the House had a right to ask for the papers proposed to be called for, because their coöperation and sanction were necessary to carry the treaty into effect, to render it *a binding instrument*, and to make it, properly speaking, *a law of the land;* because they had a full discretion to refuse that coöperation, because they must be guided in the exercise of that discretion by the merits and expediency of the treaty itself, and therefore had a right to ask for every information which could assist them in deciding that question.

"The general power of making treaties, undefined as it is, by the clause which grants it, may either be *expressly limited* by some other positive clauses of the Constitution; or it may be checked by some powers vested in other branches of the Government, which, although not diminishing, may control the treaty-making power. That the specific legislative powers delegated to Congress were limitations of the undefined power of making treaties vested in the President and Senate; and that the general power of granting money, also vested in Congress, would at all events be used, if necessary, as a check upon, and as controlling, the exercise of the powers claimed by the President and Senate."

After stating that a treaty could not repeal a law of the United States, Mr. Gallatin asked, "to what would a contrary doctrine lead? If the power of making treaties is to reside in the President and Senate unlimitedly—in other words, if in the exercise of this power the President and Senate are to be restrained by no other branch of the Government—the President and Senate may absorb all legislative power; the Executive has nothing to do but to substitute a foreign nation for the House of Representatives, and they may legislate to any extent." Mr. Gallatin further remarked that "he should not say that the treaty is unconstitutional; but he would say that it was not the supreme law of the land until it received the sanction of the legislature. That the Constitution and laws made in pursuance thereof, and treaties made under the authority of the United States, are declared to be the supreme law of the land. The words are, 'under the authority of the United States,' not 'signed and ratified by the President'; so that a treaty clashing in any of its provisions with the express powers of Congress, until it has so far obtained the sanction of Congress, is not a treaty under the authority of the United States.''

He also added that treaties were the supreme law of the land only when they came in competition with the Constitutions and laws of the individual States, but were not supreme or paramount to the laws of the United States, because it is declared, in the same clause of the Constitution, "and the judges in every State shall be bound thereby, anything in the Constitution and laws of any State to the contrary notwithstanding.''

"It would have been childish if the Constitution had confined itself to expressing the first part of the clause, because no doubt could arise whether the Constitution, laws, and treaties were the supreme law of the land; but, as the general Government sprung out of a confederation of States, it was necessary, in order to give that Government sufficient authority to provide for the general welfare, that the laws of the Union should supersede the laws of the particular States. But the clause does not compare a treaty with the law of the United States, or either of them with the Constitution; it only compares all the acts of the Federal Government with the acts of the individual States, and declares that either of the first, whether under the name of Constitution, law, or treaty, shall be paramount to, and supersede, the Constitution and laws of the individual States.''

The views of Mr. Madison on this important question were generally in accordance with those expressed by Mr. Gallatin.

MR. MADISON.—I regret that on a question of such magnitude there should be any apparent inconsistency or inexplicitness in the Constitution that could leave room for different constructions.

As the case, however, has happened, all that can be done is to examine the different constructions with accuracy and fairness, according to the rules established therefor, and to adhere to that which should be found most rational. consistent, and satisfactory.

Mr. Madison confined his remarks principally to two different constructions: one—and that supported, as he said, by the opponents of the resolution—that the treaty power was "both unlimited in its objects and completely paramount in its authority"; the other, that the congressional power was coöperative with the treaty power on the legislative subjects submitted to Congress by the Constitution.

As to the first, it is important, and appears to me to be a decisive view of the subject, that, if the treaty power alone can perform any one act for which the authority of Congress is required by the Constitution, it may perform any act for which the authority of that part of the Government is required. Congress have power to regulate trade, to declare war, to raise armies, to levy, borrow, and appropriate money, etc. If by treaty, therefore, as paramount to the legislative power, the President and Senate can regulate trade, they can also declare war, they can raise armies to carry on war, and they can procure money to support armies. I am unable to draw a line between any of the enumerated powers of Congress; and did not see but the President and Senate might, by a treaty of alliance with a nation at war, make the United States a party in that war. They might stipulate subsidies, and even borrow money to pay them: they might furnish troops to be carried to Europe, Asia, or Africa— they might even attempt to keep up a standing army in time of peace for the purpose of coöperating on given contingencies with an ally, for mutual safety, or other common objects.

The force of this reasoning is not obviated by saying that the President and Senate could only pledge the public faith, and that the agency of Congress would be necessary to carry it into operation: For, what difference does this make if the obligation imposed be, as is alleged, a Constitutional one; if Congress have no will but to obey, and if to disobey be treason and rebellion against the constituted authorities? Under a Constitutional obligation, with such sanctions to it, Congress, in case the President and Senate should enter into an alliance for war, would be nothing more than the mere heralds for proclaiming it.

He considered that construction the most consistent, most in accordance with the spirit of the Constitution, and freest from difficulties "which left with the President and Senate the power of making treaties, but required at the same time the *legislative sanction* and coöperation in those cases where the Constitution had given express and specified powers to the legislature.

It is to be presumed that in all such cases the legislature would exercise its authority with discretion, allowing due weight to the reasons which led to the treaty. Still, however, this House, in its legislative capacity, must exercise its reason; it must deliberate; for deliberation is implied in legislation. If it *must* carry all treaties into effect it would no longer exercise a legislative power; it would be the mere instrument of the will of another department, and would have no will of its own. When the Constitution contains a specific and peremptory injunction on Congress to do a particular act, Congress must, of course, do the act, because the Constitution, which is paramount over all the departments, has expressly taken away the legislative discretion of Congress. The case is essentially different when the act of one department of government interferes with a power expressly vested in another and nowhere expressly taken away: Here the latter power must be exercised according to its nature; and if it be a legislative power it must be exercised with that deliberation and discretion which are essential to legislative power.

The general doctrine of the advocates of the resolution was that the power to make treaties was limited to *such objects* as were not comprehended and included in the specified powers given to Congress, or that a treaty embracing such objects was not valid, that is, was not the supreme law of the land unless sanctioned by the House.

The advocates of the resolution also said that this was the first time this question had come before the House for their determination, and that, whatever opinions might heretofore have been expressed by individuals or by public bodies, these could have little weight.

The Constitution having fixed no precise limits to the treaty powers, the constructive limitations contended for by the advocates of the resolution were deemed totally inadmissible by its opponents. If this extensive power was liable to abuse in the hands of the President and Senate, they remarked the same might be said of all the general powers given to Congress. In answer to the limited construction given to the words "under the authority of the United States," confining their operation to the constitutions and laws of the individual States it was said that they referred to treaties already made under the Confederation, as well as those to be made under the new Government. With respect to the coöperative powers of Congress or of the House in giving validity to treaties it was asked in what way this power was to be exercised? Congress could act only in their legislative capacity, and their sanction must be given by a law. This law might be passed by a bare majority of both houses, and if not approved by the President might still be repassed by two-thirds and become a law without the assent of the President.

According to this doctrine it was also said a treaty might be sanctioned without the consent of *two-thirds* of the Senate, as a law might be passed by a bare majority of the Senate and House and be approved by the President.

WASHINGTON'S REPLY

This call for executive papers with its avowed object placed the President in a delicate situation. Satisfied after mature reflection with regard to his constitutional duty he did not hesitate as to the course to be pursued. In answer therefore on the 30th of March he sent to the House the following message, assigning his reasons for not complying with their request.

Gentlemen of the House of Representatives:

With the utmost attention I have considered your resolution of the 24th instant, requesting me to lay before your House a copy of the instructions to the minister who negotiated the treaty with the King of Great Britain, together with the correspondence and other documents relative to that treaty, excepting such of the said papers as any existing negotiation may render improper to be disclosed.

In deliberating upon this subject it was impossible to lose sight of the principle which some have avowed in its discussion, or to avoid extending my views to the consequences which must follow from the admission of that principle.

I trust that no part of my conduct has ever indicated a disposition to withhold any information which the Constitution has

enjoined upon the President as a duty to give, or which could be
required of him by either House or Congress as a right; and
with truth I affirm that it has been, as it will continue to be,
while I have the honor to preside in the Government, my constant
endeavor to harmonize with the other branches thereof, so far as
the trust delegated to me by the people of the United States, and
my sense of the obligation it imposes "to preserve, protect, and
defend the Constitution," will permit.

The nature of foreign negotiations requires caution; and their
success must often depend on secrecy; and, even when brought to
a conclusion, a full disclosure of all the measures, demands, or
eventual concessions which may have been proposed or contemplated would be extremely impolitic; for this might have a pernicious influence on future negotiations, or produce immediate
inconveniences, perhaps danger and mischief, in relation to other
powers. The necessity of such caution and security was one
cogent reason for vesting the power of making treaties with the
President, with the advice and consent of the Senate; the principle on which that body was formed confining it to a small number of members.

To admit, then, a right in the House of Representatives to demand, and to have, as a matter of course, all the papers respecting a negotiation with a foreign power would be to establish a
dangerous precedent.

It does not occur that the inspection of the papers asked for
can be relative to any purpose under the cognizance of the House
of Representatives except an impeachment, which the resolution
has not expressed. I repeat that I have no disposition to withhold any information which the duty of my station will permit,
or the public good shall require, to be disclosed; and, in fact, all
the papers affecting the negotiation with Great Britain were laid
before the Senate when the treaty itself was communicated for
their consideration and advice.

The course which the debate has taken on the resolution of
the House leads to some observations on the mode of making
treaties under the Constitution of the United States. Having
been a member of the general convention, and knowing the principles on which the Constitution was formed, I have ever entertained but one opinion on this subject; and, from the first establishment of the Government to this moment, my conduct has
exemplified that opinion that the power of making treaties is
exclusively vested in the President, by and with the advice and
consent of the Senate, provided two-thirds of the Senate present
concur; and that every treaty so made and promulgated thence-

forward becomes the law of the land. It is thus that the treaty-making power has been understood by foreign nations; and in all treaties made with them *we* have declared, and *they* have believed, that when ratified by the President, with the advice and consent of the Senate, they become obligatory.

In this construction of the Constitution every House of Representatives has heretofore acquiesced; and, until the present time, not a doubt or suspicion has appeared, to my knowledge, that this construction of the Constitution was not the true one. Nay, they have more than acquiesced; for till now, without controverting the obligation of such treaties, they have made all the requisite provisions for carrying them into effect.

There is, also, reason to believe that this construction agrees with the opinions entertained by the State conventions when they were deliberating on the Constitution; especially by those who objected to it, because there was not required in *commercial treaties* the consent of two-thirds of the whole number of the members of the Senate, instead of two-thirds of the Senators present; and because, in treaties respecting territorial and certain other rights and claims, the concurrence of three-fourths of the whole number of the members of both Houses respectively was not made necessary. It is a fact declared by the general convention, and universally understood, that the Constitution of the United States was the result of a spirit of amity and mutual concession. And it is well known that, under this influence, the smaller States were admitted to an equal representation in the Senate with the larger States; and that this branch of the Government was invested with great powers; for on the equal participation of these powers the sovereignty and political safety of the smaller States were deemed essentially to depend. If other proofs than these and the plain letter of the Constitution itself be necessary to ascertain the point under consideration, they may be found in the journals of the general convention, which I have deposited in the office of the Department of State.

In these journals it will appear that a proposition was made "that no treaty should be binding on the United States which was not ratified by a law," and that the proposition was explicitly rejected.

As, therefore, it is perfectly clear to my understanding that the assent of the House of Representatives is not necessary to the validity of a treaty, as the treaty with Great Britain exhibits in itself all the objects requiring legislative provision, and on these the papers called for can throw no light; and as it is essential to the due administration of the Government that the boundaries fixed by the Constitution between the different departments should be preserved—a just regard to the Constitution and to the duty of my office under all the circumstances of this case forbids a compliance with your request.

The House Maintains Its Position

The opinion of the President on this important constitutional question, however satisfactory it may now be to those who examine it without any particular bias, was by no means in accordance with that of the House. A resolution was submitted declaring the constitutional power of that body in relation to treaties, and on the 7th of April was adopted, 57 to 35, and entered on the journals. After referring to the section of the Constitution concerning treaties it declared:

That the House of Representatives do not claim any agency in making treaties; but that, when a treaty stipulates regulations on any of the subjects submitted by the Constitution to the power of Congress, it must depend for its *execution* as to such stipulations on a law or laws to be passed by Congress; and it is the constitutional right and duty of the House of Representatives, in all such cases, to deliberate on the *expediency* or *inexpediency* of carrying such treaty into effect, and to determine and act thereon, as in their judgment may be most conducive to the public good.

A second resolution was added, asserting that it was not necessary to the propriety of any application from the House to the executive for information desired by them, and which might relate to any constitutional functions of the House, that the purposes for which such information might be wanted, or to which it might be applied, should be stated in the application.

The opinion expressed in this resolution relative to the power of the House regarding treaties was somewhat equivocal and seemed to be confined to the *expediency* merely of making the requisite provision for carrying them into effect whenever legislative aid was necessary for that purpose.[1]

[1] The question regarding the constitutional powers of Congress or of the House, in relation to treaties, came again before Congress, when the

The President during this session had submitted to the House copies of the treaties with Spain, with the Dey and Regency of Algiers, and with the Indians northwest of the Ohio. On the 13th of April a resolution was submitted by Theodore Sedgwick [Mass.] declaring that provision ought to be made by law for carrying into effect these treaties as well as that with Great Britain.

After much altercation on the subject of thus joining all these treaties together, a division was made and the question taken on each. The resolution was amended by a majority of eighteen, so as to read "that it is *expedient* to pass the laws necessary for carrying into effect," etc.

The House Agrees to the Treaty

The subject of the British treaty was taken up on the 15th of April and debated in committee of the whole until the 29th of the same month, when the question was decided in the affirmative by the casting vote of the chairman, F. A. C. Muhlenberg [Pa.], who declared he was not satisfied with the resolution as it then stood, but should vote for it that it might go to the House and be there modified so as to meet his approbation.

The next day an amendment was proposed by Henry Dearborn (Massachusetts) by way of preamble.

"Whereas, in the opinion of this House, the treaty is highly objectionable, and may prove injurious to the United States; yet considering all circumstances relating thereto, and, particularly, that the last eighteen articles are to continue in force only during the present war, and two years thereafter; and confiding, also, in the efficiency of measures which may be taken for bring-

commercial treaty or convention with Great Britain of July, 1815, was laid before that body by the President. The House at first differed with the Senate as to the form of a law for carrying into effect that part of the convention which stipulated an equality of duties in certain cases. The House at first passed a bill equalizing the duties without referring to the convention.

The Senate negatived this, and passed a declaratory bill, to which, after a conference, the House agreed 100 to 35. This bill merely "enacted and declared that so much of any act as imposes a higher duty of tonnage or of impost on vessels and articles imported in vessels of the United States, contrary to the provisions of the convention, should be *deemed* and *taken* to be of no force and effect."

ing about a discontinuance of the violations committed on our neutral rights, in regard to vessels and seamen, therefore," etc.

After striking out the words "highly objectionable, and may prove injurious to the United States," the preamble was negatived, 50 to 49, and the resolution as reported to the House passed, 51 to 48, and bills ordered to be prepared accordingly.

AGREEMENT OF THE HOUSE TO THE TREATY

HOUSE OF REPRESENTATIVES, APRIL 15-29, 1796

Those in favor of the treaty seemed not disposed to enter into a discussion of its merits, alleging that every member had made up his mind on the subject, and that dispatch was necessary in case the treaty was carried into effect. The posts were to be delivered up on the first of June, and this required previous arrangements on the part of the American Government.

WILLIAM V. MURRAY [Md.] said "that the subject was completely understood, both by the House and country, and the time was so extremely pressing that the execution of the treaty was more valuable than any explanation which members could give. The country requires of us at this crisis acts, not speeches."

WILLIAM B. GILES [Va.], in opposition, said:

"I had hoped that a question which had already produced so much agitation would be taken up and decided upon in a manner suitable to its importance." He thought it would not be treating the public mind with a sufficient degree of respect to take a hasty vote upon the subject. He did not think that gentlemen in favor of the treaty would have wished to have got rid of it in this way. He avowed he could not discover those merits in the treaty which other gentlemen cried up; but he pledged himself that, if they would convince him the treaty was a good one, he would vote for it. He was desirous of knowing in what latent corner its good features lay, as he had not been able to find them. He thought he should be able to show features in it which were not calculated for the good, but for the mischief, of the country. He hoped, therefore, the committee would rise and suffer a proper discussion.

MR. MURRAY, in reply, "would vote for the committee to rise, as he despaired of taking a vote or hearing a word said to-day on the merits of the resolution offered. Gentlemen will, of course, come prepared, and he trusted that however terrible the treaty may have struck them in the dark, a little discussion might diminish their horrors. He could not, however, suppress his surprise that none of those, and in particular the gentleman from Virginia [Mr. Giles], who had entertained opinions so hostile to this treaty so long should be at a loss to enter on its discussion with an eagerness proportioned to their zeal and conviction of its mighty faults. But the gentleman, it seems, has left his paints and brushes at home, and cannot now attempt, though the canvas is before him, to give us those *features* of the treaty which had been so caricatured out of doors. He would agree that the committee should rise, hoping that the delay was owing to an aversion to do mischief, and relying on the effects of a night's reflection; the pillow is the friend of conscience."

With a temper and with feelings thus indicated the House entered upon the discussion of this interesting and important subject.

In this debate not only the constitutional powers of the House in relation to treaties were again discussed, but every article and every clause in the treaty examined and its merits and demerits developed. The arguments on both sides were pushed to an extreme and partook not a little of personal as well as political feelings.

The objections of those opposed to carrying the treaty into effect were generally that it wanted reciprocity—that it gave up all claim of compensation for negroes carried away contrary to the treaty of peace and for the detention of the Western posts; that it contravened the French treaty and sacrificed the interest of an ally to that of Great Britain; that it gave up in several important instances the law of nations, particularly in relation to free ships making free goods, cases of blockade, and contraband of war; that it improperly interfered with the legislative powers of Congress, especially by prohibiting the sequestration of debts, and that the commercial part gave few if any advantages to the United States.

On the other hand it was urged that the treaty had

been constitutionally made and promulgated, that a regard to public faith and the best interests of the country under all circumstances required it should be carried into effect, although not in all respects perfectly satisfactory; that it settled disputes between the two governments of a long standing, of a very interesting nature, and which it was particularly important for the United States to bring to a close; that provision also was made for a settlement of those of more recent date, not less affecting the sensibility as well as honor of the country, and in which the commercial part of the community had a deep interest; that in no case had the law of nations been given up; that the question as to provisions being contraband, although not settled, was left as before the treaty; that the conventional rights of France were saved by an express clause, and as to the sequestration of private debts it was said this was contrary to every principle of morality and good faith, and ought never to take place; that the commercial part would probably be mutually beneficial was a matter of experiment, and was to continue only two years after the close of the war in Europe. That in fine on the part of the United States the only choice left was treaty or war.

No question in Congress had ever elicited more talents or created greater solicitude than this. The loss of national character from a breach of plighted faith was strongly urged by those who believed the House bound to carry the treaty into effect. Should the treaty be rejected, war, it was also said, could not be avoided consistently with the character and honor of the American nation. The Western posts would be retained, the Indians again placed under the control of the British, millions unjustly taken from the merchants would be lost, and perhaps as many millions more added by future spoliations; redress for past, and security against future, injuries must, it was said, be obtained either by *treaty* or by *war*. It was impossible that the American people could sit down quietly without an effort to right themselves.

On these topics all the talents and all the eloquence of the advocates of the treaty were exerted and displayed. Mr. Ames in particular exceeded all his previous forensic efforts. From the peroration which dealt with the horrors of Indian warfare which might be expected if the treaty were rejected, his address received the name of the "Tomahawk Speech."

Rainbow of Peace or Meteor of War?

Speech of Fisher Ames, M. C., on Ratification or Rejection of Jay's Treaty

By rejecting the posts we light the savage fires, we bind the victims. This day we undertake to render account to the widows and orphans whom our decision will make, to the wretches that will be roasted at the stake, to our country, and, I do not deem it too serious to say, to conscience and to God. We are answerable, and if duty be anything more than a word of imposture, if conscience be not a bugbear, we are preparing to make ourselves as wretched as our country. There is no mistake in this case, there can be none. Experience has already been the prophet of events, and the cries of our future victims have already reached us. The voice of humanity issues from the shade of their wilderness. It exclaims that while one hand is held up to reject the treaty the other grasps a tomahawk. It summons our imagination to the scenes that will open. It is no great effort of the imagination to conceive that events so near are already begun. I fancy that I listen to the yells of savage vengeance, and the shrieks of torture. Already they seem to sigh in the western wind—already they mingle with every echo from the mountains.

After adverting to other probable and almost certain consequences of a rejection of the treaty—dissensions between the different branches of the Government —war abroad and anarchy at home—the orator reverses the picture:

Let me cheer the mind, weary, no doubt, and ready to despond, on this prospect, by presenting another which it is yet in our power to realize. Is it possible for a real American to look at the prosperity of this country without some desire for its continuance, without some respect for the measures which many will say produced, and, all will confess, have preserved it? Will he not feel some dread that a change of system will reverse the scene? The well-grounded fears of our citizens in 1794 were removed by the treaty, but are not forgotten. Then they deemed war nearly inevitable, and would not this adjustment have been considered at that day as a happy escape from the calamity?

The great interest and general desire of our people were to enjoy the advantage of neutrality. This instrument, however misrepresented, affords America that inestimable security. The causes of our disputes are either cut up by the roots or referred to a new negotiation after the end of the European war. This was gaining everything, because it confirmed our neutrality, by which our citizens are gaining everything. This alone would justify the engagements of the Government. For when the fiery vapors of the war lowered in the skirts of our horizon all our wishes were concentrated in this one, that we might escape the desolation of this storm. This treaty, like a rainbow on the edge of the cloud, marked to our eyes the space where it was raging, and afforded at the same time the sure prognostic of fair weather. If we reject it the vivid colors will grow pale, it will be a baleful meteor, portending tempest and war.

The speech of Mr. Ames, though delivered at nearly the close of this debate, was listened to by the House and by a crowded audience with a most silent and untired attention. Its eloquence was admired by all, though its effects were dreaded by some.

In deference to this dread, the question was postponed until the following day.

The delay occasioned by these debates had been favorable to the treaty. It gave time for reflection among those opposed, and also afforded an opportunity for an expression of their sentiments by others who had hitherto been silent, willing to leave the decision with the constituted authorities. Alexander Hamilton, Rufus King, and John Jay wrote a series of letters, thirty-five in number, signed "Camillus," in defence of the treaty, which operated powerfully to influence the public mind in its favor. Madison was eager to enter into the lists against these letters, of which it was clearly evident that Hamilton was, if not the sole author, at least the dominating spirit. Jefferson, however, dissuaded him from the attempt, saying that any reply to the defence of the treaty by the Federalist "colossus" would in the end redound to the acceptance of his arguments. The great mass of the people began seriously to reflect on the consequences of the treaty's rejection, nor could they be induced to believe that the President, who had once saved his country from the tyranny of Great Britain, had now sacrificed its best interests to the same power. During the discussion therefore numerous petitions were presented to the House from different parts of the Union, praying that the treaty might be carried into effect. This changed the votes if not the opinions of some of the members, and when the question was finally put it was decided in favor of the treaty. This action probably saved the United States from being involved in the war which then and so long afterwards desolated Europe.

John Jay —

CHAPTER III

THE BREACH WITH FRANCE

France's Displeasure over Jay's Treaty—French Directory Orders Minister Charles Cotesworth Pinckney to Leave the Country—Washington's Farewell Address: ''No Entangling Foreign Alliances''—President John Adams Proposes Arming of Merchant Vessels—Richard Sprigg, Jr. [Md.] Introduces Peace Resolutions in the House—Debate: in Favor, Abraham Baldwin [Ga.], William B. Giles [Ga.], John Nicholas [Va.], Albert Gallatin [Pa.], Edward Livingston [N. Y.]; Opposed, Samuel Sitgreaves [Pa.], Harrison Gray Otis [Mass.], Jonathan Dayton [N. J.], Robert G. Harper [S. C.], John Rutledge, Jr. [S. C.], Samuel Sewall [Mass.], Samuel W. Dana [Ct.], Nathaniel Smith [Ct.], John Williams [N. Y.], Thomas Pinckney [S. C.], John Allen [Ct.], James A. Bayard, Sr. [Del.]—Another Embassy Is Sent to France—A Treaty Is Signed and Ratified.

IN February, 1796, the French Minister of Foreign Affairs informed the American minister to that country, James Monroe, that the Directory considered the alliance between France and the United States at an end from the moment that the treaty with Great Britain was ratified, and intimated that a special envoy would be sent to announce this to the American Government. On the 2nd of July the Directory issued their celebrated decree, that ''all neutral or allied powers shall, without delay, be notified that the flag of the French Republic will treat neutral vessels, either as to *confiscation,* as to *searches,* or *capture,* in the same manner as they shall suffer the English to treat them.''

Secret orders to capture American vessels had probably been sent to the West Indies previous to this, as in June preceding a valuable ship called the Mount Vernon was captured off the capes of Delaware by a privateer from St. Domingo, commissioned by the French Republic.

The nations in Europe under the influence of France were required about the same time to pursue a similar conduct toward the Americans.

France and Spain, on the 19th of August, 1796, concluded a treaty of alliance, *offensive* and *defensive*. This treaty contained a mutual guaranty of all the states, territories, islands, and places which they respectively possessed, or should possess. France at this time was also contemplating obtaining from Spain Louisiana and the Floridas.

Washington was dissatisfied with the conduct of the American minister in France, particularly in delaying to present to the French Government an explanation of the Administration's views in concluding a treaty with Great Britain. So he recalled Monroe, and appointed Charles Cotesworth Pinckney of South Carolina to succeed him. But when Mr. Pinckney's credentials were laid before the Directory he was informed through Mr. Monroe that the French Government would "no longer recognize a minister plenipotentiary from the United States until after a reparation of the grievances demanded of the American Government, and which the French Republic has a right to expect." Mr. Pinckney was permitted to reside at Paris until about the first of February, 1797, when the Directory gave him written orders to quit the territories of the Republic.

In September, 1796, President Washington, in declining another election, had for the last time addressed his fellow citizens on subjects which he deemed highly important and intimately connected with their future political welfare.[1]

"No Entangling Foreign Alliances"

washington's farewell address

The unity of government which constitutes you one people is also now dear to you. It is justly so, for it is a main pillar in the edifice of your real independence, the support of your tranquil-

[1] James Madison stated that President Washington, four years before this, had submitted to him certain sentiments which he wished Madison to incorporate in a "farewell address," Washington at that time contemplating refusal to serve a second term as President. Accordingly Madison surmised that the President had called some one to render him a similar service in 1796—and opined that this was Alexander Hamilton, Secretary of the Treasury.

ity at home, your peace abroad, of your safety, of your prosperity, of that very liberty which you so highly prize. But as it is easy to foresee that from different causes and from different quarters much pains will be taken, many artifices employed, to weaken in your minds the conviction of this truth; as this is the point in your political fortress against which the batteries of internal and external enemies will be most constantly and actively (though often covertly and insidiously) directed, it is of infinite moment that you should properly estimate the immense value of your national union to your collective and individual happiness; that you should cherish a cordial, habitual, and immovable attachment to it; accustoming yourselves to think and speak of it as of the palladium of your political safety and prosperity, watching for its preservation with jealous anxiety; discountenancing whatever may suggest even a suspicion that it can in any event be abandoned; and indignantly frowning upon the first dawning of every attempt to alienate any portion of our country from the rest, or to enfeeble the sacred ties which now link together the various parts.

For this you have every inducement of sympathy and interest. Citizens, by birth or choice, of a common country, that country has a right to concentrate your affections. The name of American, which belongs to you in your national capacity, must always exalt the just pride of patriotism more than any appellation derived from local discriminations. With slight shades of difference you have the same religion, manners, habits, and political principles. You have, in a common cause, fought and triumphed together; the independence and liberty you possess are the work of joint councils and joint efforts, of common dangers, sufferings, and successes.

But these considerations, however powerfully they address themselves to your sensibility, are greatly outweighed by those which apply more immediately to your interest. Here every portion of our country finds the most commanding motives for carefully guarding and preserving the union of the whole.

The North, in an unrestrained intercourse with the South, protected by the equal laws of a common government, finds, in the productions of the latter, great additional resources of maritime and commercial enterprise, and precious materials of manufacturing industry. The South, in the same intercourse, benefiting by the agency of the North, sees its agriculture grow and its commerce expand. Turning partly into its own channels the seamen of the North, it finds its particular navigation invigorated; and while it contributes, in different ways, to nourish and increase the general mass of the national navigation, it looks forward to the protection of a maritime strength to which itself is unequally adapted. The East, in like intercourse with the West, already finds, and in the progressive improvement of interior communications, by land and water, will more and more find, a valuable vent for the commodities which it brings from abroad or manufactures at home. The West derives from the East supplies requisite to its growth and comfort, and, what is perhaps of still greater consequence, it must of necessity owe the secure enjoyment of indispensable outlets for its own productions to the weight, influence, and the future maritime strength of the Atlantic side of the Union, directed by an indissoluble community of interest as one nation. Any other tenure, by which the West can hold this essential advantage, whether derived from its own separate strength, or from an apostate and unnatural connection with any foreign power, must be intrinsically precarious.

While, then, every part of our country thus feels an immediate and particular interest in union, all the parts combined cannot fail to find, in the united mass of means and efforts, greater strength, greater resource, proportionably greater security from external danger, a less frequent interruption of their peace by foreign nations; and, what is of inestimable value, they must derive from union an exemption from those broils and wars between themselves which so frequently afflict neighboring countries, not tied together by the same government, which their own rivalships alone would be sufficient to produce, but which opposite foreign alliances, attachments, and intrigues would stimulate and embitter. Hence, likewise, they will avoid the necessity of those overgrown military establishments which, under any form of government, are inauspicious to liberty, and which are to be regarded as particularly hostile to republican liberty. In this sense it is that your Union ought to be considered as a main prop of your liberty, and that the love of the one ought to endear to you the preservation of the other.

These considerations speak a persuasive language to every reflecting and virtuous mind, and exhibit the continuance of the Union as a primary object of patriotic desire. Is there a doubt whether a common government can embrace so large a sphere? Let experience solve it. To listen to mere speculation, in such a case, were criminal. We are authorized to hope that a proper organization of the whole, with the auxiliary agency of governments for the respective subdivisions, will afford a happy issue to the experiment. 'Tis well worth a fair and full experiment.

With such powerful and obvious motives to union, affecting all parts of our country, while experience shall not have demonstrated its impracticability, there will always be reason to distrust the patriotism of those who, in any quarter, may endeavor to weaken its bands.

In contemplating the causes which may disturb our Union, it occurs, as a matter of serious concern, that any ground should have been furnished for characterizing parties by geographical discriminations—Northern and Southern, Atlantic and Western —whence designing men may endeavor to excite a belief that there is a real difference of local interests and views. One of the expedients of party to acquire influence within particular districts is to misrepresent the opinions and aims of other districts. You cannot shield yourselves too much against the jealousies and heart-burnings which spring from these misrepresentations; they tend to render alien to each other those who ought to be bound together by fraternal affection. . . .

To the efficacy and permanency of your Union a government for the whole is indispensable. No alliances, however strict, between the parts, can be an adequate substitute; they must inevitably experience the infractions and interruptions which alliances, in all times, have experienced. Sensible of this momentous truth, you have improved upon your first essay by the adoption of a Constitution of government better calculated than your former for an intimate union, and for the efficacious management of your common concerns. This government, the offspring of our own choice, uninfluenced and unawed, adopted upon full investigation and mature deliberation, completely free in its principles, in the distribution of its powers, uniting security with energy, and containing within itself a provision for its own amendment, has a just claim to your confidence and your support. Respect for its authority, compliance with its laws, acquiescence in its measures, are duties enjoined by the fundamental maxims of true liberty. The basis of our political systems is the right of the people to make and to alter the constitutions of government. But the Constitution, which at any time exists, until changed by an explicit and authentic act of the whole people, is sacredly obligatory upon all. The very idea of the power and the right of the people to establish a government presupposes the duty of every individual to obey the established government.

All obstructions to the execution of the laws, all combinations and associations, under whatever plausible character, with the real design to direct, control, counteract, or awe the regular deliberation and action of the constituted authorities, are destructive of this fundamental principle, and of fatal tendency. They serve to organize faction, to give it an artificial and extraordinary force, to put in the place of the delegated will of the nation the will of a party, often a small, but artful and enterprising minority of the community; and, according to the alternate triumphs of different parties, to make the public administration the mirror of the ill-concerted and incongruous projects of faction, rather than the organ of consistent and wholesome plans, digested by common councils, and modified by mutual interests.

However combinations or associations of the above description may now and then answer popular ends, they are likely, in the course of time and things, to become potent engines, by which cunning, ambitious, and unprincipled men will be enabled to subvert the power of the people, and to usurp for themselves the reins of government; destroying afterward the very engines which have lifted them to unjust dominion.

Toward the preservation of your Government and the permanency of your present happy state, it is requisite, not only that you speedily discountenance irregular opposition to its acknowledged authority, but also that you resist with care the spirit of innovation upon its principles, however specious the pretexts. One method of assault may be to effect, in the forms of the Constitution, alterations which will impair the energy of the system, and thus to undermine what cannot be directly overthrown. In all the changes to which you may be invited remember that time and habit are at least as necessary to fix the true character of governments as of other human institutions; that experience is the surest standard by which to test the real tendency of the existing constitution of a country; that facility in changes, upon the credit of mere hypothesis and opinion, exposes to perpetual change, from the endless variety of hypothesis and opinion. And remember, especially, that for the efficient management of your common interests, in a country so extensive as ours, a government of as much vigor as is consistent with the perfect security of liberty is indispensable. Liberty itself will find in such a government, with powers properly distributed and adjusted, its surest guardian. It is, indeed, little else than a name, where the government is too feeble to withstand the enterprises of faction; to confine each member of society within the limits prescribed by the laws, and to maintain all in the secure and tranquil enjoyment of the rights of person and property.

I have already intimated to you the danger of parties in the State, with particular reference to the founding of them on geographical discrimination. Let me now take a more comprehensive view, and warn you, in the most solemn manner, against the baneful effects of the spirit of party, generally.

This spirit, unfortunately, is inseparable from our nature, having its root in the strongest passions of the human mind. It exists under different shapes, in all governments, more or less stifled, controlled, or repressed. But in those of the popular form it is seen in its greatest rankness, and is truly their worst enemy.

The alternate domination of one faction over another, sharpened by the spirit of revenge, natural to party dissensions, which, in different ages and countries, has perpetrated the most horrid enormities, is itself a frightful despotism. But this leads, at length, to a more formal and permanent despotism. The disorders and miseries, which result, gradually incline the minds of men to seek security and repose in the absolute power of an individual; and sooner or later the chief of some prevailing faction, more able or more fortunate than his competitors, turns this disposition to the purposes of his own elevation on the ruins of public liberty.

Without looking forward to an extremity of this kind (which, nevertheless, ought not to be entirely out of sight) the common and continual mischiefs of the spirit of party are sufficient to make it the interest and duty of a wise people to discourage and restrain it.

It serves always to distract the public councils, and enfeeble the public administration. It agitates the community with ill-founded jealousies and false alarms; kindles the animosity of one part against another; foments occasionally riot and insurrection. It opens the door to foreign influence and corruption, which finds a facilitated access to the government itself, through the channels of party passion. Thus the policy and the will of one country are subjected to the policy and will of another.

There is an opinion that parties, in free countries, are useful checks upon the administration of the government, and serve to keep alive the spirit of liberty. This, within certain limits, is probably true; and, in governments of a monarchical cast, patriotism may look with indulgence, if not with favor, upon the spirit of party. But in those of popular character, in governments purely elective, it is a spirit not to be encouraged. From their natural tendency it is certain there will always be enough of that spirit for every salutary purpose. And, there being constant danger of excess, the effort ought to be, by force of public opinion, to mitigate and assuage it. A fire not to be quenched, it demands a uniform vigilance to prevent its bursting into a flame, lest, instead of warming, it should consume.

It is important, likewise, that the habits of thinking, in a free country should inspire caution in those intrusted with its administration to confine themselves within their respective constitutional spheres, avoiding, in the exercise of the powers of one department, to encroach upon another. The spirit of encroachment tends to consolidate the powers of all the departments in one, and thus to create, whatever the form of government, a real despotism. A just estimate of that love of power, and proneness to abuse it, which predominate in the human heart is sufficient to satisfy us of the truth of this position. The necessity of reciprocal checks in the exercise of political power, by dividing and distributing it into different depositaries, and constituting each the guardian of the public weal against invasion by the other, has been evinced by experiments ancient and modern: some of them in our country, and under our own eyes. To preserve them must be as necessary as to institute them. If, in the opinion of the people, the distribution or modification of the constitutional powers be, in any particular, wrong, let it be corrected by an amendment in the way which the Constitution designates. But let there be no change by usurpation; for though this, in one instance, may be the instrument of good, it is the customary weapon by which free governments are destroyed. The precedent must always greatly overbalance, in permanent evil, any partial or transient benefit which the use can at any time yield.

Of all the dispositions and habits which lead to political prosperity religion and morality are indispensable supports. In vain would that man claim the tribute of patriotism who should labor to subvert these great pillars of human happiness, these firmest props of the destinies of men and citizens. The mere politician, equally with the pious man, ought to respect and to cherish them. A volume could not trace all their connection with private and public felicity. Let it simply be asked, where is the security for property, for reputation, for life, if the sense of religious obligation desert the oaths which are the instruments of investigation in courts of justice? And let us with caution indulge the supposition that morality can be maintained without religion. Whatever may be conceded to the influence of refined education on minds of peculiar structure, reason and experience both forbid us to expect that national morality can prevail in exclusion of religious principles.

It is substantially true that virtue or morality is a necessary spring of popular government. The rule, indeed, extends with more or less force to every species of free government. Who, that is a sincere friend to it, can look with indifference upon attempts to shake the foundation of the fabric?

Promote, then, as an object of primary importance, institutions for the general diffusion of knowledge. In proportion as the structure of a government gives force to public opinion it is essential that public opinion should be enlightened.

As a very important source of strength and security cherish public credit. One method of preserving it is to use it as sparingly as possible; avoiding occasions of expense by cultivating peace, but remembering also that timely disbursements to prepare for danger frequently prevent much greater disbursements to repel it; avoiding likewise the accumulation of debt, not only by shunning occasions of expense, but by vigorous exertions in time of peace to discharge the debts which unavoidable wars may have occasioned, not ungenerously throwing upon posterity the burden which we ourselves ought to bear. The execution of these maxims belongs to your representatives, but it is necessary that public opinion should coöperate. To facilitate to them the performance of their duty it is essential that you should practically bear in mind that toward the payment of debts there must be revenue; that to have revenue there must be taxes; that no taxes can be devised which are not more or less inconvenient and unpleasant; that the intrinsic embarrassment inseparable from the selection of the proper objects (which is always the choice of difficulties) ought to be a decisive motive for a candid construction of the conduct of the government in making it, and for a spirit of acquiescence in the measures for obtaining revenue which the public exigencies may at any time dictate.

Observe good faith and justice toward all nations; cultivate peace and harmony with all; religion and morality enjoin this conduct; and can it be that good policy does not equally enjoin it? It will be worthy of a free, enlightened, and, at no distant period, a great nation to give to mankind the magnanimous and too novel example of a people always guided by an exalted justice and benevolence. Who can doubt that, in the course of time and things, the fruits of such a plan would richly repay any temporary advantages that might be lost by a steady adherence to it? Can it be that Providence has not connected the permanent felicity of a nation with its virtue? The experiment, at least, is recommended by every sentiment which ennobles human nature. Alas! is it rendered impossible by its vices?

In the execution of such a plan nothing is more essential than that permanent, inveterate antipathies against particular nations, and passionate attachments for others, should be excluded; and that in place of them just and amicable feelings toward all should be cultivated. The nation which indulges toward another an habitual hatred, or an habitual fondness, is in some degree a slave. It is a slave to its animosity or to its affection, either of which is sufficient to lead it astray from its duty and its interest. Antipathy in one nation against another disposes each more readily to offer insult and injury, to lay hold of slight causes of umbrage, and to be haughty and intractable, when accidental or trifling occasions of dispute occur.

Hence frequent collisions, obstinate, envenomed, and bloody contests. The nation, prompted by ill will and resentment, sometimes impels to war the government, contrary to the best calculations of policy. The government sometimes participates in the national propensity, and adopts through passion what reason would reject; at other times it makes the animosity of the nation subservient to projects of hostility instigated by pride, ambition, and other sinister and pernicious motives. The peace often, and sometimes, perhaps, the liberty, of nations has been the victim.

So, likewise, a passionate attachment of one nation for another produces a variety of evils. Sympathy for the favorite nation facilitating the illusion of an imaginary common interest in cases where no real common interest exists, and infusing into one the enmities of the other, betrays the former into a participation in the quarrels and wars of the latter, without adequate inducement or justification. It leads also to concessions to the favorite nation of privileges denied to others, which is apt doubly to injure the nation making the concessions; by unnecessarily parting with what ought to have been retained; and by exciting jealousy, ill will, and a disposition to retaliate in the parties from whom equal privileges are withheld; and it gives to ambitious, corrupted, or deluded citizens (who devote themselves to the favorite nation) facility to betray or sacrifice the interests of their own country without odium, sometimes even with popularity; gilding, with the appearances of a virtuous sense of obligation, a commendable deference for public opinion, or laudable zeal for public good, the base or foolish compliances of ambition, corruption, or infatuation.

As avenues to foreign influence, in innumerable ways, such attachments are particularly alarming to the truly enlightened and independent patriot. How many opportunities do they afford to tamper with domestic factions; to practice the arts of seduction; to mislead public opinion; to influence or awe the public councils! Such an attachment of a small or weak nation toward a great and powerful one dooms the former to be the satellite of the latter.

Against the insidious wiles of foreign influence (I conjure you to believe me, fellow-citizens) the jealousy of a free people ought to be constantly awake; since history and experience prove that foreign influence is one of the most baneful foes of republican government. But that jealousy, to be useful, must be impartial; else it becomes the instrument of the very influence to be avoided, instead of a defence against it. Excessive partiality for one foreign nation, and excessive dislike of another, cause those whom they actuate to see danger only on one side; and serve to veil and even second the arts of influence on the other. Real patriots, who may resist the intrigues of the favorite, are liable to become suspected and odious; while its tools and dupes usurp the applause and confidence of the people to surrender their interests.

The great rule of conduct for us, in regard to foreign nations, is, in extending our commercial relations, to have with them as little political connection as possible. So far as we have already formed engagements let them be fulfilled with perfect good faith. Here let us stop.

Europe has a set of primary interests, which to us have none, or a very remote, relation. Hence she must be engaged in frequent controversies, the causes of which are essentially foreign to our concerns. Hence, therefore, it must be unwise in us to implicate ourselves, by artificial ties, in the ordinary vicissitudes of her politics, or the ordinary combinations and collisions of her friendships and enmities.

Our detached and distant situation invites and enables us to pursue a different course. If we remain one people, under an efficient government, the period is not far off when we may defy material injury from external annoyance; when we may take such an attitude as will cause the neutrality we may at any time resolve upon to be scrupulously respected; when belligerent nations, under the impossibility of making acquisitions upon us, will not lightly hazard the giving us provocation; when we may choose peace or war, as our interest, guided by justice, shall counsel.

Why forego the advantages of so peculiar a situation? Why quit our own, to stand upon foreign ground? Why, by interweaving our destiny with that of any part of Europe, entangle our peace and prosperity in the toils of European ambition, rivalship, interest, humor, or caprice?

'Tis our true policy to steer clear of permanent alliances with any portion of the foreign world; so far, I mean, as we are now at liberty to do it; for let me not be understood as capable of patronizing infidelity to existing engagements. I hold the maxim no less applicable to public than to private affairs, that honesty is always the best policy. I repeat it, therefore, let those engagements be observed in their genuine sense. But, in my opinion, it is unnecessary, and would be unwise, to extend them.

Taking care always to keep ourselves, by suitable establishments, in a respectable defensive posture, we may safely trust to temporary alliances for extraordinary emergencies.

Harmony, and a liberal intercourse with all nations, are recommended by policy, humanity, and interest. But even our commercial policy should hold an equal and impartial hand; neither seeking nor granting exclusive favors or preferences; consulting the natural course of things; diffusing and diversifying, by gentle means, the streams of commerce, but forcing nothing; establishing, with powers so disposed, in order to give trade a stable course, to define the rights of our merchants, and to enable the Government to support them, conventional rules of intercourse, the best that present circumstances and mutual opinion will permit, but temporary, and liable to be, from time to time, abandoned or varied, as experience and circumstances shall dictate; constantly keeping in view that it is folly in one nation to look for disinterested favors from another; that it must pay, with a portion of its independence, for whatever it may accept under that character; that, by such acceptance, it may place itself in the condition of having given equivalents for nominal favors, and yet of being reproached with ingratitude for not giving more. There can be no greater error than to expect or calculate upon real favors from nation to nation. It is an illusion, which experience must cure, which a just pride ought to discard.

The duty of holding a neutral conduct may be inferred, without anything more, from the obligation which justice and humanity impose on every nation, in cases in which it is free to act, to maintain inviolate the relations of peace and amity toward other nations.

The inducements of interest for observing that conduct will best be referred to your own reflection and experience. With me a predominant motive has been to endeavor to gain time to our country to settle and mature its yet recent institutions, and to progress, without interruption, to that degree of strength and consistency which is necessary to give it, humanly speaking, the command of its own fortunes.

President John Adams in his inaugural address spoke only in general terms of the strained relations with France, expressing the hope that friendship might continue between the two nations. He called, however, a special session of Congress in which he delivered an address bearing fully and plainly upon the situation. As a measure of national protection, he proposed a naval establishment and asked Congress to pass such regulations as would "enable our seafaring citizens to defend themselves against violations of the law of nations," and also advised that the regular artillery and cavalry be increased and arrangements be made for forming a provisional army, and that the militia laws be revised for greater effectiveness.

The reply of the Senate heartily endorsed the President's policy. The answer of the House was in similar vein, although the opposition (Republicans) had proposed a number of amendments to the draft of the appointed committee which would cause the reply to endorse the proposals of the new administration without approving the acts of the old, and which, by going as far as possible in excusing her acts, would prevent it from irritating France.

In furtherance of a promise to Congress to reopen negotiations with France, President Adams appointed Charles Cotesworth Pinckney, John Marshall, and Elbridge Gerry envoys extraordinary to that country.

On March 19, 1798, the President informed Congress that the envoys to France had been unable to secure terms "compatible with the safety, the honor, or the essential interests of the nation," and he recommended that preparations for war be made. He also announced that he intended no longer to restrain merchant vessels from arming themselves.

This was the first time that Congress under the Constitution had been called upon to prepare for war, and a number of interesting constitutional arguments were brought forward in the discussion which ensued. The main debate was upon resolutions introduced on March 27, for the purpose of clarifying the situation, by Richard Sprigg, Jr., of Maryland. These were that it was "not expedient to resort to war against the French Republic, that the arming of merchant vessels should be restricted, and that adequate measures of defence should be adopted."

The resolutions accomplished their object by clearly dividing the House into supporters and opponents of the conduct and policy of the President. In the long and animated debate upon them they were gradually lost sight of, a more specific issue arising in the proposition to ask the President for all the papers dealing with the French relations. This proposition was carried.

The chief supporters of the Administration were Samuel Sitgreaves [Pa.], Harrison Gray Otis [Mass.], Jonathan Dayton [N. J.], Robert G. Harper [S. C.], John Rutledge, Jr. [S. C.], Samuel Sewall [Mass.], Samuel W. Dana [Ct.], Nathaniel Smith [Ct.], John Williams [N. Y.], Thomas Pinckney [S. C.], John Allen [Ct.], and James A. Bayard, Sr. [Del.].

The chief opponents of the Administration were Abraham Baldwin [Ga.], William B. Giles [Va.], John Nicholas [Va.], Albert Gallatin [Pa.], and Edward Livingston [N. Y.].

On the Peace Resolutions

House of Representatives, March 27-April 2, 1798

Mr. Sitgreaves was opposed to the resolutions of Mr. Sprigg. He said:

It is contrary to the usual and ordinary course of legislative proceeding to pass mere negative resolutions. The power of declaring war being vested in the Congress, so long as the Congress shall forbear to declare war it is a sufficient expression of their sentiment that such a declaration would be inexpedient: it is the only proper expression of such a sentiment; and it can be no more right to resolve that we will not resort to war, than it would be to pass an act to declare it would be inexpedient to make a law for the regulation of bankruptcy or any other municipal concern.

Mr. Baldwin did not believe it was intended that this House should merely be the instrument to give the sound of war; the subject seemed to be placed wholly in the hands of the legislature. This was the understanding of the country when there was no government in existence, and he believed this was the meaning of the Constitution. The country is now everywhere agitating this question of peace or war, and he trusted they would not be left to grope their way in the dark on this important question. The President had informed the House that all hopes of a negotiation were at an end. He was willing to take the information as it was given, without going into the cabinet of the executive, and to take measures accordingly. But, when some persons declare that the present state of things is already a state of war; that the country is going on in it; that the die is cast; and that we have nothing to do but to go on with it as well as we can, if the House does not believe this to be a true position, this resolution ought to be agreed to, which went to say that the House does not consider the present a state of war, but a state of peace.

MR. OTIS proposed to strike out the words "resort to" and insert "declare" as he was of opinion with the gentleman from Pennsylvania (Mr. Sitgreaves) that the only subjects fit for discussion were active measures, and that it was not regular to declare when they would not do a thing.

MR. DAYTON (the Speaker) moved to strike out the words "against the French republic" and declared that, although he deemed the whole resolution unnecessary, and considered it as not naturally growing out of the President's message, which did not call upon us to declare or make war, yet, as it must be the intenion of the mover, or of some other member, to follow it up with like declarations in relation to all other nations with whom the United States had any intercourse, provided they acted consistently, he thought it better to make the resolution a general one, even if it should be afterward negatived.

MR. HARPER seconded the motion of the gentleman from New Jersey. He was not himself disposed for war, but for peace, while peace could be preserved. But he never said, and would not say, that war was the worst thing which could happen to this country; he thought submission to the aggressions of a foreign power infinitely worse. If gentlemen meant, by agreeing to this resolution, to prevent the country from being put into a state of defence; if they meant by it to effect an entering wedge to submission, he trusted they would find themselves mistaken; for, though he believed the true interest of the country lay in peace, yet he was not disposed to recede from any measures which he thought proper through fear of war.

MR. GILES believed this the proper time to declare whether

the country should remain in peace or go to war. He thought the resolution proper as it stood, because founded on the message of the President, in which the French republic only is named. There was a part of that message, he said, which, in his opinion, amounted to a declaration of war. The President tells the House "that the situation of things is materially changed since he issued his order to prevent the arming of merchant vessels." As far as he understood the situation of the United States at that time, it was a state of neutrality. If that state is changed, and the present is not a state of neutrality, he wished to know what is. He knew only of two states: a state of neutrality and a state of war; he knew of no mongrel state between them. Therefore, if the President of the United States could declare war, we are now in war. Believing, however, that Congress had alone the power to declare war, he thought it time to declare what the state of the nation is. He did not know whether the object might not be answered by the resolution being general, as he was and always had been (notwithstanding insinuations to the contrary) against war with any nation upon the earth. He looked upon war as the greatest calamity which could befall any nation; and, whatever may be the phantoms raised in perspective of national honor and glory in such a state, they will, in the end, all prove fallacious. He believed no nation ought to go to war except when attacked; and this kind of war he should be as ready to meet as any one. He believed we were in a state which required the utmost vigor; but he thought every measure should be avoided which might involve the country in war. For, if we were to go to war with the French at present, he knew not what ever could take place which could produce peace; it must be a war of extermination.

MR. NICHOLAS considered this amendment as defeating the resolution. Was there nothing, he asked, which called for a declaration of the kind proposed? Was it not clear to every one that the country was going fast into a state of war, and was it not to be expected? Ought not the legislature, then (who alone have the power of declaring war), to determine the state of the country, and say whether they mean to go immediately to war or not? He thought the necessity of the resolution was sufficiently evident, by the motion which had been made to change the words from "resort to war," to declare war; in the one case the mischief was met, while the other meant nothing. And, if gentlemen were ready to say we were not prepared to declare war, and, at the same time, were not ready to say it is not expedient to resort to war, it proved that they thought war might be made without being declared. He asked whether gentlemen did not believe the executive had taken measures which would lead to war? And that, if he were at liberty to act upon a change of circumstances between this country and others, Congress were not brought into a situation in which they had no choice? Many discussions had heretofore taken place on the Constitution, but he had never heard it doubted that Congress had the power over the progress of what led to war, as well as the power of declaring war; but, if the President could take the measures which he had taken with respect to arming merchant vessels, he, and not Congress, had the power of making war. He was of opinion that the step taken by the President with respect to merchant vessels went to declare that we rested our cause on arms, which was not calculated to produce any good effect in our favor.

MR. RUTLEDGE said: Gentlemen asked whether war is not approaching? And whether the Executive is not hastening it? To the first question he could not answer, as it depended on France, and so versatile and uncertain is everything in that country that no dependence can be had upon it. The second question he answered in the negative. War would be a loss to this country; and to no individual more than the Executive, who is no warrior—consequently war has no laurels in store for him.

Referring to the inaction of Congress at the previous session, he thought our frigates ought not to have remained at the wharves; that our extensive seacoast, on which is much wealth, should not be unprotected: he thought our seaports, the principal depots of our revenue, ought to have been fortified. He had joined his friends in their attempts to have carried these measures, and, when they failed, he could not help thinking his country was in a degraded state and that she had lost the spirit which animated her in the year 1775. He hoped, however, that now, when France had gone to the lengths which she has gone to, there would be only one sentiment as to the propriety of the measures formerly proposed.

MR. SEWALL quoted a part of the President's message as to the decree which was proposed respecting the taking of English goods on board of neutral vessels and the carrying of which was declared to make neutral vessels good prizes. This last regulation, Mr. S. said, was a direct violation of the law of nations, and amounted to a declaration of war on the part of France against this country. But, instead of making any defence, gentlemen call upon the committee to declare we are not disposed to resort to war against the French republic; so that, after we have been injured and abused, and the common rights of humanity have been denied us, we are not to complain, but make a declaration that we will not go to war. Was, then, he asked, a question of war a card of politeness? Did a nation ever make a declaration that it was not at war? It could not say so, except it were in so degraded a state that it had no rights capable of injury. To say we are not at war was to say no more than it is light when the sun shines; but to call upon the committee to say so at this time was to degrade the nation from its independence and below its character. The present state of things, Mr. S. said, ought to be considered as a state of war, not declared by us, but against us, by the French republic; and if we want spirit to defend ourselves let us not say so. We may refrain from acting, but let us not say we receive injuries with thankfulness. But this proposition goes still further. In a moment of public danger it goes to divide and separate this House from the President of the United States. The gentleman from Virginia [Mr. Giles] had well explained this resolution when he said it was intended to interrupt the views of the President of the United States. That gentleman considered the message of the President as a declaration of war, and this resolution was to be in contradiction to it. If this was the sense in which it was to be understood, it was false in point of fact; for the President had neither declared war nor called upon Congress to declare war; no such sentiment could be found in the message. To agree to the proposition as it stands would be to give countenance to the assertion of the French Government that we are a people divided from our Government; but, taking it with the amendment, he looked upon it as a harmless thing. Mr. S. concluded by saying that he considered the conduct of France in the light of war. How far we would resent it was the question; whether offensively or defensively. He was in favor of defensive measures, as we are not equal to offensive measures (he wished to God we were). It was our weakness and the division which had appeared in our councils that had invited these attacks. He trusted they should now unite and repel them.

Mr. GALLATIN said the intention of the amendment was evidently to render the resolution as unmeaning as possible.

Every gentleman who had spoken on this subject had agreed that war is not a desirable object for the United States. He gave them credit for the assertion. But this was not the question; but whether we are prepared to resort to war under existing circumstances. It is a question of fact.

The people of the United States are informed by France that

negotiations are at an end, and that we cannot obtain redress for wrongs, but may expect a continuation of captures in consequence of the decree, which it was supposed was passed, for seizing all neutral vessels with British property, manufactures, or produce on board. Mr. G. said he differed in opinion from the gentleman last up that this was a declaration of war. He allowed it would be justifiable ground of war for this country and that, on this account, it was necessary to agree to, or reject, the present proposition in order to determine the ground intended to be taken. For, though there may be justifiable cause for war, if it is not our interest to go to war the resolution will be agreed to.

There was another reason why this resolution ought to be now decided which arose from the conduct of our executive. He has declared that a change of circumstances has taken place which has occasioned him to withdraw his order forbidding merchant vessels to arm; which amounts to this: that he now permits vessels of the United States to use means of defence against any attack which may be made upon them. Mr. G. thought it necessary, therefore, to declare whether we were to pursue measures of war or peace.

Mr. Dana said the gentleman from Pennsylvania, and two gentlemen from Virginia, had said that the message of the President amounted to a declaration that we were now in war. This idea he thought was stated very incorrectly. They did not seem to have understood the meaning of the language of the President. The state of things which existed at the time orders were issued to prevent the arming of merchant vessels was essentially different from the present; then there was an evident disposition in the owners of vessels to cruise against a foreign belligerent nation and the order was issued to prevent attack and plunder; but the desire to arm at present is for the purpose of defence merely, and not to cruise or plunder. There is a law forbidding vessels to arm for the purpose of cruising; but none forbidding merchants to arm in their own defence. This was the fair construction, he believed, of the meaning of the President.

Mr. Otis considered the message in a different view from many gentlemen. But admitting, for the sake of argument, that the President had declared an opinion upon the facts stated by him, that war was inevitable; gentlemen must consider the fact to be true; if they doubted it, they ought to demand information.

Mr. Smith looked upon the present resolution as very unimportant. It simply afforded a text from which it was intended to alarm the people with respect to war, and he wished not to indulge gentlemen in their design. He wished the question to be taken for another reason. It was suggested by the gentleman from Virginia that the message of the President was considered by the people as a declaration of war, and that reports were in circulation that a treaty, offensive and defensive, was concluded with Great Britain. After this he would call the attention of the committee to the resolution, which was, in effect, to say, we must interfere or war will be brought upon the country. Did not this go to sanction a report which was as false and malignant as even Jacobinism could invent? It did; and he hoped they would not so far sanction the report as to let the motion lie before them undecided.

Mr. GILES said the question was a question of peace or war, and yet gentlemen call it trifling. He did not mean to alarm the people of the United States, but he wished them to understand their situation. He acknowledged he was himself much alarmed. Gentlemen were willing to engage in defensive, but not in offensive, war; but, when war was once begun, it would not be in the power of the United States to keep it within the character of defensive war. Indeed, the gentleman from Massachusetts [Mr. Sewall], when he spoke of defensive war, confessed our inability for offensive war, and uttered a prayer to the Supreme Being that we were able to engage offensively; and where, he asked, with such sentiments, is the difference between offensive and defensive war? He could see none; he deprecated war of every kind.

Mr. WILLIAMS was persuaded that this negative mode of proceeding was calculated to draw on a debate to set the people against the executive. He had himself seen gentlemen write upon the late message of the President for the purpose of sending to their constituents: *"A war message against France."*

Mr. PINCKNEY said from the first period of a misunderstanding with France declarations have been made deprecating war in general terms, but particularly with that nation. A minister plenipotentiary had been sent to explain the views of this Government, and to remove any jealousies which might exist, and to make such specific propositions as were thought necessary; but our minister was rejected without a hearing. The next measure was to send special commissioners in order to settle our differences and avert the calamity of war. We have, therefore, made sufficient declarations of our pacific intentions. Indeed, he thought too much had been rested on these declarations, as nothing had been done for our defence. When we looked at our seaports and saw their defenceless condition he thought it evident sufficient attention had not been paid to them, knowing that war might at least be a possible event.

He should not have been surprised if some one, fired with the injuries we have received, had brought forward a proposition for war. But instead of this, smarting as we are under injuries, our commerce bleeding at every pore, and our country deeply humiliated, we are called upon to say: You have done everything to injure, insult, and degrade us but we have deserved it; we will do nothing to oppose you. Though God and nature have given us power we will not go to war with you, neither on the present occasion nor on any other, whatever injury you may commit upon us.

MR. GILES said that we ought not to resort to war beyond the limits of the United States. Within our own limits we are capable of making something like exertion, and there, he believed, exertions might be made to advantage. Indeed, one of the propositions which is connected with the present goes to this purpose, and therefore with what propriety could the gentleman say he, and those who were of his opinion, were not for preparing for defence till the enemy is at the door? Nor could he see anything like humiliation in this. Nay, he was convinced if we carried our preparations for defence beyond our own limits, instead of gaining glory or honor, we shall meet with nothing but disgrace, as we are not prepared to make a defence at sea. Indeed, the moment we get beyond our jurisdictional line, defence will become offence, because there will be no evidence by which it can be ascertained by whom the attack commenced. It would, therefore, be unwise to permit ourselves to be placed in this situation.

At present, said Mr. G., there is a pretty general opinion in the country (and he thought there was much ground for the opinion) that there is a disposition in a part of this House, and in part of the Government, for war; and he thought it was proper to come to a declaration upon the subject. This would not only have a good effect upon our own citizens, but it would convince European powers that, though we were preparing for defence, we were not preparing for war.

MR. HARPER said gentlemen preached about peace. They cry, "peace! peace!" as if we, holding the scale of the world, had the power to preserve it. Do not gentlemen know that peace or war is not in our power? They do know it, and that all in our power is to resist, or submit. Was not the clamor which was heard about peace in so many words saying: you must submit, not only to what injuries you have received, but to what you may hereafter receive? If peace was all that gentlemen wanted they would take the resolution in general terms, as proposed to be amended; but their opposing it shows that they have no objection to hostility, if it be not against those whom they dread. And this was the spirit of peace which they wished to preserve— a spirit which he deemed vile submission—a spirit which was afraid to complain and which met every new insult without murmur.

The committee were now told it would be time enough to prepare for war when an invasion of our country was attempted. And why were they told this? Because such an event is not likely to take place. Gentlemen know that all the hostility which France wished to commit against this country may be done by destroying our commerce.

Mr. H. said he would bring his proofs to show that those gentlemen who are now so loud in their calls for peace were heretofore the supporters of a war system. For this purpose he adduced Mr. Monroe's view of the conduct of the Executive of the United States, which, he said, was a publication which had met with the most unbounded and enthusiastic applauses from all the party; and he read from it an extract of a letter from Mr. Monroe to our Secretary of State dated Paris, September 10, 1796, in which he states it to be his opinion "that if a suitable attempt be made to engage the aid of the French Government in support of our claims upon England it may be accomplished; and that to secure success it will be necessary to take the posts and invade Canada."

Yet these are the gentlemen who now are willing to say to France: "We will not fight you; we give you license to do us all the injury you please. You may fit out half a dozen frigates which will be able to block up our ports; and we give you this notice that you may effect your purpose with little expense and not prepare a large fleet for the purpose."

MR. GILES said the gentleman from South Carolina [Mr. Harper] had said "that it had been the object of himself and his associates, but particularly of himself, since the year 1794 to go to war with Great Britain, if possible, and to enter into a treaty of alliance, offensive and defensive, with France."

From the year 1794 to the present period he had uniformly declared it to be his opinion "that war is justifiable only in case of self-defence."

Though he thought France had just ground of complaint

against this country, he did not mean to justify her conduct toward us. He thought she ought to have received our ministers; and, if they had not agreed, to have taken such measures as they thought proper. But this is supposing our ministers clothed with sufficient powers; if they were not there would be some ground of justification for their conduct. The President of the United States is in the possession of information which would satisfy the Congress and the people in this respect, but he has thought proper to withhold it, and therefore he alone is responsible. The President informed the House that he had received certain papers and says: "I have considered these papers; I have deliberated upon them; I have not sent them to you but require you to act upon them; I call upon you to take energetic measures and request you will provide sufficient revenue." The House has been thus obliged to take up the subject in the dark. Is this, said he, a desirable state for the legislature to be placed in? Is it not rather a degraded state? He thought when party rage shall subside this conduct would be deemed extraordinary. In these circumstances, said he, are the people of the United States to be led on from step to step until they are irrevocably involved in war? And are the people to be told that this is a trifling question?

MR. HARPER replied to Mr. Giles's assertion that he (Mr. G.) never proposed war against Great Britain. He knew it. The gentleman always spoke of peace, but pursued measures which led to war. He did not speak of war when he recommended sequestrations, confiscations, etc., because he loved peace. He did not talk of war; but, while he and his friends opposed measures of defence, they were in favor of every measure which led to war. While they were irritating a nation to war they opposed the building of frigates. He thought it seemed as if gentlemen believed it would be well to get to war and then rely upon their favorite nation for support.

MR. GILES renewed the assertion that he and his friends always had been willing to put the nation in a state of defence. As to the frigates, he gloried in his vote against them; but with respect to the use of them the gentleman was mistaken. They were intended to be sent against the Algerines only.

MR. ALLEN said it had been observed, and not in the most candid and proper manner, that the papers received from our commissioners ought to have been laid before the House, and the President had been charged with withholding them.

Though he was himself satisfied with the information he had at present, he believed there were many gentlemen in the

House who wished for more, because there is a paper printed in this city which is continually insinuating that there is something in these dispatches which, if they were made known, would show that the conduct of the Executive has been improper. He therefore proposed the following resolution:

"*Resolved,* That the President of the United States be requested to communicate to this House the dispatches from the envoys extraordinary of the United States to the French republic, mentioned in his message of the 19th instant, *or such parts thereof as considerations of public safety and interest in his opinion may permit.*"

Mr. GILES said that no part of the correspondence ought to be kept from Congress. He was not himself satisfied as to the sincerity of the proceedings of the Executive of the United States toward France; he wished, therefore, not only to have the correspondence of our Ministers, but the instructions which were given to them.

Mr. LIVINGSTON moved to amend the resolution by striking out all the words after the 19th instant, and insert after the words "this House" "the instructions to and."

The latter part of the resolution proposed to transfer a right to the President which it ought itself to exercise, as to judging of what it was proper to publish in consideration of the public safety and interest. If this power was given to the President he might withhold such parts of the papers as might prevent a correct judgment being formed upon them. He was not himself disposed to cede to the President the right which he was sent there to exercise for his constituents, of judging of so important a question as a question of peace or war. He could not basely surrender this right. If the papers were called for at all he hoped the whole would be called for, in order that the House might form that sound and temperate judgment for which the present crisis so loudly calls and for which the people of the United States so anxiously look. Indeed, to pass the resolution unamended would, in his opinion, be a shameful dereliction of their rights.

Mr. BAYARD thought the propriety of this call upon the President was extremely doubtful and, as it regarded the instructions given to our ministers, wholly improper. With respect to the communication of the dispatches, it was wholly a matter of executive discretion to judge whether it would be proper to communicate them or not. He was one of those who had so much confidence in the Executive as to trust to his candor, understanding, and integrity to determine upon the propriety of what he should send to, or withhold from, this House. At a time when it is not known that our negotiation with France is closed it would be extremely imprudent to have the instructions of our ministers laid before this House, as what was sent here, notwithstanding any vote of secrecy, would not long be kept secret. It would soon be in Europe and might do us essential injury by disclosing our ultimatum to France and by showing it also to the world. It was in vain, Mr. B. said, to suppose that one hundred men could keep a secret for any length of time, however important it might be. To elucidate that assertion he referred to the divulging the secret of the British treaty by a Senator.

But the gentleman from Virginia [Mr. Giles] has no confidence in the Government of this country with respect to its negotiation with France and, in order to try the sincerity of the Executive, he wishes for the papers. Does the gentleman by this mean to give the lie to the Executive? Because in his message he has told the House that he has given power to our ministers to settle our disputes with the French republic, and to "make all reasonable concessions." What more does the gentleman wish? Does he wish unreasonable concessions to be made? Surely he does not. Did anything appear in the conduct of the French Directory to show that our Ministers were not possessed of ample powers? No; the Directory never knew anything about their powers, at least so far as any official communications had been received on the subject. There could not, therefore, be any ground upon which the gentleman could rest his suspicions. He hoped, therefore, the amendment would be negatived.

Mr. Livingston's amendment was adopted. Mr. Allen's resolution was then adopted as amended by a vote of 65 to 27.

The President replied to the request of Congress by sending it every scrap of the communication he had received from the envoys in Paris. Whether he and his supporters in the House had planned the entire affair for the discomfiture of the opposition, or it had risen naturally out of the suspicions of the Republicans, its success was complete and even overwhelming. There was nothing at all revealed which excused France for her action. Indeed, the President's former communication had been singularly reserved in its statement of the ill treatment to which the American envoys had been

subjected. Congress now learned that they had been
kept six months without official recognition, during which
they had been approached unofficially by three agents of
Talleyrand, the French Minister of Foreign Affairs,
with the suggestion that bribes to the governments of
France and Holland, under the guise of "loans," might
gain their object. The agents made their proposals
under the signatures of X, Y, and Z, and from this the
whole affair became popularly known as the "X Y Z
Mission."

The envoys spurned the suggestion of the agents,
saying "we will not give you a sixpence"—a reply
which was later developed by the American people,
proud of their envoys' action, into the swelling epigram:
"Millions for defence, but not one cent for tribute."

Finding the envoys inflexible, on April 3, 1798,
Talleyrand ordered Pinckney and Marshall to quit the
country, but expressed a desire that Gerry, who he
thought, as a Republican would be more amenable to
his plans, would remain. This desire was expressed so
strongly and significantly that Gerry, fearing to precipitate war by not acceding to it, stayed on until August,
when he received imperative instructions from the
American Government to return home.

On Gerry's assigning his reasons for leaving, Talleyrand brazenly denied, with great show of indignation,
all knowledge of the X Y Z proposals. Yet he could not
deny that he himself had resorted to the old policy of the
French Government in American affairs of appealing
to the American people over the heads of their Government. In this appeal he greatly deceived himself. The
whole country flamed with warlike defiance. Mass meetings were held everywhere and addresses in support of
the President were adopted; volunteers offered themselves for war, and subscriptions of money and war vessels were made. The revolutionary badge of the time,
the black cockade, became a popular adornment of hats,
and patriotic songs, such as "Hail Columbia" and
"Adams and Liberty" were written and sung.

The Republicans, on whom Talleyrand had leaned
for support, were especially eager to avow their patriot-

ism. The French, said Jefferson, "had so far mistaken
the party as to suppose their first passion to be attachment to France and hatred of the Federal party, and not
love of their country."

Nevertheless the Republicans were put on the defensive and became greatly unpopular. In the House of
Representatives, in which they had been of equal
strength with the Federalists, all the doubtful members
and many of the former adherents of the party joined

"THE CONTRAST"

From Lossing's "Field Book of the War of 1812"

with the forces of the administration and ratified the
bills of the Federalist Senate for increasing the army
and navy, purchasing foundries, etc. On April 30 the
navy, which had heretofore been a part of the war department, was placed in a new department under Secretary Benjamin Stoddert. War vessels were authorized to capture armed French vessels committing depredations on American commerce; merchant vessels were
armed to prevent capture, and privateers were commissioned. A direct tax was imposed, and loans upon the
credit ordered, as well as a general loan of $5,000,000.
On June 13 commercial intercourse with France was
suspended, and on July 9 all treaties with that country
were declared no longer binding, as having been broken
by France.

The only one of the measures to which the Republicans offered determined opposition was that of the
increase of the army by provisional troops. It was
claimed that these were needed because of a threatened

invasion of the Southern States from the West Indies by a soldier of fortune, Victor Hugues, leading a force of negroes with the avowed intention of rousing a slave insurrection. Since the provisional troops would be officered by appointees of the Federalist administration, the Republicans declared that advantage was being taken of the "war scare" to provide salaries for Federalist politicians, and that the army might be used in party warfare, although they had the good sense not to make these charges in the course of the debate in Congress, very properly confining their objections to questions of constitutionality and military expediency.

The bill for the increase of the army was passed on May 18 by a vote of 51 to 40.

In his address at the opening of the next session of Congress (December, 1798) President Adams: (1) promised a future communication on relations with France, and for the present (2) discredited her professions of conciliatory intentions, and (3) noted that her recent decree intended ostensibly to restrain the depredations of French cruisers on American commerce was a mockery, in that the laws which were the sources of the depredations were not repealed. Therefore he recommended (4) that our vigilance be unrelaxed. He himself, he said, had refused the request of Talleyrand to reopen negotiations and send another minister, which would be an act of national humiliation. (5) Accordingly he recommended the prosecution of measures of national defence, especially the increase of the navy.

With these recommendations both the Senate and House concurred. A more stringent act to suspend commercial intercourse with France was passed, and approved on February 9, 1799; a sum not exceeding one million dollars to increase the navy, and a sum not exceeding $35,000 to increase its equipment, were appropriated on February 22; and a system for the government of the navy was enacted, and approved on March 2. A thorough reorganization of the army was made in an act approved March 3.

On February 15, 1799, the special message on relations with France, which had been promised by the

President in his opening address, was laid before Congress. It called attention to the fact that that article of the French Directory still remained in force by which, "explicitly and exclusively, American seamen were to be treated as pirates if found on board ships of the enemies of France."

In the debates on French relations during this session the Republicans continued to insist on giving the French Government the benefit of the doubt. They were, however, outvoted.

PEACE WITH FRANCE

During this session of Congress the enmity of the President toward Hamilton caused him to repudiate his firm determination not to send another minister to France. In the threat of war with France, Washington had accepted the position of lieutenant-general of the army. He appointed Alexander Hamilton, C. C. Pinckney, and Henry Knox, in respective order, as next to him in command, thus placing the three in the reverse order of their rank in the Revolution. Indeed, Washington, Hamilton, and Pinckney attended the opening of Congress in their new capacities. Now Knox, the absentee, was President Adams's choice for the position next to Washington, and the President yielded to the wish of Washington only upon the latter's express statement that he would resign unless his wishes in the matter were respected. It could not be expected that the aging dictator of the revolution would now be active in the field, and so Hamilton would practically occupy the place of commander-in-chief. As he was already the foremost minister in the cabinet, and regarded by many Federalists as the chief authority in the party, if not also in the administration, Adams clearly realized that, in event of war with France, Hamilton would in all probability become a popular hero and at the next election would be chosen President instead of himself. Therefore he determined to do all in his power to prevent the war. In the exercise of this determination he hastened the downfall of his party.

Talleyrand had signified to Adams that William Vans Murray, minister to Holland, would be acceptable to him as minister to France. Without having given any previous intimation of his intention, on February 18, 1799, the President nominated Murray as minister to France, and a few days thereafter added Oliver Ellsworth and (Patrick Henry declining) William R. Davie, Governor of North Carolina, to the commission. The friends of Hamilton in the cabinet and Senate did everything they could to defeat the appointments, but the Democratic Republicans, to whose prejudices the President appealed by stigmatizing the opposing Federalists as "the British faction," joined with the Adams Federalists and were finally able to confirm the nominations. The Federalist party, whose whole strength had been built up on the prospect of war with France, was thus left without a reason for existence.

Fortunately for the President's new policy the envoys found a new government upon their arrival in France during the autumn. Napoleon had returned from Egypt, and he became first consul. With visions of the conquest of Europe and Asia in his brain he was very glad to come to terms with America, which he did in the course of the following year. The convention, signed September 30, 1800, guaranteed the safety of American commerce for the future at the price of the abandonment by the United States of claims for damages in the past. The treaty was ratified by both parties on December 21, 1801; it abrogated all former treaties.

CHAPTER IV

THE LOUISIANA PURCHASE

Treaty with Spain for Free Navigation of the Mississippi—Retrocession of Louisiana to France by Spain—President Jefferson's Letter to Robert R. Livingston, Minister to France, on the Subject—He Determines to Purchase New Orleans—Debate in the Senate on the Forcible Seizure of New Orleans: in Favor, James Ross [Pa.], Samuel White [Del.], Gouverneur Morris [N. Y.]; Opposed, John Breckinridge [Ky.], De Witt Clinton [N. Y.], Stevens T. Mason [Va.], James Jackson [Ga.]— Purchase of Louisiana Negotiated—Constitutionality of the Act: Letter of Jefferson on the Subject; Debate in the Senate: Speakers in Favor of Constitutionality, Senator Jackson, Robert Wright [Md.], John Taylor [Va.], Wilson C. Nicholas [Va.], Senator Breckinridge, John Quincy Adams [Mass.]; Opposed, William H. Wells [Del.], Timothy Pickering [Mass.], Uriah Tracy [Ct.]—Ratification of the Treaty.

BY a striking anomaly President Jefferson, the chief advocate of the limitation of Federal powers to those expressly granted in the Constitution, was compelled by circumstances to make a greater extension of those powers than had ever before been attempted.

This action was the purchase of Louisiana, the territory owned by France about the mouth of the Mississippi, and west of that river to the Pacific ocean.

From the days of the Confederation it was the unanimous opinion of the fathers of the country that free navigation of the Mississippi was absolutely essential to the existence of the nation, and therefore they were unalterably determined to secure it. France had ceded Louisiana to Spain in 1762, who held it until 1800, when it was retroceded, in exchange for European territory, to France. During the possession by Spain that country excluded other nations from the navigation of the Mississippi. This exclusion was resisted by the United States, which was finally compelled to be satisfied with a suspension of free navigation for twenty-five

years, this being secured by John Jay, as special envoy to
Spain, in 1786. Owing to the pressure brought upon the
Federal Government by the growing population of the
western States (Kentucky and Tennessee) through proposed expeditions against New Orleans in violation of
international law, President Washington, in the summer
of 1795, sent Thomas Pinckney, then minister to Great
Britain, as an envoy extraordinary to Madrid to negotiate a treaty which should secure free navigation for the
United States at once. He arrived at a favorable time,
Spain, the ally of Great Britain in the war with France,
having been compelled by the success of French arms
to make a treaty with France. After long negotiations
a treaty between Spain and America was concluded in
October, by which the Louisiana boundary was fixed in
the middle of the Mississippi, southward to the thirty-
first degree of latitude, and navigation of the river from
source to mouth was made free to both countries, but
to no others. New Orleans was made a free port to
Americans for three years, at the expiration of which
term the privilege was to be renewed or another port
given them nearby. It was provided that free ships
should make free goods, and privateering should be
punished as piracy.

The terms of the treaty were executed in 1798, to the
measurable satisfaction of the western population, who,
however, still cherished the hope of more thoroughly
securing the right to navigate the river by annexing all
the contiguous territory.

The news of the retrocession of Louisiana to France
in 1800 was accompanied by the alarming rumor that
Napoleon Bonaparte intended to reëstablish there a
strong imperial government which would effectually
block the western development of the American republic. Late in 1801 the rumor was confirmed by the report
that Bonaparte had sent a great fleet and army ostensibly against San Domingo, which was then in insurrection, but really to take over from Spain possession of
New Orleans after they had subdued the rebellion of
the "Black Republic." This created a most uneasy
feeling in the West, which, however, was allayed by the

general confidence of that Republican region in President Jefferson. This confidence was thoroughly justified.

On April 18, 1802, the President wrote to Robert R. Livingston, minister to France, inquiring into the nature of the cession. In it he said:

"The cession of Louisiana and the Floridas by Spain to France works most sorely on the United States. It completely reverses all the political relations of the United States, and will form a new epoch in our political course. There is on the globe one single spot the possessor of which is our natural and habitual enemy. It is New Orleans, through which the produce of three-eighths of our territory must pass to market. France, placing herself in that door, assumes to us the attitude of defiance, . . . [and] seals the union of two nations who, in conjunction, can maintain exclusive possession of the ocean. From that moment we must marry ourselves to the British fleet and nation, and make the first cannon which shall be fired in Europe the signal for tearing up any settlement she [France] may have made."

According to the treaty with Spain a place of deposit for merchandise was assigned the citizens of the United States in the port of New Orleans. On October 2, 1802, this concession was abrogated by the Spanish *intendant*, to the great indignation of the Western merchants.

The President determined to solve the difficulty by purchasing New Orleans from its new owners. At his instigation the House of Representatives appropriated $2,000,000 for this purpose, and on January 11, 1803, the Senate confirmed his appointment of James Monroe as special envoy to negotiate, in collaboration with Minister Livingston, with Bonaparte, and, in collaboration with Charles Pinckney, minister to Spain, to get the necessary renunciation of the territory by his Catholic Majesty, Charles IV.

Either the ardent spirits of some of the Federalists could not wait upon the slow processes of diplomacy, or they grasped the opportunity to regain favor with the populace and at the same time discredit the Administration. They endeavored in the Senate to compel the

President to seize at once the territory and so to nullify all his peaceful negotiations. Unfortunately for the attempt the movers were Eastern and Northern Federalists who were forced to make obviously insincere pleas in behalf of the Western and Southern people, since the representatives of these were unanimous in support of the President's policy and presented proofs that their constituents were entirely satisfied to let matters take a peaceful course.

On February 16, 1803, James Ross [Pa.] introduced resolutions in the Senate to the effect that the infraction of the treaty rights in regard to Louisiana was "an aggression hostile to the honor and interest" of the United States, that it did "not consist with the dignity or safety of this Union" to hold rights "so important by a tenure so uncertain," and therefore "that the President be authorized to take possession" of a place of deposit and adopt measures necessary to secure it to the United States; and that he be authorized to call into service not over 50,000 militia, and that $5,000,000 be appropriated in order to carry out these measures.

John Breckinridge [Ky.] proposed substitute resolutions, which authorized the President only to *prepare* for such action as he might "deem necessary for the security of the territory of the United States."

Ross and Breckinridge defended their respective resolutions. Other speakers were Samuel White [Del.] and Gouverneur Morris [N. Y.], who supported Senator Ross's resolutions; and De Witt Clinton [N. Y.], Stevens T. Mason [Va.], and James Jackson [Ga.], who supported Senator Breckinridge's resolutions. The Breckinridge resolutions were adopted.

CONQUEST OR PURCHASE?

SENATE, FEBRUARY 16-25, 1903

SENATOR ROSS.—Sir, whom does this infraction of the treaty and the natural rights of this country most intimately affect? If the wound inflicted on national honor be not sensibly felt by the whole nation, is there not a large portion of your citizens exposed to immediate ruin by a continuance of this state of things? The calamity lights upon all those who live upon the western waters. More than half a million of your citizens are by this cut off from a market. What would be the language, what would be the feelings of gentlemen in this House, were such an indignity offered on the Atlantic coast? What would they say if the Chesapeake, the Delaware, or the Bay of New York were shut up and all egress prohibited by a foreign power? And yet none of these waters embrace the interests of so many as the Mississippi. The numbers and the property affected by shutting this river are greater than anything that could follow by the blockade of a river on the Atlantic coast. Every part of the Union is equally entitled to protection, and no good reason can be offered why one part should be less attended to than another.

Fortunately for this country there can be no doubt in the present case, our national right has been acknowledged and solemnly secured by treaty. The treaty has been long in a state of execution. It was violated and denied without provocation or apology. The treaty then is no security. This evident right is one the security of which ought not to be precarious: it is indispensable that the enjoyment of it shall be placed beyond all doubt. So important a right will never be secured while the mouth of the Mississippi is exclusively in the hands of the Spaniards. Caprice and enmity occasion constant interruption. From the very position of our country, from its geographical shape, from motives of complete independence, the command of the navigation of the river ought to be in our hands.

Why submit to a tardy, uncertain negotiation as the only means of regaining what you have lost: a negotiation with those who have wronged you; with those who declare they have no right at the moment they deprive you of yours? When in possession you will negotiate with more advantage. You will then be in the condition to keep others out. You will be in the actual exercise of jurisdiction over all your claims; your people will have the benefits of a lawful commerce. When your determination is known, you will make an easy and an honorable accommodation with any other claimant. The present possessors have no pretence to complain, for they have no right to the country by their own confession. The western people will discover that you are making every effort they could desire for their protection. They will ardently support you in the contest, if a contest becomes necessary. Their all will be at stake, and neither their zeal nor their courage need be doubted.

Suppose that this course be not now pursued. Let me warn gentlemen how they trifle with the feelings, the hopes, and the fears of such a body of men as those who inhabit the western waters. These men have arms in their hands; the same arms with which they proved victorious over their savage neighbors. They have a daring spirit; they have ample means of subsistence; and they have men disposed to lead them on to revenge their wrongs. Are you certain that they will wait the end of negotiations? When they hear that nothing has been done for their immediate relief, they will probably take their resolution and act. Indeed, from all we have heard, there is great reason to believe that they will or that they may have already taken that resolution.

They know the nature of the obstruction, they know the weakness of the country; they are sure of present success, and they have a bold river to bear them forward to the place of action. They want only a leader to conduct them, and it would be strange if, with such means and such a spirit, a leader should not soon present himself.

Senator Ross prophesied that such an expedition would probably result in the establishment of a new nation under French domination, and hence inimical to the United States. He feared, indeed, that it would lead to the disruption of the Union.

I say, let us go and redress ourselves; you will have the whole nation with you. On no question since the Declaration of Independence has the nation been so unanimous as upon this. It is true we have a lamentable division of political opinion among us which has produced much mischief and may produce much greater than any we have yet felt. But on this question party spirit ought to sink and disappear.

SENATOR WHITE.—We can never have permanent peace on our western waters till we possess ourselves of New Orleans and such other positions as may be necessary to give us the complete and absolute command of the navigation of the Mississippi. We have now such an opportunity of accomplishing this important object as may not be presented again in centuries, and every justification that could be wished for availing ourselves of the opportunity. Spain has dared us to the trial and now bids us defiance; she is yet in possession of that country; it is at this moment within your reach and within your power; it offers a sure and easy conquest: we should have to encounter there now only a weak, inactive, and unenterprising people; but how may a few months vary this scene and darken our prospects! Though not officially informed, we know that the Spanish provinces on the Mississippi have been ceded to the French, and that they will as soon as possible take possession of them. What may we then expect? When in the last extremity we shall be driven to arms in defence of our indisputable rights where now slumbers on his post with folded arms the sluggish Spaniard, we shall be hailed by the vigilant and alert French grenadier, and in the defenceless garrison that would now surrender at our approach we shall see unfurled the standards that have waved triumphant in Italy, surrounded by impregnable ramparts and defended by the disciplined veterans of Egypt.

But, Mr. President, what is more than all to be dreaded in such hands, it may be made the means of access and corruption to your national councils and a key to your treasury. Should Bonaparte approach the western people, not in the menacing attitude of an enemy, but under the specious garb of a protector and a friend; should he invite them to the free navigation of the river, and give them privileges in trade not heretofore enjoyed; should he send emissaries into their country to court and intrigue with them, he may seduce their affections and thus accomplish by address and cunning what even his force might not be equal to. In this way, having operated upon their passions, having enlisted in his service their hopes and their fears, he may gain an undue ascendancy over them. Should these things be effected, which God forbid—but Bonaparte in a few years has done much more—what, let me ask honorable gentlemen, will be the consequences? I fear even to look them in the face. The degraded countries of Europe that have been enslaved by the divisions and distractions of their councils, produced by similar means, afford us melancholy examples. Foreign influence will gain admittance to your national councils; the First Consul, or his interests, will be represented in the Congress of the United States; this floor may become the theater of sedition and intrigue. You will have a French faction in the Government, and that faction will increase with the rapidly increasing population of the western world. Whenever this period shall arrive it will be the crisis of American glory, and must result either in the political subjugation of the Atlantic States or in their separation from the western country; and I am sure there is no American who does not view as one of the greatest evils that could befall us the dismemberment of this Union. Honorable gentlemen may wrap themselves up in their present imaginary security and say that these things are afar off, or that they can never happen; but let me beseech of them to look well to the measures they are now pursuing, for, on the wisdom, the promptness, and energy of those measures will depend whether they shall happen or not. And let me tell them, sir, that the want of firmness or judgment in the Cabinet will be no apology for the disgrace and ruin of the nation.

SENATOR BRECKINRIDGE.—Early in the session the House of Representatives was informed by a communication from the President that the Governor of New Orleans had strongly opposed the conduct of the Intendant, declaring that he was acting without authority in refusing the deposit.

The Spanish Minister, who resides here and who stands deservedly high in the confidence of his government, was clearly of opinion that the Intendant was acting without authority, and that redress would be given so soon as the competent authority could interpose. From this state of things what is the course any civilized nation who respects her character or rights would pursue? There is but one course, which is admitted by writers on the laws of nations as the proper one, and is thus described by Vattel in his book, Secs. 336, 338:

"A sovereign ought to show, in all his quarrels, a sincere desire of rendering justice and preserving peace. He is obliged before he takes up arms, and after having taken them up also, to offer equitable conditions, and then alone his arms become just against an obstinate enemy, who refuses to listen to justice or to equity. His own advantage, and that of human society, oblige him to attempt, before he takes up arms, all the pacific methods of obtaining either the reparation of the injury, or a just satisfaction. This moderation, this circumspection, is so much the more proper, and commonly even indispensable, as the action we take for an injury does not always proceed from a design to offend us, and is sometimes a mistake rather than an act of malice: frequently it even happens that the injury is done by inferior persons, without their sovereign having any share in it; and on these occasions it is not natural to presume that he would refuse us a just satisfaction."

This is the course which the President has taken and in which the House of Representatives have expressed, by their resolution, their confidence.

But the gentleman is afraid that if we do not immediately seize the country we shall lose the golden opportunity of doing it. Would your national honor be free from imputation by a conduct of such inconsistency and duplicity? A minister is sent to the offending nation with an olive-branch for the purpose of an amicable discussion and settlement of differences and, before he has scarcely turned his back, we invade the territories of that nation with an army of fifty thousand men! Would such conduct comport with the genius and principles of our Republic, whose true interest is peace and who has hitherto professed to cultivate it with all nations? Would not such a procedure subject us to the just censure of the world, and to the strongest jealousy of those who have possessions near to us? Would such a procedure meet the approbation of even our own citizens, whose lives and fortunes would be risked in the conflict? And would it not be policy inexcusably rash to plunge this country into war to effect that which the President not only thinks can be effected but is now actually in a train of negotiation? If, on the other hand, negotiation should fail, how different will be the ground on which we stand! We stand acquitted by the world, and, what is of more consequence, by our own citizens and our own consciences. But one sentiment will then animate and pervade the whole, and from thenceforth we will take counsel only from our courage.

SENATOR CLINTON.—If I were called upon to prescribe a course of policy most important for this country to pursue, it would be to avoid European connections and wars. It is our interest and our duty to cultivate peace with sincerity and good faith. As a young nation, pursuing industry in every channel and adventuring commerce in every sea, it is highly important that we should not only have a pacific character but that we should really deserve it. If we manifest an unwarrantable ambition and a rage for conquest, we unite all the great powers of Europe against us. The security of all the European possessions in our vicinity will eternally depend, not upon their strength, but upon our moderation and justice. Look at the Canadas—at the Spanish territories to the south—at the British, Spanish, French, Danish, and Dutch West India islands—at the vast countries to the west, as far as where the Pacific rolls its waves; consider well the eventful consequences that would result if we were possessed by a spirit of conquest; consider well the impression which a manifestation of that spirit will make upon those who would be affected by it. If we are to rush at once into the territory of a neighboring nation with fire and sword for the misconduct of a subordinate officer, will not our national character be greatly injured? Will we not be classed with the robbers and destroyers of mankind? Will not the nations of Europe perceive in this conduct the germ of a lofty spirit and an enterprising ambition which will level them to the earth when age has matured our strength and expanded our powers of annoyance, unless they combine and cripple us in our infancy? May not the consequences be that we must look out for a naval force to protect our commerce; that a close alliance will result; that we will be thrown at once into the ocean of European politics, where every wave that rolls and every wind that blows will agitate our bark? Is this a desirable state of things? Will the people of this coun-

try be seduced into it by all the colorings of rhetoric and all
the arts of sophistry—by vehement appeals to their pride and
artful addresses to their cupidity? No, sir. Three-fourths of
the American people (I assert it boldly and without fear of contradiction) are opposed to this measure. And would you take
up arms with a millstone hanging around your neck? How
would you bear up, not only against the force of the enemy, but
against the irresistible current of public opinion? The thing,
sir, is impossible, the measure is worse than madness; it is wicked
beyond the powers of description

It is in vain for the mover to oppose these weighty considerations by menacing us with an insurrection of the western States,
that may eventuate in their seizure of New Orleans without
the authority of Government; their throwing themselves into
the arms of a foreign power; or in a dissolution of the Union.
Such threats are doubly improper—improper as they respect
the persons to whom they are addressed, because we are not to
be deterred from the performance of our duty by menaces of
any kind, from whatever quarter they may proceed; and it is
no less improper to represent our western brethren as a lawless,
unprincipled banditti who would at once release themselves from
the wholesome restraints of law and order, forego the sweets of
liberty, and either renounce the blessings of self-government or,
like the Goths and Vandals, pour down with the irresistible force
of a torrent, upon the countries below and carry havoc and desolation in their train. A separation by a mountain and a different
outlet into the Atlantic cannot create any natural collision between the Atlantic and western States; on the contrary, they
are bound together by a community of interests and a similarity
of language and manners—by the ties of consanguinity and
friendship and a sameness of principles. There is no reflecting
and well-principled man in this country who can view the sev-
erance of the States without horror and who does not consider it
as a Pandora's box which will overwhelm us with every calamity; and it has struck me with not a little astonishment that, on
the agitation of almost every great political question, we should
be menaced with this evil. Last session, when a bill repealing a
judiciary act was under consideration, we were told that the
eastern States would withdraw themselves from the Union if
it should obtain; and we are now informed that, if we do not
accede to the proposition before us, the western States will hoist
the standard of revolt and dismember the empire. Sir, these
threats are calculated to produce the evil they predict and they
may possibly approximate the spirit they pretend to warn us

against. They are at all times unnecessary, at all times improper, at all times mischievous, and ought never to be mentioned within these walls.

SENATOR JACKSON.—Peace is the interest of all republics, and war their destruction; it loads and fetters them with debt and entangles not only the present race but posterity. Peace, sir, has been the ruling policy of the United States throughout all her career. If we show the citizens that we are not willing to go to war and load them with taxes, they will all be with us when a necessity for war arrives. What, sir, was the policy of America from the commencement of the Revolution? At that day did we hastily go to war? No; we tried every peaceable means to avoid it, and those means induced a unanimity in the people.

At the present moment, sir, the people are averse to war; they are satisfied with the steps of the executive; they wish negotiation. If you adopt these resolutions they will be still divided; if you negotiate and fail in that negotiation—if you cannot obtain a redress of the injury which they feel as well as you, they will go all lengths with you and be prepared for any event; you will have this advantage: you will be unanimous, and America united is a match for the world. In such a case, sir, every man will be anxious to march, he would go himself if called on, and whether the sluggish Spaniard or the French grenadier commands New Orleans it must fall; they will not be able to resist the brave and numerous hosts of our western brethren, who are so much interested in the injury complained of. New Orleans must belong to the United States; it must come to us in the course of human events, it will naturally fall into our hands by gradual but inevitable causes, as sure and certain as manufactures arise from increased population and the plentiful products of agriculture and commerce. But let it be noticed that, if New Orleans by a refusal of justice falls into our hands by force, the Floridas, as sure as fate, fall with it. Good faith forbids encroachment on a pacific ally; but if hostility shows itself against us, interest demands it; Georgia in such case could not do without it. God and nature have destined New Orleans and the Floridas to belong to this great and rising empire. As natural bounds to the south are the Atlantic, the Gulf of Mexico, and the Mississippi, and the world at some future day cannot hold them from us.

SENATOR MORRIS.—In my opinion, there is nothing worth fighting for but national honor; for in the national honor is involved the national independence. I know that a State may find itself in such unpropitious circumstances that prudence may force a wise Government to conceal the sense of indignity. But the insult should be engraved on tablets of brass with a pencil of steel. And, when that time and chance which happen to all shall bring forward the favorable moment, then let the avenging arm strike him. It is by avowing and maintaining this stern principle of honor that peace can be preserved.

What is the state of things? There has been a cession of the island of New Orleans and of Louisiana to France. Whether the Floridas have also been ceded is not yet certain. Now, sir, had Spain a right to make this cession without our consent? Gentlemen have taken it for granted that she had. But I deny the position. No nation has a right to give another a dangerous neighbor without her consent. He who renders me insecure, he who hazards my peace and exposes me to imminent danger, commits an act of hostility against me and gives me the rights consequent on that act. It is among the first limitations to the exercise of the rights of property that we must so use our own as not to injure another; and it is under the immediate sense of this restriction that nations are bound to act toward each other.

But it is not this transfer alone. There are circumstances both in the time and in the manner of it which deserve attention. I ask, was this a public treaty? No. Was official notice of it given to the Government of this country? Was it announced to the President of the United States in the usual forms of civility between nations who duly respect each other? It was not. Had this transaction been intended fairly it would have been told frankly. But it was secret because it was hostile. The First Consul, in the moment of terminating his differences with you, sought the means of future influence and control. He found and secured a pivot for that immense lever by which, with potent arm, he means to subvert your civil and political institutions. Has the King of Spain, has the First Consul of France, no means of making such communication to the President of the United States? Yes, sir, we have a minister in Spain; we have a minister in France. Nothing was easier, and yet nothing has been done. Our first magistrate has been treated with contempt; and through him our country has been insulted.

With that meek and peaceful spirit now so strongly recommended we submitted to this insult and what followed? That which might have been expected—a violation of our treaty. An open and direct violation by a public officer of the Spanish Government. Furthermore, the Intendant, as if determined to try the extent of your meekness, forbids to your citizens all communication with those who inhabit the shores of the Mississippi. Though they should be starving the Spaniard is made criminal who should give them food. Fortunately the waters of the river are potable, or else we should be precluded from the common benefits of nature, the common bounty of heaven. What then, I ask, is the amount of this savage conduct? Sir, it is war. Open and direct war. And yet gentlemen recommend peace and forbid us to take up the gauntlet of defiance.

Sir, I repeat to you that I wish for peace—real, lasting, honorable peace. To obtain and secure this blessing let us by a bold and decisive conduct convince the powers of Europe that we are determined to defend our rights; that we will not submit to insult; that we will not bear degradation. This is the conduct which becomes a generous people. This conduct will command the respect of the world. Nay, sir, it may rouse all Europe to a proper sense of their situation. They see that the balance of power on which their liberties depend is, if not destroyed, in extreme danger. They know that the dominion of France has been extended by the sword over millions who groan in the servitude of their new masters. These unwilling subjects are ripe for revolt. The empire of the Gauls is not like that of Rome, secured by political institutions. It may yet be broken. But, whatever may be the conduct of others, let us act as becomes ourselves. I cannot believe, with my honorable colleague, that three-fourths of America are opposed to vigorous measures. I cannot believe that they will meanly refuse to pay the sums needful to vindicate their honor and support their independence. Sir, this is a libel on the people of America. They will disdain submission to the proudest sovereign on earth. They have not lost the spirit of seventy-six. But, sir, if they are so base as to barter their rights for gold; if they are so vile that they will not defend their honor; they are unworthy of the rank they enjoy, and it is no matter how soon they are parceled out among better masters.

SENATOR MASON.—The resolutions of the gentleman from Pennsylvania [Mr. Ross] go at once to the point of war. Indeed, he told us that it is not war—it was only going and taking peaceable possession of New Orleans! How did the gentleman mean to go, and how take peaceable possession? Would he march at the head of the *posse comitatus?* No! he would march at the head of fifty thousand militia, and he would send forth the whole naval and regular force, armed and provided with military stores. He would enter their island, set fire to their warehouses and bombard their city, desolate their farms and plantations, and, having swept all their habitations away, after wading through streams of blood, he would tell those who had escaped destruction: we do not come here to make war on you—we are a very moderate, tender-hearted kind of neighbors and are come here barely to take peaceable possession of your territory! Why, sir, this is too naked not to be an insult to the understanding of a child!

But the gentleman from New York [Mr. Morris] did not trifle with the Senate in such a style; he threw off the mask at once, and, in a downright manly way, fairly told us that he liked war—that it was his favorite mode of negotiating between nations; that war gave dignity to the species—that it drew forth the most noble energies of humanity! That gentleman scorned to tell us that he wished to take peaceable possession. No! He could not snivel; his vast genius spurned huckstering; his mighty soul would not bear to be locked up in a petty warehouse at New Orleans; he was for war—terrible, glorious havoc! He tells you plainly that you are not only to recover your rights, but you must remove your neighbors from their possessions and repel those to whom they may transfer the soil; that Bonaparte's ambition is insatiable; that he will throw in colonies of Frenchmen, who will settle on your frontier for thousands of miles round about (when he comes there); and he does not forget to tell you of the imminent dangers which threaten our good old friends, the English. He tells you that New Orleans is the lock and you must seize upon the key, and shut the door against this terrible Bonaparte or he will come with his legions, and, as Gulliver served the Lilliputians, wash you off the map. Not content, in his great care for your honor and glory, as a statesman and a warrior he turns prophet to oblige you—your safety in the present year or the next does not satisfy him—his vast mind, untrammeled by the ordinary progressions of chronology, looks over ages to come with a faculty bordering on omniscience, and conjures us to come forward and regulate the decrees of Providence at ten thousand years' distance.

We have been told that Spain had no right to cede Louisiana to France; that she had ceded to us the privilege of deposit, and had, therefore, no right to cede her territory without our consent! Are gentlemen disposed to wage war in support of this principle? Because she has given us a little privilege—a mere indulgence on her territory—is she thereby constrained from doing anything for ever with her immense possessions? No doubt if the gentleman [Mr. Morris] were to be the negotiator on this occasion he would say: "You mean to cede New Orleans; no, gentlemen, I beg your pardon, you cannot cede that, for we want it ourselves; and, as to the Floridas, it would be very indiscreet to cede that, as, in all human probability, we shall want that also in less than five hundred years from this day; and then, as to Louisiana, you surely could not think of that, for in something less than a thousand years, in the natural order of things, our population will progress toward that place also."

We are also told that the power of the Chief Consul is so great that he puts up and pulls down all the nations of the old world at discretion, and that he can do so with us. Yet we are told by the wonderful statesman who gives us this awful information that we must go to war with this maker and destroyer of governments. If, after the unceasing pursuit of empire and conquest, which is thus presented to us, we take possession of his territory, from the gentleman's own declarations, what are we to expect, only that this wonderful man—who never abandons an object; who thinks his own and the nation's honor pledged to go through whatever he undertakes—will next attack us? Does the gentleman think that this terrible picture, which his warm imagination has drawn, is a conclusive argument for proceeding to that war which he recommends?

On April 11, 1803, the day before Monroe's arrival at Paris, Bonaparte, who was greatly in need of money to prosecute his designs of European conquest, invited Minister Livingston to make an offer for the whole of the vast territory known as Louisiana. Monroe and Livingston offered $10,000,000. The price was finally fixed at $15,000,000, a sum which included $3,750,000 in claims of American citizens against France for depredations on commerce.[1] The treaty was signed on April 30, 1803.

It is probable that Bonaparte, in making the treaty, broke his faith with Spain, there having been a secret understanding on the retrocession of the territory from Spain to France that the territory would not be alienated. Spain at once protested against the sale to America, for she saw that Florida, now surrounded by an American territory, would on the first occasion fall into

---

[1] For many years afterward the settlement of these "French Spoliation Claims," as they were called, arose again and again in Congress, creating extended discussions.

the hands of the United States, and that her possession of Mexico was also greatly endangered by contiguity with the expanding American republic. Indeed, Spain did not consent to the transfer of Louisiana for a number of years, during which she preserved a hostile attitude toward the United States that, in the opinion of a number of American statesmen, justified our going to war against her. The Federalist opponents of the treaty in the Senate seized upon her protest as an argument against ratification, saying that Bonaparte was selling what he had no right to dispose of, and therefore that we were not acquiring a clear title, and that the cloud upon it might assume the proportions of a storm of war sweeping over the sea from the tricked and justly indignant Spain. The force of this argument, however, was weakened by the one they had previously made in urging the forcible seizure of New Orleans while it was yet in possession of the "sluggish Spaniard slumbering on his post," and before it was occupied by "the vigilant French grenadier."

The Democrats were exultant over the treaty, hailing it as the greatest achievement yet accomplished by the nation—one that assured for ages to come the growth and development as well as the integrity of the Union. Jefferson in private acknowledged that the act was not warranted by the national charter, asserting, however, that it could be cured of all constitutional defects by the ratification of Congress. In a letter to the Administration leader in the Senate, John Breckinridge, Jefferson wrote, on August 12, 1803:

"The Constitution has made no provision for our holding foreign territory, still less for incorporating foreign nations into our Union. The executive, in seizing the fugitive occurrence which so much advances the good of their country, have done an act beyond the Constitution. The legislature, in casting behind them metaphysical subtleties and risking themselves like faithful servants, must ratify and pay for it and throw themselves on their country for doing for them, unauthorized, what we know they would have done for themselves had they been in a situation to do it. It is the case of a guardian investing the money of his ward in purchasing an important adjacent territory and saying to him when of age, 'I did this for your good; I pretend to no right to bind you; you may disavow me and I must get out of the scrape as I can; I thought it my duty to risk myself for you.' "

The policy suggested by the President was followed by the Democratic Senators with great tactical adroitness. Fortunately for them the first Federalist speaker who opposed the treaty did so, not on the ground of the unconstitutionality of the actions of its American negotiators, but because of the cloud on the title of the purchased territory. This objection was readily answered, and the Opposition was thereby placed on the defensive, while the Administration was shown to be, on this point, exercising its constitutional right. This gave the appearance that its *main* action was constitutional, and therefore the Democrats generously admitted that, in the apparently minor points (though really major), there was room for debate as to whether or not the letter of the Constitution had been followed, and appealed to the patriotism of their opponents to waive the points, since all defects in the treaty could be removed by the Senate's action. This policy won over all but the extreme partisans among the Federalists, and the treaty was ratified by a vote of 26 to 5.

In this debate the following speakers were prominent: James Jackson [Ga.], Robert Wright [Md.], John Taylor [Va.], Wilson C. Nicholas [Va.], John Breckinridge [Ky.], and John Quincy Adams [Mass.], in the affirmative; and William H. Wells [Del.], Timothy Pickering [Mass.], and Uriah Tracy [Conn.], in the negative. Mr. Adams had recently been appointed to the Senate. Although he was nominally a Federalist his previous career as a diplomat had removed him from the evil influence of partisanship as well as inclined him to give a free rein to the President in treaty making. Accordingly he supported the treaty, while confessing the constitutional objections to it, and advising that the Constitution be so amended as to permit, without question, such territorial extension. In such recommendation he was in thorough accord with the view of the President.

CONSTITUTIONALITY OF THE LOUISIANA PURCHASE

SENATE, NOVEMBER 3, 1803

SENATOR WELLS.—There are two acts necessary to be performed to carry the present treaty into effect—one by the French Government, the other by our own. They are to deliver us a fair and effectual possession of the ceded territory; and then, and not till then, are we to pay the purchase money. We have already authorized the President to receive possession. This coöperation on our part was requisite to enable the French to comply with the stipulation they had made; they could not deliver unless somebody was appointed to receive. In this view of the subject, the question which presents itself to my mind is: who shall judge whether the French Government does, or does not, faithfully comply with the previous condition? The bill on your table gives to the President this power. I am for our retaining and exercising it ourselves. I may be asked: why not delegate this power to the President? Sir, I answer by inquiring why we should delegate it? To us it properly belongs; and, unless some advantage will be derived to the United States, it shall not be transferred with my consent. Congress will be in session at the time that the delivery of the ceded territory takes place; and, if we should then be satisfied that the French have executed with fidelity that part of the treaty which is incumbent upon them first to perform, I pledge myself to vote for the payment of the purchase money. This appears to me, arguing upon general principles, to be the course which ought to be pursued, even supposing there were attending this case no particular difficulties. But in this especial case are there not among the archives of the Senate sufficient documents, and which have been withheld from the House of Representatives, to justify an apprehension that the French Government was not invested with the capacity to convey this property to us, and that we shall not receive that kind of possession which is stipulated for by the treaty? I am not permitted, by the order of this body, to make any other than this general reference to those documents. Suffice it to say that they have strongly impressed me with an opinion that, even if possession is rendered to us, the territory will come into our hands without any title to justify our holding it.

SENATOR JACKSON.—The honorable gentleman [Mr. Wells] has said that the French have no title, and, having no title herself, we can derive none from her. Is not, I ask, the King of Spain's proclamation, declaring the cession of Louisiana to France, and his orders to his governor and officers to deliver it to France, a title? Do nations give any other?

The treaty of St. Ildefonso [whereby Spain ceded Louisiana back to France] was the groundwork of the cession, and, whatever might have been the terms to be performed by France, the King of Spain's proclamation and orders have declared to all the world that they were complied with.

Last session we were impressed with the necessity of taking immediate possession of the island of New Orleans in the face of two nations, and now we entertain doubts if we can combat the weakest of those powers; and we are further told we are going to sacrifice the immense sum of fifteen millions of dollars, and have to go to war with Spain for the country afterwards; when, last session, war was to take place at all events, and no costs were equal to the object. Gentlemen seem to be displeased because we have procured it peaceably, and at probably ten times less expense than it would have cost us had we taken forcible possession of New Orleans alone, which, I am persuaded, would have involved us in a war which would have saddled us with a debt of from one to two hundred millions, and perhaps have lost New Orleans, and the right of deposit, after all. I again repeat, sir, that I do not believe that Spain will venture war with the United States. I believe she dare not; if she dare, she will pay the costs. The Floridas will be immediately ours; they will almost take themselves. The inhabitants pant for the blessings of your equal and wise government; they ardently long to become a part of the United States. An officer, duly authorized, and armed with the bare proclamation of the President, would go near to take them; the inhabitants by hundreds would flock to his standard, the very Spanish force itself would assist in their reduction; it is composed principally of the Irish brigade and Creoles—the former disaffected, and the latter the dregs of mankind.

Exclusive, however, of the loss of the Floridas, the road to Mexico is now open to us, which, if Spain acts in an amicable way, I wish may, and hope will, be shut, as respects the United States, for ever. For these reasons, I think, sir, Spain will avoid a war in which she has nothing to gain and everything to lose.

SENATOR WRIGHT.—The honorable gentleman from Delaware [Mr. Wells] says we ought to be satisfied that the possession stipulated by the treaty shall have been delivered up before we pass this bill. Has he forgot that, by the Constitution, the President is to superintend the execution of the law? Or has he forgot that treaties are the supreme law of the land? Or why, while he professes to respect this Constitution, does he oppose the commission of the execution of this law to that organ of the Government to which it has been assigned by the Constitution? Why, I ask, does he distrust the President? Has he not been, throughout the whole of this business, very much alive to the peaceful acquisition of this immense territory, and the invaluable waters of the Mississippi? A property which, but the other day, we were told was all-important, and so necessary to our political existence that if it was not obtained the western people would sever themselves from the Union. This property, for which countless millions were then proposed to be expended, and the best blood of our citizens to be shed, and which then was to be had at all hazards, *per fas aut per nefas*, seems now to have lost its worth, and it would seem as if some gentlemen could not be satisfied with the purchase, because our title was not recorded in the blood of its inhabitants. But that this is not the wish of the American people has been unequivocally declared by their immediate representatives in Congress, as well as by this House, who had each expressed their approbation of the peaceful title we had acquired, by majorities I thought not to be misunderstood. And the gentleman, although he voted for the ratification of the treaty, now again calls on us to investigate the title. It is certainly too late.

SENATOR PICKERING.—A treaty to be obligatory must not contravene the Constitution, nor contain any stipulations which transcend the powers therein given to the President and Senate. The treaty between the United States and the French republic, professing to cede Louisiana to the United States, appeared to him to contain such an exceptionable stipulation— a stipulation which cannot be executed by any authority now existing. It is declared in the third article, that "the inhabitants of the ceded territory shall be incorporated in the Union of the United States." But neither the President and Senate, nor the President and Congress, are competent to such an act of incorporation.

The assent of each individual State is necessary for the admission of a foreign country as an associate in the Union; in like manner as in a commercial house, the consent of each member would be necessary to admit a new partner into the company; and whether the assent of every State to such an indispensable amendment is attainable is uncertain.

I have never doubted the right of the United States to acquire new territory, either by purchase or by conquest, and to govern the territory so acquired as a dependent province; and in this way might Louisiana become a territory of the United States, and receive a form of government infinitely preferable to that to which its inhabitants are now subject.

SENATOR TAYLOR.—There have been, Mr. President, two objections made against the treaty; one that the United States cannot constitutionally acquire territory; the other that the treaty stipulates for the admission of a new State into the Union; a stipulation which the treaty-making power is unable to comply with. To these objections I shall endeavor to give answers not heretofore urged.

Before confederation each State in the Union possessed a right, as attached to sovereignty, of acquiring territory, by war, purchase, or treaty. This right must be either still possessed or forbidden both to each State and to the General Government, or transferred to the General Government. It is not possessed by the States separately, because war and compacts with foreign powers and with each other are prohibited to a separate State; and no other means of acquiring territory, exist. By depriving every State of the means of exercising the right of acquiring territory, the Constitution has deprived each separate State of the right itself. Neither the means nor the right of acquiring territory are forbidden to the United States; on the contrary, in the fourth article of the Constitution, Congress is empowered "to dispose of and regulate the territory belonging to the United States." This recognizes the right of the United States to hold territory. The means of acquiring territory consist of war and compact; both are expressly surrendered to Congress and forbidden to the several States; and no right in a separate State to hold territory without its limits is recognized by the Constitution, nor any mode of effecting it possible, consistent with it. The means of acquiring and the right of holding territory, being both given to the United States, and prohibited to each State, it follows that these attributes of sovereignty once held by each State are thus transferred to the United States; and that, if the means of acquiring and the right of holding are equivalent to the right of acquiring territory, then this right merged from the separate States to the United States, as indispensably annexed to the treaty-making power, and the power of making war; or, indeed, is literally given to the General Government by the Constitution.

SENATOR TRACY.—The paragraph in the Constitution which says that "new States may be admitted by Congress into this Union" has been quoted to justify this treaty. To this two answers may be given, either of which are conclusive. First, if Congress have the power collectively of admitting Louisiana, it cannot be vested in the President and Senate alone. Secondly, Congress have no power to admit new foreign states into the Union without the consent of the old partners. The article of the Constitution, if any person will take the trouble to examine it, refers to domestic States only, and not at all to foreign states; and it is unreasonable to suppose that Congress should, by a majority only, admit new foreign states, and swallow up, by it, the old partners, when two-thirds of all the members are made requisite for the least alteration in the Constitution. The words of the Constitution are completely satisfied by a construction which shall include only the admission of domestic States, who were all parties to the Revolutionary war, and to the compact; and the spirit of the association seems to embrace no other. But, I repeat it, if the Congress collectively has this power the President and Senate cannot, of course, have it exclusively.

I think, sir, that, from a fair construction of the Constitution and an impartial view of the nature and principles of our association, the President and Senate have not the power of thus obtruding upon us Louisiana.

SENATOR BRECKINRIDGE.—No gentleman has yet ventured to deny that it is incumbent on the United States to secure to the citizens of the western waters the uninterrupted use of the Mississippi. Under this impression of duty what has been the conduct of the General Government, and particularly of the gentlemen now in the opposition, for the last eight months? When the right of deposit was violated by a Spanish officer without authority from his government, these gentlemen considered our national honor so deeply implicated, and the rights of the western people so wantonly violated, that no atonement or redress was admissible, except through the medium of the bayonet. Negotiation was scouted at. It was deemed pusillanimous, and was said to exhibit a want of fellow-feeling for the western people, and a disregard to their essential rights. Fortunately for their country the counsel of these gentlemen was rejected, and their war measures negatived. The so much scouted process of negotiation was, however, persisted in, and, instead of restoring the right of deposit and securing more effectually for the future our right to navigate the Mississippi, the Mississippi itself was acquired, and everything which appertained to it. I did suppose that those gentlemen who, at the last session, so strongly urged war measures for the attainment of this object, upon an avowal that it was too important to trust to the tardy and less effectual process of negotiation, would have stood foremost in carrying the treaty into effect, and that the peaceful mode by which it was acquired would not lessen with them the importance of the acquisition.

Permit me to examine some of the principal reasons which are deemed so powerful by gentlemen as to induce them to vote for the destruction of this treaty. Unfortunately for the gentlemen, no two of them can agree on the same set of objections; and, what is still more unfortunate, I believe there is no two of them concur in any one objection. In one thing only they seem to agree, and that is to vote against the bill. An honorable gentleman from Delaware [Mr. White] considered the price to be enormous. An honorable gentleman from Connecticut, who has just sat down [Mr. Tracy], says he has no objection whatever to the price; it is, he supposes, not too much. An honorable gentleman from Massachusetts [Mr. Pickering] says that France acquired no title from Spain, and therefore our title is bad. The same gentleman from Connecticut [Mr. Tracy] says he has no objection to the title of France; he thinks it a good one. The gentleman from Massachusetts [Mr. Pickering] contends that the United States cannot, under the Constitution, acquire foreign territory. The gentleman from Connecticut is of a different opinion, and has no doubt but that the United States can acquire and hold foreign territory; but that Congress alone have the power of incorporating that territory into the Union. Of what weight, therefore, ought all their lesser objections be entitled to when they are at war among themselves on the greater one?

The same gentleman has told us that this acquisition will, from its extent, soon prove destructive to the Confederacy.

This is an old and hackneyed doctrine: that a republic ought not to be too extensive. But the gentleman has assumed two facts and then reasoned from them: First, that the extent is too great; and, secondly, that the country will be soon populated. I would ask, sir, what is his standard extent for a republic? How does he come at that standard? Our boundary is already extensive. Would his standard extent be violated by including the island of Orleans and the Floridas? I presume not, as all parties seem to think their acquisition, in part or in whole, essential. Why not, then, acquire territory on the west as well as on the east side of the Mississippi? Is the Goddess of Liberty restrained by water courses? Is she governed by geographical limits? Is her dominion on this continent confined to the east side of the Mississippi? So far from believing in the doctrine that a Republic ought to be confined within narrow limits, I believe, on the contrary, that the more extensive its dominion the more safe and more durable it will be. In proportion to the number of hands you intrust the precious blessings of a free government to, in the same proportion do you multiply the chances for their preservation. I entertain, therefore, no fears for the Confederacy on account of its extent.

The gentleman from Connecticut [Mr. Tracy] admits explicitly that Congress may acquire territory and hold it as a territory, but cannot incorporate it into the Union. By this construction he admits the power to acquire territory, a modification infinitely more dangerous than the unconditional admission of a new State; for, by his construction, territories and citizens are considered and held as the property of the Government of the United States, and may consequently be used as dangerous engines in the hands of the Government against the States and people.

The same gentleman, in reply to the observations which fell from the gentleman from South Carolina as to the admission of new States, observes that, although Congress may admit new States, the President and Senate, who are but a component part, cannot. Apply this doctrine to the case before us. How could Congress by any mode of legislation admit this country into the Union until it was acquired? And how can this acquisition be made except through the treaty-making power? Could the gentleman rise in his place and move for leave to bring in a bill for the purchase of Louisiana and its admission into the Union? I take it that no transaction of this or any other kind with a foreign power can take place except through the executive department, and that in the form of a treaty, agreement, or convention. When the acquisition is made Congress can then make such disposition of it as may be expedient.

SENATOR ADAMS.—It has been argued that the bill ought not to pass because the treaty itself is unconstitutional, or, to use the words of the gentleman from Connecticut, an extra-constitutional act; because it contains engagements which the powers of the Senate were not competent to ratify, the powers of Congress not competent to confirm, and, as two of the gentlemen have contended, not even the legislatures of the number of States requisite to effect an amendment of the Constitution are adequate to sanction. It is, therefore, say they, a nullity; we cannot fulfill our part of its conditions, and on our failure in the performance of any one stipulation, France may consider herself as absolved from the obligations of the whole treaty on her. For my own part, I am free to confess that the third article, and more especially the seventh, contain engagements placing us in a dilemma from which I see no possible mode of extricating ourselves but by an amendment, or rather an addition, to the Constitution. The gentleman from Connecticut [Mr. Tracy], both on a former occasion and in this day's debate, appears to me to have shown this to demonstration. But what is this more than saying that the President and Senate have bound the nation to engagements which require the coöperation of more extensive powers than theirs to carry them into execution? Nothing is more common, in the negotiations between nation and nation, than for a minister to agree to and sign articles beyond the extent of his powers. This is what your ministers, in the very case before you, have confessedly done. It is well known that their powers did not authorize them to conclude this treaty; but they acted for the benefit of their country, and this House by a large majority has advised to the ratification of their proceedings. Suppose, then, not only that the ministers who signed, but the President and Senate who ratified this compact, have exceeded their powers. Suppose that the other House of Congress, who have given their assent by passing this and other bills for the fulfillment of the obligations it imposes on us, have exceeded their powers. Nay, suppose even that the majority of States competent to amend the Constitution in other cases could not amend it in this without exceeding their powers— and this is the extremest point to which any gentleman on this floor has extended his scruples—suppose all this, and there still remains in the country a power competent to adopt and sanction every part of our engagements, and to carry them entirely into execution. For, notwithstanding the objections and apprehensions of many individuals, of many wise, able, and excellent men, in various parts of the Union, yet such is the public favor attending the transaction which commenced by the negotiation of this treaty, and which, I hope, will terminate in our full, undisturbed, and undisputed possession of the ceded territory, that I firmly believe if an amendment to the Constitution, amply sufficient for the accomplishment of everything for which we have contracted, shall be proposed, as I think it ought; it will be adopted by the legislature of every State in the Union. We can therefore fulfill our part of the conventions, and this is all that France has a right to require of us.

SENATOR NICHOLAS.—The gentleman from Connecticut [Mr. Tracy] must consider the grant of power to the legislature as a limitation of the treaty-making power, for he says "that the power to admit new States and to make citizens is given to Congress, and not to the treaty-making power"; therefore an engagement in a treaty to do either of these things is unconstitutional. I cannot help expressing my surprise at that gentleman's giving that opinion, and I think myself justifiable in saying that if it is now his opinion it was not always so. The contrary opinion is the only justification of that gentleman's approbation of the British treaty, and of his vote for carrying it into effect. By that treaty a great number of persons had a right to become American citizens immediately; not only without a law but contrary to an existing law. And by that treaty many of the powers specially given to Congress were exercised by the treaty-making power. It is for gentlemen who supported that treaty to reconcile the construction given by them to the Constitution in its application to that instrument with their exposition of it at this time.

The proposal of Senator Adams to amend the Constitution in order to legalize the treaty was not supported, being out of line with the previous policy of the Federalists and not agreeable to the desires of the Democrats now that they were in power in the executive as well as legislative branches of the Government. Accordingly it was not acted upon, and thus the ratification of the Louisiana Purchase marked the greatest step forward that had yet been taken in the broad construction of the Constitution in the matter of increasing the power of the President.

CHAPTER V

THE EMBARGO

A STATE of war had existed between France and Great Britain since May 16, 1803, though actual hostilities did not begin until two years later. In May, 1805, the British Court of Appeals in the case of the captured American vessel *Essex* reversed the former rule of the British admiralty courts, viz., that in time of war "landing goods and paying duties in a neutral country breaks the continuity of the voyage, and so legalizes the trade," and held that such transshipment, *if evidently fraudulent,* did not absolve the vessel from capture and condemnation. Immediately following the decision British warships and privateers at once began to prey on American vessels which were carrying through neutral countries the trade between France and her colonies.

MESSAGES ON BRITISH AGGRESSION

President Jefferson brought the matter to the attention of Congress at its next session in December, 1805,

113

in his message. Referring to the anomaly that the commerce with France for which American vessels were captured and condemned by Great Britain was practiced with impunity by her own merchantmen, he said:

New principles have been interpolated into the law of nations, founded neither in justice nor the usage or acknowledgment of nations. According to these, a belligerent takes to itself a commerce with its own enemy which it denies to a neutral, on the ground of its aiding that enemy in the war. But reason revolts at such an inconsistency, and, the neutral having equal right with the belligerent to decide the question, the interests of our constituents, and the duty of maintaining the authority of reason, the only umpire between just nations, impose on us the obligation of providing an effectual and determined opposition to a doctrine so injurious to the rights of peaceable nations. Indeed, the confidence we ought to have in the justice of others still countenances the hope that a sounder view of those rights will, of itself, induce from every belligerent a more correct observance of them.

On January 17, 1806, the President sent a special message to the Senate on the subject, giving an account of the actions he had taken, and asking that Congress take the matter into consideration. He said:

The right of a neutral to carry on commercial intercourse with every part of the dominions of a belligerent, permitted by the laws of the country (with the exception of blockaded ports and contraband of war), was believed to have been decided between Great Britain and the United States by the sentence of their commissioners mutually appointed to decide on that and other questions of difference between the two nations, and by the actual payment of the damages awarded by them against Great Britain for the infractions of that right. When, therefore, it was perceived that the same principle was revived, with others more novel, and extending the injury, instructions were given to the Minister Plenipotentiary of the United States at the Court of London, and remonstrances duly made by him on the subject, as will appear by documents transmitted herewith. These were followed by a partial and temporary suspension only, without any disavowal of the principle. He has, therefore, been instructed to urge this subject anew, to bring it more fully to the bar of reason, and to insist on rights too evident and too important to be surrendered. In the mean time the evil is proceeding, under adjudications founded on the principle which is denied. Under these circumstances the subject presents itself for the consideration of Congress.

The Senate referred the matter to a committee, which on February 12, 1806, presented a resolution that importation of British manufactures should be prohibited until equitable arrangements had been made between Great Britain and the United States on the differences between the two governments. This was adopted on April 10, by a vote of 19 to 9.

On January 29, 1806, a similar resolution had been proposed in the House of Representatives by Andrew Gregg [Pa.]. Other resolutions of the same import were presented by Joseph Clay [Pa.] on February 5, and by Joseph B. Nicholson [Md.] on February 10. The subject came up for consideration on March 5, and was debated until March 17, when Mr. Nicholson's resolution was adopted by a vote of 87 to 35.

These measures were evidently inspired by the President and his Secretary of State, James Madison, with both of whom commercial retaliation was a favorite policy.[1]

The chief opponent of the measure was John Randolph [Va.] the free lance, who on this question allied himself with the Federalists.

[1] One of the last acts of Jefferson as Secretary of State under Washington had been the submission to Congress of a Report on American Commerce, in which he suggested the removal of European restrictions on our trade by countervailing acts where friendly arrangements could not be made. In furtherance of this recommendation Madison submitted to the House in January, 1794, his famous Commercial Resolutions, laying additional duties on manufactures of nations which had no commercial treaties with the United States. Great Britain was especially aimed at, and when, during the debate, that government seized certain American vessels trading with the French West Indies, the restrictions were laid aside in favor of the more drastic measure of an embargo. This was ordered on March 26, 1794. It prevented the embarkation for thirty days of all ships in American ports bound for foreign ports. The obnoxious orders were revoked by Great Britain, and the embargo was removed.

A very interesting report of the debates and proceedings of Congress in reference to the above matters is found in Timothy Pitkin's "Political History of the United States," Volume II, pages 406 to 412.

THE FOLLY OF RETALIATION
JOHN RANDOLPH

I am perfectly aware that on entering upon this subject we go into it manacled, handcuffed, and tongue-tied; gentlemen know that our lips are sealed on subjects of momentous foreign relations, which are indissolubly linked with the present question and which would serve to throw a great light on it in every respect relevant to it. I will, however, endeavor to hobble over the subject as well as my fettered limbs and palsied tongue will enable me to do it.

I am not surprised to hear this resolution discussed by its friends as a war measure. They say (it is true) that it is not a war measure; but they defend it on principles which would justify none but war measures, and seem pleased with the idea that it may prove the forerunner of war. If war is necessary —if we have reached this point—let us have war. But while I have life I will never consent to these incipient war measures, which, in their commencement, breathe nothing but peace, though they plunge at last into war. It has been well observed by the gentleman from Pennsylvania behind me [Mr. J. Clay] that the situation of this nation in 1793 was in every respect different from that in which it finds itself in 1806. Let me ask, too, if the situation of England is not since materially changed? Gentlemen who, it would appear from their language, have not got beyond the horn-book of politics, talk of our ability to cope with the British navy, and tell us of the war of our Revolution. What was the situation of Great Britain then? She was then contending for the empire of the British channel, barely able to maintain a doubtful equality with her enemies, over whom she never gained the superiority until Rodney's victory of the twelfth of April.[1] What is her present situation? The combined fleets of France, Spain, and Holland are dissipated, they no longer exist. I am not surprised to hear men advocate these wild opinions, to see them goaded on by a spirit of mercantile avarice, straining their feeble strength to excite the nation to war, when they have reached this stage of infatuation, that we are an overmatch for Great Britain on the ocean. It is mere waste of time to reason with such persons. They do not deserve anything like serious refutation. The proper arguments for such statesmen are a straight waistcoat, a dark room, water gruel, and depletion.

[1] Vice-Admiral George Brydges Rodney defeated the French Admiral DeGrasse in the West Indies, April 12, 1782.

What is the question in dispute? The carrying trade. What part of it? The fair, the honest, and the useful trade that is engaged in carrying our own productions to foreign markets, and bringing back their productions in exchange? No, sir. It is that carrying trade which covers enemy's property, and carries the coffee, the sugar, and other West India products, to the mother country. No, sir, if this great agricultural nation is to be governed by Salem and Boston, New York and Philadelphia, and Baltimore and Norfolk and Charleston, let gentlemen come out and say so; and let a committee of public safety be appointed from those towns to carry on the Government. I, for one, will not mortgage my property and my liberty to carry on this trade. The nation said so seven years ago—I said so then, and I say so now. It is not for the honest carrying trade of America, but for this mushroom, this fungus of war—for a trade which, as soon as the nations of Europe are at peace, will no longer exist—it is for this that the spirit of avaricious traffic would plunge us into war.

I am forcibly struck on this occasion by the recollection of a remark made by one of the ablest (if not the honestest) ministers that England ever produced. I mean Sir Robert Walpole, who said that the country gentlemen (poor meek souls!) came up every year to be sheared—that they lay mute and patient whilst their fleeces were taking off—but that if he touched a single bristle of the commercial interest the whole stye was in an uproar. It was indeed shearing the hog—"great cry and little wool."

I am averse to a naval war with any nation whatever. I was opposed to the naval war of the last administration, and I am as ready to oppose a naval war of the present administration, should they meditate such a measure. What! shall this great mammoth of the American forest leave his native element and plunge into the water in a mad contest with the shark? Let him beware that his proboscis is not bitten off in the engagement. Let him stay on shore, and not be excited by the mussels and periwinkles on the strand, or political bears in a boat, to venture on the perils of the deep. Gentlemen say, will you not protect your violated rights? and I say, why take to water, where you can neither fight nor swim? Look at France—see her vessels stealing from port to port on her own coast—and remember that she is the first military power of the earth, and as a naval people second only to England.

Let the battle of Actium be once fought and the whole line of sea coast will be at the mercy of the conqueror. The Atlantic, deep and wide as it is, will prove just as good a barrier against his ambition, if directed against you, as the Mediterranean to the power of the Cæsars. Do I mean (when I say so) to crouch to the invader? No! I will meet him at the water's edge, and fight every inch of ground from thence to the mountains—from the mountains to the Mississippi.

But, sir, I have yet a more cogent reason against going to war, for the honor of the flag in the narrow seas, or any other maritime punctilio. It springs from my attachment to the Government under which I live. I declare, in the face of day, that this Government was not instituted for the purposes of offensive war. No! It was framed (to use its own language) ''for the common defence and the general welfare,'' which are inconsistent with offensive war. I call that offensive war which goes out of our jurisdiction and limits for the attainment or protection of objects not within those limits and that jurisdiction. As in 1798 I was opposed to this species of warfare, because I believed it would raze the Constitution to its very foundation—so, in 1806, I am opposed to it, and on the same grounds. No sooner do you put the Constitution to this use—to a test which it is by no means calculated to endure—than its incompetency becomes manifest, apparent to all. I fear if you go into a foreign war, for a circuitous, unfair carrying trade, you will come out without your Constitution. Have not you contractors enough yet in this House? Or do you want to be overrun and devoured by commissaries, and all the vermin of contract? I fear, sir, that what are called ''the energy men'' will rise up again—men who will burn the parchment. We shall be told that our Government is too free; or, as they would say, weak and inefficient. Much virtue, sir, in terms! That we must give the President power to call forth the resources of the nation. That is, to filch the last shilling from our pockets—to drain the last drop of blood from our veins. I am against giving this power to any man, be he who he may. The American people must either withhold this power or resign their liberties. There is no other alternative. Nothing but the most imperious necessity will justify such a grant. And is there a powerful enemy at our doors? You may begin with a First Consul. From that chrysalis state he soon becomes an emperor. You have your choice. It depends upon your election whether you will be a free, happy, and united people at home, or the light of your Executive Majesty shall beam across the Atlantic in one general blaze of the public liberty.

Much more am I indisposed to war, when, among the first

means for carrying it on, I see gentlemen propose the confiscation of debts due by Government to individuals. Does a *bona
fide* creditor know who holds his paper? Dare any honest man
ask himself the question? 'Tis hard to say whether such principles are more detestably dishonest than they are weak and
foolish. What, sir, will you go about with proposals for opening a loan in one hand and a sponge for the national debt in the
other? If, on a late occasion, you could not borrow at a less
rate of interest than eight per cent., when the Government
avowed that they would pay to the last shilling of the public
ability, at what price do you expect to raise money with an
avowal of these nefarious opinions? God help you if these are
your ways and means for carrying on war; if your finances are
in the hands of such a chancellor of the exchequer. What are
you going to war for? For the carrying trade? Already you
possess seven-eighths of it. What is the object in dispute? The
fair, honest trade that exchanges the product of our soil for
foreign articles for home consumption? Not at all. You are
called upon to sacrifice this necessary branch of your navigation, and the great agricultural interest—whose handmaid it is—
to jeopardize your best interests for a circuitous commerce, for
the fraudulent protection of belligerent property under your
neutral flag. Will you be goaded by the dreaming calculations
of insatiate avarice to stake your all for the protection of this
trade? I do not speak of the probable effects of war on the
price of our produce. Severely as we must feel, we may scuffle
through it. I speak of its reaction on the Constitution. You
may go to war for this excrescence of the carrying trade, and
make peace at the expense of the Constitution. Your executive
will lord it over you, and you must make the best terms with
the conqueror that you can. But the gentleman from Pennsylvania (Mr. Gregg) tells you that he is for acting in this, as in
all things, uninfluenced by the opinion of any minister whatever—foreign or, I presume, domestic. On this point I am willing to meet the gentleman—am unwilling to be dictated to by
any minister, at home or abroad. Is he willing to act on the
same independent footing? I have before protested, and I again
protest, against secret, irresponsible, overruling influence. The
first question I asked when I saw the gentleman's resolution
was, "Is this a measure of the cabinet?" Not of an open declared cabinet; but of an invisible, inscrutable, unconstitutional
cabinet, without responsibility, unknown to the Constitution.
I speak of back-stairs' influence—of men who bring messages
to this House, which, although they do not appear on the jour-

nals, govern its decisions. Sir, the first question that I asked on the subject of British relations was, What is the opinion of the cabinet? What measures will they recommend to Congress?— (well knowing that whatever measures we might take they must execute them, and therefore that we should have their opinion on the subject). My answer was (and from a cabinet minister, too), *"There is no longer any cabinet."*

At the commencement of this session we received a printed message from the President of the United States, breathing a great deal of national honor and indignation at the outrages we had endured, particularly from Spain. Some of the State legislatures sent forward resolutions pledging their lives, their fortunes, and their sacred honor in support of any measures you might take in vindication of your injured rights. Well, sir, what have you done? You have had resolutions laid upon your table, gone to some expense of printing and stationery—mere pen, ink, and paper, that's all. Like true political quacks you deal only in handbills and nostrums. Sir, I blush to see the record of our proceedings; they resemble nothing but the advertisements of patent medicines. Here you have "the worm-destroying lozenges," there "Church's cough drops"; and, to crown the whole, "Sloan's vegetable specific," an infallible remedy for all nervous disorders and vertigoes of brain-sick politicians; each man earnestly adjuring you to give his medicine only a fair trial. If, indeed, these wonder-working nostrums could perform but one half of what they promise there is little danger of our dying a political death, at this time at least. But, sir, in politics as in physics, the doctor is ofttimes the most dangerous disease; and this I take to be our case at present.

But, sir, why do I talk of Spain? "There are no longer Pyrenees!" There exists no such nation, no such being as a Spanish King or minister. It is a mere juggle, played off for the benefit of those who put the mechanism into motion. You know, sir, that you have no differences with Spain; that she is the passive tool of a superior power, to whom, at this moment, you are crouching. Are your differences, indeed, with Spain? And where are you going to send your political panacea, resolutions and handbills excepted, your sole arcanum of government, your king cure all? To Madrid? No—to Paris. You know, at least, where the disease lies, and there you apply your remedy. When the nation anxiously demands the result of your deliberations you hang your head and blush to tell. You are afraid to tell. Your mouth is hermetically sealed. Your honor has received a wound which must not take air. After shrinking from the Spanish jackal, do you presume to bully the British lion? But here the secret comes out. Britain is your rival in trade, and, governed as you are by counting-house politicians, you would sacrifice the paramount interests of your country to wound that rival. For Spain and France you are carriers, and from good customers every indignity is to be endured. Yes, sir, and when a question of great national magnitude presents itself to you, it causes those who now prate about national honor and spirit to pocket any insult; to consider it as a mere matter of debit and credit; a business of profit and loss, and nothing else.

I ask any man who now advocates a rupture with England to assign a single reason for his opinion that would not have justified a French war in 1798? If injury and insult abroad would have justified it we had them in abundance then. But what did the Republicans say at that day? That, under the cover of a war with France, the executive would be armed with a patronage and power which might enable it to master our liberties. They deprecated foreign war and navies, and standing armies, and loans, and taxes. The delirium passed away—the good sense of the people triumphed, and our differences were accommodated without a war. And what is there in the situation of England that invites to war with her? It is true she does not deal so largely in perfectibility, but she supplies you with a much more useful commodity—with coarse woolens. With less profession, indeed, she occupies the place of France in 1793. She is the sole bulwark of the human race against universal dominion; no thanks to her for it. In protecting her own existence she insures theirs. I care not who stands in this situation, whether England or Bonaparte. I practice the doctrines now that I professed in 1798. I voted against all such projects under the administration of John Adams, and I will continue to do so under that of Thomas Jefferson. Are you not contented with being free and happy at home? Or will you surrender these blessings that your merchants may tread on Turkish and Persian carpets, and burn the perfumes of the East in their vaulted rooms? Gentlemen say it is but an annual million lost, and even if it were five times that amount, what is it compared with your neutral rights? Sir, let me tell them a hundred millions will be but a drop in the bucket if once they launch without rudder or compass into this ocean of foreign warfare. Whom do they want to attack? England. They hope it is a popular thing, and talk about Bunker Hill, and the gallant feats of our Revolution. But is Bunker Hill to be the theater of war? No, sir, you have selected the ocean, and the object of attack is that

very navy which prevented the combined fleets of France and
Spain from levying contribution upon you in your own seas;
that very navy which, in the famous war of 1798, stood between
you and danger. *Quem Deus vult perdere prius dementat.*[1]
Are you mad enough to take up the cudgels that have been
struck from the nerveless hands of the three great maritime
powers of Europe? Shall the planter mortgage his little crop,
and jeopardize the Constitution in support of commercial monopoly, in the vain hope of satisfying the insatiable greediness
of trade? Administer the Constitution upon its own principles;
for the general welfare, and not for the benefit of any particular
class of men.

A great deal is said about the laws of nations. What is national law but national power guided by national interest? You
yourselves acknowledge and practice upon this principle where
you can, or where you dare—with the Indian tribes for instance.
I might give another and more forcible illustration. Will the
learned lumber of your libraries add a ship to your fleet, or a
shilling to your revenue? Will it pay or maintain a single soldier? And will you preach and prate of violations of your
neutral rights, when you tamely and meanly submit to the violation of your territory [*i. e.*, by Spain]. Will you collar the
stealer of your sheep, and let him escape that has invaded the
repose of your fireside—has insulted your wife and children
under your own roof? This is the heroism of truck and traffic
—the public spirit of sordid avarice. Great Britain violates
your flag on the high seas. What is her situation? Contending, not for the dismantling of Dunkirk, for Quebec, or Pondi-
cherry, but for London and Westminster—for life; her enemy
violating at will the territories of other nations, acquiring
thereby a colossal power that threatens the very existence of her
rival. But she has one vulnerable point to the arms of her adversary, which she covers with the ensigns of neutrality; she
draws the neutral flag over the heel of Achilles. And can you
ask that adversary to respect it at the expense of her existence?
and in favor of whom? An enemy that respects no neutral territory of Europe, and not even your own. I repeat that the
insults of Spain toward this nation have been at the instigation
of France; that there is no longer any Spain. Well, sir, because the French Government does not put this in the *Moniteur*
you choose to shut your eyes to it. None so blind as those who
will not see. You shut your own eyes, and to blind those of
other people you go into conclave, and slink out again and say,

---

[1] "Whom the gods would destroy they first make mad."

"a great affair of State!"—*C'est une grande affaire d'Etat!* It seems that your sensibility is entirely confined to the extremities. You may be pulled by the nose and ears, and never feel it, but let your strong box be attacked and you are all nerve— "Let us go to war!" Sir, if they called upon me only for my little *peculium*[1] to carry it on, perhaps I might give it; but my rights and liberties are involved in the grant, and I will never surrender them while I have life. The gentleman from Massachusetts (Mr. Crowninshield) is for sponging the debt. I can never consent to it; I will never bring the ways and means of fraudulent bankruptcy into your committee of supply. Confiscation and swindling shall never be found among my estimates to meet the current expenditure of peace or war. No, sir, I have said with the doors closed, and I say so when the doors are open, "pay the public debt"; get rid of that dead weight upon your Government—that cramp upon all your measures— and then you may put the world at defiance. So long as it hangs upon you you must have revenue, and to have revenue you must have commerce—commerce, peace. And shall these nefarious schemes be advised for lightening the public burdens; will you resort to these low and pitiful shifts; dare even to mention these dishonest artifices to eke out your expenses, when the public treasure is lavished on Turks and infidels, on singing boys and dancing girls, to furnish the means of bestiality to an African barbarian?

Gentlemen say that Great Britain will count upon our divisions. How? What does she know of them? Can they ever expect greater unanimity than prevailed at the last presidential election? No, sir, it is the gentleman's own conscience that squeaks. But if she cannot calculate upon your divisions, at least she may reckon upon your pusillanimity. She may well despise the resentment that cannot be excited to honorable battle on its own ground; the mere effusion of mercantile cupidity. Gentlemen talk of repealing the British treaty. And what is all this for? A point which Great Britain will not abandon to Russia, you expect her to yield to you—Russia! indisputably the second power of continental Europe; with not less than half a million of hardy troops; with sixty sail-of-the-line, thirty millions of subjects, and a territory more extensive even than our own—Russia, sir, the storehouse of the British navy, whom it is not more the policy and the interest than the sentiment of that government to soothe and to conciliate—her sole hope of a diversion on the continent, and her only efficient ally. What this

[1] "Private property—savings."

formidable power cannot obtain with fleets and armies you will command by writ—with pothooks and hangers. I am for no such policy. True honor is always the same. Before you enter into a contest, public or private, be sure you have fortitude enough to go through with it. If you mean war, say so, and prepare for it: Look on the other side; behold the respect in which France holds neutral rights on land. And if you make the French Emperor monarch of the ocean you may bid adieu to it forever. You may take your leave, sir, of navigation— even of the Mississippi. What is the situation of New Orleans if attacked to-morrow? Filled with a discontented and repining people, whose language, manners, and religion all incline them to the invader—a dissatisfied people, who despise the miserable governor you have set over them—whose honest prejudices and basest passions alike take part against you. You have official information that the town and its dependencies are utterly defenceless and untenable. You have held that post, you now hold it, by the tenure of the naval predominance of England, and yet you are for a British naval war.

There are now but two great commercial nations—Great Britain is one, and the United States the other. When you consider the many points of contact between our interests you may be surprised that there has been so little collision. Sir, to the other belligerent nations of Europe your navigation is a convenience, I might say, a necessary. If you do not carry for them they must starve, at least for the luxuries of life, which custom has rendered almost indispensable; and if you cannot act with some degree of spirit toward those who are dependent upon you as carriers, do you reckon to browbeat a jealous rival, who, the moment she lets slip the dogs of war, sweeps you at a blow from the ocean? And *cui bono?* for whose benefit? The planter? Nothing like it. The fair, honest, real American merchant? No, sir, for renegadoes; to-day American, to-morrow Danes. Go to war when you will, the property, now covered by the American, will then pass under the Danish, or some other neutral flag. Gentlemen say that one English ship is worth three of ours; we shall therefore have the advantage in privateering. Did they ever know a nation to get rich by privateering? This is stuff, sir, for the nursery. Remember that your products are bulky, as has been stated; that they require a vast tonnage to transport them abroad, and that but two nations possess that tonnage. Take these carriers out of the market. What is the result? The manufactures of England, which (to use a finishing touch of the gentlemen's rhetoric) have received the finishing stroke of art, lie in a small comparative compass. The neutral trade can carry them. Your produce rots in the warehouse. You go to Eustatia or St. Thomas, and get a striped blanket for a joe,[1] if you can raise one. Double freight, charges, and commission. Who receives the profit? The carrier. Who pays it? The consumer. All your produce that finds its way to England must bear the same accumulated charges—with this difference, that *there* the burden falls on the home price. I appeal to the experience of the late war, which has been so often cited. What then was the price of produce, and of broadcloth?

But you are told England will not make war; that she has her hands full. Holland calculated in the same way in 1781. How did it turn out? You stand now in the place of Holland, then without her navy, and unaided by the preponderating fleets of France and Spain, to say nothing of the Baltic powers. Do you want to take up the cudgels where these great maritime states have been forced to drop them? to meet Great Britain on the ocean, and drive her off its face? If you are so far gone as this, every capital measure of your policy has hitherto been wrong. You should have nurtured the old, and devised new, systems of taxation, and have cherished your navy. Begin this business when you may, land-taxes, stamp-acts, window-taxes, hearth-money, excise, in all its modifications of vexation and oppression, must precede or follow after. But, sir, as French is the fashion of the day, I may be asked for my *projet*. I can readily tell gentlemen what I will not do. I will not propitiate any foreign nation with money. I will not launch into a naval war with Great Britain, although I am ready to meet her at the Cowpens or on Bunker's Hill—and for this plain reason we are a great land animal, and our business is on shore. I go further: I would(if anything) have laid an embargo. This would have got our own property home, and our adversary's into our power. If there is any wisdom left among us the first step toward hostility will always be an embargo. In six months all your mercantile megrims would vanish. As to us, although it would cut deep, we can stand it. Without such a precaution, go to war when you will, you go to the wall. As to debts, strike the balance to-morrow, and England is, I believe, in our debt.

I ask your attention to the character of the inhabitants of that Southern country, on whom gentlemen rely for support of their measure. Who and what are they? A simple, agricultural people, accustomed to travel in peace to market with the produce

[1] A Portuguese coin.

of their labor. Who takes it from us? Another people, devoted to manufactures—our sole source of supply. I have seen some stuff in the newspapers about manufactures in Saxony. But what became of their Dresden china? Why the Prussian bayonets have broken all the pots, and you are content with Worcestershire or Staffordshire ware. There are some other fine manufactures on the continent, but no supply, except perhaps of linens, the article we can best dispense with. A few individuals, sir, may have a coat of Louvier's cloth, or a service of Sèvres china; but there is too little, and that little too dear, to furnish the nation. You must depend on the fur trade in earnest, and wear buffalo hides and bear skins.

But, sir, it seems that we, who are opposed to this resolution, are men of no nerve, who trembled in the days of the British treaty—cowards (I presume) in the reign of terror? Is this true? Hunt up the journals; and let our actions tell. We pursue our old unshaken course. We care not for the nations of Europe, but make foreign relations bend to our political principles and subserve our country's interest. We have no wish to see another Actium, or Pharsalia, or the lieutenants of a modern Alexander playing at piquet, or all-fours, for the empire of the world. It is poor comfort to us to be told that France has too decided a taste for luxurious things to meddle with us; that Egypt is her object, or the coast of Barbary, and, at the worst, we shall be the last devoured. We are enamored with neither nation; we would play their own game upon them, use them for our interest and convenience. But with all my abhorrence of the British Government I should not hesitate between Westminster Hall and a Middlesex jury, on the one hand, and the wood of Vincennes and a file of grenadiers, on the other. That jury-trial, which walked with Horne Tooke and Hardy through the flames of ministerial persecution, is, I confess, more to my taste than the trial of the Duke d'Enghein.

I offer as apology for these undigested, desultory remarks my never having seen the treasury documents. Until I came into the House this morning I had been stretched on a sick bed. But when I behold the affairs of this nation, instead of being where I hoped, and the people believed, they were, in the hands of responsible men, committed to Tom, Dick, and Harry, to the refuse of the retail trade of politics, I do feel, I cannot help feeling, the most deep and serious concern. If the executive Government would step forward and say, "such is our plan, such is our opinion, and such are our reasons in support of it," I would meet it fairly, would openly oppose, or pledge myself to support it. But, without compass or polar star, I will not launch into an ocean of unexplored measures, which stand condemned by all the information to which I have access. The Constitution of the United States declares it to be the province and the duty of the President "to give to Congress, from time to time, information of the state of the Union, and recommend to their consideration such measures as he shall judge expedient and necessary." Has he done it? I know, sir, that we may say, and do say, that we are independent (would it were true); as free to give a direction to the executive as to receive it from him. But do what you will, foreign relations, every measure short of war, and even the course of hostilities, depend upon him. He stands at the helm, and must guide the vessel of state. You give him money to buy Florida, and he purchases Louisiana. You may furnish means; the application of those means rests with him. Let not the master and mate go below when the ship is in distress, and throw the responsibility upon the cook and the cabin-boy. I blush with indignation at the misrepresentations which have gone forth in the public prints of our proceedings, public and private. Are the people of the United States the real sovereigns of the country, unworthy of knowing what, there is too much reason to believe, has been communicated to the privileged spies of foreign governments? Let the nation know what they have to depend upon. Be true to them, and (trust me) they will prove true to themselves and to you. The people are honest—now at home at their ploughs, not dreaming of what you are about. But the spirit of inquiry, that has too long slept, will be, must be, awakened. Let them begin to think why things have been done—not to accept them as proper because they have been done—and all will be right.

Upon the passage of the Non-Importation Act, William Pinkney was appointed a special envoy to assist James Monroe, minister to Great Britain, in securing a new treaty. On December 19, 1806, the President caused the Non-Importation Act to be suspended, having arrived at the conclusion that he might thus hasten the negotiations. If this had any effect, however, it was purely psychic, since a treaty was agreed to by the representatives of the two countries on December 31, before news reached England of the suspension of the act.

This convention recognized the American contention that indirect trade should be permitted between a bel-

ligerent and its colonies by a landing made by the
carrier in a neutral country, and that provisions should
be taken from the contraband list. Monroe and Pinkney
were compelled to yield the right of search and impressment, on the understanding, however, that it would be
exercised only under extraordinary circumstances.

Owing to this concession the President declined to
submit the treaty to the Senate for confirmation, and
ordered the American envoys to continue their negotiations.

The Orders in Council

In the meantime events had occurred in the war between Great Britain and France which greatly aggravated the American grievances.

Great Britain had issued, on January 7, 1807, an
"Order in Council," by which all neutral vessels were
prohibited from trading between the ports of France
and her allies.   Then, when she further declared a
blockade of all ports from which her flag was excluded,
Napoleon retorted with his "Milan Decrees" of December 7, 1807, and January 11, 1808, which proclaimed that
any vessel which was in any way connected with British
trade, or which should submit to search by a British
commander, became thereby "denationalized" and was
a good prize for the vessels of France or of the countries
which were her allies.

But even more than the injury to their commerce
did the American people resent an outrage against the
persons of their citizens and against their flag, which
was committed on June 22, 1807, by the British frigate
Leopard in taking four sailors by force from the American frigate *Chesapeake*.

Prompted by his own sentiments as well as by the
voice of the people, the President assembled Congress
in October, 1807, in advance of its regular time of assembly, and laid before them the actions of the British
which demanded redress.

As he stated in his message, he had, without waiting
for Congress, taken instant action for redress.

MESSAGE TO CONGRESS

PRESIDENT JEFFERSON, OCTOBER 27, 1807

Circumstances, fellow-citizens, which seriously threatened the peace of our country, have made it a duty to convene you at an earlier period than usual. The love of peace, so much cherished in the bosoms of our citizens, which has so long guided the proceedings of their public councils, and induced forbearance under so many wrongs, may not insure our continuance in the quiet pursuits of industry. The many injuries and depredations committed on our commerce and navigation upon the high seas for years past, the successive innovations on those principles of public law which have been established by the reason and usage of nations as the rule of their intercourse, and the umpire and security of their rights and peace, and all the circumstances which induced the extraordinary mission to London, are already known to you.

The President here commented upon the several concessions which the embassy had been authorized to grant and the others which the treaty called for, which his own sense of honor and ideas of justice could not allow him to consider. He spoke of the consequent fruitlessness of the mission, and continued:

On the 22d day of June last, by a formal order from a British admiral, the frigate *Chesapeake,* leaving her port for a distant service, was attacked by one of those vessels which had been lying in our harbors under the indulgences of hospitality, was disabled from proceeding, had several of her crew killed, and four taken away. On this outrage no commentaries are necessary. Its character has been pronounced by the indignant voice of our citizens with an emphasis and unanimity never exceeded. I immediately, by proclamation, interdicted our harbors and waters to all British armed vessels. An armed vessel of the United States was dispatched with instructions to our ministers at London to call on that government for the satisfaction and security required by the outrage.

The aggression thus begun has been continued on the part of the British commanders, by remaining within our waters in defiance of the authority of the country, by habitual violations of its jurisdiction, and, at length, by putting to death one of the persons whom they had forcibly taken from on board the *Chesapeake*.

To former violations of maritime rights another is now added of very extensive effect. The government of that nation has issued an order interdicting all trade by neutrals between ports not in amity with them. And being now at war with nearly every nation on the Atlantic and Mediterranean seas, our vessels are required to sacrifice their cargoes at the first port they touch, or to return home without the benefit of going to any other market. Under this new law of the ocean our trade on the Mediterranean has been swept away by seizures and condemnations, and that in other seas is threatened with the same fate.

On December 18, 1807, the President, having in the meantime learned of the second ''Order in Council'' of the British Government, sent the following special message to Congress:

The communications now made, showing the great and increasing dangers with which our vessels, our seamen, and merchandise are threatened on the high seas and elsewhere, from the belligerent powers of Europe, and it being of the greatest importance to keep in safety these essential resources, I deem it my duty to recommend the subject to the consideration of Congress, who will doubtless perceive all the advantages which may be expected from an inhibition of the departure of our vessels from the ports of the United States.

Agreeably to the recommendation of the President, on December 21, Congress, in a secret session which lasted until midnight, passed an embargo act temporarily prohibiting all commerce between the United States and foreign ports.

For a time after the passage of the act the patriotism of the nation was staunch enough to approve it, in the hope that the loss of the American trade would bring Great Britain and France to terms with this country. Many State legislatures passed approving resolutions, and the suffering shipowners and merchants for a while bore their losses in grim silence. In three or four months, however, opposition to the act began to assert itself both in and out of Congress.

Nor could the opponents be accused of lack of patriotism in view of the fact that no indication had yet appeared that the purpose of the embargo would be accomplished. Indeed, Great Britain professed to be pleased with its effects, chief of which was the surrender of the carrying trade to her own marine and the upbuilding of her American colonies. Napoleon, too, praised it highly, and in characteristic fashion enforced his professions by another proclamation, the "Bayonne Decree" of April 17, 1808, which righteously supported the embargo by ordering the seizure and sale of all American vessels which should enter the ports of France or its allies in violation of the act.

The first strong attack in Congress upon the embargo came from a representative of the President's own State. John Randolph, who had advocated an embargo in substitution for the Non-Importation Act, now permitted his hostility to the Administration to get the better of his consistency and, on April 7, 1808, in opposing a bill to increase the army in view of the prospect of a war with Great Britain, included the embargo among the objects of his reprobation. As for some reason, probably the great number and length as well as incoherence of his speeches, all of his remarks were not reported in the succeeding debate, his attack on the embargo in the army debate is presented in connection with the embargo debate.

On April 8, George W. Campbell, of Tennessee, in the interest of the Administration moved that the President have the right to suspend the act in view of certain contingencies (*i. e.,* the settlement of difficulties with Great Britain and France) which might arise during the coming recess of Congress.

During the debates the speakers who chose the opportunity to denounce the embargo as wrong in principle and ineffective in practice were John Randolph [Va.], Josiah Masters [N. Y.], and Philip B. Key [Md.]; and those who defended it were Richard M. Johnson [Ky.], John Love [Va.], James Fisk [Vt.], and Mr. Campbell.

The bill giving the President the desired power was passed on April 19, 1808, by a vote of 54 to 33.

SUSPENSION OF THE EMBARGO

HOUSE OF REPRESENTATIVES, APRIL 8-19 1808

MR. RANDOLPH.—The non-importation law might be called the edge of the wedge, the embargo the center, and the standing army the butt [of the President's policy for the aggrandizement of his power], and it is all about to be driven to the hilt.

We quarreled about impressed American seamen, and commenced a system which produced consequences the remedy for which is an embargo; and we give up all our seamen, for they are not to be embargoed; they will slip out. Great Britain has now not only all her own seamen, but a great many of ours. I am not surprised to learn that in England the embargo is a most popular measure; that they are glad to see the patriotism with which we bear it, and hope it will not fail us.

The British West Indies, so long verging to ruin, are at last relieved. Year after year they have petitioned Parliament, complaining that they are undersold by the enemies' colonies, whose produce is carried in neutral bottoms (chiefly American) free of war risks and charges. We have done more for them than their own government could do. We have given them the monopoly of the supply of Europe; and to the mother country the monopoly of the carrying trade also.

I therefore am not one of those who approve the embargo; and so far permit me to differ with my friend from South Carolina (Mr. D. R. Williams) in considering the embargo a halfway measure. Not so. It is up to the hilt; commerce and agriculture are lingering and must die under its operation. A halfway measure indeed! It gives up to Great Britain all the seamen and all the commerce; their feet are not now upon your decks, for your vessels are all riding safely moored along your slips and wharves; and this measure absolutely gives agriculture a blow which she cannot recover till the embargo is removed.

Mr. Randolph then entered into a constitutional argument against the measure, making a distinction between a permanent and a temporary embargo, and saying that because it affected exportation the measure was in the same category as export duties, which were prohibited by the Constitution.

Mr. Johnson answered the first of these arguments.

If we have power to lay an embargo for one day, have we not the power to renew it at the end of that day? If for sixty days, have we not the power to lay it again? Would it not amount to the same thing? If we pass a law to expire within a limited term, we may renew it at the end of that term; and there is no difference between a power to do this and a power to pass laws without specified limit.

Mr. Randolph said he would just remind his friend from Kentucky that he had never conceded the right of Congress to lay even a temporary embargo.

Mr. Johnson resumed:

The gentleman has told us that the embargo is well received in Great Britain. Do we not know the warm discussions which have taken place in the British Parliament? Have we not seen the petitions of the people of England, and from our minister himself do we not know that if we are plunged into a war the whole world will say that the cause of America is just? If we are upon wrong ground let us retract; if not, let us have bare justice, and I for one will be satisfied.

Mr. Love answered the second of Mr. Randolph's constitutional arguments:

But to lay an embargo is unconstitutional, because Congress cannot lay an export duty! And it is argued by the same gentleman that the lesser power being thus provided against the exercise of the greater must of course be included in the prohibition; the minor forming an objection, the major is, *a fortiori*, inadmissible. How easily, sir, is this argument of inference retorted on the gentleman; for, according to a familiar and certainly plain course of reasoning, it would seem that, if the subjects are the same as is said, when the framers of our Constitution made an exception of the lesser power, if they had intended also to except the greater, they would not have forgotten it.

The reasons which influenced the framers of that instrument to provide against the power of laying an export duty were obvious; the provision was adopted in that spirit of mutual accommodation which was so necessary to the harmony of the whole. It would be difficult, it was easily foreseen, to devise an export duty which would not bear harder on some of the States than others; it was better therefore not to resort at all to a mode of taxation which would afford so fruitless a source of contention. The policy, too, of taxing exports was perhaps radically inadmissible; yet I cannot, for my life, discern how an export duty has been drawn into analogy with an embargo.

That the embargo was a curse, sir, and continues to be a most calamitous one to us all, I have heard no one deny; but until now I have not heard the assertion advanced that our Government, by its conduct, was the author of that cause. Yes, sir, many evils which the injustice of other nations has inflicted on the peace and honor of the United States are acknowledged to be curses of the most irritating and affecting nature; but the gentleman has said more for England and France than either of them have before said for themselves, when he attributes to his own government the misconduct which has produced those evils. It was scarcely to be expected that any state of internal division or any views of whatever description would have produced on this floor an assertion which has thus put a new argument in the hands of our enemies in justification of their aggressions on us; it is more than our enemies have asserted. We have heard indeed from France and England that their decrees and orders, which make the present voluntary retirement from the seas necessary on our part, were the effect of an unjustifiable attack, which each has attributed in the first instance to the other. Each criminates the other, and not America, with being the author of the peculiar mode of warfare which has proved so destructive to the rights of neutrals. The very language of their orders and decrees assumes this position, and they are all prefaced with the declaration that their orders are enacted in the spirit of retaliation on each other, and not, sir, for any offence which our Government has been the author of, as the gentleman now tells the American people; for what purpose let the nation judge.

Remove the embargo and we must arm our vessels, and war is at once declared. Compare the evils, both of great extent. I admit, by the embargo, we lose half the value of the products of our country, or the receipt of it is suspended; by war, to admit the effect in this particular, no worse, at least it could be no better; but have we counted the costs of the armies we are to raise, and to pay, of the supplies we are to furnish, of the loss of our blood, and the diminution of our strength, of the reduction of the profits of agriculture itself, by calling men from their domestic occupations, and lessening the number of hands for tillage—have we calculated the thousand other evils which follow in the train of war? To plunge into war, sir, to escape the curse of the embargo, would be truly fulfilling the adage of old —"out of the frying-pan into the fire."

THE EMBARGO

Mr. Masters censured President Jefferson for his refusal to ratify the treaty with Great Britain which
had been signed by James Monroe and William Pinkney.
He said:

Mr. Chairman, I shall not undertake to say that the rejected
treaty is so advantageous as we had a right to expect. But I do
not hesitate to declare that it, or even Jay's treaty, is preferable
to the present state of our affairs. Can we expect that nation,
whose navy commands the seas, will sacrifice that navy, or any
part of her power, by conceding the point of search for her seamen on board of neutral vessels? It is inconsistent with their
interest, and it is inconsistent with their superiority. My wish
is to raise the embargo and arm our vessels. The nation cannot
bear the pressure. The embargo virtually inhibits all intercourse with foreign nations; the effects are and will be pernicious to the agricultural productions of this country, and
produce will fall to the lowest ebb, and enforce the most unparalleled distress on the community. Commerce ought always to
be left to the merchant, unshackled and unembarrassed, as much
as possible. Our commercial intercourse is the principal resource, both of revenue and commercial opulence. The embargo
will tear up by the roots and annihilate the commerce of this
country. And the effects will be heavy taxes, an exhausted
treasury, a diminished and ruined revenue. It weakens your
own power, fetters your operations, and deludes your citizens;
it devours not only the fruits but the seeds of industry. It will
sink down and depress the nation to an absence of hope and a
want of resources; it will be felt by the nation as a calamity,
without deciding the general question of dispute. Prove to me
the embargo is consistent with common sense, and will be the
means of adjusting our differences with the belligerent powers,
and I will then be an advocate for it. It may be good in theory,
but it is chimerical in practice, a mere speculative proposition.
Search all the histories of the world and you will not find eleven
hundred thousand tons of shipping, of one of the greatest commercial nations, embargoed for an unlimited time.

If you entertain a sense of the many blessings which you
have enjoyed; if you value a continuance of that commerce
which is the source of so much opulence; if you wish to preserve
that high state of prosperity by which the country has, for some
years past, been so eminently blessed, you lose all these advantages by continuing the embargo and neglecting to arm your
vessels. Restore, then, confidence and vigor to commerce. You

are at war with your own interest and every idea of policy; instead of protecting commerce you destroy it.

In whatever view the embargo presents itself it appears to me to be fraught with impolicy; it was laid at midnight; that miserable scene was closed under the darkness which suits with it, and under the secret shelter of our own walls. If we are to go to war, you have, instead of warlike preparations and exerting every sinew of national ability, laid an embargo, and obtained just nothing.

The policy of France, as regards Great Britain, is to make a warlike non-intercourse, and we have, by a side-wind, fallen into the measure, adopted and sanctioned it; we have abandoned the great highway of nations: our dispute with Great Britain is about commercial rights; we have given them up.

Is this country at that crisis when we shall surrender all those rights her citizens hold most dear? God forbid! I have contemplated upon the embargo, which is hazardous and impolitic, with great pain and anxiety, and I turn my face from it with horror. If there are any who improperly foster and countenance the threatening storm, and whatever consequences may follow, they are answerable to their country and their God.

All the advocates of the embargo on this floor have admitted that it was oppressive and a curse. Take away this *curse* and arm your vessels. It does not follow, as the gentleman from Virginia [Mr. Love] supposes, that arming will involve us in a war. When Great Britain finds we resist the French decrees she will revoke her orders of council. When France sees she cannot bring us into her views she will revoke her decrees.

MR. FISK.—The gentleman last up and the gentleman from Virginia [Mr. Randolph] yesterday have expressed sentiments which, if they once take root in this nation, will prostrate your liberties and rights at the feet of foreign governments. The gentleman who just took his seat has observed that the subject of impressment was the main block in the way of negotiation. Very true, it was, sir; it goes to the personal liberty and security of your citizens; and, if you surrender that right, what do you expect those citizens will say to you? Do you expect they will greet you with, "well done thou good and faithful servant?" What can the gentleman think when he recollects the sensation displayed at New York on the death of Pierce, in consequence of the exercise by Britain of the right of impressment? Were those tears and lamentations feigned, or were they the sincere effusions of citizens feeling the injury done them, and burning with indignation at seeing their fellow-citizens murdered almost before their face? If we could believe what the gentleman now suggests we should suppose that the liberties and lives of our citizens were of no value compared with commerce.

I am a little surprised to hear gentlemen telling us that arming our merchant vessels would not produce war. Why arm, if they are not to defend themselves? If the belligerents defend their proceedings, will they not resist our vessels arming against their orders? Could it be done without being met by a declaration of war? But the gentleman from New York has told us that if we suffer our merchants to arm the British would consider it a sufficient token of our resistance to the French decrees, and remove their orders of council. You have seen all the decrees and orders which make innovations on the law of nations and subject our commerce to plunder. Look at the treaty which our Government is on this floor condemned for not signing, with the note annexed, declaring that, if we submit to the decrees of France, His Britannic Majesty would consider himself bound not to observe the treaty.

What do the British ministers offer us? If we will trade as they please, and pay them a duty on all our exports, we may carry on our commerce. Is it possible that any man who professes himself an American could accede to this? The spirit of 1776, refusing to pay a duty of two per cent. on tea, would certainly not now yield that for which they then contended, and become again tributary to the British Government. And yet gentlemen wish us to raise the embargo, to embrace these regulations, open all our ports to this fettered commerce, and will not place it in the power of the Executive to suspend the embargo. I am a little astonished that gentlemen who consider the embargo as the heaviest curse which could befall this nation should be against any measure for removing its pressure. But so it is. Here permit me to say that I admire the flexibility of the sentiments of the gentleman from Virginia (Mr. Randolph) who, in combating the non-importation law, said that if we take measures at all they should be strong measures; none of your milk-and-water measures, but an *embargo;* which would be an efficient measure.

MR. KEY.—Mr. Chairman, let us review this law and its effects. In a commercial point of view it has annihilated our trade. In an agricultural point of view it has paralyzed industry. I have heard that the touch of Midas converted everything into gold; but the embargo law, like the head of Medusa, turns everything into stone. Our most fertile lands are re-

duced to sterility, so far as it respects our surplus product. As
a measure of political economics it will drive (if continued) our
seamen into foreign employ, and our fishermen to foreign sand-
banks. In a financial point of view it has dried up our revenue,
and if continued will close the sales of Western lands, and the
payment of instalments of past sales; for unless produce can be
sold payments cannot be made. As a war measure the embargo
has not been advocated.

It remains, then, to consider its effects as a peace measure—
a measure inducing peace. I grant, sir, that if the friends of
the embargo had rightly calculated its effects; if it had brought
the belligerents of Europe to a sense of justice and respect for
our rights, through the weakness and dependence of their West
India possessions, it would have been infinitely wise and desirable, and that they voted for it with such noble views I have no
doubt. But, sir, the experience of near four months has not produced that effect; and I have endeavored to show from the
situation of our country, the manner in which the law is executed, the demand for subsistence, the consequent rise in price,
and the facility of supply, that the West Indies (British) will
be supplied.

If that be the case, if such should be the result, then will the
embargo of all measures be the most acceptable to Britain; by
occluding our ports you give to her ships the exclusive use of
the ocean; and you give to her despairing West India planter
the monopoly of sugar and rum and coffee to the European
world. But, sir, what are we? A peaceable agricultural people, of simple and I trust virtuous habits, of stout hearts and
willing minds, and a brave, powerful, but badly disciplined
militia, unarmed, and without troops; and whom are we to come
in conflict with? The master of continental Europe in the full
career of universal domination, and the mistress of the ocean
contending for self-preservation; nations who feel power and
forget right. What man can be weak enough to suppose that
a sense of justice can repress or regulate the conduct of Bonaparte? We need not resort to other nations for examples. Has
he not, in a manner as flagrant as flagitious, directly, openly,
publicly violated and broken a solemn treaty entered into with
us? Did he not stipulate that our property should pass free
even to enemy ports, and has he not burnt our ships at sea
under the most causeless pretexts? Look to England; see her
conduct to us; do we want any further evidence of what she will
do in the hour of impending peril than the attack on Copen-
hagen? That she prostrates all rights that come in collision

with her self-preservation? Strangely infatuated would she be, to make our repealing the embargo to depend on the acts of governments, which will be annulled whenever their interest or their danger prompt them. No, sir; let us pursue the steady line of rigid impartiality; let us hold the scales of impartial neutrality with a high and steady hand, and export our products to, and bring back supplies from, all who will trade with us. Much of the world is yet open to us, and let us profit of the occasion.

At present we exercise no neutral rights; we have quit the ocean; we have abandoned our rights; we have retired to our shell. Sooner than thus continue our merchantmen should arm to protect legitimate trade. Sir, I believe war itself, as we could carry it on, would produce more benefit and less cost than the millions lost by the continuance of the embargo.

Mr. Campbell.—It is true, sir, we have abandoned our commerce *with* Great Britain, but not *to her;* we have retired from the ocean, and in retiring have carried with us almost the whole commerce of the European world. The belligerent powers cannot carry on commerce with each other, and there are no neutrals in Europe with which they can trade—what commerce, then, is abandoned by us to Great Britain? There is scarcely a merchant vessel that sails the ocean—she can hardly find a solitary ship to pursue—we had carried on almost the whole of the neutral trade—we were forced to abandon it—we did so—we retired, and left the great Leviathan of the ocean to roam about without a solitary object upon which to prey. Let gentlemen, then, inform us what commerce Great Britain has acquired by this measure; they can point out none; they cannot designate a single branch of trade of any importance which Great Britain has got by our retiring. But let us notice what the first statesmen in that country say on this subject—and they seem to have furnished the full to what was said on this floor, as has frequently been the case, with only this difference, that they stated the whole case, whereas a part only was stated here. They say that, in consequence of *their* orders of council, you have abandoned your commerce, as you ought to have done; and yet they inquire what is the commerce thus abandoned? They admit they have all that is left, but they inquire what that is; they cannot ascertain it; they say there is none, and in this they are correct. With regard to the effect of the embargo they state what has been before, in substance, stated on this floor, what was always considered, and so stated, would be the effect of this measure. They say the French West India islands will starve; but, supposing this to be the case, they inquire what will become of their own islands, whose sole dependence for subsistence is on the commerce and productions of America. They say *they* must also starve; they inquire if a famine must be produced in England, in order to supply their islands with provisions, which they could not even then effect. They pursue the picture, which every one must have seen; they describe the distresses that must be produced in Great Britain itself, as well as in the islands; and ascribe the whole of these misfortunes to the orders of council of their own government. This does not go to prove that the embargo was the very measure which Great Britain wanted; nor does it show that she acquired any real or valuable acquisition of commerce by our retiring from the ocean; it contradicts the assertion that the embargo has failed in its object, and proves, in a very decided manner, that it is in full operation, and in a fair way toward effecting the object for which it was laid; and that its pressure is severely felt by both the great belligerent powers.

MR. RANDOLPH.—The embargo power, which now holds in its palsying gripe all the hopes of this nation, is distinguished by two characteristics of material import, in deciding what control shall be left over it during our recess. I allude to its greatness and its novelty.

As to its greatness, nothing is like it. Every class of men feels it. This power resembles not the mild influences of an intelligent mind, balancing the interests and conditions of men, and so conducting a complicated machine as to make inevitable pressure bear upon its strongest parts. But it is like one of the blind visitations of nature; a tornado or a whirlwind. It sweeps away the weak; it only strips the strong. The humble plant, uprooted, is overwhelmed by the tempest. The oak escapes with the loss of nothing except its annual honors. It is true the sheriff does not enter any man's house to collect a tax from his property. But want knocks at his door and poverty thrusts his face into the window. And what relief can the rich extend? They sit upon their heaps and feel them mouldering into ruins under them. The regulations of society forbid what was once property to be so any longer. For property depends on circulation; on exchange; on ideal value. The power of property is all relative. It depends not merely upon opinion here, but upon opinion in other countries. If it be cut off from its destined market much of it is worth nothing, and all of it is worth infinitely less than when circulation is unobstructed.

But the magnitude of the embargo power is not more remarkable than its novelty. An experiment such as is now making,

was never before—I will not say tried—it never before entered
into the human imagination. There is nothing like it in the
narrations of history or in the tales of fiction. All the habits
of a mighty nation are at once counteracted. All their property
depreciated. All their external connections violated. Five millions of people are engaged. They cannot go beyond the limits
of that once free country; now they are not even permitted to
thrust their own property through the grates. I am not now
questioning its policy, its wisdom, or its practicability, I am
merely stating the fact. And I ask if such a power as this, thus
great, thus novel, thus interfering with all the great passions
and interests of a whole people, ought to be left for six months
in operation without any power of control, except upon the occurrence of certain specified and arbitrary contingencies? Who
can foretell when the spirit of endurance will cease? Who,
when the strength of nature shall outgrow the strength of your
bonds? Or, if they do, who can give a pledge that the patience
of the people will not first be exhausted? I make a supposition,
Mr. Chairman—you are a great physician; you take a hearty,
hale man, in the very pride of health, his young blood all active
in his veins, and you outstretch him on a bed; you stop up all
his natural orifices, you hermetically seal down his pores, so that
nothing shall escape outward, and that all his functions and all
his humors shall be turned inward upon his system. While
your patient is laboring in the very crisis of this course of treatment you, his physician, take a journey into a far country, and
you say to his attendant, "I have a great experiment here in
process, and a new one. It is all for the good of the young man,
so do not fail to adhere to it. No attention is to be paid to any
internal symptom which may occur. If the patient be convulsed
you are to remove none of my bandages. But in case something
external should happen, if the sky should fall, and larks should
begin to appear, if three birds of Paradise should fly into the
window, the great purpose of all these sufferings is answered.
Then, and then only, have you my authority to administer
relief."

OPPOSITION TO THE EMBARGO

During the following recess of Congress the feeling
against the embargo became extreme in certain parts
of the country, particularly New England.

The Federal courts there began to find it difficult to
secure convictions from juries of even flagrant violations of the act, and smuggling over the Canadian bor-

der became a safe and profitable and extensive trade. Indeed, some of the State courts decided that the embargo was unconstitutional, since it went beyond the regulation of commerce to its *annihilation*. The State legislatures, too, following the precedent of the Ken-

THE AMERICAN SNAPPING-TURTLE

[Cartoon on the Embargo.]

From the collection of the New York Historical Society

tucky and Virginia resolutions, which they had formerly denounced, expressed their condemnation of the embargo, intimating that it was a sectional measure, passed by the agricultural Middle and Southern States at the expense of commercial New England.

At the next session of Congress memorials against the embargo poured in upon that body from various interests injured by the act. It appeared that every industry but domestic manufacture was suffering.

The President in his message reported that the embargo had not yet been effective in securing the revocation of the obnoxious decrees of Great Britain and France, but that it had been the means of "saving our mariners, and our vast mercantile property, as well as of affording time for prosecuting the defensive and provisional measures called for by the occasion." He added:

It has demonstrated to foreign nations the moderation and firmness which govern our councils, and to our citizens the necessity of uniting in support of the laws and the rights of their country, and has thus long frustrated those usurpations and spoliations which, if resisted, involved war, if submitted to, sacrificed a vital principle of our national independence.

He therefore left the matter with Congress to decide. On November 21, 1808, James Hillhouse [Conn.] offered a resolution in the Senate to repeal the embargo. The arguments were much the same as those presented in the House in the preceding debate, and therefore need not be repeated. There were, however, brought forward in the course of the debate opposing views of the effectiveness of an appeal to the patriotism of the country when this is at the sacrifice of its financial interests, which has a psychological import not limited to the special crisis, and therefore is deserving of presentation. Senator Hillhouse and Senator William B. Giles [Va.] were the antagonists.

PUBLIC HONOR vs. PRIVATE INTEREST

THE SENATE, NOVEMBER 21-24, 1808

SEN. HILLHOUSE.—This embargo, instead of operating on those nations which had been violating our rights, was fraught with evils and privations to the people of the United States. They were the sufferers. And have we adopted the monkish plan of scourging ourselves for the sins of others? He hoped not; and that, having made the experiment and found that it had not produced its expected effect, they would abandon it, as a measure wholly inefficient as to the objects intended by it, and as having weakened the great hold which we had on Great Britain, from her supposed dependence on us for raw materials.

Some gentlemen appeared to build up expectations of the efficiency of this system by an addition to it of a non-intercourse law. Mr. H. treated this as a futile idea. He said he was young when the old non-intercourse took place, but he remembered it well, and had then his ideas on the subject. The British army was then at their door, burning their towns and ravaging the country, and at least as much patriotism existed then as now; but British fabrics were received and consumed to almost as great an extent as before the prohibition. When the country was in want of clothing, and could get it for one-fourth price from the British, what was the consequence? Why, all the zealous patriots—for this work of tarring and feathering, and meeting in mobs to destroy their neighbor's property, because he could not think quite as fast as they did, which seemed to be coming in fashion now, had been carried on then with great zeal—these patriots, although all intercourse was penal, carried on commerce notwithstanding. Now, Mr. H. wanted to know how a non-intercourse law was to be executed by us with a coast of fifteen hundred miles open to Great Britain by sea, and joining her by land? Her goods would come through our courts of admiralty by the means of friendly captors; they would be brought in, condemned, and then naturalized, as Irishmen are now naturalized, before they have been a month in the country.

SEN. GILES.—Sir, I have always understood that there were two objects contemplated by the embargo laws. The first, precautionary, operating upon ourselves. The second, coercive, operating upon the aggressing belligerents. Precautionary, in saving our seamen, our ships, and our merchandise, from the plunder of our enemies, and avoiding the calamities of war. Coercive, by addressing strong appeals to the interests of both the belligerents. The first object has been answered beyond my most sanguine expectations.

The President of the United States, ever watchful and anxious for the preservation of the persons and property of all our fellow-citizens, but particularly of the merchants, whose property is most exposed to danger, and of the seamen whose persons are also most exposed, recommended the embargo for the protection of both; and it has saved and protected both.

But, sir, these are not the only good effects of the embargo. It has preserved our peace—it has saved our honor—it has saved our national independence. Are these savings not worth notice? Are these blessings not worth preserving?

Mr. President, the eyes of the world are now turned upon us; if we submit to these indignities and aggressions, Great Britain herself would despise us; she would consider us an outcast among nations; she would not own us for her offspring; France would despise us; all the world would despise us; and, what is infinitely worse, we should be compelled to despise our-

selves! If we resist we shall command the respect of our enemies, the sympathies of the world, and the noble approbation of
our own consciences.

Mr. President, our fate is in our own hands; let us have
union and we have nothing to fear. So highly do I prize union,
at this awful moment, that I would prefer any one measure of
resistance with union to any other measure of resistance with
division; let us, then, sir, banish all personal feelings; let us
present to our enemies the formidable front of an indissoluble
band of brothers; nothing else is necessary to our success. Mr.
President, unequal as this contest may seem; favored as we are
by our situation, and under the blessing of a beneficent Providence, who has never lost sight of the United States in times of
difficulty and trial, I have the most perfect confidence that if
we prove true to ourselves we shall triumph over our enemies.
Deeply impressed with these considerations, I am prepared to
give the resolution a flat and decided negative.

The views of statesmen such as Giles were still predominant, and on January 9, 1809, a drastic enforcing
act supplementary to the embargo was passed. This
act was published by many newspapers in New England inclosed in black borders and headed by such mot-
toes as "Liberty Is Dead!"

John Quincy Adams, who had resigned from the Senate because he could not conscientiously represent his
State on the question of the embargo, informed the Government in February, 1809, that execution of the enforcing act in New England might result in the secession of its five States from the Union,—indeed, that un-
official negotiations were already in progress for British
assistance to that end.

An opportunity was afforded the President to "back
water" on the subject by intimations received from the
British Government that its objectionable Orders in
Council would be withdrawn if the United States met it
half way. Accordingly the administration secured the
passage by Congress of a "Non-Intercourse Bill," which
repealed the embargo after May 20, 1809, and gave the
President power to open trade with either Great Britain
or France upon the repeal of its oppressive decrees in
so far as these related to the United States. The bill

was passed by the Senate on February 21, and by the House on February 27, and approved by the President on March 1, 1809.

This Non-Intercourse Bill was to continue to the end of the next session of Congress. Owing to circumstances hereinafter related it was renewed, and continued until abolished by the Treaty of Ghent in 1814.

The last speaker on the subject in the House (James Sloan, of New Jersey) expressed the prevalent opinion both of the embargo and the device by which it had been repealed, as follows:

Gentlemen could not detest the bill more than he did; and yet he should vote for it for this reason, that the people, as well as himself, were so heartily tired of the embargo that they would be glad to get anything else in place of it. Another reason was that it contained a limitation to the embargo laws, and he hoped that the embargo would expire at the time limited, never again to be resuscitated; that it would be *dead, dead, dead.*

CHAPTER VI

RESISTANCE OR SUBMISSION TO GREAT BRITAIN?

The British Minister, D. M. Erskine, Withdraws the "Orders in Council"— His Government Repudiates the Action—Election of a Militant Congress —Message of President James Madison—Report of the Committee on Foreign Relations—Debate: in Favor of War Measures, Richard M. Johnson [Ky.], Robert Wright [Md.], John C. Calhoun [S. C.]; Opposed, John Randolph [Va.]—The President Recommends an Embargo as Preliminary to War—Debate as to Its Good Faith: in Favor, Henry Clay [Ky.]; Opposed, Mr. Randolph, Josiah Quincy, 3rd [Mass.].

THE administration of James Madison began under most favorable auspices in respect to foreign relations. On April 19, 1809, the British minister at Washington, D. M. Erskine, withdrew the "Orders in Council," and on the same day President Madison proclaimed the full renewal of trade with that country after June 10, 1809.

The satisfaction over this agreement was, however, short-lived, since the British Government repudiated the action of its minister as unauthorized and recalled him in disgrace. Accordingly, on August 9, 1809, President Madison by proclamation reëstablished the rescinded part of the Non-Intercourse Law which related to Great Britain. F. J. Jackson, the successor of Erskine, charged that the agreement with his predecessor had been obtained by trickery, and the Secretary of State, Robert Smith, refused to hold communications with him.

The Non-Intercourse Act was equally ineffective in bringing France to terms.

In January, 1810, Napoleon informed John Armstrong, our minister to France, that the repeal of his various "Decrees" was dependent on the withdrawal by Great Britain of her blockade of the European continent, and on March 23, 1810, he issued his "Rambou-

147

illet Decree," by which 132 American vessels, of a value of $8,000,000, which had entered the ports of France and her allies, were condemned and sold.

On May 1, 1810, Congress replaced the Non-Intercourse Act, which was shortly to expire, with one which removed all restrictions from commerce but excluded 248 British and French ships of war from the harbors of the United States until either country should withdraw its restrictions on American commerce. This bill contained a proviso that if either belligerent withdrew its decrees before March 3, 1811, and the other should fail to do so within three months thereafter, the President would restore the Non-Intercourse Act against the delinquent alone.

Napoleon seized the opportunity thus afforded him to involve the United States in war with Great Britain. On August 5, 1810, he informed Minister Armstrong that he had revoked his obnoxious decrees, on the understanding that Great Britain would revoke her Orders in Council or, on her failure to do so, the United States would assert her rights in the matter.

On November 2 the President accepted this arrangement. The British Government refused to revoke its orders, denying that Napoleon had made a *bona fide* revocation because he retained the money for which the vessels seized under the Rambouillet Decree had been sold, and because the French prize courts refused to consider any of the former decrees revoked.

Notwithstanding this protest, the Non-Intercourse Act went into effect against Great Britain alone on March 2, 1811.

In the elections to the succeeding Congress, the people of the country, weary of temporizing measures, had replaced many of the old "peace-at-any-price" statesmen with younger men of a more violent temper. Among these may be mentioned Henry Clay [Ky.], who entered the House of Representatives by the unusual door of the Senate, and John C. Calhoun [S. C.]. Clay, owing to the prestige he had gained in the Upper House, was elected Speaker by the new element.

The President convened Congress at an early date.

In his message he reviewed the events which had taken place in the recess of the national legislature, and recommended that action be taken to maintain the nation's rights.

MESSAGE TO CONGRESS

PRESIDENT MADISON, NOVEMBER 5, 1811

The period is arrived which claims from the legislative guardians of the national rights a system of more ample provisions for maintaining them. Notwithstanding the scrupulous justice, the protracted moderation, and the multiplied efforts on the part of the United States to substitute for the accumulating dangers to the peace of the two countries all the mutual advantages of reëstablished friendship and confidence, we have seen that the British Cabinet perseveres, not only in withholding a remedy for other wrongs, so long and so loudly calling for it, but in the execution, brought home to the threshold of our territory, of measures which, under existing circumstances, have the character, as well as the effect, of war on our lawful commerce.

With this evidence of hostile inflexibility, in trampling on rights which no independent nation can relinquish, Congress will feel the duty of putting the United States into an armor and an attitude demanded by the crisis, and corresponding with the national spirit and expectations.

On November 29 Peter B. Porter, chairman of the Committee on Foreign Relations, made the following report:

ARMED RESISTANCE AGAINST GREAT BRITAIN

REPORT OF COMMITTEE ON FOREIGN RELATIONS, HOUSE OF REPRESENTATIVES, NOVEMBER 29, 1811

Without recurring to the multiplied wrongs of which we have so just cause of complaint against the two great belligerents, your committee will only call your attention, at this time, to the systematic aggression of those powers, authorized by their edicts against neutral commerce—a system which, as regarded its principles, was founded on pretensions that went to the subversion of our national independence; and which, although now abandoned by one power, is, in its broad and destructive operation, as still enforced by the other, sapping the foundation of our prosperity.

It is more than five years since England and France, in violation of those principles of justice and public law held sacred
by all civilized nations, commenced this unprecedented system
by seizing the property of the citizens of the United States,
peaceably pursuing their lawful commerce on the high seas.   To
shield themselves from the odium which such outrage must incur, each of the belligerents sought a pretext in the conduct of
the other—each attempting to justify his system of rapine as a
retaliation for similar acts on the part of his enemy.   As if the
law of nations, founded on the eternal rules of justice, could
sanction a principle which, if ingrafted into our municipal code,
would excuse the crime of one robber upon the sole plea that
the unfortunate object of his rapacity was also a victim to the
injustice of another.   The fact of priority could be true as to
one only of the parties, and, whether true or false, could furnish
no ground of justification.

The United States, thus unexpectedly and violently assailed
by the two greatest powers in Europe, withdrew their citizens
and property from the ocean: and, cherishing the blessing of
peace, although the occasion would have fully justified war,
sought redress in an appeal to the justice and magnanimity of
the belligerents.   When this appeal had failed of the success
which was due to its moderation, other measures, founded on the
same specific policy, but applying to the interests instead of the
justice of the belligerents, were resorted to.   Such was the character of the non-intercourse and non-importation laws, which
invited the return of both powers to their former state of amicable relations, by offering commercial advantages to the one
who should first revoke his hostile edicts, and imposing restrictions on the other.

A year has elapsed since the French decrees were rescinded,
and yet Great Britain, instead of retracing *pari passu* that
course of unjustifiable attack on neutral rights in which she
professed to be only the reluctant follower of France, has advanced with bolder and continually increasing strides.   To the
categorical demands lately made by our Government for the
repeal of her Orders in Council, she has affected to deny the
practical extinction of the French decrees, and she has, more-
over, advanced a new and unexpected demand, increasing in
hostility the orders themselves.   She has insisted, through her
accredited minister at this place, that the repeal of the Orders
in Council must be preceded, not only by the practical abandonment of the decrees of Berlin and Milan, so far as they infringe
the neutral rights of the United States; but by the renunciation

on the part of France of the whole of her system of commercial warfare against Great Britain, of which those decrees originally formed a part.

This system is understood to consist in a course of measures adopted by France and the other powers on the Continent subject to, or in alliance with, her, calculated to prevent the introduction into their territories of the produce and manufactures of Great Britain and her colonies; and to annihilate her trade with them. However hostile these regulations may be on the part of France toward Great Britain, or however sensibly the latter may feel their effects, they are, nevertheless, to be regarded only as the expedients of one enemy against another, for which the United States, as a neutral power, can, in no respect, be responsible; they are, too, in exact conformity with those which Great Britain has herself adopted and acted upon in time of peace as well as war. And it is not to be presumed that France would yield to the unauthorized demand of America what she seems to have considered as one of the most powerful engines of the present war.

Such are the pretensions upon which Great Britain founds the violation of the maritime rights of the United States—pretensions not theoretical merely, but followed up by a desolating war upon our unprotected commerce. The ships of the United States, laden with the products of our own soil and labor, navigated by our own citizens, and peaceably pursuing a lawful trade, are seized on our own coasts, at the very mouths of our harbors, condemned, and confiscated.

Your committee are not, however, of that sect whose worship is at the shrine of a calculating avarice. And, while we are laying before you the just complaints of our merchants against the plunder of their ships and cargoes, we cannot refrain from presenting to the justice and humanity of our country the unhappy case of our impressed seamen. Although the groans of these victims of barbarity for the loss of (what should be dearer to Americans than life) their liberty; although the cries of their wives and children, in the privation of protectors and parents, have, of late, been drowned in the louder clamors at the loss of property; yet is the practice of forcing our mariners into the British navy, in violation of the rights of our flag, carried on with unabated rigor and severity. If it be our duty to encourage the fair and legitimate commerce of this country by protecting the property of the merchant; then, indeed, by as much as life and liberty are more estimable than ships and goods, so much more impressive is the duty to shield the persons of our seamen, whose hard and honest services are employed equally with those of the merchants in advancing, under the mantle of its laws, the interests of their country.

To sum up, in a word, the great causes of complaint against Great Britain, your committee need only say that the United States, as a sovereign and independent power, claim the right to use the ocean, which is the common and acknowledged highway of nations, for the purposes of transporting, in their own vessels, the products of their own soil and the acquisitions of their own industry, to a market in the ports of friendly nations, and to bring home, in return, such articles as their necessities or convenience may require—always regarding the rights of belligerents as defined by the established laws of nations. Great Britain, in defiance of this incontestable right, captures every American vessel bound to, or returning from, a port where her commerce is not favored; enslaves our seamen, and, in spite of our remonstrances, perseveres in these aggressions.

To wrongs so daring in character, and so disgraceful in their execution, it is impossible that the people of the United States should remain indifferent. We must now tamely and quietly submit, or we must resist by those means which God has placed within our reach.

Your committee would not cast a shade over the American name by the expression of a doubt which branch of this alternative will be embraced. The occasion is now presented when the national character, misunderstood and traduced for a time by foreign and domestic enemies, should be vindicated. If we have not rushed to the field of battle like the nations who are led by the mad ambition of a single chief, or the avarice of a corrupted court, it has not proceeded from a fear of war, but from our love of justice and humanity. That proud spirit of liberty and independence which sustained our fathers in the successful assertion of their rights against foreign aggression is not yet sunk. The patriotic fire of the Revolution still burns in the American breast with a holy and unextinguishable flame, and will conduct this nation to those high destinies which are not less the reward of dignified moderation than of exalted valor.

But we have borne with injury until forbearance has ceased to be a virtue. The sovereignty and independence of these States, purchased and sanctified by the blood of our fathers, from whom we received them, not for ourselves only, but as the inheritance of our posterity, are deliberately and systematically violated. And the period has arrived when, in the opinion of your committee, it is the sacred duty of Congress to call forth the patriotism and resources of the country. By the aid of these, and with the blessing of God, we confidently trust we shall be enabled to procure that redress which has been sought for by justice, by remonstrance, and forbearance, in vain.

Your committee, reserving for a future report those ulterior measures which, in their opinion, ought to be pursued, would, at this time, earnestly recommend, in the words of the President, "that the United States be put into an armor and attitude demanded by the crisis, and corresponding with the national spirit and expectations."

The committee recommended an increase of the army, a refitting of the navy, and resort to privateering.

These recommendations were adopted after long and heated debates, of which the first, that on the increase of the army, contained the leading arguments, *pro* and *con.*

In this debate the following were the chief speakers in the affirmative: Richard M. Johnson [Ky.], Robert Wright [Md.], and John C. Calhoun [S. C.]. John Randolph [Va.], the free lance, was a member of the committee and the only one who dissented from the resolution, being vehement in opposition to the measure when it was brought before the House. By a vote of 110 to 22 the House resolved to increase the army.

On Preparations for War

House of Representatives, December 6-16, 1811

JOHN RANDOLPH.—In the days of terror we shrunk at standing armies; and what is the object now—defence? Who? Freemen who would not defend themselves. Are seven millions of Americans to be protected in their lives and liberties by ten thousand vagabonds who are fit food for gunpowder? It will be necessary to know the ulterior views of the committee on this point. It will be proper, before a vote is taken on this resolution, to know for what purpose these additional troops are wanted. The House ought not to commit itself on a question of such magnitude without detailed information. I am as much opposed to raising standing armies now as in the reign of terror. I have seen too much of the corruptions attendant on those establishments not to disclaim all share in the creation of them.

The people of the United States can defend themselves, if necessary, and have no idea of resting their defence on mercenaries, picked up from brothels and tippling houses—pickpockets who have escaped from Newgate, etc., and sought refuge in this asylum of oppressed humanity. This resolution contains an unconstitutional proposition, and the standing army now in the service of the United States is maintained in the very teeth of that part of the Constitution which declares that no money for the support of a standing army should be appropriated for more than two years. I ask again what is the object of the army now proposed to be raised? If the President says they are necessary for the protection of New Orleans, to be employed against the Indians, or to repel incursions from Canada (although this seems not to be much thought of), I shall not refuse to grant them. I know not how gentlemen calling themselves republicans can advocate such a war. What was their doctrine in 1798-'9, when the command of the army—that highest of all possible trusts in any government, be the form what it may—was reposed in the bosom of the Father of his Country, the sanctuary of a nation's love, the only hope that never came in vain! When other worthies of the Revolution—Hamilton, Pinckney, and the younger Washington—men of tried patriotism, of approved conduct and valor, of untarnished honor, held subordinate command under him; Republicans were then unwilling to trust a standing army even to his hands who had given proof that he was above all human temptation. Where now is the Revolutionary hero to whom you are about to confide this sacred trust? To whom will you confide the charge of leading the flower of our youth to the Heights of Abraham? Will you find him in the person of an acquitted felon?[1] What; then you were unwilling to vote an army where such men as had been named held high command! when Washington himself was at the head—did you then show such reluctance, feel such scruples; and are you now nothing loth, fearless of every consequence? Will you say that your provocations were less then than now? When your direct commerce was interdicted—your ambassadors hooted with derision from the French Court—tribute demanded—actual war waged upon you!

Those who opposed the army then were indeed denounced as the partisans of France; as the same men—some of them at least—are now held up as the advocates of England; those firm and undeviating Republicans who then dared, and now dare, to cling to the ark of the Constitution, to defend it even at the

General James Wilkinson, tried with Aaron Burr for treason.

expense of their fame, rather than surrender themselves to the wild projects of mad ambition! There is a fatality attending plenitude of power. Soon or late some mania seizes upon its possessors—they fall from the dizzy height through the giddiness of their own heads. Will not the same causes produce the same effects now as then? Sir, you may raise this army, you may build up this vast structure of patronage, this mighty apparatus of favoritism; but—"lay not the flattering unction to your souls"—you will never live to enjoy the succession. You sign your political death warrant.

An insinuation has fallen from the gentleman from Tennessee (Mr. Grundy) that the late massacre of our brethren on the Wabash has been instigated by the British Government. Has the President given any such information? has the gentleman received any such, even informally, from any officer of this Government? Is it so believed by the Administration? I have cause to think the contrary to be the fact; that such is not their opinion. This insinuation is of the grossest kind—a presumption the most rash, the most unjustifiable. Show but good ground for it, I will give up the question at the threshold—I am ready to march to Canada. It is indeed well calculated to excite the feelings of the Western people particularly, who are not quite so tenderly attached to our red brethren as some modern philosophers; but it is destitute of any foundation, beyond mere surmise and suspicion.

This war of conquest, a war for the acquisition of territory and subjects, is to be a new commentary on the doctrine that republics are destitute of ambition—that they are addicted to peace, wedded to the happiness and safety of the great body of their people. But it seems this is to be a holiday campaign—there is to be no expense of blood, or treasure, on our part—Canada is to conquer herself—she is to be subdued by the principles of fraternity. The people of that country are first to be seduced from their allegiance, and converted into traitors, as preparatory to the making them good citizens. Although I must acknowledge that some of our flaming patriots were thus manufactured, I do not think the process would hold good with a whole community. It is a dangerous experiment. We are to succeed in the French mode by the system of fraternization—all is French; but how dreadfully it might be retorted on the Southern and Western slaveholding States. I detest this subornation of treason. No—if he must have them, let them fall by the valor of our arms, by fair, legitimate conquest; not become the victims of treacherous seduction.

I am not surprised at the war spirit which is manifesting itself in gentlemen from the South. In the year 1805-'6, in a struggle for the carrying trade of belligerent colonial produce, this country had been most unwisely brought into collision with the great powers of Europe. By a series of most impolitic and ruinous measures,[1] utterly incomprehensible to every rational, sober-minded man, the Southern planters, by their own votes, had succeeded in knocking down the price of cotton to seven cents, and of tobacco (a few choice crops excepted) to nothing —and in raising the price of blankets (of which a few would not be amiss in a Canadian campaign), coarse woolens, and every article of first necessity, three or four hundred per cent. And now that, by our own acts, we have brought ourselves into this unprecedented condition, we must get out of it in any way but by an acknowledgment of our own want of wisdom and forecast. But is war the true remedy? Who will profit by it? Speculators—a few lucky merchants, who draw prizes in the lottery—commissaries and contractors. Who must suffer by it? The people. It is their blood, their taxes, that must flow to support it.

I am gratified to find gentlemen acknowledging the demoralizing and destructive consequences of the non-importation law —confessing the truth of all that its opponents foretold when it was enacted. And will you plunge yourselves in war because you have passed a foolish and ruinous law, and are ashamed to repeal it? "But our good friend the French Emperor stands in the way of its repeal," and as we cannot go too far in making sacrifices to him, who has given such demonstration of his love for the Americans, we must, in point of fact, become parties to his war. "Who can be so cruel as to refuse him this favor?" My imagination shrinks from the miseries of such a connection. I call upon the House to reflect whether they are not about to abandon all reclamation for the unparalleled outrages, "insults and injuries" of the French Government, to give up our claim for plundered millions; and I ask what reparation or atonement they can expect to obtain in hours of future dalliance, after they have made a tender of their person to this great deflowerer of the virginity of republics. We have by our own wise (he would not say *wise-acre*) measures, so increased the trade and wealth of Montreal and Quebec that at last we begin to cast a wishful eye at Canada. Having done so much toward its improvement by the exercise of "our restrictive energies," we begin to think the laborer worthy of his hire, and to put in claim

[1] Non-importation, non-intercourse, embargo.

for our portion. Suppose it ours, are we any nearer to our point? As his minister said to the King of Epirus, "may we not as well take our bottle of wine before as after this exploit?" Go! march to Canada! leave the broad bosom of the Chesapeake and her hundred tributary rivers—the whole line of seacoast from Machias to St. Mary's—unprotected! You have taken Quebec—have you conquered England? Will you seek for the deep foundations of her power in the frozen deserts of Labrador?

> "Her march is on the mountain wave,
> Her home is on the deep!"

Will you call upon her to leave your ports and harbors untouched, only just till you can return from Canada to defend them? The coast is to be left defenceless, while men of the interior are reveling in conquest and spoil. But grant for a moment, for mere argument's sake, that in Canada you touched the sinews of her strength, instead of removing a clog upon her resources—an encumbrance, but one which, from a spirit of honor, she will vigorously defend. In what situation would you then place some of the best men of the nation? As Chatham and Burke, and the whole band of her patriots, prayed for her defeat in 1776, so must some of the truest friends to their country deprecate the success of our arms against the only power that holds in check the arch-enemy of mankind.

Our people will not submit to be taxed for this war of conquest and dominion. The Government of the United States is not calculated to wage offensive foreign war—it was instituted for the common defence and general welfare; and whosoever should embark in a war of offence would put it to a test which it was by no means calculated to endure. I am unwilling to embark in common cause with France and be dragged at the wheels of the car of some Burr or Bonaparte.

What is the situation of the slaveholding States? During the war of the Revolution, so fixed were the habits of subordination of the blacks that when the whole Southern country was overrun by the enemy, who invited them to desert, no fear was ever entertained of an insurrection of the slaves. During the war of seven years, with our country in possession of the enemy, no such danger was ever apprehended. But should we therefore be unobservant spectators of the progress of society within the last twenty years—of the silent and powerful change wrought by time and chance upon its composition and temper? When the fountains of the great deep of abomination were broken up even the poor slaves had not escaped the general deluge. The French Revolution had polluted even them. Nay, there had not been wanting men in that House, witness their legislative *Legendre,* the butcher who once held a seat there, to preach upon that floor these imprescriptible rights to a crowded audience of blacks in the galleries—teaching them that they are equal to their masters; in other words, advising them to cut their throats. Similar doctrines were disseminated by peddlers from New England and elsewhere, throughout the Southern country—and masters have been found so infatuated as by their lives and conversation, by a general contempt of order, morality, and religion, unthinkingly to cherish these seeds of self-destruction to them and their families. What was the consequence? Within the last ten years repeated alarms of insurrection among the slaves—some of them awful indeed. From the spreading of this infernal doctrine the whole Southern country has been thrown into a state of insecurity. Men dead to the operation of moral causes have taken away from the poor slave his habits of loyalty and obedience to his master, which lightened his servitude by a double operation; beguiling his own cares and disarming his master's suspicions and severity; and now, like true empirics in politics, you are called upon to trust to the mere physical strength of the fetter which holds him in bondage. You have deprived him of all moral restraint, you have tempted him to eat of the fruit of the tree of knowledge, just enough to perfect him in wickedness; you have opened his eyes to his nakedness; you have armed his nature against the hand that has fed, that has clothed him, that has cherished him in sickness; that hand which, before he became a pupil of your school, he had been accustomed to press with respectful affection. You have done all this—and then show him the gibbet and the wheel, as incentives to a sullen, repugnant obedience. God forbid, sir, that the Southern States should ever see an enemy on their shores, with these infernal principles of French fraternity in the van! While talking of taking Canada, some of us are shuddering for our own safety at home. The night-bell never tolls for fire in Richmond that the mother does not hug her infant more closely to her bosom. I have been a witness of some of the alarms in the capital of Virginia.

Strange! that we should have no objection to any people or government, civilized or savage, in the whole world other than the British. The great Autocrat of all the Russias receives the homage of our high consideration. The Dey of Algiers and his Divan of Pirates are very civil, good sort of people, with whom we find no difficulty in maintaining the relations of peace and amity—"Turks, Jews, and Infidels"; Mellimelli, or the Little Turtle; barbarians and savages of every clime and color are welcome to our arms. With chiefs of banditti, negro or mulatto, we can treat and can trade. Name, however, but England, and all our antipathies are up in arms against her. Against whom? Against those whose blood runs in our veins; in common with whom we claim Shakespeare, and Newton, and Chatham for our countrymen; whose form of government is the freest on earth, our own only excepted; from whom every valuable principle of our own institutions has been borrowed—representation, jury trial, voting the supplies, writ of habeas corpus—our whole civil and criminal jurisprudence—against our fellow Protestants, identified in blood, in language, in religion with ourselves. In what school did the worthies of our land, the Washingtons, Henrys, Hancocks, Franklins, Rutledges of America, learn those principles of civil liberty which were so nobly asserted by their wisdom and valor? And American resistance to British usurpation has not been more warmly cherished by these great men and their compatriots; not more by Washington, Hancock, and Henry, than by Chatham and his illustrious associates in the British Parliament. It ought to be remembered, too, that the heart of the English people was with us. It was a selfish and corrupt ministry, and their servile tools, to whom we were not more opposed than they were. I trust that none such may ever exist among us—for tools will never be wanting to subserve the purposes, however ruinous or wicked, of kings and ministers of state.

I acknowledge the influence of a Shakespeare and Milton upon my imagination, of a Locke upon my understanding, of a Sidney upon my political principles, of a Chatham upon qualities which, would to God! I possessed in common with that illustrious man—of a Tillotson, a Sherlock, and a Porteus, upon my religion. This is a British influence which I could never shake off. I allow much to the just and honest prejudices growing out of the Revolution. But by whom have they been suppressed when they ran counter to the interests of his country? By Washington. By whom, would you listen to them, are they most keenly felt? By felons escaped from the jails of Paris, Newgate, and Kilmainham, since the breaking out of the French Revolution—who, in this abused and insulted country, have set up for political teachers, and whose disciples give no other proof of their progress in republicanism except a blind devotion to the most ruthless military despotism that the world ever saw. These are the patriots who scruple not to brand with the epithet of Tory the men (looking toward the seat of Col. Stuart) by whose blood your liberties have been cemented. These are they who hold in so keen remembrance the outrages of the British armies, from which many of them were deserters. Ask these self-styled patriots where they were during the American war (for they are for the most part old enough to have borne arms), and you strike them dumb—their lips are closed in eternal silence. If it were allowable to entertain partialities, every consideration of blood, language, religion, and interest would incline us toward England; and, yet, shall they be alone extended to France and her ruler, whom we are bound to believe a chastening God suffers as the scourge of a guilty world! On all other nations he tramples—he holds them in contempt—England alone he hates; he would, but he cannot, despise her—fear cannot despise. And shall we disparage our ancestors?—shall we bastardize ourselves by placing them even below the brigades of St. Domingo? with whom Mr. Adams had negotiated a sort of treaty, for which he ought to have been and would have been impeached if the people had not previously passed sentence of disqualification for their service upon him. This antipathy to all that is English must be French.

The outrages and injuries of England, bred up in the principles of the Revolution, I myself never palliate, much less defend. I well remember flying with my mother and her new-born child from Arnold and Phillips—and how they had been driven by Tarleton and other British pandours from pillar to post, while her husband was fighting the battles of his country. The impression is indelible on my memory—and yet (like my worthy old neighbor, who added seven buckshot to every cartridge at the battle of Guilford, and drew a fine sight at his man) I must be content to be called a Tory by a patriot of the last importation. Let us not get rid of one evil (supposing it to be possible) at the expense of a greater—*mutatis mutandis*.[1] Suppose France in possession of the British naval power—and to her the trident must pass should England be unable to wield it—what would be your condition? What would be the situation of your seaports and their seafaring inhabitants? Ask Hamburg, Lubec. Ask Savannah. What, sir! when their privateers are pent up in our harbors by the British bulldogs, when they receive at our hands every rite of hospitality, from which their enemy is excluded, when they capture within our own waters, interdicted to British armed ships, American vessels; when such is their deportment toward you, under such circum-

---

[1] "The necessary changes having been made."

stances, what could you expect if they were the uncontrolled lords of the ocean? Had those privateers at Savannah borne British commissions, or had your shipments of cotton, tobacco, ashes, and what not to London and Liverpool been confiscated and the proceeds poured into the English exchequer—my life upon it!—you would never have listened to any miserable wire-drawn distinctions between "orders and decrees affecting our neutral rights," and "municipal decrees" confiscating in mass your whole property. You would have had instant war! The whole land would have blazed out in war.

And shall republicans become the instruments of him who has effaced the title of Attila to the "Scourge of God!" Yet even Attila, in the fallen fortunes of civilization, had, no doubt, his advocates, his tools, his minions, his parasites in the very countries that he overran—sons of that soil whereon his horse had trod; where grass could never after grow.

I beseech the House, before they run their heads against this post Quebec, to count the cost. My word for it, Virginia planters will not be taxed to support such a war—a war which must aggravate their present distresses; in which they have not the remotest interest. Where is the Montgomery, or even the Arnold, or the Burr who is to march to Point Levi?

I call upon those professing to be republicans to make good the promises held out by their republican predecessors when they came into power—promises which, for years afterwards, they had honestly, faithfully fulfilled. We had vaunted of paying off the national debt, of retrenching useless establishments; and yet had now become as infatuated with standing armies, loans, taxes, navies, and war as ever were the Essex Junto. What republicanism is this?

RICHARD M. JOHNSON.—For the first time since my entrance into this body there now seems to be but one opinion with a great majority—that with Great Britain war is inevitable; that the hopes of the sanguine as to a returning sense of British justice have expired; that the prophecies of the discerning have failed; and, that her infernal system has driven us to the brink of a second revolution as important as the first. Upon the Wabash, through the influence of British agents, and within our territorial sea by the British navy, the war has already commenced. Thus, the folly, the power, and the tyranny of Great Britain have taken from us the last alternative of longer forbearance.

We must now oppose the farther encroachments of Great Britain by war, or formally annul the Declaration of our Independence and acknowledge ourselves her devoted colonies. The people whom I represent will not hesitate which of the two courses to choose; and, if we are involved in war to maintain our dearest rights and to preserve our independence, I pledge myself to this House and my constituents to this nation, that they will not be wanting in valor nor in their proportion of men and money to prosecute the war with effect. Before we relinquish the conflict I wish to see Great Britain renounce the piratical system of paper blockade; to liberate our captured seamen on board her ships of war; relinquish the practice of impressment on board our merchant vessels; to repeal her orders in Council; and cease in every other respect to violate our neutral rights; to treat us as an independent people. The gentleman from Virginia [Mr. Randolph] has objected to the destination of this auxiliary force—the occupation of the Canadas and the other British possessions upon our borders where our laws are violated, the Indians stimulated to murder our citizens, and where there is a British monopoly of the peltry and fur trade. I should not wish to extend the boundary of the United States by war if Great Britain would leave us to the quiet enjoyment of independence; but, considering her deadly and implacable enmity, and her continued hostility, I shall never die contented until I see her expulsion from North America, and her territories incorporated with the United States.

The waters of the St. Lawrence and the Mississippi interlock and the great Disposer of Human Events intended those two rivers should belong to the same people.

But it has been denied that British influence had any agency in the late dreadful conflict and massacre upon the Wabash; and this is said to vindicate the British nation from so foul a charge. Sir, look to the book of the Revolution. See the Indian savages in Burgoyne's army urged on every occasion to use the scalping-knife and tomahawk—not in battle, but against old men and women, and children, in the night, when they were taught to believe an omniscient eye could not see their guilty deeds; and, thus hardened in iniquity, they perpetrated the same deeds by the light of the sun when no arm was found to oppose or protect. And when this crying sin was opposed by Lord Chatham in the House of Lords,[1] the employment of these Indians was justified by a speech from one of the ministry. Thus we see how the principles of honor, of humanity, of Christianity were violated and justified in the face of the world. Therefore I can have no doubt of the influence of British agents

[1] See Volume I, page 217.

in keping up Indian hostility to the people of the United States, independent of the strong proofs on this occasion; and I hope it will not be pretended that these agents are too moral or too religious to do the infamous deed. So much for the expulsion of Great Britain from her dominions in North America and their incorporation into the United States of America.

The gentleman from Virginia says we are identified with the British in religion, in blood, in language, and deeply laments our hatred to that country, who can boast of so many illustrious characters. This deep-rooted enmity to Great Britain arises from her insidious policy, the offspring of her perfidious conduct toward the United States. Her disposition is unfriendly; her enmity is implacable; she sickens at our prosperity and happiness. If obligations of friendship do exist, why does Great Britain rend those ties asunder and open the bleeding wounds of former conflicts? Or does the obligation of friendship exist on the part of the United States alone? I have never thought that the ties of religion, of blood, of language, and of commerce would justify or sanctify insult and injury—on the contrary, that a premeditated wrong from the hand of a friend created more sensibility and deserved the greater chastisement and the higher execration. What would you think of a man to whom you were bound by the most sacred ties who would plunder you of your substance, aim a deadly blow at your honor, and, in the hour of confidence, endeavor to bury a dagger in your bosom? Would you, sir, proclaim to the world your affection for this miscreant of society after this conduct, and endeavor to interest your audience with the ties of kindred that bound you to each other? So let it be with nations, and there will be neither surprise nor lamentation that we execrate a government so hostile to our independence—for it is from the government that we meet with such multiplied injury, and to that object is our hatred directed. As to individuals of merit, whether British or French, I presume no person would accuse the people of the United States of such hatred to them, or of despising individuals who might not be instrumental in the maritime despotism which we feel; and this accounts for the veneration we have for Sidney and Russell, statesmen of whom the gentleman has spoken; they are fatal examples why we should love the British Government. The records of that government are now stained with the blood of these martyrs in freedom's cause, as vilely as with the blood of American citizens; and certainly we shall not called upon to love equally the murderer and the victim. For God's sake let us not again be told of the ties of religion, of laws, of blood, and of customs which bind the two nations together, with a view to extort our love for the English Government, and, more especially, when the same gentleman has acknowledged that we have ample cause of war against that nation—let us not be told of the freedom of that corrupt government whose hands are washed alike in the blood of her own illustrious statesmen for a manly opposition to tyranny and the citizens of every other clime. But I would inquire into this love for the British Government and British institutions, in the gross, without any discrimination. Why love her rulers? Why kiss the rod of iron which inflicts the stripes without a cause? When all admit we have just cause of war such attachments are dangerous and encourage encroachment. I will venture to say that our hatred of the British Government is not commensurate with her depredations and her outrages on our rights, or we should have waged a deadly war against her many years past. The subject of foreign attachments and British hatred has been examined at considerable length. I did not intend to begin that discussion, but I will pursue it, and, though I make no charge of British attachments, I will, at all times, at every hazard, defend the Administration and the Republican party against the charge of foreign partialities— French or Spanish, or any other kind—when applied to the measures of our Government. This foreign influence is a dangerous enemy; we should destroy the means of its circulation among us—like the fatal tunic, it destroys where it touches. It is insidious, invisible, and takes advantage of the most unsuspecting hours of social intercourse. I would not deny the good will of France nor of Great Britain to have an undue influence among us. But Great Britain alone has the means of this influence to an extent dangerous to the United States. It has been said that Great Britain was fighting the battles of the world—that she stands against universal dominion threatened by the arch-fiend of mankind. I should be sorry if our independence depended upon the power of Great Britain. If, however, she would act the part of a friendly power toward the United States I should never wish to deprive her of power, of wealth, of honor, of prosperity. But, if her energies are to be directed against the liberties of this free and happy people, against my native country, I should not drop a tear if the fast-anchored isle would sink into the waves, provided the innocent inhabitants could escape the deluge and find an asylum in a more favorable soil.

And as to the power of France, I fear it as little as any

other power; I would oppose her aggressions under any circumstances as soon as I would British outrages.

The ties of religion, of language, of blood, as it regards Great Britain, are dangerous ties to this country, with her present hostile disposition—instead of pledges of friendship they are used to paralyze the strength of the United States in relation to her aggressions. There are other ties equally efficacious. The number of her commercial traders within our limits, her agents, etc., the vast British capital employed in our commerce and our moneyed institutions, connected with her language, ancestry, customs, habits, and laws. These are formidable means for estranging the affections of many from our republican institutions, and producing partialities for Great Britain.

The gentleman from Virginia has called the military regular forces mercenaries. If, by this appellation, any reproach or degradation is intended, its justice and propriety is denied. In times like the present, when dangers thicken upon us, at the moment when we are compelled by most wanton tyranny upon the high seas, and upon land may be added, to abandon our peaceful habits for the din of arms, officers and soldiers in this country are governed by the noble feelings of patriotism and of valor. The history of the world may be ransacked; other nations may be brought in review before us, and examples of greater heroism cannot be quoted than shall be performed in battle by our officers and soldiers, military and naval and marine. The deeds of their ancestors would be before them; glory would animate their bosoms, and love of country would nerve the heart to deeds of mighty fame. If, therefore, there should not be a diminution of respect for those who entertain an opinion so degrading to our army, it should at least be understood that such opinions do not lessen the confidence due to those who faithfully serve their country, and who would lay down their lives for it. This reflection brings to memory the late memorable conflict upon the Wabash. Governor Harrison pitched his tents near the Prophet's town; and, although this fanatic and his followers collected, and the American forces were anxious to finish the work by an open and daylight engagement, if there was a necessity to resort to arms, their impetuous valor was easily stayed, when they were informed that the white flag of peace was to be hoisted next morning, and the effusion of blood was to be spared. But in the silent watches of the night, relieved from the fatigues of valor, and slumbering under the perfidious promises of the savages, who were infuriated and made drunk by British traders, dreaming of the tender smile of a mother, and the fond embraces of affectionate wives, and of prattling children upon their knees, on their return from the fatigues of a campaign!—the destroyers came with the silent instruments of death—the war-club, the scalping-knife, the tomahawk, and the bow and arrow; with these they penetrate into the heart of our forces—they enter the tents of our officers—many close their eyes in death—it was a trying moment for the rest of our heroes, but they were equal to the dreadful occasion. The American forces flew to arms; they rallied at the voice of their officers, and soon checked the work of death. The savages were successively and successfully charged and driven until daylight, when they disappeared like the mist of morning. In this dreadful conflict many were killed and wounded on both sides; and the volunteers and the regiment under Colonel Boyd acted and fought with equal bravery and to their immortal honor. The volunteers from Kentucky were men of valor and worth—young men of hopeful prospects, and married men of reputation and intelligence, governed by no mercenary views—honor prompted them to serve their country. Some of these fallen heroes were my acquaintances, my friends: one not the least conspicuous lived in my district—Colonel Owens; Colonel Daviess, a neighbor. You, Mr. Speaker, know the worth of some of these men; and I regret that you are not in my place to speak their praise. So long as the records of this transaction remain, the 9th of November will not be forgotten, and time shall only brighten the fame of the deeds of our army, and a tear shall be shed for those who have fallen.

ROBERT WRIGHT.—I, sir, shall take the liberty of varying the question from the honorable member from Virginia [Mr. Randolph] who, yesterday, considered it a question of peace or war. I shall consider it as a question of war or submission, dire alternatives, of which, however, I trust no honest American can hesitate in choosing when the question is correctly stated and distinctly understood. The gentleman from Virginia contends that it is a dispute about the carrying trade, brought on us by the cupidity of the American merchants, in which the farmer and planter have little interest; that he will not consent to tax his constituents to carry on a war for it; that the enemy is invulnerable on the "mountain wave," the element of our wrongs, but should they violate the *natale solum*[1] he would point all the energies of the nation and avenge the wrong. Was that gentleman stricken on the nose by a man so tall that he could not reach his nose, I strongly incline to think his manly

[1] "Native soil."

pride would not permit him to decline the conflict. Sir, the honorable member is incorrect in his premises, and, of course, in his conclusions. I will endeavor to convince him of this, and shall be gratified if I can enlist his talents on the side of a bleeding country. Sir, the violations of the commercial rights of which we complain do not only embrace the carrying trade, properly so called, but also the carrying of the products of our own soil, the fruits of our own industry; these, although injurious only to our property, are just causes of war. But, sir, the impressment of our native seamen is a stroke at the vitals of liberty itself, and, although it does not touch the *"natale solum,"* yet it enslaves the *"nativos filios"*—the native sons of America; and, in the ratio that liberty is preferable to property, ought to enlist the patriotic feelings of that honorable member and make his bosom burn with that holy fire that inspired the patriots of the Revolution.

Sir, the carrying trade—by which I mean the carrying of articles, the growth, produce, or manufacture of a foreign clime —except articles contraband of war—is as much the right of the American people as the carrying of the products of their own soil, and is not only secured by the law of nations, but by the positive provisions of the British treaty. To us, sir, it is an all-important right. We import from the West Indies, annually, property to the amount of forty millions of dollars, for which we pay in the products of our own soil; of this, ten millions are consumed in the United States and the surplus thirty millions are exported to foreign countries, on which the American merchant pays three per cent. on the duties to the United States, obtains the profits on the freight of thirty millions of dollars, and furnishes a market for American productions to the same amount.

Mr. Speaker, the gentleman from Virginia has declared that, if he could believe that the late massacre of the troops in the attack on Governor Harrison by the Indians under the Prophet was the effect of British agency he would unite with us, heart and hand, and personally assist to avenge the bloody deed. I feel a confidence that, if the gentleman will attend to the circumstances of this case and take a retrospective view of the conduct of the British Government, he will feel no doubt of the fact.

At the late great council with Governor Harrison the chiefs of many tribes were convened, all of whom, except Tecumseh, the Prophet's brother, in their speeches avowed their friendly dispositions and their devotion to peace with the United States.

Tecumseh, who, with a number of his tribe, came from Fort Malden in Canada, declared his hostile intentions against the United States, left the council with that avowed intention, and returned again to Fort Malden. Shortly after this the Shawanees assembled a large body in arms in the Indian Territory under the Prophet, and committed the assault on the troops of Governor Harrison, though they have paid for their temerity. This, I trust, connected as it is with the immorality and extraordinary pretensions of that government at this crisis, will satisfy, not only the gentleman from Virginia, but this House, of a British agency in the case.

Mr. Speaker, I regret that the gentleman from Virginia should ascribe to gentlemen of the West a disposition for war, with a view to raise the price of their hemp; or to the gentlemen of the North, with a view to raise the price of their beef and flour. These, sir, are selfish motives, and such I cannot for a moment believe will be taken into consideration; they will, with every other section of the Union, unite in deciding it on its merits; they will count the wrongs we have sustained; they will reflect that the honor, the interest, and the very independence of the United States are directly attacked; they will, as guardians of the nation's rights, agreeably to the advice of the administration "put the United States into an armor and an attitude demanded by the crisis, and correspondent with the national spirit and expectations"; they will prepare to chastise the wrongs of the British cabinet which, the President tells us, "have the character as well as the effect of war on our commercial rights which no independent nation can relinquish." They will decide, with the President, the executive organ of the nation's will, "that these wrongs are no longer to be endured." They will decide, with the Committee of Foreign Relations, "that forbearance longer to repel these wrongs has ceased to be a virtue," and I hope they will decide with me that submission is a crime; and, sir, if they will examine a document on that table, I mean the returns of the Twelfth Congress, and compare them with the eleventh, they will find nearly one-half of the eleventh Congress removed. This, sir, may correctly be considered as the sentence of the nation against the doctrine of submission; it is certainly an expression of the nation's will in a language not to be misunderstood and too serious in its application not to be respected.

Mr. Speaker, the gentleman from Virginia says he expects to be charged with being under British influence; however, he disregarded it. I assure him I shall not be one of his accusers;

I believe him governed by *himself*, and influenced by pure American motives, and that, if he saw the subject as I do, his bosom would burn with the same sacred fire to avenge our wrongs; and were I to hear him charged in his absence with British influence I should repel it, notwithstanding he has told us, in a prideful manner, that he had descended from British ancestors; that, from a Shakespeare he had formed his taste, from a Locke his mind, from a Chatham his politics, from a Sydney his patriotism, from a Tillotson his religion. Mr. Speaker, had I been that honorable member I should have boasted a nobler line of ancestry; I should have claimed my descent from the beardless Powhatan and the immortal Pocahontas,[1] and I should have taken as models, from my own State, a Henry for my eloquence, a Jefferson for my politics, a Washington for my patriotism, and a Madison, or rather the Oracles of Revolution, for my religion. But, sir, I am myself so much a Roman that I can truly say, in their language:

"Aut genus aut proavos, aut qua non fecimus ipse, vix ea nostra voco."[2]

"Honor and shame from no condition rise,
  Act well your part, there all the honor lies."

Sir, the charge of foreign influence and the recrimination of one political party by the other are unpleasant things. I should rejoice to see the curtain of oblivion drawn over them and all uniting under the nobler distinction of American.

Mr. Calhoun.—Sir, I am not insensible to the weighty importance of this question, for the first time submitted to this House, as a redress of our long list of complaints against one of the belligerents; but, according to my mode of thinking on this subject, however serious the question, whenever I am on its affirmative side my conviction must be strong and unalterable. War, in this country, ought never to be resorted to but when it is clearly justifiable and necessary; so much so as not to require the aid of logic to convince our reason, nor the ardor of eloquence to inflame our passions. There are many reasons why this country should never resort to it but for causes the most urgent and necessary. It is sufficient that, under a government like ours, none but such will justify it in the eye of the nation; and, were I not satisfied that such is the present case, I certainly would be no advocate of the proposition now before the House.

---

[1] Randolph was a descendant of these Indians.
[2] "Neither race, nor ancestors, nor aught save what I myself have accomplished hardly do I call mine."

Sir, I might prove the war, should it ensue, justifiable by the express admission of the gentleman from Virginia; and necessary by facts undoubted and universally admitted, such as that gentleman did not pretend to controvert. The extent, duration, and character of the injuries received; the failure of those peaceful means heretofore resorted to for the redress of our wrongs, is my proof that it is necessary. Why should I mention the impressment of our seamen; depredation on every branch of our commerce, including the direct export trade, continued for years, and made under laws which professedly undertake to regulate our trade with other nations; negotiation resorted to time after time, till it is become hopeless; the restrictive system persisted in to avoid war, and in the vain expectation of returning justice? The evil still grows, and in each succeeding year swells in extent and pretension beyond the preceding. The question, even in the opinion and admission of our opponents, is reduced to this single point—which shall we do, abandon or defend our own commercial and maritime rights, and the personal liberties of our citizens employed in exercising them? These rights are essentially attacked, and the war is the only means of redress. The gentleman from Virginia has suggested none—unless we consider the whole of his speech as recommending patient and resigned submission as the best remedy. Sir, which alternative this House ought to embrace it is not for me to say. I hope the decision is made already by a higher authority than the voice of any man. It is not for the human tongue to instill the sense of independence and honor. This is the work of nature—a generous nature, that disdains tame submission to wrongs.

This part of the subject is so imposing as to enforce silence even on the gentleman from Virginia. He dared not to deny his country's wrongs, or vindicate the conduct of her enemy.

Only one point of that gentleman's argument had any, the most remote, relation to this point. He would not say we had not a good cause of war, but insisted that it was our duty to define that cause. If he means that this House ought, at this stage of the proceeding, or any other, to enumerate such violations of our rights as we are willing to contend for, he prescribes a course which neither good sense nor the usage of nations warrants. When we contend, let us contend for all our rights; the doubtful and the certain, the unimportant and essential. It is as easy to struggle, or even more so, for the whole as a part. At the termination of the contest secure all that our wisdom and valor and the fortune of the war will permit. This is the dictate of common sense; such, also, is the usage of nations. How, then, could the gentleman, after his admissions, with the facts before him and the nation, complain? The causes are such as to warrant, or rather make it indispensable in any nation not absolutely dependent to defend its rights by force. Let him, then, show the reasons why we ought not so to defend ourselves. On him, then, is the burden of proof. This he has attempted; he has endeavored to support his negative. Before I proceed to answer the gentleman particularly, let me call the attention of the House to one circumstance: that is, that almost the whole of his arguments consisted of an enumeration of evils always incident to war, however just and necessary; and that, if they have any force, it is calculated to produce unqualified submission to every species of insult and injury. I do not feel myself bound to answer arguments of the above description; and, if I should touch on them, it will be only incidentally and not for the purpose of serious refutation. The first argument of the gentleman which I shall notice is the unprepared state of the country. Whatever weight this argument might have in a question of immediate war it surely has little in that of preparation for it. If our country is unprepared, let us remedy the evil as soon as possible. Let the gentleman submit his plan; and, if a reasonable one, I doubt not it will be supported by the House. But, sir, let us admit the fact and the whole force of the argument, I ask whose is the fault? Who has been a member for many years past, and has seen the defenceless state of his country even near home, under his own eyes, without a single endeavor to remedy so serious an evil? Let him not say: "I have acted in a minority." It is no less the duty of the minority than a majority to endeavor to serve our country. For that purpose we are sent here, and not for that of opposition. We are next told of the expenses of the war, and that people will not pay taxes. Why not? Is it a want of capacity? What, with one million tons of shipping, a trade of near $100,000,000, manufactures of $150,000,000, and agriculture of thrice that amount, shall we be told the country wants capacity to raise and support ten thousand or fifteen thousand additional regulars? No; it has the ability, that is admitted; but will it not have the disposition? Is not the course a just and necessary one? Shall we, then, utter this libel on the nation? Where will proof be found of a fact so disgraceful? It is said in the history of the country twelve or fifteen years ago. The case is not parallel. The ability of the country is greatly increased since. The object of that tax was unpopular. But on this, as well as my memory and almost infant observation at that time serve me, the objection was not to the tax or its amount, but the mode of collection. The eye of the nation was frightened by the number of officers; its love of liberty shocked with the multiplicity of regulations. We, in the vile spirit of imitation, copied from the most oppressive part of European laws on that subject, and imposed on a young and virtuous nation all the severe provisions made necessary by corruption and long growing chicane. If taxes should become necessary I do not hesitate to say the people will pay cheerfully. It is for their Government and their cause, and it would be their interest and duty to pay. But it may be, and I believe was, said that the nation will not pay taxes because the rights violated are not worth defending, or that the defence will cost more than the profit. Sir, I here enter my solemn protest against this low and "calculating avarice" entering this hall of legislation. It is fit only for shops and counting-houses, and ought not to disgrace the seat of sovereignty by its squalid and vile appearance. Whenever it touches sovereign power, the nation is ruined. It is too short-sighted to defend itself. It is an unpromising spirit, always ready to yield a part to save the balance. It is too timid to have in itself the laws of self-preservation. It is never safe but under the shield of honor.

Sir, I know of only one principle to make a nation great, to produce in this country not the form but real spirit of union, and that is to protect every citizen in the lawful pursuit of his business. He will then feel that he is backed by the Government; that its arm is his arms; and will rejoice in its increased strength and prosperity. Protection and patriotism are reciprocal. This is the road that all great nations have trod. Sir, I am not versed in this calculating policy; and will not, therefore, pretend to estimate in dollars and cents the value of national independence or national affection. I cannot dare to measure, in shillings and pence, the misery, the stripes, and the slavery of our impressed seamen; nor even to value our shipping, commercial, and agricultural losses under the Orders in Council and the British system of blockade. I hope I have not condemned any prudent estimate of the means of a country before it enters on a war. This is wisdom, the other folly. Sir, the gentleman from Virginia has not failed to touch on the calamity of war; that fruitful source of declamation by which pity becomes the advocate of cowardice; but I know not what we have to do with that subject. If the gentleman desires to repress the gallant ardor of our countrymen by such topics, let me inform him that true courage regards only the cause—that it is just and necessary—and that it despises the pain and danger of war. If he really wishes to promote the cause of humanity, let his eloquence be addressed to Lord Wellesley or Mr. Percival, and not the American Congress. Tell them, if they persist in such daring insult and injury to a neutral nation, that, however inclined to peace, it will be bound in honor and interest to resist; that their patience and benevolence, however great, will be exhausted; that the calamity of war will ensue; and that they, in the opinion of wounded humanity, will be answerable for all its devastation and misery. Let melting pity and regard to the interest of humanity stay the hand of injustice, and, my life on it, the gentleman will not find it difficult to call off his country from the bloody scenes of war.

We are next told of the danger of war! I believe we are all ready to acknowledge its hazard and accidents; but I cannot think we have any extraordinary danger to contend with, at least so much as to warrant an acquiescence in the injuries we have received. On the contrary, I believe no war can be less dangerous to internal peace or national existence. But we are told of the black population of the South. As far as the gentleman from Virginia speaks of his own personal knowledge I will not pretend to contradict him; I only regret that such is the dreadful state of his particular part of the country. Of the Southern section I, too, have some personal knowledge, and can say that in South Carolina no such fears in any part are felt. But, sir, admit the gentleman's statement; will a war with Great Britain increase the danger? Will the country be less able to repress insurrection? Had we any thing to fear from that quarter, which I sincerely disbelieve, in my opinion, the precise time of the greatest safety is during a war in which we have no fear of invasion—then the country is most on its guard; our militia the best prepared; and standing force the greatest. Even in our Revolution no attempts were made by that portion of our population; and, however the gentleman may frighten himself with the disorganizing effects of French principles, I cannot think our ignorant blacks have felt much of their baneful influence. I dare say more than one-half of them never heard of the French Revolution.

But, as great as is the danger from our slaves, the gentleman's fears end not there—the standing army is not less terrible to him. Sir, I think a regular force, raised for a period of actual hostilities, cannot be called a standing army. There is a just distinction between such a force, and one raised as a peace establishment. Whatever may be the composition of the latter, I hope the former will consist of some of the best materials of the country. The ardent patriotism of our young men, and the reasonable bounty in land which is proposed to be given, will impel them to join their country's standard and to fight her battles; they will not forget the citizen in the soldier, and, in obeying their officer, learn to contemn their Constitution. In our officers and soldiers we will find patriotism no less pure and ardent than in the private citizen; but, if they should be depraved, as represented, what have we to fear from twenty-five or thirty thousand regulars? Where will be the boasted militia of the gentleman? Can one million of militia be overpowered by thirty thousand regulars? If so, how can we rely on them against a foe invading our country? Sir, I have no such contemptuous idea of our militia—their untaught bravery is sufficient to crush all foreign and internal attempts on their country's liberties.

But we have not yet come to the end of the chapter of dangers. The gentleman's imagination, so fruitful on this subject, conceives that our Constitution is not calculated for war, and that it cannot stand its rude shock. This is rather extraordinary —we must depend upon the pity or contempt of other nations for our existence. The Constitution, it seems, has failed in its essential part, "to provide for the common defence." No, says the gentleman from Virginia, it is competent for a defensive, but not an offensive, war. It is not necessary for me to expose the error of this opinion. Why make the distinction in this instance? Will he pretend to say that this is an offensive war; a war of conquest? Yes, the gentleman has dared to make this assertion; and for reasons no less extraordinary than the assertion itself. He says our rights are violated on the ocean, and that these violations affect our shipping and commercial rights, to which the Canadas have no relation. The doctrine of retaliation has been much abused of late by an unnatural extension; we have now to witness a new abuse. The gentleman from Virginia has limited it down to a point. By his system, if you receive a blow on the breast, you dare not return it on the head, you are obliged to measure and return it on the precise point on which it was received. If you do not proceed with mathematical accuracy it ceases to be just self-defence; it becomes an unprovoked attack. In speaking of Canada the gentleman from Virginia introduced the name of Montgomery with much feeling and interest. Sir, there is danger in that name to the gentleman's argument. It is sacred to heroism! It is indignant of submission! This calls my memory back to the time of our Revolution; to the Congress of '74 and '75. Supposing a speaker of that day had risen and urged all the arguments which we have heard on this subject; had told that Congress: "your contest is about the right of laying a tax, and that the attempt on Canada had nothing to do with it; that the war would be expensive; that danger and devastation would overspread our country; and that the power of Great Britain was irresistible." With what sentiment, think you, would such doctrines have been received? Happy for us, they had no force at that period of our country's glory. Had they been then acted on, this hall would never have witnessed a great nation convened to deliberate for the general good; a mighty empire, with prouder prospects than any nation the sun ever shone on would not have risen in the West. No; we would have been vile, subjected colonies; governed by that imperious rod which Great Britain holds over her distant provinces.

The gentleman from Virginia is at a loss to account for what he calls our hatred to England. He asks how can we hate the country of Locke, of Newton, Hampden, and Chaham; a country having the same language and customs with ourselves, and descending from a common ancestry. Sir, the laws of human affections are uniform. If we have so much to attach us to that country powerful indeed must be the cause which has overpowered it.

Yes, sir, there is a cause strong enough. Not that occult courtly affection which he has supposed to be entertained for France; but it is to be found in continued and unprovoked insult and injury. A cause so manifest that the gentleman from Virginia had to exert much ingenuity to overlook it. But, sir, here I think the gentleman, in his eager admiration of that country, has not been sufficiently guarded in his argument. Has he reflected on the cause of that admiration? Has he examined the reasons of our high regard for her Chatham? It is his ardent patriotism; the heroic courage of his mind that could not brook the least insult or injury offered to his country, but thought that her interest and honor ought to be vindicated at every hazard and expense.

[Here Mr. Calhoun indulged in a rather ungenerous comparison between Lord Chatham and Mr. Randolph, the Representative from Virginia having challenged it, which, on reflection, the young member from South Carolina caused to be omitted from the recorded speech.]

MR. RANDOLPH.—The nation has been brought into its present alarming and unprecedented situation by means in nowise unaccountable—by steps as direct and successive as Hogarth's celebrated series of prints, "The Rake's Progress," beginning at the gaming table and ending in a jail, or in bedlam. We commenced our system somewhat on the plan of Catharine of Russia, when she lent her nominal aid to the coalition; we had dealt even more profusely than she in manifestoes; we began, under the instigation of mercantile cupidity, to contend by proclamations and resolutions for the empire of the ocean. But, instead of confining ourselves as she had done to this bloodless warfare, we must copy the wise example of her successors, and, after our battle of Friedland, I suppose we also shall have our peace of Tilsit.

The gentleman from Maryland has expressed surprise at my manner of speaking of our origin from an English stock. We were vastly particular about the breed of our horses, cattle, and sheep, but careless of the breed of human nature. And yet to our Anglo-Saxon origin we owe our resistance to British tyranny. Whence, but from that origin came all the blessings of life, so far as political privileges are concerned? To what is it owing that we are at this moment deliberating under the forms of a free representative government? Had we sprung from the loins of Frenchmen (he shuddered at the thought!) where would have been that proud spirit of resistance to ministerial encroachment on our rights and liberties which achieved our independence? In what school had the illustrious men of the Revolution formed those noble principles of civil liberty asserted by their eloquence and maintained by their arms? Among the grievances stated in their remonstrance to the King a "standing army" met us at the threshold. It was curious to see in that list of wrongs so many that had since been self-inflicted by us.

I will forever stand up for the militia. It is not in the scoffs of the epaulette gentry, who, for any service they have seen, are the *rawest militia,* to degrade them in my eyes. Who are they? Ourselves—the country. Arm them and you are safe, beyond the possibility of danger. Yearly did the standing army sweep off the money, while the militia received empty praise. I would rather see the thing reversed. But there will forever be a court and country party. The standing army is the devoted creature of the court. It must forever be so. Can we wonder that it should be cherished by its master? I will ever uphold the militia; but I detest standing armies as the profligate instruments of despotism, as the bloodhounds of hell. They would support any and every existing government. In all history I remember only one instance of their deserting their government and taking part with the people: and that was when the Duke of Orleans had bribed the army of the last of the Bourbon Kings. A mercenary soldier is disgusting to our senses; odious and detestable to the eye of reason, republicanism, and religion. Yet, that "mere machine of murder," rude as it is, was the manufacturer of all the Cæsars and Cromwells, and Bonapartes of the earth; consecrated by a people's curse, not loud but deep, to the infernal gods. As from the filth of the kennel and common sewer spread the pestilence that carried havoc through a great city, so from this squalid, outcast, homeless wretch springs the scourge of military despotism. And yet we are told that there is no danger from an army of thirty or forty thousand men. With five thousand Cæsar had passed the Rubicon. With twenty-two thousand he fought the battle of Pharsalia which rendered him master of the world. To come to later times— what number had Bonaparte when, deserting his companions in arms, he returned a solitary fugitive from Egypt, to overturn that government which, if it had possessed one particle of energy, if it had been possible for the civil authority to cope with military power, would have cashiered him for having ruined one of the best-appointed fleets and armies that ever sailed from a European port? Well might the father of political wisdom (Lord Chatham) say to the Parliament of England: "entrench yourselves in parchment to the teeth, the sword will find a passage to the vitals of the constitution." As good a Republican as ever sat on that floor (Andrew Fletcher of Saltoun) had dissolved his political friendship with the Earl of Sunderland when he found him supporting an army; and the event justified his sagacity. Cromwell, the affected patron of liberty, always encouraged the army. We know the consequence. It was a fundamental principle of free government that a legislature which would preserve its liberty must avoid that canker, a standing army. Are we to forget, as chimerical, our notions of this institution which we imbibed from our very cradles, which are imprinted on our bills of rights and Constitutions, which we avowed under the reign of John Adams? Are they to be scourged out of us by the birch of the unfledged political pedagogues of the day? If I were the enemy of this Government, could I reconcile it to my principles, I would follow the example set me in another quarter and say to the majority, *go* to your inevitable destruction! I liken the people under this joint operation of the two parties, ministerial and federal, to the poor client between two lawyers, or the cloth between the tailor's shears.

I am glad to hear that this is not to be a party war. When the last additional force bill was raised, to which this was about to be superadded, it was an indispensable preliminary to an appointment to sign, or to promise to sign, the thirty-nine articles of the creed of the reigning political church. But now the political millennium was at hand—already had John Adams and Citizen Genet laid down, like the lion and the lamb, in the same fold. And, if they were not joined by their fellow-laborer in Newgate, it was his keeper's fault, not that of his inclination. Citizen *Genet*, now an American patriot of the first order, who extols "*our* Washington"; the champion of the laws of nations; the vindicator of American rights against foreign (and, of course, French) aggression!

I am glad to hear that it is not to be a war for the protection of manufactures. To domestic manufactures, in the true sense of the term, I have always been, and ever shall be, a friend; I have taken a pride in clothing myself in them until it was attempted to be made a political test. I abhor tests of all sorts, political and religious, and never will submit to them. I am sick of this cant of patriotism which extends to a man's victuals, drink, and clothes. I have, from a sort of obstinacy that belongs to me, laid aside the *external* use of these manufactures; but I am their firm friend, and of the manufacturers also. They are no new things to me; no Merino hobby of the day; I have known them from my infancy.

On April 1, 1812, President Madison, reverting to his favorite weapon of commercial restrictions, sent a confidential message to Congress which proposed as "expedient under existing circumstances and prospects" a general embargo for sixty days.

This was discussed in executive session, the proceedings, however, being printed later by order of the House.

The debate centered upon the question as to whether the embargo was what it was evidently intended to mean, namely, a genuine preparation for war, or whether it was another measure in the long series of commercial restrictions on which the Government had thus far vainly relied to bring Great Britain to terms. Henry Clay

[Ky.], the Speaker of the House, upheld the former view. He was opposed by John Randolph and Josiah Quincy, 3rd [Mass.].

The War Embargo

House of Representatives, April 1-3, 1812

Mr. Clay warmly expressed his satisfaction and full approbation of the message, and the proposition now before the committee. He approved of it because it is to be viewed as a direct precursor to war. Sir, said Mr. C., after the pledges we have made, and the stand we have taken, are we now to cover ourselves with shame and indelible disgrace by retreating from the measures and grounds we have taken? He said what would disgrace an individual under certain circumstances would disgrace a nation. And what would you think of one individual who had thus conducted to another, and should then retreat? He said there was no intrinsic difficulty or terror in the war: there was no terror except what arises from the novelty. Where are we to come in contact with our enemy? On our own continent. If gentlemen please to call these sentiments Quixotic he would say he pitied them for their sense of honor. We know no pains have been spared to villify the Government. If we now proceed we shall be supported by the people. Many of our people have not believed that war is to take place. They have been wilfully blinded. He was willing to give them further notice. It remains for us to say whether we will shrink or follow up the patriotic conduct of the President. As an American and a member of this House he felt a pride that the Executive had recommended this measure.

Mr. Randolph was confident in declaring that this was not a measure of the Executive—that it was engendered by an extensive excitement upon the Executive. Whose ever measure it is the people of the United States will consider it as a subterfuge for war; as a retreat from the battle. We some years ago resolved that we must have *war, embargo,* or *submission*—we have not had war or submitted—we must therefore have embargo. It appears to be limited to sixty days; at the expiration of that time will any one say we shall be prepared for war? Sir, we are in the situation of a debtor who promises to pay his note at the bank in sixty days—we shall prolong the time sixty days, and sixty days after that, until deferred hope makes the heart sick. He would tell the honorable Speaker that, at the end of sixty days, we shall not have war, and the reason is the

Executive dare not plunge the nation into a war in our unprepared state.

Are the majority, in consequence of having been goaded by the presses, to plunge the people into a war by bringing them first to the whipping-post and then by exciting their spirit? He would assure the House the spirit of the people is not up to it at this time; if so, there would be no necessity of those provocations to excite this false spirit—this kind of Dutch courage. If you mean war, if the spirit of the country is up to it, why have you been spending five months in idle debate?

JOSIAH the FIRST.

From Lossing's "Field Book of the War of 1812"

MR. QUINCY expressed in strong terms his abhorrence of the measure. He said that his objection was that it was not what it pretended to be; and was what it pretended not to be. That it was not embargo preparatory to war; but that it was embargo as a substitute for the question of declaring war.

But it is said "we must protect our merchants." Heaven help our merchants from *embargo-protection!* It is also said that "the present condition of things has been brought upon the country by the merchants; that it was their clamor, in 1805 and 1806, which first put Congress upon this system of coercive restriction, of which they now so much complain." It is true that, in those years, the merchants did petition, not for embargo, not for commercial embarrassment and annihilation, but for protection. They, at that time, really thought that this national Government was formed for protection, and that it had at heart the prosperity of all the great interests of the country. If "it was a grievous fault, grievously have *the merchants* answered it." They asked you for relief and you sent them embarrassment. They asked you for defence and you imposed embargo. They "asked bread *and you* gave them a stone." They "asked a fish *and you* gave them a serpent." Grant that the fault was great, suppose that they did mistake the nature and character of the Government, is the penalty they incurred by this error never to be remitted? Permit them once to escape and, my word for it, they will never give you an apology for this destructive protection. If they do they will richly deserve all the misery which, under the name of protection, you can find means to visit upon them. Your tender mercies are cruelties. The merchants hate and spurn this ruinous defence.

Seeing the war spirit in Congress President Madison laid aside his pet remedy of commercial retaliation against British aggression, and reluctantly resorted to armed resistance.

CHAPTER VII

THE SECOND WAR WITH GREAT BRITAIN

President Madison's Message on Relations with Great Britain—Declaration of War—Protest of the Minority—The President's Message on "The Justice of the War"—Debate on Bill to Raise Additional Troops; It Develops into One on the Justice and Expediency of the War: in Favor of the War: Felix Grundy [Tenn.], Henry Clay [Ky.]; Opposed, Joseph Pearson [N. C.], Timothy Pitkin, Jr. [Conn.], Josiah Quincy, 3rd [Mass.], John Randolph [Va.]—New England State Governments Oppose Call for Troops as Unconstitutional—Debate in the House of Representatives Between Daniel Webster [N. H.], in Opposition to the War, and John C. Calhoun [S. C.] in Its Defence—The Hartford Convention —The Treaty of Ghent.

O N June 1, 1812, the President sent a message to Congress which, exhaustively reviewing our relations with Great Britain, summed up the situation as follows:

We behold, in fine, on the side of Great Britain, a state of war against the United States; and, on the side of the United States, a state of peace toward Great Britain.

Whether the United States shall continue passive under these progressive usurpations, and their accumulating wrongs, or, opposing force to force in defence of their national rights, shall commit a just cause into the hands of the Almighty Disposer of Events, avoiding all connections which might entangle it in the contest or views of other powers, and preserving a constant readiness to concur in an honorable reëstablishment of peace and friendship, is a solemn question which the Constitution wisely confides to the legislative department of the Government. In recommending it to their early deliberation, I am happy in the assurance that the decision will be worthy the enlightened and patriotic councils of a virtuous, a free, and a powerful nation.

DECLARATION OF WAR

The message was referred to a committee of which John C. Calhoun was chairman. On June 3 he brought in the report of the committee which reviewed the case against Great Britain even more fully than the President had done, and concluded with the recommendation of an immediate appeal to arms.

"Your committee, believing that the free-born sons of America are worthy to enjoy the liberty which their fathers purchased at the price of so much blood and treasure, and seeing, in the measures adopted by Great Britain, a course commenced and persisted in, which must lead to a loss of national character and independence, feel no hesitation in advising resistance by force; in which the Americans of the present day will prove to the enemy and to the world that we have not only inherited that liberty which our fathers gave us, but also the will and power to maintain it. Relying on the patriotism of the nation, and confidently trusting that the Lord of Hosts will go with us to battle in the righteous cause and crown our efforts with success, your committee recommend an immediate appeal to arms."

On June 16, 1812, the Senate passed a bill declaring war with Great Britain. It was concurred in by the House on June 18, and approved by the President on the same day.

The minority in the House of Representatives drew up the following protest against the declaration, which they addressed to their constituents:

The momentous question of war with Great Britain is decided. On this topic, so vital to your interests, the right of public debate, in the face of the world, and especially of their constituents, has been denied to your Representatives. They have been called into secret session on this most interesting of all your public relations, although the circumstances of the time and of the nation afforded no one reason for secrecy, unless it be found in the apprehension of the effect of public debate on public opinion; or of public opinion on the result of the vote.

Except the message of the President of the United States, which is now before the public, nothing confidential was communicated. That message contained no fact not previously known. No one reason for war was intimated but such as was of a nature public and notorious. The intention to wage war and invade Canada had been long since openly avowed. The object of hostile menace had been ostentatiously announced. The inadequacy of both our army and navy for successful invasion, and the insufficiency of the fortifications for the security of our seaboard, were everywhere known. Yet the doors of Congress were shut upon the people. They have been carefully kept in ignorance of the progress of measures, until the purposes of the administration were consummated and the fate of the country sealed. In a situation so extraordinary the undersigned have deemed it their duty by no act of theirs to sanction a proceeding so novel and arbitrary. On the contrary, they made every attempt in their power to attain publicity for their proceedings. All such attempts were vain. When this momentous subject was stated as for debate, they demanded that the doors should be opened.

This being refused, they declined discussion; being perfectly convinced, from indications too plain to be misunderstood, that, in the House, all argument with closed doors was hopeless, and that any act giving implied validity to so flagrant an abuse of power would be little less than treachery to the essential rights of a free people.

A RIGHTEOUS WAR

MESSAGE TO CONGRESS BY PRESIDENT MADISON

In his annual message to Congress at its next session, in November, 1812, the President, after stating the military operations which had been undertaken, and recommending measures of war proper to the circumstances, said:

Above all, we have the inestimable consolation of knowing that the war in which we are actually engaged is a war neither of ambition nor of vain glory; that it is waged, not in violation of the rights of others, but in the maintenance of our own; that it was preceded by a patience without example, under wrongs accumulating without end: and that it was finally not declared until every hope of averting it was extinguished by the transfer of the British scepter into new hands clinging to former councils; and, until declarations were reiterated to the last hour, through the British envoy here, that the hostile edicts against our commercial rights and our maritime independence would not be revoked; nay, that they could not be revoked without violating the obligations of Great Britain to other powers, as well as to her own interests. To have shrunk, under such circumstances, from manly resistance would have been a degradation blasting our best and proudest hopes; it would have struck us from the high ranks where the virtuous struggles of our fathers had placed us, and have betrayed the magnificent legacy which we hold in trust for future generations. It would have acknowledged that, on the element which forms three-fourths of the globe we inhabit, and where all independent nations have equal and common rights, the American people were not an independent people, but colonists and vassals. It was at this moment, and with such an alternative, that war was chosen. The nation felt the necessity of it and called for it. The appeal was accordingly made, in a just cause, to the just and all-powerful Being who holds in His hand the chain of events and the destiny of nations. It remains only that, faithful to ourselves, entangled in no connections with the views of other powers, and ever ready to accept peace from the hand of justice, we prosecute the war with united counsels and with the ample faculties of the nation, until peace be so obtained and as the only means, under the Divine blessing, of speedily obtaining it.

A bill to raise an additional military force which it was intended to use for the conquest of Canada (a pet plan of the Administration) was introduced in the House of Representatives on December 24, 1812, by David R. Williams, of South Carolina, chairman of the Committee on Military Affairs. It was debated from December 29, 1812, to January 14, 1813, when it was passed by a vote of 77 to 42.

Of this debate Senator Benton says, in his "Debates of Congress":

This debate, although arising on a subject which implied a limited discussion, soon passed beyond its apparent bounds, and, instead of being confined to the simple military question of raising additional troops, expanded into a discussion of the whole policy, objects, and causes of the war, and became the principal debate of the session. All the leading members of the House took part in it; and many new members, then young, and whose names have since become famous, then took their start.

The chief speakers in favor of a continuance of the war were: Felix Grundy [Tenn.] and Henry Clay [Ky.]. Leading opponents of the war were: Joseph Pearson [N. C.], Timothy Pitkin, Jr. [Conn.], Josiah Quincy, 3rd [Mass.], and John Randolph [Va.].

THE CONTINUANCE OF THE WAR

HOUSE OF REPRESENTATIVES, DECEMBER 29, 1812-JANUARY 14, 1813

MR. PEARSON.—Mr. Speaker: Whatever may have been the original causes for the declaration of this war, we are now taught to believe that the question in contest is reduced to a single point. The British Orders in Council were repealed on the 21st of June, three days after our declaration of war; and, of course, without a knowledge of that event, the blockade of May, 1806, had long ceased to exist. The sole avowed cause, therefore, remaining, and for which the war is now carried on, is the practice of impressment from on board our merchant vessels. This subject has for many years engaged the attention of both nations; it has been a fruitful theme of execration and declamation for almost every editor and orator of the age. Great as our cause of complaint may have been (and I am not disposed to palliate it), it must be admitted by all who understand the nature and true bearing of the question that it had been subjected to much exaggeration. Permit me, sir, to remark that, notwithstanding the importance, the difficulty, and delicacy which have been justly attributed to this subject, and the unwillingness at all times manifested on the part of the British Government to abandon or derogate from the *abstract* right of impressing her own seamen from on board neutral merchant vessels, it is very far from being certain that she has not been willing to enter into such arrangement with this Government as would place the question of impressment on a basis both safe and honorable to this nation. By a reference to the correspondence of Messrs. Monroe and Pinkney with the British Commissioners, which preceded the treaty concluded by those gentlemen in the year 1806, but which was unfortunately rejected by the then President, it is evident that the interest of impressment was, in the opinion of those gentlemen, placed on a footing well calculated to secure our own seamen from the abuse against which we had complained, and against which it was our duty to protect them. This opinion was not only expressed in forcible and decisive language at the time of entering into the arrangement, but repeated by Mr. Monroe more than a year after, in a formal letter to the Secretary of State.

Thus, sir, as we have conclusive evidence of a disposition on the part of the British Government, at one period at least, to advance considerable length toward an adjustment of this long-contested question and as we have no evidence that different principles and claims are now asserted from those then advanced, I think it fair to conclude that it is still in our power to put an end to this controversy with safety to our seamen and advantage to the nation. Instead, then, of passing this bill, and spending the blood and treasure of our countrymen in the prosecution of this war, I conceive it our duty to make an effort for the sanction of our just rights, and the restoration of peace, without a further appeal to force. It is my decided opinion that such an effort, if fairly and liberally made by this House, and the executive branch of the Government, would not fail in producing the desired effect.

This is what I ask you now to do—pass a law effectually to exclude all British subjects from the public and private maritime service of the United States; let the law be well guarded against the possibility of violation or evasion; and let us be determined rigidly to enforce it; place this law in the hands of your Executive; let him immediately appoint one or more honest, able, independent commissioners; give them ample powers to form a treaty or arrange the sole question which is now the pivot on which this war depends. Do all this; do it faithfully, and I venture to predict you will obtain a peace and secure your just rights more speedily, more effectually, and more satisfactorily to the people of this country than by all the military operations in the compass of your power.

Mr. Pitkin.—On the subject of impressments, for which alone the war is now to be continued, what, let me ask, is the principle for which our Government contends? It is this, sir: that the flag of the merchant vessel shall cover all who sail under it; or, in other words, that our flag shall protect all the foreigners our merchants may think proper to employ in their service, whether naturalized or not. Before we raise immense armies, before we sacrifice any more of the lives of American citizens, let us inquire—

1st. Whether the principle, if yielded to us to-morrow, would benefit our native seamen, or would promote the real permanent interests of their country.

2d. Whether there is a probability of obtaining a recognition of this principle by a continuance of the war.

The foreigners employed in our service are those who have not been naturalized, and those who have taken the benefit of our naturalization laws. The former constitute nearly the whole: the latter class is very inconsiderable. The foreigners of the first description, of course, are in competition with our native seamen, and either exclude them from employment, or lessen the rate of their wages. In this way, then, the employment of foreign seamen is an injury to our native seamen; and, in a national point of view, it may well be questioned whether their employment subserves the permanent and solid interest of the country.

Is it not, sir, of the first importance to us, as a commercial and maritime nation, especially when we may be engaged in a war with a great naval power, to be able to have a sufficient number of native seamen employed in our service? Seamen who shall be attached by every tie to this country, and on whom we can depend for its defence in time of danger?

The situation in which we now are proves the correctness, as well as the importance, of the position. We are now at war with Great Britain. And, at the very time when this war was declared, thousands of British seamen who had not been naturalized in this country were, and they still continue, in our employment. These seamen (I am speaking, sir, of those not naturalized) are now claimed as British subjects, and, indeed, by our own laws, are now considered as alien enemies.

With respect to foreigners who have been naturalized under our laws, the question is of a more distinct nature and presents greater difficulties. We ought, undoubtedly, to fulfill all our obligations toward them. I presume, however, the number of naturalized British seamen now in our employ does not exceed two or three hundred. Shall we, sir, continue the war for these men?

I am aware, sir, that, with respect to impressment from our merchant vessels, abuses have happened; that, although the right of taking American citizens is not claimed, the British commanders have not been scrupulous whether they took British subjects or American citizens. Sir, these abuses I never can, and I never will, justify. I am satisfied, however, that they have been exaggerated.

But, sir, let me ask if we have not really intended to protect foreign seamen under our flag, if we have not been guilty of gross negligence, to say the least of it, toward our native seamen?

In 1796 Congress passed an act for the relief and protection of American seamen. By this act the collectors of the several ports were directed, on application, to enter the names of seamen, being citizens of the United States, to grant them certificates, in a form given in the act. Have those certificates, or protections, as they are commonly called, been confined to *bona fide* American citizens? No, sir; we cannot, we ought not, to shut our eyes against facts too notorious to be concealed or denied. Under this act, made expressly for the protection of American seamen, every foreign seaman, almost, at the moment of setting his feet on our shores, has obtained a certificate from some collector that he is a citizen of the United States; and, with this certificate in his pocket, although perhaps a deserter from his own government, he enters a public or private vessel as an American seaman. Not only have these protections been thus obtained by fraud and perjury, but they have also, long since, been an object of barter; they have been bought and sold, and transferred from one to another, not only in this country, but in foreign countries. When we ourselves place no confidence in these certificates, when we know that they are thus obtained by fraud and perjury, can we expect that foreign nations will give credit to them? Instead of being a shield and protection to the real American sailor, they have become a dangerous weapon of offence.

MR. QUINCY.—When war against Great Britain was proposed at the last session there were thousands in these United States, and I confess to you I was myself among the number, who believed not one word of the matter. I put my trust in the old-fashioned notions of common sense and common prudence. That a people which had been more than twenty years at peace should enter upon hostilities against a people which had been twenty years at war; that a nation whose army and navy were little more than nominal should engage in a war with a nation possessing one of the best appointed armies and the most powerful marine on the globe; that a country to which neutrality had been a perpetual harvest should throw that great blessing away for a controversy in which nothing was to be gained and everything valuable put in jeopardy; from these, and innumerable like considerations, the idea seemed so absurd that I never once entertained it as possible. And now, after war has been declared, the whole affair seems so extraordinary and so utterly irreconcilable to any previous suggestions of wisdom and duty that I know not what to make of it or how to believe it. Even at this moment my mind is very much in the state of certain Pennsylvania Germans, of whom I have heard it asserted that

they are taught to believe, by their political leaders, and do at
this moment consider the allegation, that war is at present existing between the United States and Great Britain to be a "Federal falsehood."

It was just so with respect to the invasion of Canada. I
heard of it last June. I laughed at the idea, as did multitudes
of others, as an attempt too absurd for serious examination. I
was in this case again beset by common sense and common prudence. That the United States should precipitate itself upon
the unoffending people of that neighboring colony, unmindful
of all previously subsisting amities, because the parent state,
three thousand miles distant, had violated some of our commercial rights; that we should march inland, to defend our
ships and seamen; that with raw troops, hastily collected, miserably appointed, and destitute of discipline, we should invade a
country defended by veteran forces, at least equal, in point of
numbers, to the invading army; that bounty should be offered
and proclamations issued, inviting the subjects of a foreign
power to treason and rebellion, under the influences of a quarter of the country upon which a retort of the same nature was
so obvious, so easy, and, in its consequences, so awful; in every
aspect the design seemed so fraught with danger and disgrace
that it appeared absolutely impossible that it should be seriously entertained. Those, however, who reasoned after this
manner were, as the event proved, mistaken. The war was declared. Canada was invaded. We were in haste to plunge into
these great difficulties, and we have now reason, as well as
leisure enough, for regret and repentance.

The great mistake of all those who reasoned concerning the
war and the invasion of Canada, and concluded that it was impossible that either should be seriously intended, resulted from
this, that they never took into consideration the connection of
both those events with the great election for the chief magistracy which was then pending. It never was sufficiently considered by them that plunging into war with Great Britain was
among the conditions on which the support for the Presidency
was made dependent. They did not understand that an invasion
of Canada was to be in truth only a mode of carrying on an
electioneering campaign. But since events have explained
political purposes there is no difficulty in seeing the connections
between projects and interests. It is now apparent to the most
mole-sighted how a nation may be disgraced, and yet a cabinet
attain its desired honors. All is clear. A country may be
ruined in making an Administration happy.

Concerning the invasion of Canada as a means of carrying
on the subsisting war, it is my duty to speak plainly and decidedly, not only because I herein express my own opinions upon
the subject, but, as I conscientiously believe, the sentiments also
of a very great majority of that whole section of country in
which I have the happiness to reside. I say then, sir, that I
consider the invasion of Canada as a means of carrying on this
war as cruel, wanton, senseless, and wicked.

You will easily understand, Mr. Speaker, by this very statement of opinion, that I am not one of that class of politicians
which has for so many years predominated in the world on both
sides of the Atlantic. You will readily believe that I am not one
of those who worship in that temple where Condorcet is the
high priest and Machiavel the God. With such politicians the
end always sanctifies the means; the least possible good to
themselves perfectly justifies, according to their creed, the inflicting the greatest possible evil upon others. In the judgment of such men, if a corrupt ministry at three thousand miles'
distance shall have done them an injury, it is an ample cause to
visit with desolation a peaceable and unoffending race of men,
their neighbors, who happen to be associated with that ministry
by ties of mere political independence. What though these
colonies be so remote from the sphere of the questions in controversy that their ruin or prosperity could have no possible influence upon the result? What though their cities offer no plunder? What though their conquest can yield no glory? In
their ruin there is revenge. And revenge to such politicians is
the sweetest of all morsels. With such men neither I nor the
people of that section of country in which I reside hold any
communion. There is between us and them no one principle of
sympathy either in motive or action.

That wise, moral, reflecting people, which constitute the
great mass of the population of Massachusetts—indeed, of all
New England—look for the sources of their political duties nowhere else than in those fountains from which spring their
moral duties. According to their estimate of human life and
its obligations, both political and moral duties emanate from
the nature of things, and from the essential and eternal relations
which subsist among them. True it is that a state of war gives
the right to seize and appropriate the property and territories
of an enemy. True it is that the colonies of a foreign power
are viewed, according to the law of nations, in the light of its
property. But, in estimating the propriety of carrying desolation into the peaceful abodes of their neighbors, the people of

New England will not limit their contemplation to the mere circumstance of abstract right, nor ask what lawyers and juris-prudists have written or said, as if this was conclusive upon the subject. That people are much addicted to think for themselves, and, in canvassing the propriety of such an invasion, they will consider the actual condition of those colonies, their natural relations to us, and the effect which their conquest and ruin will have, not only upon the people of those colonies, but upon them-selves and their own liberties and Constitution. And above all, what I know will seem strange to some of those who hear me, they will not forget to apply to a case occurring between na-tions, as far as is practicable, that heaven-descended rule which the great author and founder of their religion has given them for the regulation of their conduct toward each other. They will consider it the duty of these United States to act toward those colonies as they would wish those colonies to act, in exchange of circumstances, toward these United States.

The actual condition of those colonies, and the relation in which they stood to the United States antecedent to the declara-tion of war, were of this nature. Those colonies had no con-nection with the questions in dispute between us and their parent state. They had done us no injury. They meditated none to us. Between the inhabitants of those colonies and the citizens of the United States the most friendly and mutually useful intercourse subsisted. The borderers on this, and those on the other side of the St. Lawrence, and of the boundary line, scarcely realized that they were subjects of different govern-ments. They interchanged expressions and acts of civility. In-termarriages took place among them. The Canadian sometimes settled in the United States; sometimes our citizens emigrated to Canada.

After the declaration of war, had they any disposi-tion to assail us? We have the reverse expressly in evidence. They desired nothing so much as to keep perfect the then sub-sisting relations of amity. Would the conquest of those colonies shake the policy of the British cabinet? No man has shown it. On the contrary, nothing was more obvious than that an invasion of Canada must strengthen the ministry of Great Britain, by the excitement and sympathy which would be occasioned in the people of that country in consequence of the sufferings of the innocent inhabitants of those colonies, on account of a dis-pute in which they had no concern, and of which they had scarcely a knowledge. All this was anticipated—all this was frequently urged to this House, at the last and preceding sessions, as the necessary effect of such a measure. The event has justified those predictions. The late elections in Great Britain have terminated in the complete triumph of the friends of the British ministry.

As there was no direct advantage to be hoped from the conquest of Canada, so also there was none incidental. Plunder there was none—at least, none which would pay the cost of the conquest. Glory there was none. Could seven millions of people obtain glory by precipitating themselves upon half a million, and trampling them into the dust? A giant obtain glory by crushing a pigmy? That giant must have a pigmy's spirit who could reap, or hope, glory from such an achievement.

Show any advantage which justifies that dreadful vial of wrath which, if the intention of the American Cabinet had been fulfilled, would, at this day, have been poured out upon the heads of the Canadians. It is not owing to the tender mercies of the American Administration if the bones of the Canadians are not at this hour mingled with the ashes of their habitations. It is easy enough to make an excuse for any purpose. When a victim is destined to be immolated every hedge presents sticks for the sacrifice. The lamb who stands at the mouth of the stream will always trouble the water, if you take the account of the wolf who stands at the source of it. But show a good to us bearing any proportion to the multiplied evils proposed to be visited upon them. There is none. Never was there an invasion of any country worse than this, in point of moral principle, since the invasion of the West Indies by the Buccaneers or that of the United States by Captain Kidd. Indeed, both Kidd and the Buccaneers had more apology for their deed than the American Cabinet. They had at least the hope of plunder; but in this case there is not even the poor refuge of cupidity. We have heard great lamentations about the disgrace of our arms on the frontier. Why, sir, the disgrace of our arms on the frontier [1] is terrestrial glory in comparison with the disgrace of the attempt. The whole atmosphere rings with the utterance, from the other side of the House, of this word "glory"—"glory" in connection with this invasion. What glory? Is it the glory of the tiger, which lifts his jaws, all foul and bloody, from the bowels of his victim, and roars for his companions of the wood to come and witness his prowess and his spoils? Such is the glory of Genghis Khan and of Bonaparte. Be such glory far, very far, from my country. Never, never may it be accursed with such fame.

[1] General Hull had surrendered Detroit without resistance on August 16, 1812.

"Fame is no plant that grows on mortal soil,
    Nor in the glistering foil
Set off to the world, nor in broad rumor lies,
But lives and spreads aloft, by those pure eyes,
And perfect witness of all-judging Jove,
As he pronounces lastly on each deed."
May such fame as this be my country's meed!

The army which advances to the walls of Quebec, in the present condition of Canadian preparation, must be veteran. And a veteran army, under a popular leader, flushed with victory, each individual realizing that while the body remains combined he may be something, and possibly very great; that, if dissolved, he sinks into insignificance; will not be disbanded by vote. They will consult with one another, and with their beloved chieftain, upon this subject; and not trouble themselves about the advice of the old people who are knitting and weaving in the chimney corners at Washington. Let the American people receive this as an undoubted truth, which experience will verify. Whoever plants the American standard on the walls of Quebec conquers it for himself, and not for the people of the United States. Whoever lives to see that event—may my head be low in the dust before it happen!—will witness a dynasty established in that country by the sword. He will see a king or an emperor, dukedoms, and earldoms, and baronies, distributed to the officers, and knights' fees bestowed on the soldiery. Such an army will not trouble itself about geographical lines in portioning out the divisions of its new empire; and will run the parallels of its power by other steel than that of the compass. When that event happens the people of New England, if they mean to be free, must have a force equal to defend themselves against such an army. And a military force equal to this object will itself be able to enslave the country.

Mr. Speaker—when I contemplate the character and consequences of this invasion of Canada; when I reflect upon its criminality and its danger to the peace and liberty of this once happy country; I thank the great Author and Source of all virtue that through His grace that section of country in which I have the happiness to reside is, in so great a degree, free from the iniquity of this transgression. I speak it with pride, the people of that section have done what they could to vindicate themselves and their children from the burden of this sin. That whole section has risen, almost as one man, for the purpose of driving from power, by one great constitutional effort,[1] the guilty authors of this war. If they have failed it has not been

---

[1] The presidential election.

through the want of will or of exertion, but in consequence of the weakness of their political power. When in the usual course of Divine Providence, who punishes nations as well as individuals, His destroying angel shall on this account pass over this country—and sooner or later, pass it will—I may be permitted to hope that over New England his hand will be stayed. Our souls are not steeped in the blood which has been shed in this war. The spirits of the unhappy men who have been sent to an untimely audit have borne to the bar of divine justice no accusations against us.

This opinion, concerning the principles of this invasion of Canada, is not peculiar to me. I believe this sentiment is entertained, without distinction of parties, by almost all the moral sense, and nine-tenths of the intelligence, of the whole Northern section of the United States. I know that men from that quarter of the country will tell you differently. Stories of a very different kind are brought by all those who come trooping to Washington for place, appointments, and emoluments; men who will say anything to please the ear, or do anything to please the eye of majesty, for the sake of those fat contracts and gifts which it scatters; men whose fathers, brothers, and cousins are provided for by the departments; whose full-grown children are at suck at the money-distilling breasts of the treasury; the little men who sigh after great offices; those who have judgeships in hand or judgeships in promise; toads that live upon the vapor of the palace, that swallow great men's spittle at the levees; that stare and wonder at all the fine sights which they see there; and most of all wonder at themselves—how they got there to see them. These men will tell you that New England applauds this invasion.

But, Mr. Speaker, look at the elections. What is the language they speak? The present tenant of the chief magistracy rejected, by that whole section of country, with the exception of a single State unanimously. And for whom? In favor of a man [1] out of the circle of his own State without much influence, and personally almost unknown. In favor of a man against whom the prevailing influence in New England had previously strong political prejudices; and with whom, at the time of giving him their support, they had no political understanding; in favor of a man whose merits, whatever in other respects they might be, were brought into notice, in the first instance, chiefly so far as that election was concerned, by their opinion of the utter want of merit of the man whose reëlection they opposed.

[1] De Witt Clinton.

I have taken some pains to learn the sentiments which prevail in New England, and particularly among its yeomanry, the pride and the hope of that country. I have conversed with men, resting on their spades and leaning on the handles of their ploughs, while they relaxed for a moment from the labor by which they support their families, and which gives such a hardihood and character to their virtues. They asked—"What do we want of Canada? We have land enough. Do we want plunder? There is not enough of that to pay the cost of getting it. Are our ocean rights there? Or is it there our seamen are held in captivity? Are new States desired? We have plenty of those already. Are they to be held as conquered territories? This will require an army there. Then, to be safe, we must have an army here. And with a standing army what security for our liberties?"

These are no fictitious reasonings. They are the suggestions I doubt not of thousands and tens of thousands of our hardy New England yeomanry; men who, when their country calls, at any wise and real exigency, will start from their native soils and throw their shields over their liberties, like the soldiers of Cadmus, "armed in complete steel"; yet men who have heard the winding of your horn to the Canada campaign with the same apathy and indifference with which they would hear in the streets the trilling of a jewsharp or the twirring of a banjo.

MR. GRUNDY.—At the last session of Congress, when every hope of obtaining justice in any other way was lost, the United States declared war, not to procure a repeal of the Orders in Council only, but to obtain redress for the unjust spoliations which had been committed on the property of American citizens, and to cause Great Britain to cease the practice of impressment. Other causes of irritation existed, but these were the prominent causes of the war. You are now asked to lay down the sword before you have obtained any of the objects of the war, except the abolition of these obnoxious orders. I request gentlemen to reflect whether this is not, in point of fact, an abandonment of the other points in dispute? Do you not, by ceasing to prosecute the war which is already commenced, declare, in the strongest possible terms, that you will not make war for the injuries which remain unredressed? Can any man persuade himself that you will obtain that by negotiation for which you have determined you will not fight! and that, too, from a nation at all times disposed to depress this growing country? That politician must have a very imperfect knowledge of the considerations which influence all cabinets who does not know that the strongest inducement which can be brought to operate in favor of an injured nation is the apprehension of retaliation, or fear of war, entertained by the other party.

If you now say that you will not prosecute the war, the enemy must view it as a decision pronounced by this Government that war shall not be waged by the American nation for the impressment of her citizens, or for depredations committed on commerce. It might as well be said in plain, intelligible language that the ocean is to be abandoned by the people of the United States, except so far as depends on the will of Great Britain. If both the property and liberty of American citizens on the ocean are subject to her disposal, you cease to possess the rights of a sovereign and independent nation. For my own part, if we have the right to claim security for the liberty and property of our citizens against that nation, of which no man dare express a doubt, I am for asserting it until the object is attained, or the ability of this nation fails; of the latter I have no fear.

It is pretended that this Government is not desirous of peace, and that this is a war of conquest and ambition. I beg gentlemen to refrain from making statements which they themselves do not believe. After the declaration of war, what has been the conduct of the Executive? Through Mr. Russell, our *chargé des affaires* at London, they have offered to conclude an armistice on terms which would remove every pretext for complaint on the part of Great Britain. He proposed that this country should exclude from her service British seamen. It is true that Lord Castlereagh urged Mr. Russell's want of powers, and stated that the American Congress alone could make the necessary provisions on that subject. If, however, sincerity had existed with the British ministry, a temporary arrangement could have been made by which hostilities would have been suspended until the legitimate authorities of this country could have expressed an opinion.

MR. CLAY.—If gentlemen would only reserve for their own government half the sensibility which is indulged for that of Great Britain, they would find much less to condemn. Restriction after restriction has been tried; negotiation has been resorted to until longer to have negotiated would have been disgraceful. While these peaceful experiments are undergoing a trial, what is the conduct of the opposition? They are the champions of war; the proud, the spirited, the sole repository of the nation's honor; the exclusive men of vigor and energy. The Administration, on the contrary, is weak, feeble, and pusillanimous—"incapable of being kicked into a war." The maxim, "not a cent for tribute, millions for defence," is loudly proclaimed. Is the Administration for negotiation? The Opposition is tired, sick, disgusted with negotiation. They want to draw the sword and avenge the nation's wrongs. When, at length, foreign nations, perhaps emboldened by the very opposition here made, refused to listen to the amicable appeals made, and repeated and reiterated by the Administration, to their justice and to their interests; when, in fact, war with one of them became identified with our independence and our sovereignty, and it was no longer possible to abstain from it, behold the opposition become the friends of peace and of commerce. They tell you of the calamities of war; its tragical events; the squandering away of your resources; the waste of the public treasure, and the spilling of innocent blood. They tell you that honor is an illusion! Now we see them exhibiting the terrific forms of the roaring king of the forest! Now the meekness and humility of the lamb! They are for war, and no restrictions, when the Administration is for peace; they are for peace and restrictions when the Administration is for war. You find them, sir, tacking with every gale, displaying the colors of every party, and of all nations, steady only in one unalterable purpose: to steer, if possible, into the haven of power.

During all this time the parasites of opposition do not fail by cunning sarcasm or sly innuendo to throw out the idea of French influence, which is known to be false; which ought to be met in one manner only, and that is by the lie direct. The Administration of this country devoted to foreign influence! The Administration of this country subservient to France! Great God! how is it so influenced? By what ligament, on what basis, on what possible foundation, does it rest? Is it on similarity of language? No! we speak different tongues; we speak the English language. On the resemblance of our laws! No! the sources of our jurisprudence spring from another and a different country. On commercial intercourse? No! we have comparatively none with France. Is it from the correspondence in the genius of the two governments? No! here alone is the liberty of man secure from the inexorable despotism which everywhere else tramples it under foot. Where, then, is the ground of such an influence? But, sir, I am insulting you by arguing on such a subject. Yet, preposterous and ridiculous as the insinuation is, it is propagated with so much industry that there are persons found foolish and credulous enough to believe it. You will, no doubt, think it incredible (but I have nevertheless been told the fact) that an honorable member of this House, now in my eye, recently lost his election by the circulation of a story in his district that he was the first cousin of the Emperor Napoleon. The proof of the charge was rested on a statement of facts which was undoubtedly true. The gentleman in question it was alleged had married a connection of the lady of the President of the United States, who was the intimate friend of Thomas Jefferson, late President of the United States, who, some years ago, was in the habit of wearing red French breeches. Now, taking these premises as established, you, Mr. Chairman, are too good a logician not to see that the conclusion necessarily followed!

Throughout the period he had been speaking of the opposition had been distinguished, amid all its veerings and changes, by another inflexible feature—the application of every vile epithet, which our rich language affords, to Bonaparte. He has been compared to every hideous monster and beast, from that of the *Revelations* to the most insignificant quadruped. He has been called the scourge of mankind, the destroyer of Europe, the great robber, the infidel, and—Heaven knows by what other names. Really, gentlemen remind me of an obscure lady in a city, not very far off, who also took it into her head, in conversation with an accomplished French gentleman, to talk of the affairs of Europe. She, too, spoke of the destruction of the balance of power, stormed and raged about the insatiable ambition of the emperor; called him the curse of mankind—the destroyer of Europe. The Frenchman listened to her with perfect patience, and, when she had ceased, said to her, with ineffable politeness: "Madam, it would give my master, the emperor, infinite pain if he knew how hardly you thought of him."

Sir, gentlemen appear to me to forget that they stand on American soil; that they are not in the British House of Commons, but in the Chamber of the House of Representatives of the United States; that we have nothing to do with the affairs of Europe—the partition of territory and sovereignty there—except in so far as these things affect the interests of our own country. Gentlemen transform themselves into the Burkes, Chathams, and Pitts, of another country, and forgetting, from honest zeal, the interests of America, engage, with European sensibility, in the discussion of European interests. If gentlemen ask me if I do not view with regret and sorrow the concentration of such vast power in the hands of Bonaparte, I reply that I do. I regret to see the Emperor of China holding such immense sway over the fortunes of millions of our species. I regret to see Great Britain possessing so uncontrolled a command over all the waters of our globe. And if I had the ability to distribute among the nations of Europe their several portions of power and of sovereignty, I would say that Holland should be resuscitated and given the weight she enjoyed in the days of her De Witts. I would confine France within her natural boundaries—the Alps, the Pyrenees, and the Rhine—and make her a secondary naval power only. I would abridge the British maritime power, raise Prussia and Austria to first-rate powers, and preserve the integrity of the Empire of Russia. But these are speculations. I look at the political transactions of Europe, with the single exception of their possible bearing upon us, as I do at the history of other countries or other times. I do not survey them with half the interest that I do the movements in South America. Our political relation is much less important than it is supposed to be. I have no fears of French or English subjugation. If we are united we are too powerful for the mightiest nation in Europe, or all Europe combined. If we are separated, and torn asunder, we shall become an easy prey to the weakest of them. In the latter dreadful contingency our country will not be worth preserving.

In one respect there is a remarkable difference between Administration and the Opposition—it is in a sacred regard for personal liberty. When out of power, my political friends opposed the violation of the freedom of the press, in the sedition law; they opposed the more insidious attack upon the freedom of the person, under the imposing garb of an alien law. The party now in opposition, then in power, passed those two laws. True to our principles, we are now struggling for the liberty of our seamen against foreign oppression. True to theirs, they oppose the war for this object. They have indeed lately affected tender solicitude for the liberties of the people, and talk of the danger of standing armies, and the burden of taxes. But it is evident to you, Mr. Chairman, that they speak in a foreign idiom. Their brogue betrays that it is not their vernacular tongue. What! the opposition, who in 1798 and 1799 could raise a useless army to fight an enemy three thousand miles distant from us, alarmed at the existence of one raised for a known specified object—the attack of the adjoining provinces of the enemy? The gentleman from Massachusetts [Mr. Quincy], who assisted by his vote to raise the army of twenty-five thousand, alarmed at the danger of our liberties from this very army!

I mean to speak of another subject which I never think of

but with the most awful considerations. The gentleman from Massachusetts [Mr. Quincy] has entertained us with cabinet plots, presidential plots, which are conjured up in the gentleman's own perturbed imagination. I wish, sir, that another plot of a much more serious kind—a plot that aims at the dismemberment of our Union—had only the same imaginary existence. But no man who had paid any attention to the tone of certain prints, and to transactions in a particular quarter of

PRESIDENT MADISON AND HIS SNAPPING TURTLE
"To the Grave Go Sham Protectors of 'Free Trade and Sailors' Rights'— and All the People Say Amen!"
From the collection of the New York Public Library

the Union for several years past, can doubt the existence of such a plot. The project is not brought forward openly, with a direct avowal of the intention. No, the stock of good sense and patriotism in that portion of the country is too great to be undisguisedly encountered. It is assailed from the masked batteries of friendship to peace and commerce on the one side, and by the groundless imputation of opposite propensities on the other. The affections of the people are to be gradually undermined. The project is suggested or withdrawn; the diabolical parties in this criminal tragedy make their appearance or exit as the audience to whom they address themselves are silent, applaud, or hiss.

The war was declared because Great Britain arrogated to

herself the pretension of regulating foreign trade, under the delusive name of retaliatory Orders in Council—a pretension by which she undertook to proclaim to American enterprise, "Thus far shalt thou go, and no farther." Orders which she refused to revoke after the alleged cause of their enactment had ceased; because she persisted in the act of impressing American seamen; because she had instigated the Indians to commit hostilities against us; and because she refused indemnity for her past injuries upon our commerce. I throw out of the question other wrongs. The war in fact was announced, on our part, to meet the war which she was waging on her part. So undeniable were the causes of the war; so powerfully did they address themselves to the feelings of the whole American people, that when the bill was pending before this House gentlemen in the opposition, although provoked to debate, would not, or could not, utter one syllable against it.

I am far from acknowledging that had the Orders in Council been repealed, as they have been, before the war was declared, the declaration would have been prevented. In a body so numerous as this, from which the declaration emanated, it is impossible to say with any degree of certainty what would have been the effect of such a repeal. Each member must answer for himself. I have no hesitation, then, in saying that I have always considered the impressment of American seamen as much the most serious aggression. But, sir, how have those Orders at last been repealed? Great Britain, it is true, has intimated a willingness to suspend their practical operation, but she still arrogates to herself the right to revive them upon certain contingencies, of which she constitutes herself the sole judge. She waives the temporary use of the rod, but she suspends it *in terrorem* over our heads. Supposing it was conceded to gentlemen than such a repeal of the Orders in Council as took place on the 23d of June last, exceptionable as it is, being known before the war, would have prevented the war, does it follow that it ought to induce us to lay down our arms without the redress of any other injury? Does it follow, in all cases, that that which would have prevented the war in the first instance should terminate the war? By no means. It requires a great struggle for a nation prone to peace as this is to burst through its habits and encounter the difficulties of war. Such a nation ought but seldom to go to war. When it does it should be for clear and essential rights alone, and it should firmly resolve to extort, at all hazards, their recognition. The war of the Revolution is an example of a war begun for one object and prosecuted for another. It was waged in its commencement against the right asserted by the parent country to tax the colonies. Then no one thought of absolute independence. The idea of independence was repelled. But the British Government would have relinquished the principle of taxation. The founders of our liberties saw, however, that there was no security short of independence, and they achieved our independence. When nations are engaged in war those rights in controversy, which are acknowledged by the treaty of peace, are abandoned. And who is prepared to say that American seamen shall be surrendered, the victims to the British principle of impressment? And, sir, what is this principle? She contends that she has a right to the services of her own subjects: that, in the exercise of this right, she may lawfully impress them, even although she finds them in our vessels, upon the high seas, without her jurisdiction. Now, I deny that she has any right, without her jurisdiction, to come on board our vessels on the high seas, for any other purpose but in pursuit of enemies, or their goods, or goods contraband of war. But she further contends that her subjects cannot renounce their allegiance to her and contract a new obligation to other sovereigns. I do not mean to go into the general question of the right of expatriation. If, as is contended, all nations deny it, all nations at the same time admit and practice the right of naturalization. Great Britain, in the very case of foreign seamen, imposes perhaps fewer restraints upon naturalization than any other nation. Then, if subjects cannot break their original allegiance, they may, according to universal usage, contract a new allegiance. What is the effect of this double obligation? Undoubtedly, that the sovereign having possession of the subject would have a right to the services of the subject. If he return within the jurisdiction of his primitive sovereign he may resume his right to his services, of which the subject by his own act could not divest himself. But his primitive sovereign can have no right to go in quest of him, out of his own jurisdiction into the jurisdiction of another sovereign, or upon the high seas, where there exists either no jurisdiction, or it belongs to the nation owning the ship navigating them. But, sir, this discussion is altogether useless. It is not to the British principle, objectionable as it is, that we are alone to look; it is to her practice—no matter what guise she puts on. It is in vain to assert the inviolability of the obligation of allegiance. It is in vain to set up the plea of necessity, and to allege that she cannot exist without the impressment of her seamen. The truth is, she comes, by her press gangs, on board of our vessels, seizes our native seamen, as well as naturalized, and drags them into her service. It is the case, then, of the assertion of an erroneous principle, and a practice not conformable to the principle— a principle which, if it were theoretically right, must be forever practically wrong. If Great Britain desires a mark by which she can know her own subjects, let her give them an ear mark. The colors that float from the mast head should be the credentials of our seamen. There is no safety to us, and the gentlemen have shown it, but in the rule that all who sail under the flag (not being enemies) are protected by the flag. It is impossible that this country should ever abandon the gallant tars who have won for us such splendid trophies. Let me suppose that the Genius of Columbia should visit one of them in his oppressor's prison and attempt to reconcile him to his wretched condition. She would say to him, in the language of the gentlemen on the other side, "Great Britain intends you no harm; she did not mean to impress you, but one of her own subjects; having taken you by mistake, I will remonstrate, and try to prevail upon her by peaceable means to release you, but I cannot, my son, fight for you." If he did not consider this mockery he would address her judgment, and say, "You owe me, my country, protection; I owe you in return obedience. I am no British subject, I am a native of old Massachusetts, where live my aged father, my wife, and my children. I have faithfully discharged my duty. Will you refuse to do yours?" Appealing to her passions, he would continue, "I lost this eye in fighting under Truxton with the *Insurgent;* I got this scar before Tripoli; I broke this leg on board the *Constitution* when the *Guerrière* struck."

I will not imagine the dreadful catastrophe to which he would be driven by an abandonment of him to his oppressor. It will not be, it cannot be, that his country will refuse him protection!

The honorable gentleman from North Carolina [Mr. Pearson] supposes that if Congress would pass a law prohibiting the employment of British seamen in our service, upon condition of a like prohibition on their part, and repeal the act of non-importation, peace would immediately follow. Sir, I have no doubt if such a law were passed, with all the requisite solemnities, and the repeal to take place, Lord Castlereagh would laugh at our simplicity. No, sir, Administration has erred in the steps which it has taken to restore peace, but its error has been not in doing too little, but in betraying too great a solicitude for that event. An honorable peace is attainable only by an efficient war. My plan would be to call out the ample resources of the country, give them a judicious direction, prosecute the war with the utmost vigor, strike wherever we can reach the enemy, at sea or on land, and negotiate the terms of a peace at Quebec or Halifax. We are told that England is a proud and lofty nation that, disdaining to wait for danger, meets it half-way. Haughty as she is, we once triumphed over her, and if we do not listen to the counsels of timidity and despair we shall again prevail. In such a cause, with the aid of Providence, we must come out crowned with success; but, if we fail, let us fail like men—lash ourselves to our gallant tars, and expire together in one common struggle, fighting for "seamen's rights and free trade."

Mr. Randolph rose, apparently laboring under the effects of a serious indisposition, and addressed the Chair.

The war in Europe brought to this country, among other birds of passage, a ravenous flock of neutralized carriers, which interposed the flag of neutrality, not only between the property, but even between the persons of the two belligerent powers; and it was their clamor principally, aided by the representations of those of our merchants who saw and wished to participate in the gains of such a commerce, that the first step was taken in that policy of restriction which it was then foreseen would lead to the disastrous condition in which we now find ourselves. Yes, it was then foreseen and foretold. What was then prophesied is now history. It is so. "You," said the prophet, "are prospering beyond all human example. You, favorites of Almighty God, while all the rest of the world are scourged, and ravaged, and desolated by war, are about to enter into a policy called *preventive* of war; a policy which comes into this House in the garb of peace, but which must end in war." And in war it *has* ended. Yes, sir, we have been tortured, fretted, goaded, until at last, like some poor man driven from his family by discord at home, who says to himself, "anything, even exile, is better than this," we have said that we will take war; we will take *anything* for a change. And, when war came, what said the people? *They* said, "anything for a change!"

Regardless of every consequence, we went into war with England as an inconsiderate couple go into matrimony, without considering whether they have the means of sustaining their own existence, much less that of any unfortunate progeny that should happen to be born of them. The sacrifice was made. The blood of Christians enjoying the privileges of jury trial, of the writ of *habeas corpus*, of the freedom of conscience, of the blessings of civil liberty, citizens of the last republic that ambition has left upon the face of a desolate earth—the blood of such a people was poured out as an atonement to the Moloch of France. The Juggernaut of India is said to smile when it sees the blood flow from the human sacrifice which its worship exacts; the Emperor of France might now smile upon us. But, no, sir, our miserable offering is spurned. The French monarch turns his nose and his eyes another way. He snuffs on the plains of Moscow a thousand hecatombs, waiting to be sacrificed on the shrine of his ambition; and the city of the Czars, the largest in the world, is to be at once the altar and the fire of sacrifice to his miserable ambition. And what injury has the Emperor of Russia done to him? For what was he contending? For national existence; for a bare existence; for himself and the people who are subject to his sway. And what, sir, are you doing? Virtually fighting the battles of his foes; surrendering yourself to the views of his adversary, without a plea—without anything to justify your becoming the victims of his blasting ambition.

Yes, sir, after having for years attempted to drive us by menace into war with England, when he has seen us fairly embarked in it, and the champions of human rights bleeding in his cause, the ruler of France has turned with contempt from your reclamations. Is there anything yet wanting to fill up the full measure of injustice you have sustained? Gentlemen on all sides are obliged to admit that the provocation which we have received from France is ample; that the cup of it is overflowing. And yet, what is our situation in relation to that destroyer of mankind—him who, devising death to all that live, sits like a cormorant on the tree of life; who cannot be glutted, nor tired, with human carnage; the impersonation of death; himself an incarnate death? At this moment, when it is well known that it would not require one additional man in the army or navy to make good, in the eye of nations, your character as an independent and high-spirited people, you are prostrate at the feet of your's and the world's undoer.

A word, now, on the subject of impressment. Our foreign trade had grown beyond the capacity of either our tonnage or seamen to manage. Our mercantile marine was an infant Hercules; but it was overloaded beyond its strength: the crop was too abundant to be gathered by our hands alone. The consequence was, and a natural one, too, that not only the capitalists flocked into our country from abroad to share in our growing commerce, but the policy also of our Government was adapted to it, and a law was passed to enable us to avail ourselves of the services of British seamen and seamen of other countries. And, in doing this, we availed ourselves of the pretext—which, as long as the countries to which they belonged winked at it, was fair for us to use—of taking these British seamen for Americans. It was in 1796 that commenced the act to which reference has been made, and that system of "protections," as they were called, the very mention of which, at this day, causes a burst of honest indignation in the breast of citizens whose situation enables them to ascertain their true character. If these "protections," so termed, have not been forged all over Europe, it is only for the reason that the notes of a certain bank of which I have heard have not been forged, viz: that, the bank being broke, its notes were so worthless that people would not even steal them. The "protections" are attainable by everybody; by men of all ages, countries, and descriptions. They are a mere farce. The issuing of them has gone far to disgrace the character of the country, and has brought into question and jeopardy the rights of real American citizens. Sir, there is a wide difference between the character of American seamen and seamen of every other country on earth. The American seaman has a home on the land, a domicile, a wife and children, to whom he is attached, to whom he is in the habit of returning after his voyages; with whom he spends, sometimes, a long vacation from the toils of maritime life. It is not so with the seamen of other countries. For the protection of men of the first description I am disposed, if necessary, to use the force of the country, but for no other. I know, indeed, that some gentlemen who have spoken much on the subject of the principle of impressment will tell you that the right to take from a neutral vessel one seaman, if carried to its extent, involves a right to take any or all seamen. Why, sir, in like manner, it might be argued that the taking illegally of one vessel at sea involves the right to take every vessel. And yet, sir, who ever heard of two nations *going to war* about a single case of capture, though admitted not to be justified by the laws? Such a case never did and never will occur.

Of one thing we are certain: it rests upon no doubtful ground: that Great Britain, rather than surrender the right of impressing her own seamen, will nail her colors to the mast, and go down with them. And she is right, because, when she does surrender it, she is Samson shorn of his strength: the sinews of her power are cut. The right of Great Britain to take her own

seamen from your merchant vessels (if it be a right) is one
which she has exercised ever since you were a people, wherever
occasions for its exercise have occurred. Will you not only go
to war, but wage a *bellum ad internecinum* for it? Will you
wage an endless war of extermination for this right which, you
have known for two and twenty years of your national existence,
she will not relinquish?

But it may be said that the right of search cannot be endured; that the protection of our flag must be held inviolate;
that if a search of our ships be permitted for British seamen
they may actually take American seamen. Sir, there is no doubt
of the fact that by mistake, sometimes perhaps by wilful misconduct, on the part of officers engaged in the search, such a
thing may happen. But, should we not think it exceedingly
strange that the misconduct of an officer of the American Government, in one case in twenty if you will, should be a cause of
war for any nation against us? It is one of those cases which
does occur, and will forever occur, to a neutral power, whenever
a general war is lighted up. It is one of the prices which this
country has to pay for its rapid accession of wealth, such as is
unheard of in the annals of any other nation but our own. And
this, sir, is the state of things in which we have undertaken, in
children's language, to quarrel with our bread and butter; and
to identify ourselves with one of the belligerents in a war in
which we have no proper concern.

The right of search has been acknowledged by all nations.
The President of the United States and his Secretary of State,
as great masters of the law of nations, will be among the first
to acknowledge it; they *have* acknowledged it, and by our
treaties with foreign powers this country has heretofore
acknowledged it, so far as concerns the right to search
for contraband goods and enemy's property. There is
no doubt that, under the color of the right of search—
for I am advocating its lawful purposes only—abuses have been
committed on neutrals; and as long as men exist it will be so.
The liability to abuse of this right is the price which neutrals
pay for the advantages which they derive from their neutrality;
and I should like to know whether it would be for me to join in
the contest in which these belligerents are engaged for the re-
covery of my *neutral* rights. Where are those rights when great
maritime powers become belligerent? There are neutral rights
undoubtedly, but there are also neutral duties. And shall a
neutral nation, a nation which has in that character prospered
and flourished more than any people on the face of the globe,

sacrifice those rights and those advantages, and resort to war against one of those belligerents—and for what? For a point of honor! Yet, while in this Quixotic spirit, we have gone to war with England; although we have been robbed, reviled, contemned throughout by the Emperor of France, we can see no cause of war with him!

What shall we say of the *French* doctrine in relation to this subject of impressment? That all who spoke the English language should be treated as Englishmen, unless they could give proof to the contrary; the *onus probandi* lying on those who spoke the language of Locke, and Newton, and Milton, and Shakespeare. Yes, sir, while the English Government establishes no such doctrine, the French Government acts upon the principle that speaking the English language is *prima facie* evidence of your being a British subject, and would justify their treating you as an enemy, the burden of the proof to the contrary being thrown upon yourself.

Is it fitting that the only two nations among whom the worship of the true God has been maintained with anything like truth and freedom from corruption; that the only two nations among whom this worship has been preserved unstained shall be the two now arrayed against each other in hostile arms in a conflict in which, let who will conquer in the fight, his success in one point, if that be an object, will have been attained: so much of human life, liberty, and happiness will have perished in the affray—in the service of this scourge with which it has pleased God, in his wisdom and justice, not in his mercy, to inflict mankind? Is it fitting that those hands which unite in giving to idolaters and to the heathen the Word of God, the Book of Life —that those hands, and those alone, should be thus drenched in each other's blood? Will you unite as a Christian with your Protestant brother across the Atlantic for these noble purposes, and then plunge the dagger into his breast with whom you are associated in a cause so holy—one so infinitely transcending the low, the little, the dirty business we are called upon here to transact? I hope that the sacrifice may be stopped. Let us join in the worship of the true and living God, instead of spilling the blood of His people on the abominable altar of the French Moloch.

NEW ENGLAND'S OPPOSITION TO THE WAR

From the first outbreak of hostilities with Great Britain the center of opposition to the war had been New England. Indeed, the State governments of Connecticut and Massachusetts had refused to contribute their quotas of militia for the service of the United States, characterizing the requisitions of Congress as unconstitutional.

In reference to this refusal President Madison, in his message to Congress on November 4, 1812, said:

This refusal is founded on a *novel* and *unfortunate exposition* of the provisions of the Constitution relating to the militia. It is obvious that if the authority of the United States to call into service and *command the militia* for the public defence can be thus frustrated, even in a state of declared war, and of course *under apprehensions of invasion preceding war,* they are not one nation for the purpose most of all requiring it; and that the public safety may have no other resource than in those large and permanent military establishments which are forbidden by the principles of our free Government, and against the necessity of which the militia were meant to be a constitutional bulwark.

Among the many New England statesmen antagonistic to the war was Daniel Webster, elected to the House of Representatives from New Hampshire in 1812. Before the close of his term he assumed the position of leader of the anti-war faction.

On January 14, 1814, in the course of a debate on a bill for the encouragement of enlistments, he attacked the Administration for its un-American policy of conducting an *offensive* war (*i. e.,* for the conquest of Canada) instead of a *defensive* war (*i. e.,* on the sea). He was replied to on the following day by John C. Calhoun of South Carolina.

OFFENSIVE VS. DEFENSIVE WAR

HOUSE OF REPRESENTATIVES, JANUARY 14-15, 1814

MR. WEBSTER.—You have prosecuted this invasion [of Canada] for two campaigns. They have cost you vastly more, upon the average, than the campaigns of the Revolutionary war. The project has already cost the American people nearly half as much as the whole price paid for independence. The result is before us. Who does not see and feel that this result disgraces us? Who does not see in what estimation our martial prowess must be by this time holden by the enemy and by the world? Administration has made its master effort to subdue a province three thousand miles removed from the mother country; scarcely equal in natural strength to the least of the States of this confederacy, and defended by external aid to a limited extent. It has persisted two campaigns, and it has failed. Let the responsibility rest where it ought. The world will not ascribe the issue to want of spirit or patriotism in the American people. The possession of those qualities, in high and honorable degrees, they have heretofore illustriously evinced, and spread out proof on the record of their Revolution. They will be still true to their character, in any cause which they feel to be their own. In all causes they will defend themselves. The enemy, as we have seen, can make no permanent stand in any populous part of the country. Its citizens will drive back his forces to the line. But at that line, at the point where defence ceases and invasion begins, they stop. They do not pass it because they do not choose to pass it. Offering no serious obstacle to their actual power, it rises, like a Chinese wall, against their sentiments and their feelings.

It is natural, sir, such being my opinion, on the present state of things, that I should be asked what, in my judgment, ought to be done. In the first place, then, I answer, withdraw your invading armies and follow counsels which the national sentiment will support. In the next place, abandon the system of commercial restriction. That system is equally ruinous to the interests and obnoxious to the feelings of whole sections and whole States. They believe you have no constitutional right to establish such systems. They protest to you that such is not, and never was, their understanding of your powers. They are sincere in this opinion, and it is of infinite moment that you duly respect that opinion, although you may deem it to be erroneous. These people, sir, resisted Great Britain, because her minister, under pretence of regulating trade, attempted to put his hand into their pockets and take their money. There is that, sir, which they then valued, and which they still value, more than money. That pretence of regulating trade they believed to be a mere cover for tyranny and oppression. The present embargo, which does not vex and harass and embarrass their commerce, but annihilates it, is also laid by color of a power to regulate trade. For if it be not laid by virtue of this power, it is laid by virtue of no power. It is not wonderful, sir, if this should be viewed by them as a state of things not contemplated when they came into the national compact.

The humble aid which it would be in my power to render to measures of Government shall be given cheerfully if Government will pursue measures which I can conscientiously support. Badly as I think of the original grounds of the war, as well as of the manner in which it has been hitherto conducted, if even now, failing in an honest and sincere attempt to procure just and honorable peace, it will return to measures of defence and protection, such as reason and common sense and the public opinion all call for, my vote shall not be withholden from the means. Give up your futile projects of invasion. Extinguish the fires that blaze on your inland frontiers. Establish perfect safety and defence there, by adequate force. Let every man that sleeps on your soil sleep in security. Stop the blood that flows from the veins of unarmed yeomanry and women and children. Give to the living time to bury and lament their dead, in the quietness of private sorrow.

Having performed this work of beneficence and mercy on your inland border, turn, and look with the eye of justice and compassion on your vast population along the coast. Unclench the iron grasp of your embargo. Take measures for that end before another sun sets upon you. With all the war of the enemy on your commerce, if you would cease to war on it yourselves you would still have some commerce. That commerce would give you some revenue. Apply that revenue to the augmentation of your navy. That navy, in turn, will protect your commerce. Let it no longer be said that not one ship of force, built by your hands since the war, yet floats upon the ocean. Turn the current of your efforts into the channel which national sentiment has already worn broad and deep to receive it. A naval force, competent to defend your coast against considerable armaments, to convoy your trade, and perhaps raise the blockade of your rivers, is not a chimera. It may be realized. If, then, the war must be continued, go to the ocean. If you are seriously contending for maritime rights go to the theater where alone those rights can be defended. Thither every indication of your fortune points you. There the united wishes and exertions of the nation will go with you. Even our party divisions, acrimonious as they are, cease at the water's edge. They are lost in attachment to national character on the element where that character is made respectable. In protecting naval interests by naval means you will arm yourselves with the whole power of national sentiment, and may command the whole abundance of the national resources. In time you may enable yourselves to redress injuries, in the place where they may be offered, and, if need be, to accompany your own flag throughout the world with the protection of your own cannon.

Mr. Calhoun.—Gentlemen contend that this is not a defensive but an offensive war; and under that character undertake its denunciation, without ever condescending to state what in their opinion constitutes the characteristic difference between them. The people of this country have an aversion to an of-

JOHN BULL STUNG TO AGONY BY THE "WASP" AND "HORNET"
From the collection of the New York Historical Society

fensive war; which I suppose interprets the meaning of the vehemence of the Opposition on this subject; while they readily acknowledge the possible necessity and justice of one that is defensive. It is therefore proper that our ideas on this point should be fixed with precision and certainty. I would lay it down as a universal criterion that a war is offensive or defensive, not by the *mode* of carrying it on, which is an immaterial circumstance, but by the *motive* and *cause* which led to it. If it has its origin in ambition, avarice, or any of the like passions, then is it offensive; but if, on the contrary, to repel insult, injury, or oppression, it is of an opposite character, and is defensive. In the view which I have presented the difference between an offensive and defensive war is of the moral kind; and the American sense of justice accounts for their feelings. Their exemption from ambition and love of justice preserve them from the former, while their manly spirit and good sense will always make them cheerfully meet the other whenever it becomes necessary. What, then, is the character of the war in which we are now engaged? Was it dictated by avarice or love of conquest? I appeal to our opponents for a decision. They have already decided. When the resolutions of the gentleman from New Hampshire were under discussion, at the last session, it was repeated till the ear was fatigued by every one on that side of the House who took any part in the debate that if the repeal of the Berlin and Milan decrees had been communicated in time to the British Government the Orders in Council would have been repealed; and, had the last even happened, the war would not have been declared. They then have acknowledged that the Orders in Council, and not the conquest of Canada, as they now pretend, was the cause of the war; and it would be idle to inquire whether to resist them is in its nature offensive or defensive. It would be to inquire whether they are or are not an injury to our commerce; a point I have never heard denied by the most obstinate debater. It would be equally so to examine whether the cause of continuing the war, to prevent our seamen from impressment, is of an offensive or defensive character.

Very few have the hardihood to deny that it is an injury of the most serious kind, both as it regards the Government and the unhappy subjects of its operations. It involves the most sacred obligation which can bind the body politic to the citizen; I mean that of protection, due alike to all; to the beggar in the street—much more, if susceptible of degrees, to our sailors, that class of the community who have added so much to the wealth and renown of this country. Having thus established the character of the war in its origin and continuance, I would lay down as a rule not less clear that a defensive war does not become offensive by being carried beyond the limits of our territory. The motive and cause will ever give character; all the rest are mere essential incidents. When once declared, the only question, even in a defensive war, is how can it be carried on with the greatest effect. The reverse of this involves the most glaring absurdity. It supposes that we had determined to compel our enemy to respect our rights; and at the same time voluntarily renounced what is acknowledged to be the best and most effectual mode of producing that effect. On this point, as well as the cause of the war, the opinion of our opponents may be arrayed against themselves. What have they advised as to the mode of carrying on the war? Withdraw your troops from Canada, reduce your army, and limit your operations to the ocean. What! to the ocean? Carry the war beyond our own territory! make it offensive! The gentlemen surely do not intend to support an offensive war. To use their own language, it is too immoral for a virtuous and religious people. It is then admitted that it does not cease to be offensive by its being waged at sea; how, then, can the carrying it into Canada change its character?

It now remains to consider the defence which gentlemen have made for their opposition to the war and the policy of their country; a subject which I conceive is of the greatest importance, not only as affecting the result of the present contest, but the lasting peace and prosperity of our country. They assume as a fact that opposition is in its nature harmless; and that the calamities which have afflicted free States have originated in the blunders and folly of the Government, and not from the perverseness of opposition. Opposition simply implies contrariety of opinion; and, when used in the abstract, it admits neither censure nor praise. It cannot be said to be either good or bad; useful or pernicious. It is not from itself, but from the connected circumstances, that it derives its character. When it is simply the result of that diversity in the structure of our intellect which conducts to different conclusions on the same subject, and is confined within those bounds which love of country and political honesty prescribe, it is one of the most useful guardians of liberty. It excites gentle collision, prompts to due vigilance, a quality so indispensable, and at the same time so opposite to our nature, and results in the establishment of an enlightened policy and useful laws. Such are its qualities when united with patriotism and moderation. But in many instances it assumes a far different character. Combined with faction and ambition it bursts those limits within which it may usefully act, and becomes the first of political evils. If, sir, the gentlemen on the other side of the House intend to include this last species of opposition, as I am warranted to infer from their expression, when they spoke of its harmless character, then have they made an assertion in direct contradiction to reason, experience, and all history. A factious opposition is compounded of such elements that no reflecting man will ever consider it as harmless. The fiercest and most ungovernable passions of our nature, ambition, pride, rivalry, and hate, enter into its dangerous composition— made still more so by its power of delusion, by which its projects against government are covered in most instances, even to the eyes of its victims, by the specious show of patriotism. Thus constituted, who can estimate its force? Where can benevolent and social feelings be found sufficiently strong to counteract its progress? Is love of country? Alas! the attachment to a party becomes stronger than that to our country. A factious opposition sickens at the sight of the prosperity and success of the country. Common adversity is its life; general prosperity its death. Nor is it only over our virtuous sentiments that this bane of freedom triumphs. Even the selfish passions of our nature, planted in our bosom for our individual safety, afford no obstacle to its progress. It is this opposition which gentlemen call harmless, and treat with so much respect; it is this moral treason which has in all ages and countries ever proved the most deadly foe to freedom.

Nor is it then only dangerous, when it breaks forth into open treason and rebellion. Without resort to violence it is capable in a thousand ways to counteract and deaden all the motions of Government; to render its policy wavering, and to compel it to submit to schemes of aggrandizement on the part of other governments; or, if resistance is determined on, to render it feeble and ineffectual. Do gentlemen ask for instances? Unhappily, they are but too numerous. Where shall they not be found? Admired and lamented republics of antiquity!—Athens, Carthage, and Rome—you are the victims and witnesses of the fell spirit of factious opposition. Fatal fields of Zama and Chæronea! you can attest its destructive cruelty. What is the history of Polybius, and that of the other historians of the free states of antiquity? What the political speeches of Cicero, and the orations of Demosthenes, those models of eloquence and wisdom, but volumes of evidence, attesting that an opposition founded in faction, unrestrained by moderation and a regard to the general welfare, is the most dangerous of political evils. Nor does antiquity alone testify. The history of modern times is pregnant with examples. What, I would ask, have become of the free states of modern Italy, which once flourished in wealth and power—Florence, Genoa, Venice, and many others? What of the United Provinces and Switzerland? Gone; perished under the deadly feuds of opposition. Even England, with her deep-rooted and powerful executive, has not been free from its pernicious effect. What arrested the war of Marlborough, when France was so humbled that, had it been continued, Europe might have been free from the danger which she has experienced from that power? What stayed the conquering hand of Chatham, when before his genius and power the throne of the Bourbons trembled to its center? The spirit of factious opposition, that common cause of calamity, that without which liberty might be eternal, and free states irresistible.

THE HARTFORD CONVENTION

In the congressional elections in the autumn of 1814 the opponents of the war elected all the representatives from New England except three. Emboldened thereby the Massachusetts legislature, on October 18, 1814, proposed a convention of the New England States "to lay the foundation of a radical reform in the national compact by inviting to a future convention a deputation from all the other States in the Union."

Agreeably to this proposition delegates from Massachusetts, Rhode Island, Connecticut, and the Federalist counties of New Hampshire and Vermont met at Hartford, Conn., on December 15, 1814. In this convention, which deliberated for three weeks, a report to the legislatures and counties represented was adopted, in which a number of constitutional amendments were proposed; but news of the signing of a treaty of peace with Great Britain was received before any of the recommendations could be acted upon.

[For a discussion of the Hartford convention in its bearing upon the question of secession, see Volume V, Chapter I.]

APPOINTMENT OF PEACE COMMISSIONERS

Early in 1813 the Emperor of Russia offered himself as a mediator in order to facilitate peace between Great Britain and the United States. At the opening of Congress in May, 1813, the President announced that he had appointed James A. Bayard, Henry Clay, and Albert Gallatin as envoys extraordinary to act with John Quincy Adams, minister to Russia, and Jonathan Russell, *chargé des affaires* of the United States at London, as peace commissioners.

The British Government, on one pretext or another, delayed appointing commissioners to negotiate with the

American envoys. Indeed it was not until the summer of 1814 that the British commissioners, Lord Gambier, Henry Goulburn, and William Adams, were appointed. On August 6 the commissioners of both countries met at Ghent, in Belgium, and proceeded to their negotiations, which terminated on December 24, 1814, with the signing of the treaty.

THE FALL OF WASHINGTON, OR MADDY [MADISON] IN FULL FLIGHT
British caricature
From the collection of the New York Historical Society

The delay had been profitable to Great Britain. The failure of the military policy of the American Government, the great expense of the war, and the rapidly increasing strength of the opposition made it imperative that peace should be secured as quickly as possible, and, if necessary, at a sacrifice, even of principles. Hence, even before the commissioners met at Ghent, the American Government had instructed its representatives to omit, at their discretion, any stipulation on the subject of impressment which appeared likely to be the point of irreconcilable difference.

The American commissioners therefore, after contending for as long as it seemed wise for the assertion of "sailors' rights," for the maintenance of which the war had really been fought, at last agreed to accept Great Britain's relinquishment of the practice (now that there was peace in Europe) in lieu of her humiliating recantation of the principle. The question of neutral rights also was not pressed by the American commissioners for the same reason.

The main provisions of the treaty were:

1. Restoration to its former ownership of territory captured by either party.

2. Settlement of disputed territory, and establishment of boundary by joint commissions.

3. Suppression by the earnest efforts of both parties of the slave trade, as being a practice "irreconcilable with the principles of humanity and justice."

Although the objects for which the United States had begun the war were not mentioned in the treaty, they were practically secured by the contest. Thereafter, knowing that such actions would result in war, Great Britain did not attempt to enforce against this country her peculiar construction of neutral rights, the right of search, and the impressment of sailors.

CHAPTER VIII

RECOGNITION OF SOUTH AMERICAN REPUBLICS

[THE MONROE DOCTRINE]

Revolt of Latin America—Resolution in the House of Representatives to Send a Minister to La Plata Republics; Speeches in Favor: Henry Clay [Ky.], Thomas B. Robertson [La.], John Floyd [Va.]—Motion Negatived—President James Monroe's Message in Favor of Recognizing Independence of South American Republics—Resolution of the House to This Effect; in Favor, David Trimble [Ky.]; Opposed, Robert S. Garnett [Va.]—Motion Carried—The President Declares Against European Colonization of the Americas and Interference in American Affairs—The Occasion of the Declaration—Strict and Broad Construction of the Doctrine—President John Quincy Adams Accepts Invitation to Send Delegates to the Panama Congress—Debate in the Senate: in Favor, Josiah S. Johnston [La.]; Opposed, Robert Y. Hayne [S. C.], Levi Woodbury [N. H.]—The Action Is Ratified—John Branch [N. C.] Introduces Resolution in the Senate Protesting Against the President Acting in Such Matters Without the Consent of the Senate—John Randolph [Va.] Attacks the President and Secretary of State (Henry Clay): "Blifil and Black George"—Duel Between Randolph and Clay.

D URING the first quarter of the nineteenth century there occurred a general revolt under the leadership of General Simon Bolivar against Spanish rule throughout Latin America. Among the first of the former colonies of Spain to establish a fairly stable government under the republican form were the provinces of the River Plata. The question arose in Congress as to the recognition of these governments. The Spanish minister, Señor Onis, opposed this action. On March 24, 1818, Henry Clay [Ky.] proposed in the House of Representatives to appropriate money to send a minister to Buenos Aires, and on the next day supported his resolution by a speech. Thomas B. Robertson [La.] and John Floyd [Va.] also spoke in favor of the motion. On March 27 the resolution for prudential reasons was negatived by a vote of 115 to 45.

THE SOLIDARITY OF AMERICAN REPUBLICS

HOUSE OF REPRESENTATIVES, MARCH 24-27, 1818

MR. CLAY.—I am no propagandist. I would not seek to force upon other nations our principles and our liberty, if they did not want them. I would not disturb the repose even of a detestable despotism. But if an abused and oppressed people will their freedom; if they seek to establish it; if, in truth, they have established it, we have a right, as a sovereign power, to notice the fact and to act as circumstances and our interest require. I would say, in the language of the venerated Father of our Country: "Born in a land of liberty, my anxious recollections, my sympathetic feelings, and my best wishes are irresistibly excited whensoever, in any country, I see an oppressed nation unfurl the banners of freedom."[1] Whenever I think of Spanish America, the image irresistibly forces itself upon my mind of an elder brother, whose education has been neglected, whose person has been abused and maltreated, and who has been disinherited by the unkindness of an unnatural parent. And when I contemplate the glorious struggle which that country is now making, I see in my mind that brother rising, by the power and energy of his fine native genius, to the manly rank which nature and nature's God intended for him.

We are the natural head of the American family. I would not intermeddle in the affairs of Europe. We wisely keep aloof from their broils. I would not even intermeddle in those of other parts of America farther than to exert the incontestable rights appertaining to us as a free, sovereign, and independent power; and, I contend, the accrediting of a Minister from the new Republic is such a right. We are bound to receive their Minister, if we mean to be really neutral. If the Royal belligerent were represented and heard at our Government, the Republican belligerent ought also to be heard. Give M. Onis his congé, or receive the Republican Minister. Unless you do so, your neutrality is nominal.

MR. ROBERTSON.—I do not consider the direct pecuniary ad-

[1] Washington's answer to the French Minister's address, on his presenting the colors of France, in 1796.

vantages to our country, however great and certain they may
be, as of so much importance as the political and moral effects
growing out of a liberal and manly policy toward the South
American people. It will have a tendency to give us confidence
in the firmness and virtue of Government—it will prove that
it is not forgetful of the high character which belongs to us
as a powerful and free people—that the reputation we have
acquired, at the expense of so much blood and treasure is not
to be sacrificed by timidity, or an undue spirit of accommodation toward the monarchs of Europe—that we will do what our
principles require, in spite of imaginary terrors, artfully excited
by the enemies of freedom—in fine, that, cautious of giving just
cause of offence, we will pursue the path of fidelity and honor
in defiance of the views and wishes of those whose political
institutions make them necessarily hostile to human happiness
and human rights—that we dare at least do what we are sustained in by right and truth in favor of the liberties of mankind without being deterred by those who promote, with un-
hallowed violence, at the expense of every sacred obligation, the
dogmas of priest-craft and the doctrines of despotism. And,
if we are asked by the officious and intermeddling representatives of kings why it is that we not only feel but manifest
sympathy for a people struggling to be free, let us refer them
to their own unholy combinations, in support of the execrable
principles of their government—let us tell them of their wars
for thirty years past against liberty—that if the safety of
monarchies in Europe depends on the annihilation of republics,
the security of a republic in America will not be injured by
other republics growing up by its side.

MR. FLOYD.—The grand object and advantage of establishing an independent policy for America would be that we
might be disenthralled—that we might not feel the effects of
that political plexus which has so entangled the nations of
Europe, by producing those intimate connections and combinations by which the movements and operations of one power are
so felt by all as to influence their councils and produce corresponding motions. When now we negotiate, it is in Europe;
when we are inconvenienced here, we send off an ambassador
there; they are governed by the principles and policy of continental Europe, and not by anything here. Do difficulties arise
in Canada, they are adjusted in London. Do the same difficulties arise in Mexico, the province of Texas, or in Florida, they
are settled in Madrid. Thus are we compelled to negotiate all
our affairs upon the basis of European policy, because even the

best interests of the colonists must give way to the policy of the mother country.

But when the independence of the South Americans shall be acknowledged, and they take their stand among the great nations of the earth, there will then be an American policy, and a European policy, which may, in negotiation upon just and honorable principles, be fairly opposed to each other. Then, if, unhappily, difficulties should arise exclusively on this side the ocean, there will be no European convenience to consult, delay, or obstruct their adjustment in terms of complete reciprocity.

On March 8, 1822, President Monroe in his message expressed it as his opinion that the American provinces of Spain which had declared their independence and were in enjoyment of it should be recognized by the United States as independent nations. On March 28 a motion to extend this recognition was introduced into the House of Representatives. David Trimble [Ky.] made the chief speech in its support. It was passed by a vote of 167 to 1. Robert S. Garnett [Va.] cast the single vote in opposition, and, suffering from odium for his action, on March 30 he asked to have his reasons for dissent to an otherwise unanimous opinion entered on the Journal of Congress. His request was refused by a vote of 49 to 51. On April 1, however, when the feeling of the House was somewhat sobered, the vote was reconsidered and the desired permission was granted, 89 yeas to 71 nays, those who voted in the negative doing so in order not to establish a precedent that might encumber the minutes.

RECOGNITION OF SOUTH AMERICAN INDEPENDENCE

HOUSE OF REPRESENTATIVES, MARCH 28-30, 1822

MR. TRIMBLE.—The nations of America have suffered more from the severity of commercial interdictions and colonial monopoly, than they have from the cruelty of arbitrary power— that commercial vassalage has been more oppressive to them than political dependence; and that they are as deeply interested in the establishment of free trade as they are of free government. The radical change made in their political condition will necessarily be attended with a corresponding change in their commercial intercourse and maritime relations. Their case, in all its aspects, is similar to that of the United States, and will terminate in similar results. The entire emancipation of the new from the old continent can only be effected by two great revolutions: the one political, the other commercial. Both had commenced in the United States under the most favorable auspices, and are progressing southward in the "full tide of successful experiment." These revolutions have been preceded by a "wide-spread range" of moral reformation. The new hemisphere has produced a new catalog of civil maxims—a new family of political institutions—a new code of commercial regulations. All civilized nations were under the dominion of two great social systems, differing widely from each other. One is established in the *Occidental,* the other in the *Oriental* world. The spirit of the age is against the European system. The American system has invaded Europe, and spreads alarm and consternation everywhere among its kings and emperors. A coalition of crowned heads is created to oppose it and two millions of armed men embodied to expel it from that continent.

And what are these systems? What is the American system? Why is it that it agitates two worlds? Why should kings shudder at it, while their subjects bid it welcome? Of what is it composed? What is the element that thus, when unresisted, operates unseen, but, when opposed, launches its thunderbolts at diadems and shakes the nations like an earthquake? It has two aspects, two essential principles—one political, the other commercial. The first is known and distinguished by written constitutions, representative government, religious toleration, freedom of opinion, of speech, and of the press. The second, by sailors' rights, free trade, and freedom of the seas.

Contrast it with the European system. The political character of that system is aristocracy, monarchy, imperial government, arbitrary power, passive obedience, and unconditional submission. Its commercial character is prohibition, restriction, interdiction, impressment, colonial monopoly, and maritime domination. These systems are the antipodes of each other. They are sworn enemies, and cannot harmonize.

The American system is free government and free trade; monarchy and monopoly is that of Europe. But the European system is artificial, and will perish with the spurious causes that produced it. The American system is natural, and, therefore, durable—natural, because it springs from public opinion —from the embodied will of nations acting freely for themselves; durable, because it reposes upon written constitutions.

Its first appearance struck the despots with dismay. Our Revolution gave it birth. Its nativity was cast among these States. It grows with their growth, and strengthens with their strength. The impulse of the age accelerates its motion. Nothing can impede its march because it moves in the majesty of national opinion and public opinion is a power that cannot be resisted. From every zone we hear of congresses, elected by the people, assembled and assembling to establish written constitutions. The system spreads like light—its rays fall everywhere. The nations hail it as the harbinger of peace and happiness. They act wisely in laboring to adopt it, seeing that the people of this Union have prospered under it beyond all former parallel.

The tendency of the American system is manifest to every statesman. Its political progress and extension can be seen by every observer, and time will develop its maritime results. A single instance will explain its commercial operation. The continent is free; not so the Islands. Europe, as to them, will continue its system of colonial monopoly—its system of interdictions, prohibitions, and restrictions. These will act and re-act upon all the Americas, but more especially upon Colombia, Mexico, and the United States. Those powers will retaliate, and unite in their retaliation. The common injury will find a common remedy. They will adopt the counter-check of navigation laws, and, by simultaneously protecting regulations, exclude all foreign tonnage from their ports and harbors. A blow like that would be decisive. It would forever prostrate the colonial system and open a free trade to all the Islands. The measure, when adopted, would finish the commercial revolution. It would subvert the whole system of maritime domination, and restore the freedom of the seas. And thus the Americas, by the reaction of internal laws and regulations, well concerted and well directed, may enforce their system of free trade. Thus, without the waste of blood or treasure, they may sustain the general system, and vindicate the rights and honor of the continent. Hitherto, he said, the American system of free trade had been struggling, single-handed, with the European system of colonial monopoly, and had maintained itself against the fearful odds. Hereafter, all the Americas will coöperate. The subject ought to have their prompt attention. It required a careful examination, because the course of policy to be adopted by them would settle, finally and forever, whether the American system shall prevail, or that of Europe triumph over it.

Shall the people of this continent forego the advantages of free and friendly intercourse, to indulge the mother country in her love of dominion? Shall we, as a nation, stifle all our sympathies in favor of free governments, to gratify the vain-glorious pride of Spain? If we do, we shall betray the rights and interests of republics. Heaven, in giving freedom to us first, made it our primal eldest duty to go forth first, and acknowledge it in others. Honor and duty call alike upon us to perform the rightful obligation. The same Providence that gave us succor in the perils of our Revolutionary struggle is conducting the other nations of America, through bloody wars, to peace and independence. Our approbation may inspire them with fresh confidence, and stimulate their love of liberty. If there are any who have fears that the proposed acknowledgment will produce a war with Spain, let them remember that Cuba is a hostage for her peace. The moment she fires a gun at us, we shall occupy that island and her dominion over it will cease forever. And England, in aiding Spain, would only hasten the downfall of her favorite colonial system—a coalition between Colombia, Mexico, and the United States would convince her of her folly. It would be better for us if our statesmen would look less eastward, and more southward than they do at present.

Some statesmen hold that nations whose political principles and opinions have been formed in the school of despotism must undergo long periods of probationary preparation before they can be qualified to manage the affairs of self-government. This is but a modification of the exploded maxim, "that the people know not how to govern,"—that kings must save them from their worst enemies, themselves. Such opinions, if true, form no argument against the policy or justice of acknowledging the nations of America. If true, in former ages, and on the old continent, they are more than doubtful in modern times, and in the new hemisphere. The fact is that the present and past ages are alike in nothing. The whole civilized world is under the dominion of a different mind. Men and nations are shaking off their mental imbecilities and preparing themselves to regulate their own affairs. It was necessary that moral regeneration should precede political reform; and thus it has happened. A great moral revolution has occurred, and is occurring. The spirit of the age is busy—reformation is everywhere at work, and upon all subjects. We see the beginning, not the end of revolutions. No statesman, no nation, should mistake the character and fashion of the times. Every thing in fifty years has changed, and every thing is changing. "Nothing of the future will resemble what is past." We live in the crisis of all ages. The whole civilized world is laboring in a crisis—a great moral crisis—a great political crisis—a great commercial crisis. Nations have changed their moral characters, and political opinions and governments must change their form and purpose. Formerly the sword was umpire of the world; and then the maxim grew that nations were incapable of self-command. Now public opinion is the great chancellor of nations. All tongues and kindreds own its jurisdiction, and kings and subjects are submissive to its rule; none dare oppose its high authority—none with impunity resist its just decrees. Wars were fought formerly for families and dynasties; for the rights of thrones and prerogatives of crowns; and then the people were assuredly their own worst enemies. Now men fight for written constitutions; for the rights of man and prerogatives of nations; and, fighting, learn to govern for themselves. The contest now is not between dynasties and diadems, but between creeds, and principles, and institutions.

Nations formerly had no volition; kings thought and acted for them, rudely pretending that their subjects had no capacity for affairs of state. But now the will of nations has supremacy of rank, and speaks by delegation in assembled Congresses; and now we find more talent—more patriotic feeling—more public virtue—more every thing, that strengthens and improves the social system. Time was when kings held power by arrogation, and used it at their pleasure and discretion; and then the people were denounced as "a many-headed monster." The people now reclaim all power as inherent in themselves, and delegate it only as a trust; and now nations are more peaceful, more prosperous, more happy, and more just than formerly. History speaks only of alliances, or wars, between contemporary despots—now nothing is talked of but congresses, and constitutions, and representative governments. And do we find things changing for the worse? The spirit of the age is, peace and moderation. It is the spirit of free government and written constitutions. Its conservative principles are—widespread knowledge, equality of rights, freedom of opinion, and frequent and free elections.

The spirit of past ages was war and domination. The trade of man, of all the sons of men, was war—from the first conqueror down to '76. It was the storm of empires. It raged unspent and unabated. It swept along the field of time, and all was desolation that was left. It had no limits but the margin of the world. Its stream of blood flowed on from age to age; its sources, like the Nile, unknown, lost in the desert of forgotten years; but still, the stream rolled on, increasing with a

thousand tributary torrents, and spreading far and wide its
overwhelming floods. Such was the history of past times, and
of the olden world. Our continent, on the contrary, is the
chosen land of liberty—vineyard of the God of peace; and we,
its husbandmen, selected by the unseen will of Providence to
till the soil, and feed the famished nations with the food of
independence. Let us perform the sacred trust impartially.
It is our duty, as a free people, not to sanction but refute the
heresies that nations are incapable of managing their own
concerns. They have disabused themselves by illustrious examples, and we should be careful not to weaken their effect.

It is the will of Providence that this continent should be the
arena of successive revolutions—of moral, and political, and
commercial revolutions—the theater of man's political regeneration—the hemisphere in which nations should be reinstated in
their rights, and reinvested of their "long-lost liberty." On
the 4th of July, 1776, the Congress of the thirteen States declared their independence. On this day (28th March, 1822)
the assembled Congress of the Union will announce the independence of all the nations of America. These are glorious
epochs. Let history commemorate them as coessential in the
works of reformation. Freemen are this day called upon to
fraternize with freemen; nations to fraternize with nations.
All the Americas are summoned to embrace as friends and
equals, and make a lasting covenant of peace. It is not the
flight of a false prophet, or the foundation of a city, the birthday of a petty chieftain, or an heir-apparent that we are assembled here to celebrate; no; a continent has disenchained
itself, and stands unfettered and erect. It is the birthday of a
hemisphere redeemed. It is the jubilee of nations. Let the
world rejoice.

If experience and long suffering can create the faculties of
self-government, then the people of America are prepared to
manage and control their own affairs. For three long centuries
they "clanked the chains" of lawless power; for three long
lingering ages they felt the "keen lash" and galling yoke of
despotism—each generation leaving its manacles to posterity as
their only heritage. Continued agonies had worn away the
memory of better times. The light of hope had left the Children
of the Sun, and dark despair, like soporific drugs, had stupefied
the powers of will and faculties of life. They slept to mitigate
their pain; for nations sleep and never die. But the day of
their deliverance was at hand. The Spirit of God was abroad
in the sky. It called, and the slumbering nations awoke. It

breathed the electric fire of freedom on the air, and a whole continent ran simultaneously to arms! One great, one godlike purpose animated all—it was death or independence! Like us, they pledged their lives, their fortunes, and their sacred honor, to live as freemen, or die in its defence. They fought from field to field. A thousand battles left the cause in doubt; a thousand passions mingled in the fray; and all that history has told of savage cruelty, ferocious vengeance, rapine, plunder, treachery, cold-blooded massacre, and every violence and every crime that shocks humanity was perpetrated over and over again upon all ages, sexes, and conditions. But the God of Battles fought on freedom's side, and, sickening at the scene of carnage and of desolation, and hastening to end it, he took a Bolivar and consecrated him a Washington, and, putting in his hand a flaming sword, commanded him to go forth to the uttermost ends of the continent, conquering and to conquer, until oppression should surcease, and man learn tyranny no more. And behold the work is finished, and Colombia is free, and all the Americas are free—free as ourselves; for there all power is acknowledged in the people, and vassalage abolished, and unknown; for there all officers are elective, and held by the tenure of the law and the constitution; for there, free in their property, their persons, and religion—

> "They own no Lord but Him in heaven,
> No power but what consent has given."

Mr. Garnett submitted the following declaration of his reasons for not voting to recognize the republics:

I voted against the recognition of the late American provinces of Spain, not because I am opposed to their independence; on the contrary, I rejoice in its accomplishment, and believe that it would be even better for them to be independent with a worse form of government than to be dependent with a better. But I voted against it because I am of opinion that recognition must be either the mere formal declaration of a fact which will be inoperative, and therefore useless, or it must be substantial, and propose some advantage to one or both of the parties—that, if it be substantial, it must be intended either to impart to the party recognized the physical means, or the moral force, necessary to accomplish their revolution, or to establish relations for the mutual benefit of both the parties concerned—that the idea of assistance, to consummate a revolution, concedes that it is not completed, and is incompatible with the neutral obligations to the country claiming jurisdiction; and that the second alternative of mutual benefit reduces it to a question of policy in which it is only necessary to balance the good with the evil:

That we have no right to recognize nations because they have adopted forms of government congenial with our own, if our recognition would not otherwise be proper; and to maintain this doctrine would be to assert the odious principle of legitimacy, that nations have a right to interfere with the internal concerns of each other, which must be beneficial or injurious accordingly as free principles or despotism happens to prevail in the world; and that, for this reason also, the present is a question of policy, not of principle:

That, the period having past when our recognition of the independent Governments of South America could be of any substantial benefit to them, their independence being already firmly established, it is impolitic in us, for the sake of any advantages which either party is likely to derive from an intercourse at this time, to risk those we already possess.

That, if Spain only, through mistaken pride, resents our act, though perhaps too feeble to carry on a war with us, she may interdict our commerce with her remaining colonies, and thus deprive us of a trade more valuable than any we can expect to substitute, for a long time, with the independent provinces:

That, if the importance of this trade to those colonies should induce them to revolt, or our recognition itself should produce in them revolutionary movements, the island of Cuba, the most valuable to us, will either fall under the dominion of the colored population, or of our jealous and ambitious rival, England, or we must occupy it ourselves, at the expense of a war with that rival, who will certainly seek to prevent that occupation at the same cost:

And, finally, that circumstances do not warrant precipitancy —that the great interests of both parties will be endangered without any adequate motive for the risk; and that the temporary *éclat* which priority of recognition may obtain for us is not to be put in opposition to the great permanent interests of both countries, which will be best promoted by adhering, on their part, to the sage monitions inculcated in the language of one of their most distinguished patriots, Rivadavia, who declared, as late as September last, "that they did not seek the recognition of other nations, because it must operate, if unsuccessful, to the humiliation of the provinces, and, if successful, to mislead the people, by persuading them that such recognition was all-sufficient to their political existence and happiness; that the most efficacious system would be to establish order and wise institutions of government throughout the provinces, and to show themselves worthy of the fraternity of other nations, when it would be voluntarily offered''; and, on our part, by abstaining to propose that fraternity, until the elements of their political society, purified from the crimes and corruption engendered by former oppression, have settled down into order, and they have fully demonstrated their capacity for self-government, and until we are mutually in a condition to derive advantages from a free intercourse, which will overbalance the considerations of the evil which immediate recognition presents, without a prospect of good.

In his message of December 2, 1823, President Monroe announced the famous doctrine that bears his name. It consisted of two declarations which appeared in widely separated parts of the message:
The first declaration was:

That the American continents, by the free and independent condition which they have assumed and maintain, are henceforth not to be considered as subjects for future *colonization* by any European power.

The occasion for this declaration was as follows: Russia claimed the Pacific coast as far southward as 51 degrees north latitude. Great Britain and the United States opposed this claim, from 54 degrees and 40 minutes southward, and disputed between themselves the possession not only of the coast but of the interior Western country, the former claiming that its southern boundary was 46 degrees (the line of the mouth of the Columbian river), and the latter that its northern boundary was 54 degrees and 40 minutes. In 1818 Great Britain and the United States agreed by treaty to a joint occupancy for ten years of the disputed territory. Early in this period Great Britain began to explore the country, presumably preparatory to settling it, and thereby acquiring the ''nine points of the law'' by the time of adjudicating the ownership.
On July 2, 1823, John Quincy Adams, Secretary of

State, wrote to Richard Rush, American Minister to Great Britain, a declaration for Rush to present to the British Government that the continent of America "is occupied by civilized nations and is accessible to Europeans and to each other on that footing alone," meaning by this that no more original titles could be secured by discovery, exploration, or settlement. Five months later, without the knowledge of the rest of the Cabinet, Secretary Adams caused President Monroe to insert the declaration to this effect in his message.

The British Government denied that the declaration was in accord with facts, asserting that there still remained land on the American continent to which no original title had been acquired.

The second declaration of the Monroe Doctrine, as we shall see, was also inspired, and was also in thorough accord with the maxim "America for Americans" which had been and was to continue the guiding principle of the President's foreign policy. It ran:

In the wars of the European powers, in matters relating to themselves, we have never taken any part, nor does it comport with our policy so to do. It is only when our rights are invaded, or seriously menaced, that we resent injuries, or make preparation for our defence. With the movements in this hemisphere, we are, of necessity, more immediately connected, and by causes which must be obvious to all enlightened and impartial observers. The political system of the allied powers is essentially different, in this respect, from that of America. This difference proceeds from that which exists in their respective Governments. And to the defence of our own, which has been achieved by the loss of so much blood and treasure, and matured by the wisdom of their most enlightened citizens, and under which we have enjoyed unexampled felicity, this whole nation is devoted. We owe it, therefore, to candor and to the amicable relations existing between the United States and those powers to declare that we should consider any attempt on their part to extend their system to any portion of this hemisphere as dangerous to our peace and safety. With the existing colonies or dependencies of any European power we have not interfered, and shall not interfere. But, with the Governments who have declared their independence, and maintained it, and whose independence we have, on great consideration, and on just principles, acknowledged, we could not view any interposition for the purpose of oppressing them, or controlling, in any other manner, their destiny, by any European power, in any other light than as the manifestation of an unfriendly disposition toward the United States. In the war between those new Governments and Spain, we declared our neutrality at the time of their recognition, and to this we have adhered, and shall continue to adhere, provided no change shall occur, which, in the judgment of the competent authorities of this Government, shall make a corresponding change, on the part of the United States, indispensable to their security.

The occasion of this declaration was the proposition of the Holy Alliance at its congress at Verona in 1822, that the allied European powers should check the spread of republicanism throughout the world by interfering with its greatest source of propagation, namely, America. This portended that the monarchies of Europe would either assist Spain to recover her revolted colonies by force, would seize them for themselves, or would establish them as dependent monarchies, and even that the greatest exemplar of the blessings of popular government, the United States, might be ruined by such means as discriminations in trade, if not actual warfare.

When the declaration of Verona became known the British secretary of foreign affairs, George Canning, wrote to Mr. Rush, the American minister, urging the United States to oppose the proposed European intervention in the affairs of the South American republics. Rush sent the letter to Washington, and the President, after consultation with Thomas Jefferson, followed its advice by the enunciation of his celebrated Doctrine.

The determined attitude of the United States effectively strengthened the British Government in blocking the proposal of European absolutism to destroy republicanism in America, and was the earnest of Canning's famous prophecy that "the New World had been called into existence to redress the balance of the Old, and would in time outweigh and topple over the fabrics of kingcraft upon which so many wise men had labored for thousands of years."

The South American republics were greatly delighted with the declaration which, their wish being father to the thought, they construed as pledging the United States actively to defend their territories from European colonization, instead of encouraging each country to defend its own integrity. This view was chiefly instrumental in causing the countries, early in 1825, to call a congress of all the American republics, including the United States, to meet in Panama to discuss questions of mutual concern. This broad construction of the Doctrine was from the beginning also the popular one, and has become, by an increasing extension of the principle in such cases as Yucatan (1848), Mexico (1861-65), and Venezuela (1895), the official construction, and as such is acquiesced in even by some European powers. It will be interesting for the reader to note, in the debates upon these cases, the early opposition to the Doctrine, even in its mildest construction, gradually disappearing until the broadest construction is scarcely contested.

THE PANAMA CONGRESS

In his first message to Congress (December 6, 1825) President John Quincy Adams announced that he had accepted an invitation from the South American republics to send delegates to a Pan-American Congress to be held at Panama, these delegates to take part in the deliberations "as far as may be compatible with that neutrality from which it is neither our intention nor the desire of the other American states that we depart." Colombia, the foremost of the republics, had voiced the invitation. Among the subjects for consideration which it suggested for the congress was "the means of making effectual" the Monroe Doctrine.

Great opposition to taking part in this congress as likely to embroil us in foreign disputes at once became apparent, and the President, who was ardently in favor of the project, on December 26 sent a special message on the subject to the Senate, which was intended to allay objections. It said "an agreement between all the parties represented at the meeting *that each will guard by its own means* against the establishment of any future European colony within its borders may be advisable.''

On March 14, 1826, the Senate began the discussion on the advisability of sending delegates to the congress. The debate was in secret, but with the understanding that each speaker might publish his speech after the question had been decided. Of this privilege several senators availed themselves. Says Senator Thomas H. Benton, in his ''Debates of Congress'':

It was the principal debate of the session, and entered largely into the contest, then hot, for party supremacy—the Administration staking itself upon the mission, as the opposition did against it. It was carried through both Houses of Congress, but deprived of its *prestige* under the heavy blows which it received; and became abortive from the failure of the congress ever to meet. Losing, as it has, the hot interest derived from party contention, the debate (stripped of temporary topics) retains a permanent value from the ability which it developed, and the views of national policy which it opened.

The measure was passed by a vote of 24 to 19, and delegates were appointed to the congress. One of these, however, died, and the other failed to reach Panama in time for the first session of the congress. Owing to disappointment of the South American republics at the conservative attitude of the United States a second session was not held.

A leading speaker in support of the measure was Josiah S. Johnston [La.]. It was strenuously opposed by Robert Y. Hayne [S. C.] and Levi Woodbury [N. H.].

THE PANAMA MISSION

SENATE, MARCH 14-16, 1826

SENATOR HAYNE.—No man can deny that the Congress of Panama is to be composed of deputies from belligerent States, and that its objects are essentially belligerent. These objects are not concealed but are publicly avowed, and known to the world. It is to be an assembly of confederates, differing very little from the old Congress under our Articles of Confederation, to which, indeed, it bears a striking resemblance.

The question arises whether a neutral state can join in such a council without violating its neutrality? Can the United States lawfully send deputies to a congress of the confederated Spanish American states?—a congress which not only has objects confessedly connected with the prosecution of the war, but when it is notorious that these belligerent objects create the very occasion of its assembling? Can we do so without departing from our neutral relations toward Spain? Is it possible, Mr. President, that this can be seriously questioned It will not bear an argument. There can be no difference under the law of nations—for there is none in reason or justice—between aiding a belligerent in council or in action—between consulting with him in respect to belligerent measures or furnishing the men and money to accomplish them. A strict and honorable neutrality must keep us out of any meeting not having peaceful objects exclusively. The law of nations in this respect cannot differ from those rules of municipal law founded in the common sense of mankind which involve in a common guilt all who associate with those engaged in any unlawful enterprise. It is not permitted to individuals, nor can it be permitted to nations, to excuse themselves for acting with those engaged in belligerent enterprises by alleging that their own purposes are peaceful. Sir, I hold that, if you go into council at all with such powers, you become answerable for all their acts.

But an attempt is made to remove all our apprehensions on this subject (and it comes from a high quarter, too) by the assurance that Spain is just about to acknowledge the independence of her former colonies, under our mediation. The Secretary of State, in his report which accompanies the President's message of the 9th January, in answer to our call for information, transmits a mass of documents to show that our Government has invoked the aid of Russia; that the emperor has interfered at our request; and that there is a flattering prospect of speedy and entire success. So says Mr. Middleton—so says Mr. Clay. But, Mr. President, it fortunately happens that the Senate, on the 30th January, made another call for information on this point, and the answer of the President, of the 1st of February, dispels the illusion entirely. The three letters of Mr. Everett, there disclosed, demonstrate that there is no hope, whatever, of a peace. The Minister of the Spanish Government (Mr. Zea) declares that the determination of the king, on that subject, is unalterable—he will stand upon his naked right and look to Providence, should all other means fail. But this is not all. The Russian Minister concurs in the views of Mr. Zea, and the British Minister will not interfere.

The first great subject to which our attention at this congress is to be called arises out of the pledge which Mr. Monroe is supposed to have given ''not to permit any foreign power to interfere in the war between Spain and her colonies''; and it appears from the correspondence to be the special object of the new states to get us to enter into treaties to redeem that pledge, according to the construction they have chosen to put upon it, and in which, I am sorry to add, the Executive seems to have acquiesced. Mr. Obregon tells us that the United States are only expected to take part in those matters which the ''late Administration pointed out as being of general interest, for which reason,'' says he, ''one of the subjects which will occupy the attention of the congress will be the resistance or opposition to the interference of any neutral nation in the question and war of independence between the new powers of the continent and Spain''; and ''that, as the powers of America are of accord as to resistance, it behooves them to discuss the means of giving to that resistance all possible force, that the evil may be met, if it cannot be avoided; and the only means of accomplishing this object is by a previous concert as to the mode in which each of them shall lend its coöperation: for, otherwise, resistance would operate partially and in a manner much less certain and effective.

''The opposition to colonization in America by the European powers will be another of the questions which may be discussed, and which is in like predicament with the foregoing.''

Mr. Salazar holds language on this subject still more explicit.

Now I do positively deny that Mr. Monroe ever pledged this nation to go to war, or make treaties, to prevent the interference of any European nation in the present contest. I deny that he had a right to make any such pledge; and most of all do I deny that any sanction has been given to such an idea by the Senate, the House of Representatives, by the States, or by the people of the United States. The language of Mr. Monroe is extremely vague and indefinite. That great and good man well knew that he had no power to use any but a moral force on that question; and beyond this moral influence over the councils of the nations of Europe he neither attempted nor desired to go. He well knew—every intelligent man in the United States knows—that this nation is not now and never has been prepared to go to war for the independence of South

America. The new states have always carried with them our warmest wishes for their success—but beyond the indulgence of a sincere and friendly sympathy we have never been willing to proceed. Mr. Monroe's declaration, I repeat, was intended to produce a moral effect abroad; he designed it for the atmosphere of Europe, and therefore it was couched in such terms that, while it did not commit us to any overt acts, it left foreign nations under a vague impression of what we might do if the event alluded to should ever happen. The substance of Mr. Monroe's statement was "that he should consider any attempt on their part (the powers of Europe) to extend their system to any portion of this hemisphere as dangerous to our peace and safety," and as "the manifestation of an unfriendly disposition toward the United States." It is obvious that we are left by this pledge altogether free to act in any emergency according to circumstances and a sense of our own interests. We have incurred no obligations to others by the declaration; and it is our policy to incur none. But it now appears that the new states have conceived themselves entitled to our aid whenever foreign interference shall be threatened, and (what is truly unfortunate) it further appears that the new Administration have acknowledged their claims and admitted our obligations; they have acted, and are now about to act, on the presumption that the Spanish American states may rightfully claim, and that we are bound to grant, our assistance against all nations who may "hereafter interfere in any way whatever in the question and war of independence." Nay, so far have our Government gone in this respect that they have actually claimed commercial privileges from these states on the ground that we are to be considered as "one of the American nations," and "within the pale of the great American system"; that we are "prepared to bear the brunt of the contest which will arise should any foreign power attempt to interfere."

To show how far our Government have proceeded in this course I must be permitted to read a few pages from the documents before us. In the letter of our minister to Mexico to the Secretary of State, dated 28th September, 1825, after giving an account of the difficulties which had arisen in making a treaty with Mexico, in consequence of the desire of that government to introduce an article putting it in their power to grant special commercial privileges to the other Spanish American states, he informs us that he insisted that we should be entitled to similar privileges because "we were bound to them by similar fraternal ties." To some objections urged against our claims on the ground that we had not yet taken part in the war, our minister replied in the following words, viz: "To these observations I replied that, against the power of Spain, they had given sufficient proof that they required no assistance, and the United States had pledged themselves not to permit any other power to interfere either with their independence or form of government; and that, as in the event of such an attempt being made by the powers of Europe, we would be compelled to take the most active and efficient part, and to bear the brunt of the contest, it was not just that we should be placed on a less favorable footing than the other republics of America, whose existence we were ready to support at such hazards." The minister then goes on to state that, after explaining what we had already done, he declared "what further we were ready to do in order to defend their rights and liberties; but that this could only be expected from us, and could only be accomplished by a strict union of all the American republics on terms of perfect equality and reciprocity; and repeated that it was the obvious policy of Europe to divide us into small confederacies, with separate and distinct interests, and as manifestly ours to form a single great confederacy, which might oppose one united front to the attacks of our enemies."

And now, sir, I must put the question directly and seriously to the Senate, whether they are prepared to send ministers to the congress of Panama for the purpose of making effectual this pledge of the President of the United States, as construed by the present Administration and understood by the Spanish American states? Whatever may be the opinion of others, I, for one, have no hesitation in declaring that I am not prepared for any such proceeding; I am not ready now to declare that I will involve my country in all the horrors of war for the establishment of South American independence; and even if I were prepared to say that, rather than permit the interference of any foreign nation in the contest, "we must fight," still I should think it wise and prudent not to commit ourselves by treaties or compacts, but to reserve the right to act when the contingency shall happen, as our feelings or interests may then dictate. It is of the last importance that we should reserve this privilege to ourselves; that we should enter into no stipulations whatever with other nations on such a subject. But should we send ministers to Panama for these objects we will not be free to pursue this course. If our ministers go there with our sanction, committed as we know the President to be, we must either sanction the compacts which may be entered into or disappoint the just expectations which we will have raised. In the one case our interests will be sacrificed, and in the other our friendly relations with the new states will be interrupted. Let us, then, avoid this dilemma by not placing ourselves voluntarily in a situation which will leave us only a choice of difficulties and impose upon us the hard necessity of offending our friends or injuring ourselves.

Connected with this object is another bearing a close resemblance to it: "the opposition to colonization in America" by any European power. If by this it is to be understood that we are to interfere to obstruct the settlement of the territories in America owned by Russia or England, it must speedily involve us in an unjust and unnecessary war. But if the design is to enter into compacts with the South American states not to permit any colonization within our respective limits, or if we are to make common cause in resisting all such attempts, then I must boldly declare that the scheme is, in the one case, derogatory to our honor, and, in the other, dangerous to our safety. What! is it come to this, that the United States of America are to come under obligations to others; to bind themselves to nations of yesterday, to preserve their own territories from invasion and their homes and their altars from pollution? Nay, are we, at this period of our history, to enter into solemn vows that we will neither permit ourselves to be conquered nor to be sold? Sir, the idea of treaty stipulations against colonization is degrading and unmeaning, unless it is intended that we shall guarantee to the new states the possession of their territories; and, if that is the plan, it is as unwise as it is dangerous.

I proceed next to consider the great object (which seems to lie so near to the hearts of some of our statesmen) of building up what they are pleased to call "an American system"—terms which, when applied to our domestic policy, mean restriction and monopoly, and, when applied to our foreign policy, mean "entangling alliances," both of them the fruit of that prurient spirit which will not suffer the nation to advance gradually in the development of its great resources and the fulfilment of its high destinies, but would accelerate its march by the most unnatural and destructive stimulants. "As Europe (says Mr. Canas) has formed a continental system, America should form a system for herself." "The mere assembling (says Mr. Salazar) of the congress, by showing the ease with which America can combine, will increase our political importance." In plain terms, Mr. President, we are called upon to form a Holy Alliance on this side of the water, as a counterpoise to the Holy

Alliance on the other side of it. Are the people of this country prepared for that? What is there in the history or character of the Holy Alliance that makes it a fit subject for our imitation? This combination of nations at peace, to maintain certain principles and institutions, contains the most atrocious violation of the natural and social rights of man that the world has ever seen. It is wrong—most fatally wrong—and it makes no difference, in reason or justice, what the principles to be maintained are. It is of the essence of national independence that every country should be left free to adopt and to change its principles and its policy according to its own views of its own interests; and from the very bottom of my soul I abhor the idea of combinations among sovereign states for any purpose whatever. Great Britain, the only nation in Europe that possesses the shadow of freedom, has refused to join the Holy Alliance. I hope we shall follow her example in having nothing to do with this "great American Confederacy."

I have given to this subject, Mr. President, the most dispassionate consideration, and I am free to confess that, whether I consider the measure itself, the form of the invitation, or the course which has been pursued in relation to it, my mind is filled with the most unqualified astonishment. That the President should have committed himself, committed us, and committed the nation, and that the question should have been brought before us, will form, it appears to me, a curious page in the history of this country, which will hereafter be referred to with peculiar interest.

SENATOR WOODBURY.—The Secretary of State to Mr. Poinsett, October 25, 1825, says, no longer than about three months ago, when an invasion by France of the Island of Cuba was believed at Mexico, the United Mexican Government promptly called on the Government of the United States, through you, to fulfil the memorable pledge of the President of the United States, in his message to Congress, of December, A. D. 1823. What they would have done, had the contingency happened, may be inferred from a dispatch to the American Minister at Paris. Then follows that dispatch, dated October 25, 1825, in which he deliberately avows that "we could not consent to the occupation of those islands by any other European power than Spain under any contingency whatever." The same sentiment is repeated to Mr. Middleton, December 26, 1825, "we cannot allow a transfer of the island (of Cuba) to any European power." Has it indeed come to this, that we are to tell the autocrat of fifty millions he has not the same right to take a transfer of Porto Rico as we had to take a transfer of Florida? Is this republicanism, equal rights, and received national law; or is it some marvelous discovery of the present age? And are we prepared, by this mission, to back up by a war the menace to France, that in no contingency whatever shall she be allowed to occupy Cuba, although she buy it of Spain by as fair and as honest a treaty as that by which we purchased Louisiana of France herself?

Are these the doctrines of the American Congress, or of the American people, or do they savor of the Holy Alliance?

Where, also, is the crisis—where the emergency to justify such an extraordinary measure? "Why quit our own, to stand on foreign ground?" Why join our fortunes in any case, much less in a useless war with powers of another origin—another tongue—another faith? Have we become incompetent to our self-defence? Are we in need of foreign "councils" and foreign "deliberations" to manage our own concerns? Or are we so moonstruck, or so little employed at home as, in the eloquent language of our President on another occasion—when the sentiments expressed found a response in every patriot heart—as to wander abroad in search of foreign monsters to destroy? Speaking of America and her foreign policy, he observed, "she has abstained from interference in the concerns of others even when the conflict has been for principles to which she clings as to the last vital drop which visits the heart." "Whenever the standard of freedom and independence has been or shall be unfurled, there will her heart, her benedictions, and her prayers be. But she goes not abroad in search of monsters to destroy. She is the well-wisher to the freedom and independence of all. She is the champion and vindicator only of her own."—(Adams' Oration, 4th July, 1821.) This is the first time that the legislative department of our Government has ever been distinctly appealed to for its sanction to the new notions thus ably denounced by him; and if we now approve the Panama congress, whose chief object is to enforce them, we at once adopt and approve the principle that Spain has not, by such alliances as national law warrants, and as were formed on both sides in our own Revolution, any right to attempt to reconquer and recolonize South America; and, further, that she has not, by such sales as national law warrants and as we ourselves have partaken, any right to transfer Cuba or Porto Rico to any European power with whom she can agree upon the purchase money; and that these unprecedented and unjust positions we are willing to maintain at any sacrifice of blood and treasure.

SENATOR JOHNSTON.—These Spanish American states have been engaged in a war of revolution. They have achieved their independence; all the force of Spain has been driven from the continent. But, as Spain refuses all terms with them and may renew the war upon either the most exposed or the most feeble; as she will concentrate all her power upon a given point; as the occupation of any position on the continent will form a basis of operations on which to act against all the rest; as it will become the rallying point of all her adherents and enable them to prolong the war—it became necessary to unite for the common defence of all and mutually to guarantee peace, security, and independence.

In such a compact it was not our duty, our policy, or inclination to engage; and, accordingly, we find that no proposition was made to us to become a party, and all the communications speak with the most guarded precautions and the most explicit avowals. To believe that they intended to unite us in their councils or to draw us into their measures would be to arrive at this conclusion not only without evidence but against all evidence and in the face of the most solemn assurances. This alliance of Spanish American states is already formed. The parties that compose it, the principles on which it is based, the obligations it imposes, and the means to be employed are fully set forth in the convention before us; to which I confidently refer.

But suppose we were to take part in the discussion of belligerent measures, what part should we take? It is our interest and our duty to keep Cuba as it is: a movement there would be dangerous to us. The Secretary of State has said we desire to see Cuba remain as it is. The President has, on a memorable occasion, said: "We cannot view with indifference the interposition of any European nation." We should, therefore, advise them to husband their strength and resources—to secure what they have gained. We should dissuade them from striking at that island—a measure, perhaps, fatal to them and injurious to us.

How, then, can we participate in any belligerent measure? or any act prejudicial to Spain? or any act inconsistent with our faith, our honor, or our neutrality?

Mr. President, much has been said about a pledge. It is now the policy to make an impression that some secret understanding has taken place; some unknown and mysterious arrangement, which the Government will now be bound in honor and good faith, if this mission is sent, to carry into effect.

The gentleman from South Carolina [Senator Hayne] intimates strongly that this Government has given a pledge. The declaration of the President admonished neutral nations not to interfere with Spain and her colonies. It was a distinct and positive enunciation of the views of this Government. It was supposed, at the time, to mean something. By some it has been termed a protest; by others a pledge; but more properly designated as the memorable declaration. No other or different assurance has been given to strengthen the connections with these new states. But admit there was: all motive to treat on that subject now has ceased; there is now no danger, or even expectation, that the contingency will ever happen; and, if we cannot rely upon the assurance of the President that no alliance will be formed, we may rely upon the fact that no pledge has been given, by the inference arising from the fact that Mexico refused to place us on the footing of the most favored nations. If we had given the pledge to protect her independence, there would have existed no reason for the distinction taken between us and the other American states.

Among the events of greatest magnitude and most anxious concern to this country is the future condition of Cuba. We know that Colombia and Mexico have long contemplated the independence of that island. It has probably been delayed by want of concert and by our mediation to produce peace. But we now know that the fortune of that island is now to be settled. They have waited for a favorable moment to attack them with a certainty of success by the greater forces which the alliance of all the sections of the South and Mexico will procure. The final decision is now to be made, and the combination of forces and plan of attack to be formed.

With regard to the effect of that mission upon us there is no difference of opinion. It is deprecated by all as equally dangerous to our peace and their safety. What, then, at such a crisis becomes the duty of this Government? Send your ministers instantly to this diplomatic assembly where this measure is maturing. Advise with them—remonstrate—menace them, if necessary, against a step so dangerous to us and perhaps fatal to them. Urge them to be satisfied with what they have achieved —to establish their governments—consolidate their union—improve their resources. Guard them against the madness and folly of this enterprise. Warn them of the danger of provoking the allies to take part with Spain. Admonish them of their duty and obligation they owe to themselves, to us, and to all Europe—not to disturb the peace and repose of the world. Our advice will be respected and the danger averted.

I trust I have shown that, if this mission is not due to courtesy, it is due to a just estimate of our essential interests. It is due to friendship, to peace, to commerce, to our principles; it can do no injury—it may do good—it *will* do good.

It was in connection with the Panama mission that John Randolph made his celebrated attack on the President and Henry Clay, whom Adams had appointed Secretary of State—as the result, many opponents of the Administration claimed, of a "corrupt bargain" whereby Adams had won the presidency.

On March 30, 1826, John Branch [N. C.] introduced a resolution in the Senate protesting against the competency of the President to have appointed ministers to the congress of Panama without the advice and consent of the Senate. It was to this motion that Randolph spoke.

BLIFIL AND BLACK GEORGE

ATTACK ON ADAMS AND CLAY BY JOHN RANDOLPH

Sir, in what parliamentary debate was it that, upon a certain union between Lord Sandwich, one of the most corrupt and profligate of men in all the relations of life, and the sanctimonious, puritanical Lord Mansfield, and the other ministerial leaders, that Lord Chatham said that it reminded him of the union between Blifil and Black George? I, who am no professional man, but only a planter: I, whose reading has not gone very deep into black letter, though I do know some little of that, too; I do believe there is more wisdom, after the Bible, Shakespeare, and Milton—I do believe that in Don Quixote, Gil Blas, and Tom Jones there is contained a greater body of wisdom than is to be found in the same number of pages in the whole collection of English and foreign literature.

I will prove, if the Senate will have the patience to listen to me—I will prove to their satisfaction that the President has clapped an extinguisher on himself. If I don't prove it, I will sit down infamous and contented for the rest of my life. And how, sir, has he extinguished himself? He has done it by the aid and instrumentality of this very new ally. I shall not say which is Blifil and which is Black George. I do not draw my pictures in such a way as to render it necessary to write under them, "this is a man, this is a horse." I say this new ally has been the means of extinguishing him, and for what? Sir, we hear a great deal about the infirmity of certain constitutions— not paper constitutions—we hear a great deal of constitutional infirmity. Seven years is too long for some of us to wait; and if the President can be disposed of at the end of three years, then, being extinguished, may they not, by some new turning up of trumps, expect to succeed him? Whatever the motive may have been, the fact is that there is a discrepancy in the communications of the Executive to Congress; and I will state another thing when I come to it. It is that I do believe—though I do not pledge myself to prove—but I will pledge myself to make out a very strong case, such as would satisfy a jury in the county of Charlotte—and I would put myself on that jury, and be tried by God and my country—I then say, sir, that there is strong reason to believe that these South American communications which have been laid before us were manufactured here at Washington, if not by the pens, under the eye of our own ministers, to subserve their purposes. Sir, though in one respect I am like the great Earl of Warwick, the king-maker, and a little unlike him in unmaking one king—though between two hawks I can tell which flies the higher pitch—between two dogs, which has the deeper mouth—between two horses, which bears him best—between two blades, which hath the better temper— between two girls, which hath the merrier eye—yet, in matters of law, I am like the unlearned Earl Goodlack. One thing has my attention been turned to—language—words—the counters of wise men, the money of fools—that machine and material with which the lawyer, the priest, the doctor, the charlatan of every sort and kind pick the pocket and put the fetters upon the planter and upon the slaveholder. It is by a dexterous cutting and shuffling of this pack that the business is done. They who can shuffle the whole pack are often quite ignorant of any foreign language, even of their own, and, in their attempts to write and talk finely, they only betray their poverty, like the fine ladies in the Vicar of Wakefield by their outrageous attempts to be very genteel. The first thing that struck me in these documents was how wonderfully these Spaniards must have improved in English in their short residence in the United States. It reminded me of a remark in one of Scott's novels, in the part about old Elspeth, of the Craigburnfoot: "Aye," says old Edie, "she's ar well educate woman; and an she win to her English, as I hae heard her do at an orra time, she may come to fickle us a'." These Spaniards have got to their English, and we are all fickled. But I shall be told—not as I have been told—but as I am prepared to be told—because I have kept this thing locked up here to bring it out here in this Senate—I shall be told that these English letters were translations from the Spanish, made in the office of the Secretary of State. I hope not—I should be sorry to see any such tokens of affinity, and consanguinity, and good understanding; but they have the footprints and the flesh-marks of the style of that office.

Now, sir, John Quincy Adams coming into power under these inauspicious circumstances, and with these suspicious allies and connections, has determined to become the apostle of liberty, of universal liberty, as his father was, about the time of the formation of the Constitution, known to be the apostle of monarchy. It is no secret—I was in New York when he first took his seat as Vice-President. I recollect—for I was a schoolboy at the time, attending the lobby of Congress when I ought to have been at school—I remember the manner in which my brother was spurned by the coachman of the then Vice-President for coming too near the arms blazoned on the scutcheon of the vice-regal carriage. Perhaps I may have some of this old animosity rankling in my heart, and, coming from a race[1] who are known never to forsake a friend or forgive a foe—I am taught to forgive my enemies, and I do from the bottom of my heart, most sincerely, as I hope to be forgiven; but it is my enemies—not the enemies of my country; for, if they come here in the shape of the English, it is my duty to kill them; if they come here in a worse shape—wolves in sheep's clothing—it is my duty and my business to tear the sheepskins from their backs, and, as Windham said to Pitt, open the bosom and expose beneath the ruffled shirt the filthy dowlas. Adams determined to take warning by his father's errors, but in attempting the perpendicular he bent as much the other way. Who would believe that Adams, the son of the sedition-law President, who held office under his father—who, up to December 6, 1807, was the undeviating, stanch adherent to the opposition to Jefferson's administration, then almost gone—who would believe he had selected for his pattern the celebrated Anacharsis Cloots, "orator of the human race"? As Anacharsis was the orator of the human race, so Adams was determined to be the President of the human race. He has come out with a speech and a message, and with a doctrine that goes to take the whole human family under his special protection. Now, sir, who made him his brother's keeper? Who gave him, the President of the United States, the custody of the liberties, or the rights, or the interests of South America, or any other America, save only the United States of America, or any

---

[1] Randolph was descended from Pocahontas.

other country under the sun? He has put himself, we know, into the way, and I say God send him a safe deliverance and God send the country a safe deliverance from his policy. I quitted the Senate ten minutes before the vote was taken. After twenty-six hours' exertion it was time to give in. I was defeated, horse, foot, and dragoons—cut up—and clean broke down—by the coalition of Blifil and Black George—by the combination, unheard of till then, of the puritan with the blackleg.

Secretary Clay, understanding from the report of the speech that Randolph had charged him with deliberately forging public documents, challenged him to a duel, which Randolph accepted. Neither contestant was wounded at the first fire, and at the second Randolph discharged his pistol in the air and had the skirt of his coat ripped by Clay's bullet. Randolph then stepped up to Clay and saying, "You owe me a coat, Mr. Clay," he extended his hand, which Clay took, saying "I am glad the debt is no greater"; and so the "high-toned" duel, as Senator Benton, Randolph's second, termed it, ended in good feeling between the duellists.

CHAPTER IX

SYMPATHY WITH EUROPEAN REVOLUTIONISTS [GREEK]

Resolution of Daniel Webster [Mass.] in Sympathy with Greek Independence —Debate on the Resolution: in Favor, Daniel Webster; Opposed, John Randolph [Va.].

IN the same message in which he announced his famous Doctrine (December, 1823) President Monroe made the revolution in Greece the subject of a paragraph, and on the 8th of December Daniel Webster [Mass.] moved the following resolution in the House of Representatives:

"*Resolved,* That provision ought to be made by law for defraying the expense incident to the appointment of an agent or commissioner to Greece, whenever the President shall deem it expedient to make such appointment."

The resolution was brought up for discussion in the House on January 19, 1824, when Mr. Webster spoke upon it. John Randolph [Va.] replied to him on January 24. The resolution never went into effect, although its expression, the first official utterance favorable to the independence of Greece uttered by any of the governments of Christendom, no doubt contributed toward the creation of that feeling throughout the civilized world which eventually led to the battle of Navarino and the liberation of a portion of Greece from the Turkish yoke.

RECOGNITION OF GREEK INDEPENDENCE

HOUSE OF REPRESENTATIVES, JANUARY 19-24, 1824

MR. WEBSTER.—I wish to take occasion of the struggle of an interesting and gallant people, in the cause of liberty and Christianity, to draw the attention of the House to the circumstances which have accompanied that struggle, and to the principles which appear to have governed the conduct of the great states of Europe in regard to it; and to the effects and consequences of these principles upon the independence of nations, and especially upon the institutions of free governments. What I have to say of Greece, therefore, concerns the modern, not the ancient; the living, and not the dead. It regards her not as she exists in history, triumphant over time, and tyranny, and ignorance; but as she now is, contending against fearful odds for being and for the common privileges of human nature.

As it is never difficult to recite commonplace remarks and trite aphorisms, so it may be easy, I am aware, on this occasion, to remind me of the wisdom which dictates to men a care of their own affairs, and admonishes them, instead of searching for adventures abroad, to leave other men's concerns in their own hands. It may be easy to call this resolution quixotic, the emanation of a crusading or propagandist spirit. All this, and more, may be readily said; but all this, and more, will not be allowed to fix a character upon this proceeding until that is proved which it takes for granted. Let it first be shown that in this question there is nothing which can affect the interest, the character, or the duty of this country. Let it be proved that we are not called upon, by either of these considerations, to express an opinion on the subject to which the resolution relates. But, in my opinion, this cannot be shown. In my judgment, the subject is interesting to the people and the Government of this country, and we are called upon, by considerations of great weight and moment, to express our opinions upon it. These considerations, I think, spring from a sense of our own duty, our character, and our own interest. I wish to treat the subject on such grounds, exclusively, as arc truly American. Let it embrace everything that fairly concerns America. Let it comprehend not merely her present advantage but her permanent interest, her elevated character as one of the free states of the world, and her duty toward those great principles which have hitherto maintained the relative independence of nations, and which have, more especially, made her what she is.

At the commencement of the session the President, in the discharge of the high duties of his office, called our attention to the subject to which this resolution refers. "A strong hope," says that communication, "has been long entertained, founded on the heroic struggle of the Greeks, that they would succeed in their contest and resume their equal station among the nations of the earth. It is believed that the whole civilized world takes a deep interest in their welfare. Although no power has declared in their favor, yet none, according to our information, has taken part against them. Their cause and their name have protected them from dangers which might ere this have overwhelmed any other people. The ordinary calculations of interest, and of acquisition with a view to aggrandizement, which mingle so much in the transactions of nations, seem to have had no effect in regard to them. From the facts which have come to our knowledge, there is good cause to believe that their enemy has lost forever all dominion over them; that Greece will become again an independent nation.''

If the sentiments of the message in respect to Greece be proper, it is equally proper that this House should reciprocate those sentiments. The present resolution is designed to have that extent, and no more. If it pass, it will leave any future proceeding where it now is, in the discretion of the executive Government.

I take it for granted that the policy of this country, springing from the nature of our Government and the spirit of all our institutions, is, so far as it respects the interesting questions which agitate the present age, on the side of liberty and enlightened sentiments. We are placed, by our good fortune and the wisdom and valor of our ancestors, in a condition in which we *can* act no obscure part. Be it for honor, or be it for dishonor, whatever we do is sure to attract the observation of the world. As one of the free states among the nations, as a great and rapidly rising republic, it would be impossible for us, if we were so disposed, to prevent our principles, our sentiments, and our example from producing some effect upon the opinions and hopes of society throughout the civilized world. It rests probably with ourselves to determine whether the influence of these shall be salutary or pernicious.

It cannot be denied that the great political question of this age is that between absolute and regulated governments. The substance of the controversy is whether society shall have any part in its own government. Whether the form of government shall be that of limited monarchy, with more or less mixture of hereditary power, or wholly elective or representative, may perhaps be considered as subordinate. The main controversy is between that absolute rule which, while it promises to govern well, means, nevertheless, to govern without control, and that constitutional system which restrains sovereign discretion and asserts that society may claim as matter of right some effective power in the establishment of the laws which are to regulate it. The spirit of the times sets with a most powerful current in favor of these last-mentioned opinions. It is opposed, however, whenever and wherever it shows itself, by certain of the great potentates of Europe; and it is opposed on grounds as applicable in one civilized nation as in another, and which would justify such opposition in relation to the United States as well as in relation to any other state or nation if time and circumstances should render such opposition expedient.

Our place is on the side of free institutions. From the earliest settlement of these States, their inhabitants were accustomed, in a greater or less degree, to the enjoyment of the powers of self-government; and for the last half-century they have sustained systems of government entirely representative, yielding to themselves the greatest possible prosperity, and not leaving them without distinction and respect among the nations of the earth. This system we are not likely to abandon; and, while we shall no farther recommend its adoption to other nations, in whole or in part, than it may recommend itself by its visible influence on our own growth and prosperity, we are, nevertheless, interested to resist the establishment of doctrines which deny the legality of its foundations. We stand as an equal among nations, claiming the full benefit of the established international law; and it is our duty to oppose, from the earliest to the latest moment, any innovations upon that code which shall bring into doubt or question our own equal and independent rights.

I have a most deep and thorough conviction that a new era has arisen in the world, that new and dangerous combinations are taking place, promulgating doctrines and fraught with consequences wholly subversive in their tendency of the public law of nations and of the general liberties of mankind. Whether this be so or not is the question which I now propose to examine, upon such grounds of information as are afforded by the common and public means of knowledge.

Here Mr. Webster recited the history of the "Holy Alliance."

It is not a little remarkable that a writer of reputation upon the public law described, many years ago, not inaccurately, the character of this alliance. I allude to Puffendorf. "It seems useless," says he, "to frame any pacts or leagues, barely for the defence and support of universal peace; for by such a league nothing is superadded to the obligation of natural law, and no agreement is made for the performance of anything which the parties were not previously bound to perform; nor is the original obligation rendered firmer or stronger by such an addition.

"If one engage to serve another, he does not set it down expressly and particularly among the terms and conditions of the bargain that he will not betray nor murder him, nor pillage nor burn his house. For the same reason, that would be a dishonorable engagement in which men should bind themselves to act properly and decently, and not break the peace."[1]

How nearly Puffendorf had anticipated the case of the Holy Alliance will appear from the preamble to that alliance. After stating that the allied sovereigns had become persuaded, by the events of the last three years, that "their relations with each other ought to be regulated exclusively by the sublime truths taught by the eternal religion of God the Savior," they solemnly declare their fixed resolution "to adopt as the sole rule of their conduct, both in the administration of their respective states and in their political relations with every other government, the precepts of that holy religion, namely, the precepts of justice, charity, and peace, which, far from being applicable to private life alone, ought, on the contrary, to have a direct influence upon the counsels of princes, and guide all their steps, as being the only means of consolidating human institutions and remedying their imperfections."

This measure, however, appears principally important as it was the first of a series, and was followed afterward by others of a more marked and practical nature. These measures, taken together, profess to establish two principles which the Allied Powers would introduce as a part of the law of the civilized world; and the establishment of which is to be enforced by a million and a half of bayonets.

The first of these principles is that all popular or constitutional rights are held no otherwise than as grants from the crown. Society, upon this principle, has no rights of its own; it takes good government, when it gets it, as a boon and a concession, but can demand nothing. It is to live by that favor which emanates from royal authority, and, if it have the misfortune to lose that favor, there is nothing to protect it against any degree of injustice and oppression. It can rightfully make no endeavor for a change, by itself; its whole privilege is to receive the favors that may be dispensed by the sovereign power, and all its duty is described in the single word *submis-*

[1] Law of Nature and Nations, Book II., Chap. 2, Sec. 11.

sion. This is the plain result of the principal Continental state papers; indeed, it is nearly the identical text of some of them.

I need not stop to observe, Mr. Chairman, how totally hostile are these doctrines to the fundamental principles of our Government. They are in direct contradiction; the principles of good and evil are hardly more opposite. If these principles of the sovereigns be true, we are but in a state of rebellion or of anarchy, and are only tolerated among civilized states because it has not yet been convenient to reduce us to the true standard.

But the second, and, if possible, the still more objectionable, principle avowed in these papers is the right of forcible interference in the affairs of other states. A right to control nations in their desire to change their own government, wherever it may be conjectured or pretended that such change might furnish an example to the subjects of other states, is plainly and distinctly asserted.

No matter what be the character of the government resisted, no matter with what weight the foot of the oppressor bears on the neck of the oppressed, if he struggle or if he complain he sets a dangerous example of resistance—and from that moment he becomes an object of hostility to the most powerful potentates of the earth. I want words to express my abhorrence of this abominable principle. I trust every enlightened man throughout the world will oppose it, and that, especially, those who, like ourselves, are fortunately out of the reach of the bayonets that enforce it will proclaim their detestation of it in a tone both loud and decisive. What is to be the limit to such a principle, or to the practice growing out of it? What, in any case but sovereign pleasure, is to decide whether the example be good or bad? And what, under the operation of such a rule, may be thought of our example? Why are we not as fair objects for the operation of the new principle as any of those who may attempt a reform of government on the other side of the Atlantic?

M. de Chateaubriand, in his speech in the French Chamber of Deputies, in February last, declared that he had a conference with the Emperor of Russia at Verona, in which that august sovereign uttered sentiments which appeared to him so precious that he immediately hastened home and wrote them down while yet fresh in his recollection. "The Emperor declared," said he, "that there can no longer be such a thing as an English, French, Russian, Prussian, or Austrian policy; there is henceforth but one policy, which, for the safety of all, should be adopted both by people and kings. It was for me first to show myself convinced of the principles upon which I founded the alliance; an occasion offered itself—the rising in Greece. Nothing certainly could occur more for my interests, for the interests of my people; nothing more acceptable to my country, than a religious war in Turkey. But I have thought I perceived in the troubles of the Morea the sign of revolution, and I have held back. Providence has not put under my command eight hundred thousand soldiers to satisfy my ambition, but to protect religion, morality, and justice, and to secure the prevalence of those principles of order on which human society rests. It may well be permitted that kings may have public alliances to defend themselves against secret enemies.''

If it be true that there is hereafter to be neither a Russian policy, nor a Prussian policy, nor an Austrian policy, nor a French policy, nor even, which yet I will not believe, an English policy, there will be, I trust in God, an American policy. If the authority of all these governments be hereafter to be mixed and blended, and to flow, in one augmented current of prerogative, over the face of Europe, sweeping away all resistance in its course, it will yet remain for us to secure our own happiness by the preservation of our own principles; which I hope we shall have the manliness to express on all proper occasions, and the spirit to defend in every extremity. Human liberty may yet, perhaps, be obliged to repose its principal hopes on the intelligence and the vigor of the Saxon race.

This asserted right of forcible intervention in the affairs of other nations is in open violation of the public law of the world. On the basis of the independence of nations has been reared the beautiful fabric of international law. On this principle the great commonwealth of civilized states has been hitherto upheld. There have been occasional departures or violations, and always disastrous, as in the case of Poland; but, in general, the harmony of the system has been wonderfully preserved. In the production and preservation of this sense of justice, this predominating principle, the Christian religion has acted a main part. Christianity and civilization have labored together; it seems, indeed, to be a law of our human condition that they can live and flourish only together.

It may now be required of me to show what interest *we* have in resisting this new system. The thunder, it may be said, rolls at a distance. The wide Atlantic is between us and danger; and, however others may suffer, *we* shall remain safe.

I think it is a sufficient answer to this to say that we are one of the nations of the earth; that we have an interest, therefore, in the preservation of that system of national law and national intercourse which has heretofore subsisted so beneficially for all. Our system of government, it should also be remembered, is, throughout, founded on principles utterly hostile to the new code; and, if we remain undisturbed by its operation, we shall owe our security either to our situation or our spirit. The enterprising character of the age, our own active, commercial spirit, the great increase which has taken place in the intercourse among civilized and commercial states, have necessarily connected us with other nations, and given us a high concern in the preservation of those salutary principles upon which that intercourse is founded. We have as clear an interest in international law as individuals have in the laws of society.

But apart from the soundness of the policy, on the ground of direct interest, we have, sir, a duty connected with this subject which I trust we are willing to perform. What do *we* not owe to the cause of civil and religious liberty? to the principle of lawful resistance? to the principle that society has a right to partake in its own government? As the leading republic of the world, living and breathing in these principles, and advanced by their operation with unequaled rapidity in our career, shall we give *our* consent to bring them into disrepute and disgrace? It is neither ostentation nor boasting to say that there lies before this country, in immediate prospect, a great extent and height of power. We are borne along toward this without effort and not always even with a full knowledge of the rapidity of our own motion. Circumstances which never combined before have coöperated in our favor, and a mighty current is setting us forward which we could not resist even if we would, and which, while we would stop to make an observation, and take the sun, has set us, at the end of the operation, far in advance of the place where we commenced it. Does it not become us, then, is it not a duty imposed on us, to give our weight to the side of liberty and justice, to let mankind know that we are not tired of our own institutions, and to protest against the asserted power of altering at pleasure the law of the civilized world?

It may, in the next place, be asked, perhaps, Supposing all this to be true, what can *we* do? Are we to go to war, Are we to interfere in the Greek cause, or any other European cause? Are we to endanger our pacific relations? No, certainly not. What, then, the question recurs, remains for us?

Sir, this reasoning mistakes the age. The time has been, indeed, when fleets and armies and subsidies were the principal reliances even in the best cause. But, happily for mankind, a great change has taken place in this respect. Moral causes come into consideration, in proportion as the progress of knowledge is advanced; and the public opinion of the civilized world is rapidly gaining an ascendency over mere brutal force. It is already able to oppose the most formidable obstruction to the progress of injustice and oppression; and as it grows more intelligent and more intense, it will be more and more formidable. It may be silenced by military power, but it cannot be conquered. It is elastic, irrepressible, and invulnerable to the weapons of ordinary warfare. It is that impassible, unextinguishable enemy of mere violence and arbitrary rule, which, like Milton's angels,

> "Vital in every part, . . .
> Cannot, but by annihilating, die."

Until this be propitiated or satisfied, it is vain for power to talk either of triumphs or of repose. No matter what fields are desolated, what fortresses surrendered, what armies subdued, or what provinces overrun. In the history of the year that has passed by us, and in the instance of unhappy Spain, we have seen the vanity of all triumphs in a cause which violates the general sense of justice of the civilized world. It is nothing that the troops of France have passed from the Pyrenees to Cadiz; it is nothing that an unhappy and prostrate nation has fallen before them; it is nothing that arrests and confiscation and execution sweep away the little remnant of national resistance. There is an enemy that still exists to check the glory of these triumphs. It follows the conqueror back to the very scene of his ovations; it calls upon him to take notice that Europe, though silent, is yet indignant; it shows him that the scepter of his victory is a barren scepter; that it shall confer neither joy nor honor, but shall molder to dry ashes in his grasp. In the midst of his exultation, it pierces his ear with the cry of injured justice; it denounces against him the indignation of an enlightened and civilized age; it turns to bitterness the cup of his rejoicing, and wounds him with the sting which belongs to the consciousness of having outraged the opinion of mankind.

Sir, what has been the conduct pursued by the Allied Powers in regard to the contest in Greece? When the revolution broke out the sovereigns were assembled in congress at Laybach; and the papers of that assembly sufficiently manifest their sentiments. They proclaimed their abhorrence of those "criminal combinations which had been formed in the eastern parts of Europe.'' Now it must be remembered that Russia was a leading party in this denunciation, yet it is notorious that within the last half-century she has again and again excited the Greeks to rebellion against the Porte, and that she has constantly kept alive in them the hope that she would one day, by her own great power, break the yoke of their oppressor. The Grecian revolution has been discouraged, discountenanced, and denounced, solely because it *is* a revolution.

Now it is upon this practical result of the principle of the Continental powers that I wish this House to intimate its opinion. The great question is a question of principle. Greece is only the signal instance of the application of that principle. If the principle be right, if we esteem it comfortable to the law of nations, if we have nothing to say against it, or if we deem ourselves unfit to express an opinion on the subject, then, of course, no resolution ought to pass. If, on the other hand, we see in the declarations of the Allied Powers principles not only utterly hostile to our own free institutions, but hostile also to the independence of all nations, and altogether opposed to the improvement of the condition of human nature; if, in the instance before us, we see a most striking exposition and application of those principles, and if we deem our opinions to be entitled to any weight in the estimation of mankind—then I think it is our duty to adopt some such measure as the proposed resolution.

I close, sir, with repeating that the object of this resolution is to avail ourselves of the interesting occasion of the Greek revolution to make our protest against the doctrines of the Allied Powers, both as they are laid down in principle and as they are applied in practice. I think it right, too, sir, not to be unseasonable in the expression of our regard and, as far as that goes, in a manifestation of our sympathy with a long oppressed and now struggling people. I am not of those who would, in the hour of utmost peril, withhold such encouragement as might be properly and lawfully given, and, when the crisis should be past, overwhelm the rescued sufferer with kindness and caresses. The Greeks address the civilized world with a pathos not easy to be resisted. They invoke our favor by more moving considerations than can well belong to the condition of any other people. They stretch out their arms to the Christian communities of the earth, beseeching them, by a generous recollection of their ancestors, by the consideration of their desolated and ruined cities and villages, by their wives and children sold into an accursed slavery, by their blood, which they seem willing to pour out like water, by the common faith, and in the name which unites all Christians, that they would extend to them at least some token of compassionate regard.

MR. RANDOLPH.—It is with serious concern and alarm that I have heard doctrines broached in this debate fraught with consequences more disastrous to the best interests of this people than any that I ever heard advanced during the five and twenty years since I have been honored with a seat on this floor. They imply, to my apprehension, a total and fundamental change of the policy pursued by this Government, *ab urbe condita*—from the foundation of the Republic to the present day. Are we, sir, to go on a crusade, in another hemisphere, for the propagation of two objects as dear and delightful to my heart as to that of any gentleman in this or in any other assembly—Liberty and Religion—and in the name of those holy words—by this powerful spell, is this nation to be conjured and beguiled out of the highway of Heaven—out of its present comparatively happy state, into all the disastrous conflicts arising from the policy of European powers, with all the consequences which flow from them? Liberty and Religion, sir!—things that are yet dear, in spite of all the mischief that has been perpetrated in their name. I believe that nothing similar to this proposition is to be found in modern history, unless in the famous decree of the French National Assembly, which brought combined Europe against them, with its united strength, and, after repeated struggles, finally effected the downfall of the French power. Sir, I am wrong—there is another example of like doctrine; and you find it among that strange and peculiar people—in that mysterious book, which is of the highest authority with them (for it is at once their gospel and their law), the Koran, which enjoins it to be the duty of all good Moslems to propagate its doctrines at the point of the sword; by the edge of the scimitar. Sir, these Moslems were encamped, where we now find them, before this country was discovered, and their title to the country which they occupy is at least as good as ours. They hold their possessions there by the same title by which all other countries are held—possession obtained at first by a successful employment of force, confirmed by time, by usage, by prescription —the best of all possible titles. Their policy has been, not tortuous, like that of other states of Europe, but straightforward; they have invariably appealed to the sword, and have held by the sword. And, in consequence of this straightforward policy, this peculiar people could boast of being the only one of all the powers of continental Europe whose capital had never been insulted by the presence of a foreign military force.

I would respectfully ask the gentleman from Massachusetts whether in his very able and masterly argument he himself has not furnished an answer to his speech? The gentleman lays down, from Puffendorf, in reference to the honeyed words and pious professions of the Holy Alliance, that these are all surplusage, because nations are always supposed to be ready to do what justice and national law require. Well, sir, if this be so, why may not the Greek presume—why are they not, on this principle, bound to presume that this Government is disposed to do all, in reference to them, that they ought to do, without any formal resolutions to that effect? I ask the gentleman from Massachusetts whether the doctrine of Puffendorf does not apply as strongly to the resolution as to the declaration of the Allies—that is, if there be not something behind this nothing which divides this House into two unequal parts, one the advocate of a splendid system of crusades, the other the friends of peace and harmony, the advocates of a *fireside policy;* for, as has truly been said, as long as all is right at the fireside, there cannot be much wrong elsewhere?

But, sir, we have already done more than this. The President of the United States, the only organ of communication which the people have seen fit to establish between us and foreign powers, has already expressed all, in reference to Greece, that the resolution goes to express. *Actum est*—it is done—it is finished—there is an end.

If the great master of the political philosophy could arise from the dead, or had his valuable life been spared till now, he would not only have been relieved from all his terrors on the subject of a regicide peace, but also have witnessed a return of the age of chivalry and the banishment of calculation even from the estimates of statesmen which that great man could never have foreseen; for the proposition now under consideration is that something new under the sun which Solomon himself never dreamed of. Is this all? No, sir; if that was all I should not have thrown myself upon your attention. But this is not all. Cases have already been stated, to which the principle of the resolution equally applies as to that of the Greeks. In addition to those already put, I will take the case of Canada, if you will. It is known to everybody that discontents have for some time existed in the Canadian Provinces with the mother country and the measures of its government. Suppose the people of the British colonies to the north of us undertake to throw off the yoke—I will not put the case of Jamaica, because they, unhappily, are slaveholders. Are you ready to stake the peace and welfare and the resources of this nation in support of Canadian independence? Your doctrine goes that length—you cannot stop short of it. Where, in that case, will be the assistance of Great Britain, already referred to in debate as being the only spot in the world in which liberty resides except our own country? There is another people—in valorous achievements and daring spirit on a footing with these Greeks themselves—who have achieved their independence from a bondage far heavier than that of the Greeks to the Turks. How is it, sir, that we have never sent an envoy to our sister republic of Hayti? Here is a case that fits—a case beyond dispute. It is not that of a people who have "almost" (aye, sir! *almost*, but not *altogether*)—who have *almost* but perfectly achieved their independence. To attempt to show that these cases are equally within the range of the principle of the resolution would be to show a disrespect to the intellects of those around me. The man who cannot pursue the inference would not recognize my picture, though, like the Dutchman's painting, were written under it, *"This* is the man, *that* the horse."

Among other cases forcibly put by the gentleman from Massachusetts, why he would embark in this incipient crusade against Mussulmen, he stated this as one—that they hold human beings as property. Ah, sir, and what says the Constitution of the United States on this point? Unless, indeed, that instrument is wholly to be excluded from consideration—unless it is to be regarded as a mere useless parchment, worthy to be burned, as was once actually proposed. Does not that Constitution give its sanction to the holding of human beings as property? Sir, I am not going to discuss the abstract question of liberty or slavery, or any other abstract question. I go for matters of fact. But I would ask gentlemen in this House who have the misfortune to reside on the wrong side of a certain mysterious parallel of latitude to take this question seriously into consideration—whether the Government of the United States is prepared to say that the act of holding human beings as property is sufficient to place the party so offending under the ban of its high and mighty displeasure?

Sir, the objections to this resolution accumulate as I proceed—*vires acquirit eundo.*[1] If I should attempt to go through with a statement of them all, and had strength to sustain me, I

[1] "It gathers powers in its going."

should do what I promised I would not do—I should worry and exhaust the patience of this committee.

Sir, what are we now asked to do? To stimulate the Executive to the creation of embassies. And what then? That we, or our friends, may fill them. Sir, the sending ambassadors abroad is one of the great prerogatives, if you will, of our Executive authority; and we are, I repeat, about to stimulate the President to the creation of a new, and, I must be permitted to say, an unnecessary, embassy—a diplomatic agency to Greece—that we, or our friends, may profit by it. For, sir, it is a matter of notoriety that all these good things are reserved for men who either have been or are *de facto* members of this or of the other House. No doubt we shall be able to find some learned Theban, or some other Bœotian, willing to undertake this mission—perfectly willing to live upon the resources of the people rather than his own. But then recurs the old-fashioned question, *Cui bono?* His own, undoubtedly, but surely not that of this nation.

But it is urged that we have sent and received ministers from revolutionary France. True, we have; but what was revolutionary France? Our own ancient and very good ally; a substantive power, if any such exist on the continent of Europe, whose independent existence no one could doubt or dispute, unless, indeed, the disciples of Berkeley, who deny that there is any such thing as matter. Sir, let these Greeks send a minister to us, and then we will deliberate on the question whether we will accredit him or not. If, indeed, there was a minister of Greece knocking at the door of the President's antechamber for admittance, and that admittance was denied, the question of Grecian independence would be more legitimately before us; but I greatly doubt if even that case would be sufficient to call for the interference of this House.

But there is one aspect of this question which ought to be conclusive on the minds of all, viz: That Russia, whose designs on Turkey have been unremittingly prosecuted ever since the days of Peter the Great for more than a century; that Russia, allied to the Greeks in religious faith—identified in that respect; that Russia, unassailable territorially, and dividing with us (according to the gentleman from Massachusetts) the dread and apprehension of the Allied Powers—even Russia, in "juxtaposition" (to use the words of the mover of the resolution) to Turkey—even Russia dare not move. But we, who are separated first by the Atlantic Ocean and then have to traverse the Mediterranean Sea to arrive at the seat of conflict—we, at the distance of five thousand miles, are to interfere in this quarrel

—to what purpose? To the advantage solely of this very colossal power which has been held up as the great object of our dread, and of whom it is difficult to say whether it is more to be dreaded for its physical force or its detestable principle.

Permit me, sir, to ask why, in the selection of an enemy to the doctrines of our Government, and a party to those advanced by the Holy Alliance, we should fix on Turkey? She, at least, forms no party to that alliance; and I venture to say that, for the last century, her conduct, in reference to her neighbors, has been much more Christian than that of all the "Most Christian," "Most Catholic," or "Most Faithful" Majesties of Europe—for she has not interfered, as we propose to do, in the internal affairs of other nations.

But, sir, we have not done. Not satisfied with attempting to support the Greeks, one world, like that of Pyrrhus or Alexander, is not sufficient for us. We have yet another world for exploits: we are to operate in a country distant from us eighty degrees of latitude, and only accessible by a circumnavigation of the globe, and to subdue which we must cover the Pacific with our ships, and the tops of the Andes with our soldiers. Do gentlemen seriously reflect on the work they have cut out for us? Why, sir, these projects of ambition surpass those of Bonaparte himself.

It has once been said of the dominions of the King of Spain —thank God! it can no longer be said—that the sun never set upon them. Sir, the sun never sets on ambition like this: they who have once felt its scorpion sting are never satisfied with a limit less than a circle of our planet. I have heard, sir, the late coruscation in the heavens attempted to be accounted for by the return of the lunar cycle, the moon having got back into the same relative position in which she was nineteen years ago. However this may be, I am afraid, sir, that she exerts too potent an influence over our legislation, or will have done so if we agree to adopt the resolution on your table. I think about once in seven or eight years, for that seems to be the term of our political cycle, we may calculate upon beholding some redoubted champion—like him who prances into Westminster Hall, armed cap-a-pie, like Sir Somebody Dimock, at the coronation of the British king, challenging all who dispute the title of the sovereign to the crown—coming into this House, mounted on some magnificent project such as this. But, sir, I never expected that, of all places in the world (except Salem) a proposition like this should have come from Boston!

Sir, I am afraid that, along with some most excellent attri-

butes and qualities—the love of liberty, jury trial, the writ of
habeas corpus, and all the blessings of free government, that
we have derived from our Anglo-Saxon ancestors, we have got
not a little of their John Bull, or rather John Bull Dog spirit—
their readiness to fight for anybody and on any occasion. Sir,
England has been for centuries the gamecock of Europe. It is
impossible to specify the wars in which she has been engaged
for contrary purposes; and she will, with great pleasure, see us
take off her shoulders the labor of preserving the balance of
power. We find her fighting now for the Queen of Hungary—
then for her inveterate foe, the King of Prussia—now at war
for the restoration of the Bourbons—and now on the eve of war
with them for the liberties of Spain. These lines on the subject
were never more applicable than they have now become—

> "Now Europe's balanced—neither side prevails;
> For nothing's left in either of the scales."

If we pursue the same policy, we must travel the same road
and endure the same burdens under which England now groans.
But, glorious as such a design may be, a President of the United
States would, in my apprehension, occupy a prouder place in
history who, when he retires from office, can say to the people
who elected him, I leave you without a debt, than if he had
fought as many pitched battles as Cæsar, or achieved as many
naval victories as Nelson. No, sir. Let us abandon these
projects. Let us say to those seven millions of Greeks: "We
defended ourselves when we were but three millions against a
power in comparison to which the Turk is but as a lamb. Go
and do thou likewise." And so with respect to the governments of South America. If, after having achieved their independence, they have not valor to maintain it, I would not commit the safety and independence of this country in such a cause.

Let us adhere to the policy laid down by the second, as well
as the first, founder of our Republic—by him who was the
Camillus, as well as the Romulus, of the infant state;—to the
policy of peace, commerce, and honest friendship with all nations, entangling alliances with none: for to entangling alliances we must come if you once embark in projects such as this.

CHAPTER X

SYMPATHY WITH EUROPEAN REVOLUTIONISTS [HUNGARIAN AND IRISH]

American Sympathy with the Hungarian Revolutionists—President Taylor Sends Secret Agent to Hungary—His Report; Controversy Over It by Baron Hülsemann, Austrian *Chargé d'Affaires*, and Daniel Webster, Secretary of State—Government Brings Louis Kossuth, Hungarian Revolutionist, in a War Vessel to America—Henry S. Foote [Miss.] Moves in the Senate that the Government Give Kossuth a Reception—John P. Hale [N. H.] Moves to Amend the Resolution by Expressing Sympathy with ''Victims of Oppression Everywhere''—Debate on Resolution and Amendment: William C. Dawson [Ga.], Hale, Foote, Lewis Cass [Mich.]—Resolutions Are Withdrawn—Resolution of Senator Foote to Intervene with Great Britain in Behalf of Condemned Irish Patriots—Debate: in Favor of Intervention, General James Shields [Ill.], William H. Seward [N. Y.], Senator Cass; Opposed, George E. Badger [N. C.]—John H. Clarke [R. I.] Introduces in the Senate Resolutions against Intervention in Foreign Affairs; Substitutes Are Offered by Senators Seward and Cass; Debate on the Subject Between Clarke, in Favor of Non-Intervention, and Cass and Seward, in Favor of Intervention.

DURING the time when Hungary was striving for independence from Austria many refugee Hungarian patriots had come to America in 1848-49, and their presence and appeals for aid concentrated the sympathy which this country has always felt toward republicans throughout the world into a demand that the Government do what it could in helping the revolutionists. In June, 1849, President Taylor sent a secret agent to Hungary to obtain information of the situation with a view to recognizing the independence of the country. This information Taylor laid before Congress, whereupon the Austrian *chargé d'affaires*, Baron Hülsemann, entered protest to the State Department. About this time Fillmore succeeded to the Presidency, and Webster to the head of the department. In December, 1850, Webster in an able paper argued that the United States

Government had violated no principle of international law, saying: "This sympathy (for nations struggling for institutions like their own), so far from being necessarily a hostile feeling toward any of the parties to these great national struggles, is quite consistent with amicable relations with them all."

He did not forbear gratuitous remarks offensive to the dignity of Austria.

"The power of this Republic, at the present moment, is spread over a region one of the richest and most fertile on the globe, and of an extent in comparison with which the possessions of the house of Hapsburg are but as a patch on the earth's surface."

In a letter to his friend, George Ticknor, Webster gave the following as his reasons for the "high hand" he had taken in the matter:

"If you say that my Hülsemann letter is boastful and rough, I shall own the soft impeachment. My excuse is twofold: 1. I thought it well enough to speak out, and tell the people of Europe who and what we are, and awaken them to a just sense of the unparalleled growth of this country. 2. I wished to write a paper which should touch the national pride, and make a man feel sheepish and look silly who should speak of disunion."

This paper fulfilled both objects, greatly angering Austria and rousing to a high pitch the national pride of the United States. There was a strong desire to bring to America the exiled Hungarian leader, Louis Kossuth. On February 17, 1851, Henry S. Foote [Miss.] moved in the Senate a joint resolution empowering the President to send a ship to Turkey, which was harboring the exiles, in order to fetch Kossuth and his companions to this country. This was adopted on February 26, and concurred in by the House on March 3. Kossuth arrived in New York on the *Mississippi* in December, and met with an enthusiastic reception from the city.

On the first day of the session of Congress in December Senator Foote offered a joint resolution for the reception of Kossuth by the United States Government. On the next day (December 3, 1851) a debate occurred on the resolution, which is noteworthy because of the manner in which the irrepressible question of slavery was obtruded in a matter with which it had no seeming connection. An amendment offered by John P. Hale [N. H.], apparently innocent of all design to bring forward the burning issue but really intended to do so, precipitated an angry discussion, in which Hale was denounced for his duplicity by Senator Foote and Lewis Cass [Mich.].

William C. Dawson [Ga.] began the debate by opposing official recognition of Kossuth.

THE RECEPTION OF KOSSUTH

SENATE, DECEMBER 3, 1851

SENATOR DAWSON.—I see nothing in the character of this distinguished individual which should make the Government of the United States get up a great pageant on his account, and distinguish him from all other men who have ever lived. Has he ever been connected with our institutions? Has he ever rendered any particular service to this country to entitle him to this mark of distinction? Not at all. It is true he is a great man, but he is not greater than many men who now live, and who have lived. His position is such as to call into exercise our sympathies for him and his associates as men. That sympathy this Government has already shown to an extent almost unparalleled by sending one of the national vessels to receive him and his associates, if they were willing to come to this country. Have we not done enough to show our sympathies and our good feelings? I think we have. Against the man's character and course I utter not a word. The American heart is open for his reception. It is the people who will receive him. It is the people and not the Government that ought to receive him. Lafayette, when he came to this country, was received in a manner which was justifiable on the part of the Government of that day, because he was connected with the Revolution which gave us the liberties which we enjoy.

SENATOR HALE.—I move to amend the resolution by adding the following words:

"And also to assure him and his associates in exile of the

sympathy of the Congress and people of the United States with the victims of oppression everywhere, and that their earnest desire is that the time may speedily arrive when the rights of man shall be universally recognized and respected by every people and government of the world.''

If this be added to the resolution I think it will obviate the objection of the Senator from Georgia; because then, instead of being personal to Kossuth, it would apply to the victims of oppression everywhere, without any distinction.

SENATOR FOOTE.—Sir, the gentleman from Georgia seems to overlook the fact that there is a great struggle going on at this moment in all parts of the civilized world between the principles of freedom and the principles of slavery. The tyrants of the earth have combined for the overthrow of liberty. In some instances open attempts are made to break down political and religious freedom. In others the means employed by the enemies of freedom are more disguised and insidious, but not at all less dangerous. At such a moment does it behoove the American people to join the side of despotism or to stand by the cause of freedom? We must do one or the other. We cannot avoid the solemn alternative presented. Those who are not for us are against us. Those who are not for freedom are for slavery.

The eminent personage [Louis Kossuth] whose claims upon our respect and sympathy I have endeavored to make manifest has commended himself especially to my regard by the delicate and discreet forbearance which he has elsewhere exercised in avoiding all indecent interference with the domestic institutions of other countries than his own. While in monarchical England he did not hesitate to avow his decided partiality for republican institutions, yet no one can accuse him of uttering a word upon any occasion which was in the least degree calculated to awaken popular discontent or to foment civil discord; and I venture to predict, sir, that if the vicious and contriving factionists who have so fiercely struggled for several years past to disturb the domestic quiet of the Republic should attempt to enlist Louis Kossuth in their unholy designs, they will incur such a withering rebuke from his lips as will make them wish, for a moment, at least, that the Almighty in his providence had never permitted such miscreants to pollute the pure air of heaven with their pestilential breath.

SENATOR HALE.—What is this amendment? Why, that we shall assure to this illustrious man, as dear to my affections as to his—dear to my affections for the principles which he has advocated, and for the maintenance and advocacy of which he is now an exile—that we shall assure him and his associates in exile of the sympathy of the Congress and the people of the United States not only with them but with the victims of oppression everywhere. Is there any intimation there that the honorable Senator means to find fault with? Does he mean to intimate that in this land there is a place where the rights of man are not respected and recognized? If he does, he utters a fouler slander upon the country and upon some of the States of the Confederacy than I would allow myself to utter in this place.

I wish Kossuth to come here, in his very person, a living reproach to despotism of whatever name and wherever it may be. I want him to go about among the people of the land, the living advocate of the rights of man, so that everybody, wherever he may be, who feels in his own breast that he is guilty of any invasion or infraction of these rights when he looks into the face of Kossuth may see there the lineaments that speak out reproach. That is the reason why I honor him, and that is the reason why I wish him to come here.

There are other victims of oppression. There are the victims of English oppression. The people of this country have been moving lately to get the kind offices of this Government to interfere in behalf of O'Brien, Mitchell, and their associates. I want this resolution to reach them. I want to let it go just exactly as far as the history of the United States goes. I want it to go, as was eloquently said by a distinguished orator of this country to Lafayette when he was here, speaking to him of the voice of Washington that was raised in his behalf, that that voice of sympathy could reach him even in the dungeons of Austria. Well, if there are victims of oppression in the dungeons of Austria, or of any other government on earth, I want this expression of the sentiments of the American people to be broad enough to reach them. I want Kossuth, and Mitchell, and O'Brien, and everybody else that is suffering in the great cause of human rights and human liberty, to feel that here, without division and without partiality, there is the entertainment of an honest and earnest and zealous respect for the course they have pursued.

Owing to the opposition which Foote met, both from Southerners and Northerners, he withdrew his resolutions, whereat Kossuth openly expressed his opinion of a Government that had invited him to be its guest and almost immediately afterward had refused him and his cause official recognition.

Sympathy with Ireland

The question of extending sympathy to the Irish victims of English oppression, to which Senator John P. Hale [N. H.] referred in the previous debate, had been brought forward in the Senate on December 2, 1851, by Henry S. Foote [Miss.] in a joint resolution ''expressive of the sympathy of Congress for the exiled Irish patriots, Smith O'Brien and Thomas F. Meagher, and their associates.'' This resolution authorized a correspondence in which appeal should be made to the magnanimity of the British Government and people requesting the liberation of these persons from their present confinement and offering to receive them ''upon the hospitable shores of the United States.''

On January 29 General James Shields [Ill.] offered in the Senate this amendment to the resolution:

''Disclaiming all intention to interfere in the internal affairs of the Kingdom of Great Britain and Ireland, we would regard this act of clemency as a new proof of the friendly disposition of the British Government toward our Republic, and as calculated to strengthen the bonds of affection now happily existing between the people of the United States and of the United Kingdom of Great Britain and Ireland.''

On February 7 General Shields supported the motion and his amendment in an eloquent speech. William H. Seward [N. Y.] and Lewis Cass [Mich.] spoke in similar vein in favor of the motion, and George E. Badger [N. C.] opposed it.

Liberation of the Irish Patriots

Senate, February 7-11, 1852

GENERAL SHIELDS.—Mr. President, I have prepared the amendment which I now take the liberty of offering as a substitute for the original resolution offered by a Senator [Mr. Foote], now no longer a member of this body. I am exceedingly anxious for its passage because, as it now stands, I think it preserves the dignity of this Government and can give no reasonable offence to the English Government; and I firmly believe it will effect a humane and Christian object—the liberation of those unfortunate men from captivity. I may as well state that O'Brien, Meagher, and O'Donahoe were convicted of treason and sentenced to be hanged, drawn, and quartered—which sentence was afterward commuted, by virtue of an express statute, into transportation for life. Mitchell, Martin, and O'Dougherty were convicted of sedition—an offence made felony and a species of treason by a statute expressly enacted for the occasion, and they were sentenced to be transported—Mitchell for fourteen years and Martin and O'Dougherty for ten years each. These six persons are now in captivity in Van Diemen's Land. The punishment is not so cruel as it is degrading; but, to men like these, death would be more acceptable than degradation. And what can be more degrading than to confine, and in a measure confound, such noble spirits with the vilest convicted criminals of the British empire? If this resolution has the effect, as I hope it will, of restoring these Irish patriots to liberty, it will be a work of beneficence, and the action of this Government will be to them like the interposition of an angel of mercy. But if it even fails to accomplish this object, it will still be successful in another respect: it will sound like a voice of encouragement to the captives—the voice of a great people. It will give consolation and hope; and, if it waft them nothing but hope, it will lighten their captivity and brighten their dreary existence in that far-distant land. As one of the friends of these Irish exiles, I take this occasion to state to the Senate—and I think I interpret the wishes of all their friends when I make this statement—that if they have the good fortune to ever reach our shores, we have no wish to see them welcomed with any public demonstration or display like that which has been just rendered to the illustrious Kossuth. We ask nothing of that kind. We wish to see them receive no other welcome or reception than that which the generous American heart always renders to the noble unfortunate.

In the passage of this resolution all we declare is that the liberation of these Irish patriots would be gratifying to the people of the United States. Surely there can be no reasonable objection to this. We ask that they be permitted to emigrate to this country—to incorporate themselves with our citizens, and live here quietly and peacefully under the protection of our free Constitution. There are strong natural reasons for the interest which the people of this country take in the fate of Ireland and Irishmen. Not only are millions of native Irishmen citizens of this country at this time, but Irish blood runs warmly in the veins of more than half the people of the United States. There is still another and a higher view of this matter, and one which seems to me to rise above all the etiquette of diplomacy. In one sense the people of this country and of Great Britain and Ireland may be considered as one great distinct family of the human race, connected by strong natural and traditional relations, which exist to the same extent among no other people on earth —blood, language, literature, the memories of the past and the hopes of the future. America may be considered not only the second home but the ultimate home of millions who are born under the British flag. How, then, can it even be suspected that under all these circumstances an application of this kind could offend the British Government? So far from being offensive, sir, in my humble opinion it is complimentary to that Government. The British Government has nothing to gain by continuing these men in confinement, and nothing to risk in their liberation. It has nothing to fear from Irish agitation now. Ireland is at this moment as feeble, helpless, and hopeless as the most anti-Irish heart can desire. Her nationality is gone; her hopes are crushed; her ancient generous race is becoming extinct. She has no future—or, if she has, it is a dark one. At such a time, and under such circumstances, how can any government, great and powerful as the English Government is, retain the last defenders of such a nation in captivity?

At this age of the world I think it is generally admitted that to punish a man for a political offence, without a very strong political necessity, is not an act of justice or self-defence, but, on the contrary, an act of cruel, useless, and impolitic vengeance. The British Government is too proud and powerful to stoop to the wicked weakness of vengeance. I think the present a very favorable time for moving in this affair and for preferring this request. The most friendly relations exist at this time between this country and Great Britain. There is a strong feeling of mutual regard and common interest, and, perhaps I may add, a sense of common danger uniting the people of both countries at this moment in close and intimate connection. The English people, so far as I can observe, are beginning to appreciate the character, resources, and institutions of this country, and to look with something like admiration upon the growth of this continental republic. Not only England but the world begins to see and acknowledge that this nation is destined to future supremacy.

The example of England herself would be, perhaps, the best argument we could use in favor of this resolution, or to enforce this request. Her history, in fact, is full of examples, not only of intercession but of interference in the internal affairs of other nations. England interfered directly in behalf of Kossuth and his companions—while we merely intercede for Smith O'Brien and his associates. She defended these Hungarians against Austria and Russia; we only appeal to her own clemency for the liberation of Irish patriots. She contributed to the liberation of Austrian subjects, although they are, in a certain sense, still dangerous to the Austrian Government. We simply request the liberation of British subjects whose freedom, in my opinion, at this time will serve to strengthen the English Government. We all recollect the universal delight with which the American people witnessed the first interference of England in behalf of the Hungarian exiles. When the British fleet appeared at the mouth of the Dardanelles—when the Red Cross of England joined the Crescent of Mahomet, and blazed in defence of the exile and the unfortunate—all America, with one voice, shouted glory and honor to the flag of Old England. She acted gloriously on that occasion. Her conduct called forth the applause of the liberal world. But now we have to moderate this applause when we think of Van Diemen's Land. We give her credit for her generosity abroad, but we are sorry to be compelled to refuse her equal credit for her clemency at home. Patriotism cannot be a virtue in Hungary and a crime in Ireland. England may be able to make some distinction between the two cases, but the world will refuse to recognize it. She will raise her national character in the estimation of the world— she will establish her disinterestedness before the tribunal of history and posterity—if she follow up her conduct toward the Hungarians with the liberation of the Irish exiles. As it is, her conduct is severely criticized on the continent of Europe. The Austrians and Russians especially accuse her of hypocrisy—of violating the great law of moral and political consistency—of traversing half the globe in defence and support of Hungarian patriots, while at the same time she proscribes, banishes, and imprisons Irish patriots. They say English philanthropy is like the philanthropy of the elder Mirabeau, who was styled *"The Friend of Man,"* for his universal benevolence, while he practiced at the same time, within the bosom of his own family, the most cruel, heartless, and unrelenting tyranny.

This is the kind of indictment the Continent prefers against England at this time. I am not prepared to endorse it. On the contrary, I am thoroughly convinced she will avail herself of the first favorable opportunity to clear her reputation from any such reproach. I am inclined to think she will feel thankful to this Government for supplying her with a fair occasion, a graceful pretext, to perform a humane and politic act. The world will then see that she is not governed, either in her foreign or domestic policy, by jealousy of Russia or hatred of Austria, but by a great principle of philanthropy and humanity.

If we weigh the conduct of these Irish patriots, not in legal but in moral scales, we will find much to justify their attempt. They loved their native country. There is no moral guilt in this. On the contrary, the love of country is one of the noblest sentiments of our nature. When this sentiment fades from the soul, the soul has lost its original brightness. In Ireland, however, this sentiment is almost considered a political offence. There is something so unnatural in this state of things, that what the English law denounces as treason the Irish heart recognizes as patriotism. An Irish patriot hears himself pronounced guilty in what is called the sanctuary of justice, while he feels in the sanctuary of his heart that he stands guiltless before God and his country.

Poor Ireland! Her history is a sad one. It is written in the tears and blood of her children. Her sons have been so long accustomed to injustice that they regard themselves as aliens and outcasts in the very land that God gave them as a heritage. Yet they love their country with all the fervor of the Irish heart. The more she suffers the more they love her. This love has become almost a part of their religion and of their fervent devotion to their God. As her own sweet poet [Thomas Moore] has so truly and beautifully said:

> "Her chains as they rankle, her blood as it runs,
> But make her more painfully dear to her sons."

Ireland has always been an incorrigible and irreconcilable rebel against power; but when her oppressors became unfortunate she became loyal; when they became friendless and helpless, she drew the sword and poured out her blood for them in the hour of their adversity. The Stuarts at the head of the empire were her cruel and constant oppressors; yet Ireland sacrificed herself for the last monarch of that ungrateful race, when, abandoned by his favorites and betrayed by his family, he fled from his throne—an exile, a wanderer, friendless and unfortunate.

I hope it will be allowable on this occasion to refer to the conduct of the Irish in your own glorious Revolution. History attests that during that whole period of trial and struggle a single Irish Tory was not to be found in the thirteen colonies. Both here and in Ireland, at home and abroad, the Irish heart declared openly and fearlessly in favor of the colonies. Who defended their cause in the British Parliament with more eloquent ability than Edmund Burke? And who defended it in the hour of danger with more unselfish devotion than the brave Montgomery? The Irish were true to this country then, and they are true to it still; they have always proved true, in word and deed, to the republican institutions of this country.

I would appeal to the people of England for justice to Ireland as quickly at this moment as I would to any other people on earth except the American people. Ireland has never been governed by the English people. It has been governed by an Anglo-Irish oligarchy—an oligarchy that has had no instinct but selfishness; no passion but the preservation of its own class. The government of Ireland was the government of a *caste*,— the very abstraction of an evil government. Such a government would have ruined any other country as well as Ireland. There was certain ruin in the very principle upon which it governed. That principle was to anglicize Ireland—to force an English government on the Irish race, an English church on Irish consciences, and English habits on Irish hearts,—in a word, to transform Irishmen into Englishmen. Of course the experiment has failed.

There is a national as well as a personal individuality. No people can be improved or elevated except through the medium of their own nationality. To develop a people we must respect the scruples of the national conscience—the virtues of the national heart, and the aspirations and even prejudices, of the national mind. National varieties are as necessary to improve and develop the human race as individual varieties. And political systems ought to be as various as the varieties of national character. A political system to improve and develop a people must grow out of the habits and circumstances of that people. It must be the natural product of the country.

The first requirement for Ireland is religious liberty; not toleration, but full, equal, absolute religious liberty. She will never be satisfied until she obtains this boon. There is nothing so dangerous to a government in a perilous crisis as a powerful, dissatisfied religious party, like the Roman Catholic party of the British Empire; and nothing so harmless as religious sects or parties, when a government abolishes all religious distinctions and gives full, perfect, and absolute religious liberty to all. If you want to put down religious agitation and destroy clerical influence, give the people equal and universal religious liberty. This is a truth very well understood in this country, yet, strange to say, it has hitherto escaped the penetration of the first statesmen of Europe.

Ireland also requires political liberty and an equitable share of all the advantages of the British Government and British Empire, and above all, the Irish people require an absolute interest in the soil of their country. As it is, Ireland may be considered a vast warren—a hunting ground for absentee nobility; and, unhappily, the spoils of the chase are the hearts, hopes, and lives of the Irish peasantry. I have long watched and waited to see some great English statesman arise, who could grapple with this monster difficulty.

But, after all, Ireland must be the great agent of her own regeneration; she must not depend upon England, or upon America, or upon the Continent. If she looks to the absolutists of Europe for support, as I apprehend she does at this moment, she will be deceived and disappointed and betrayed. There is not a despot in Europe, large or small, from the Czar of Russia to the King of Naples, who would not, at this moment, sell and sacrifice Ireland and all her hopes to purchase the friendship of the English Government.

I know it is difficult to form a correct judgment of the true policy of a distant nation; but, after long reflection upon this subject, I have arrived at the conclusion that the present policy of Ireland is to abandon all idea of a political separation from England. Her own nationality is gone. She can never recover or restore either her old language or her old nationality. If she were an independent nation this moment, her great effort should be to build up a *new* nationality conformable to her present moral, social, and political condition. Her policy now is to make the most of her present political connection, and to avail herself of all the political, commercial, industrial, and intellectual advantages of the British Empire. She should coöperate on all occasions with the most liberal English party. She should throw her whole weight into the scale of liberalism. Her movement should be an imperial one; and by acting in this manner she would raise and regenerate herself in contributing to elevate and liberalize the whole empire.

SENATOR SEWARD.—I am told that we may lawfully sympathize, as individuals, in the misfortunes of these unhappy men, and of their more unhappy country; but that to us as a political body—a state or nation—or as the representatives—the government of a nation—such sympathy is forbidden. This seems to me equivalent to saying that we may indulge sentiments of generous compassion, but we shall never carry them into beneficent action. The sympathy of the several members of this Senate, or of this Congress, or of the individual citizens of the United States will be unavailing. If that sympathy is truly felt by the nation, it can only be effectually expressed in the manner in which national sympathies and determinations of the national will are always made effective—by the action of the Government. And, sir, let me say that there is only one code of morals for mankind, and its obligations bind them equally, whether they be individuals, subjects, citizens, states, or nations.

I shall be told that we may not intervene in this which is a domestic affair of a foreign government. It is true that we may not intervene in the affairs of any government for unjust purposes, nor can we intervene by force for even just or benevolent purposes. But this is the only restraint imposed on us by the law of nations. That law, while it declares that every government has the absolute right to deal with its own citizens, according to its own laws, independently of any other, affords a large verge and scope for the exercise of offices of courtesy, kindness, benevolence, and charity. It is Montesquieu who says that "the law of nations is founded upon the principle that every nation is bound in time of peace to do to every other nation all the good it possibly can, and in time of war the least evil it possibly can consistently with its own real interests." It is upon this humane principle that diplomatic intercourse is maintained among the civilized nations of the earth, all of whom are by the law of nations regarded as constituting one great commonwealth.

But, Mr. President, it will be said that, if we adopt this resolution, it will, however harmless it be in itself, furnish a precedent for mischievous intervention, either by ourselves in the affairs of other states or by other states in our affairs hereafter. To admit this argument is to admit distrust of ourselves. We certainly do not distrust our own sense of justice. We do not distrust our own wisdom. So long as we remain here, then, we shall be able to guard against any such abuse of this precedent. Let us also be generous instead of egotistical, and let us believe that neither wisdom nor justice will die with those who occupy these places now, but that our successors will be as just and as wise as we are. So far as the objection anticipates an abuse of this precedent by foreign states, I have only to say that if a foreign state shall ask of us just what we now propose, and no more, we shall have no difficulty and no ground of complaint. If it shall ask more, we shall be free to reject what is asked, as the British Government is free to reject our application.

Sir, this proposition involves a view of the relations of the parties concerned. The people of Ireland are affiliated to us, as we are to the people of Great Britain. Surely there can be no offence given by a younger member in offering mediation between the elder brethren of the same family upon a point of difference between them.

But what if Great Britain should take offence at this suggestion? What then? Why, then England would be in the wrong, and we in the right. The time has passed when this country can be alarmed by fear of war in such a case. No one will confess that he indulges any such apprehension. Sir, Great Britain will not take offence. She knows that her greatness and her fame are well assured. She has no motive whatever to affect wounded sensibility. She will receive this suggestion in the same fraternal spirit in which it is made. Nor will she refuse the boon. She knows as well as we do that rigor protracted beyond the necessity of security to the state reacts. She knows full well that for the present, at least, sedition sleeps profoundly in Ireland, and that the granting of this appeal will protract its slumbers. Great Britain will be thankful to us for our confidence in her generosity, for her motto is *"Parcere subjectis et debellare superbos."*[1]

The points of Senator Cass, who followed, will be found as quoted by Senator Badger, the next speaker.

SENATOR BADGER.—After every examination which I have been able to give this subject, I cannot persuade myself that it is proper that the Congress of the United States should pass the resolution in any of the forms in which it has been proposed to our consideration. If I could vote for the resolution in any form, I would undoubtedly vote for it in that which it has assumed upon the suggestion of the honorable Senator from Illinois [Mr. Shields]; and if anything could persuade me to forego the exercise of my own deliberate judgment and put myself under the mastery of those feelings which are apt to be excited by discussions of this kind, to favor the adoption of the resolution, it would be the speech delivered on last Saturday by the honorable Senator from Illinois, full as it was of everything that can do honor to a man's head and heart.

But whatever my feelings of attachment, consideration, or

[1] "To spare the abject and war down the proud."

sympathy for the other nations and races of the world—and I trust I am not deficient in those feelings of consideration and sympathy—I must prefer my own country, my own race, the people and institutions among which I was born and in which I have been reared, to all other nations and all other races in the world. I cannot, therefore, consent to give my support to any measure, however commended to us by high considerations of sympathy, which, in my judgment, is capable of having an unjust and injurious operation upon the country to which I belong.

This resolution proposes that the Congress of the United States shall express, and that the Congress of the United States shall declare, and that we feel it our duty to express an earnest desire that the Queen of Great Britain will extend her royal clemency to certain Irish prisoners now confined, under a sentence, to Van Diemen's Land. Now, in the first place, I do not feel myself called upon by my duty as an American Senator to express any sentiment upon that subject. But that would be—that is—the smallest of the difficulties that press upon my mind. Though I cannot recognize the duty, yet if no evil consequences could be readily imagined to result from it, I might, nevertheless, be willing to give expression to the wish. But, sir, I ask you, who have had no little experience in the state and condition of our foreign affairs, and the management of our diplomatic relations with other countries, and the reciprocal operations of proceedings of this kind, whether we can affirm that there is no danger from the precedent which we are now setting?

My honorable friend from Michigan [Mr. Cass], in the remarks which he addressed to the Senate—remarks conceived and expressed, I will not say with a force and clearness that were not usual with him but certainly with great force and clearness—has laid down some propositions to which I wish to invite the attention of the Senate, and to show, if I can, that the mode by which he undertakes to defend the proceedings now recommended to us is one that must, or, at all events, one that may, lead to mischievous counterinterference with our concerns; and that the suggestions which he has thrown out for the purpose of dissipating the fear of such a result, when properly considered, are entitled to no weight.

First, the Senator laid down a proposition in these words:

"Mr. President, a great change has taken place in the opinions of the world on the subject of political offences. They nowhere carry with them reproach or shame. They violate, indeed, existing laws; but they generally originate in the most praiseworthy motives, and are pursued at the hazard of every earthly good, as Washington and a host of other industrious men in ancient and modern days pursued their patriotic enterprises.''

Again, he says:

''They'' (alluding to political offenders) ''are recognized as being unfortunate but not vicious. Indeed, they are often noble men, as are those whose case engages our attention, and who deserve the kind interest of the world, both from their motives and their character, and also from the position, once high, but now low, to which they have fallen, and in consequence of an effort, made, not for themselves, but for their country. It cannot be—there is not the slightest danger of it—that such a national application will ever be made, in any case but in one like this, which is as far from moral guilt as innocence is from crime. Let no one fear that this example will ever be used, or abused, for the purpose of intermeddling in the ordinary criminal proceedings of other powers.''

Again, the honorable Senator says:

''As to improper interference, it seems to me an entire misconstruction of the term to apply it to a case like this. It is not interference at all; it is intercession. It is a simple request, made from the best motives, in the best spirit, and presented in the most unexceptionable language; and it leaves the British Government free to act its own pleasure, without giving us the slightest offence should the result be unsuccessful.''

Now, I wish to say, in the first place, that this is interference. Intercession is one mode of interference. It is not an offensive mode of interference; but it is a mode of interference. He who undertakes to intercede between the judge and the offender—between the sovereign and his convicted subject, undoubtedly interferes. It seems to me that the honorable Senator is entirely mistaken in supposing that intercession is not interference. It is true that all interference is not intercession, because we may interfere by threats, by violence, by blows; but it is no less true that every intercession is an interference. Then I am not exactly prepared to admit the fundamental, the original proposition, from which the argument of the honorable Senator from Michigan starts, which is that political offences, though they violate existing laws, are yet offences accompanied with no moral guilt. I can conceive of such a thing as a political offence which, though violating municipal laws, is not accompanied with moral guilt; but I do not think it is regularly or generally the case, or can be affirmed as a proposition either universal or with but few exceptions. But, assuming it to be so:

then the honorable Senator says we come forward and do not interfere, but intercede for these political offenders upon the ground that they are persons free from moral guilt; that they are noble patriots who have been condemned to a grievous imprisonment—originally condemned to the forfeiture of life—for the discharge of high acts of patriotic duty to their country; and that the noblest motives influenced them in what they had done; and that they are not to be considered as affected with any species of moral guilt.

Now, be it so. Assume that it is so, and that we wish it to be so. How was the transaction viewed by the British Government? That Government prosecuted these men as traitors—for an attempt to overturn the existing government of the United Kingdom of Great Britain and Ireland. For this offence they were convicted. For this offence they received the sentence of death; but the sentence was afterward commuted to an expatriation or exile in Van Diemen's Land. It seems to me that the English Government will scarcely think that when they have prosecuted these men for an offence of this kind, pronounced by their laws to be capital, when after conviction and judgment they have not thought proper to pardon the convicts but have exchanged the sentence of death to that of banishment from the realm, that they are honorable and noble men, who have been influenced by high and patriotic motives in what they have done. The British Government looks upon them in a far different light and description. Well, that being the case, how does it follow that we have no reason to fear that if we set this example, we shall not have it followed with a very unpleasant and disagreeable interference in the administration of our own laws?

Now, let us suppose for one moment that some of the actors in the Christiana riot [for the liberation of fugitive slaves] had been found guilty of high treason. They were indicted for that crime. High treason is a political offence. I pray you, sir, if that case would not in a few sympathizing minds, on the other side of the water, have presented a case with all the claims which the honorable Senator from Michigan brings forward in behalf of these Irish exiles, for the interference of the masses, or the governments, or the parliaments, or the other legislative assemblies on the other side of the water, under the strong feelings of modern humanity and general sympathy for the oppressed everywhere? Why, to those people these Christiana rioters would have appeared noble men—guilty, it is true, of committing the little technical offence of violating the municipal laws of the country, convicted, to be sure, of what was called treason against the United States, but influenced by high and noble motives, under the full inspiration of the "higher law" enthusiasm, which prompted them to come forward and at every hazard, not for the benefit of themselves, but, as my friend from Michigan said with regard to these gentlemen, for the benefit of their country, to relieve the oppressed, and to prevent the wronged and hunted wayfarer from being dragged back into the captivity from which he had luckily escaped. They would be looked upon as men influenced by a high and lofty spirit of hospitality, who, with outstretched arms, were willing, even at the hazard of destroying the Constitution of their country, to carry into effect the high, noble, and generous purposes and impulses of their nature. If we think that it is our duty to interpose, because we look upon these persons who have been sentenced to this punishment by a foreign nation as meritorious and noble men, entitled to our sympathies and accompanied with no moral blame—how can we resist the right of a foreign state, of a foreign parliament or legislative body, to interfere in precisely the same mode with regard to citizens of ours whom we may think worthy of the extremest punishment, but which they regard as occupying the same relation to moral guilt which we attribute to the persons in whose behalf this resolution is now proposed? We should cut ourselves off, by adopting this proceeding, from any right to object. I see not where the thing would end. Resolutions of the British Parliament may be passed and sent to us, or communicated to us, in a kind of indirect, secret, and unostentatious mode, to which the Senator has referred, through their minister in this country.

Upon this subject I wish to practice upon the old-fashioned morality of doing as I would be done by. I want no interference of foreign states or governments in our internal affairs anywhere, and therefore I am not willing to set a practical example of such an interference on our behalf with their internal concerns. I know that this resolution springs from the highest and best motives. I know that my honorable friend from Illinois [Mr. Shields], who has moved it, has, at least in my judgment, no superior in the honorable, the fine, and elevated sentiments that belong to the human heart. But it was well remarked, as I think Sallust or some of those old Roman writers told us, that Cæsar once said in the Roman Senate that there was never any course of measures which had brought ruin upon a country which, at the first outset, did not spring from some good motive, and in the initiative were intended to accomplish some good end.

The honorable Senator from New York [Mr. Seward] in the remarks which he submitted to the Senate this morning, after reassuring us that there was no danger that Great Britain would take any offence at this proceeding, became exceedingly bold, and held in very slight regard and estimation any, even the most serious, displeasure of that power. I am not a very valiant man, and I confess myself to have a pretty large share of that extreme reluctance as well to cutting the throats of other people as to having my own cut which is denominated by the word fear. And I go one step further. In my representative capacity I have a great deal of fear of involving this country in collisions with the great powers of the earth. Who should not fear it? Is not war a dreadful evil? Is not a war with the greatest naval and commercial power of the earth a fearful evil?

I fear putting ourselves wrong in the outset of such a proceeding. If we must have a conflict with Great Britain, or any other nation, let us be right in the commencement, in the prosecution, and throughout the whole conflict. And rely upon it, sir, that when such a conflict comes, if come it must, which God forbid, those who have some little salutary fear beforehand of the coming emergency will not be found the least resolute to do what that emergency may require.

I have, however, an objection to this resolution of another and different kind from that suggested by the Senator from New York. It has been said by the Senator from Michigan that Great Britain will not regard this in the light of an officious intermeddling with her concerns. We hear from various quarters that the probability is that the British Government, acting upon this intimation of the wishes of the American people, will gladly interpose and discharge these gentlemen from their hard captivity. For one, I should be sorry that the British Government should, at our interposition, and as a favor to us, set these gentlemen at liberty. And why? Because it is very obvious that that places us under an obligation to the British Government. It not only entitles them to interfere, by way of interceding in behalf of our people, if any of them should be convicted of offences similar to that to which I have referred, but it also entitles them to come with a claim upon us that they should be heard. I, for one, am not willing that this country should lay itself under any such obligation to the clemency, or courteousness, or kindness of the British Queen.

Let us have a little common sense in the regulation of our concerns. Do not let us be carried away captive with emotions which, however generous and noble in themselves, do not furnish the proper guides for representative conduct. A man, in the private transactions of life, may allow a profuse generosity and inability to refuse any applicants for help to exhaust his purse and beggar himself for life; and when this is done, however severely we may disapprove of it, we are obliged to have a sympathy for him who, under such generous impulses, has sacrificed himself; but representatives and nations are bound, in my judgment, to have all their sympathies and feelings under thorough and complete control—to regulate themselves by understanding—to let common sense weigh, in all their deliberations, because they are not like a generous man who squanders his own, for, if they yield themselves up to these unguided impulses, they squander what is not their own—the wealth, the power, the resources of the state of which they are only the representatives. They sacrifice not themselves, but their country.

Non-Intervention in Foreign Affairs

As a result of the debates on the Kossuth reception and the resolution of sympathy with the Irish patriots, John H. Clarke [R. I.], on January 19, 1852, introduced in the Senate the following resolutions:

Resolved, That Congress recognizes and reaffirms these manifest truths: "That governments are instituted among men to secure the inalienable rights of life, liberty, and the pursuit of happiness, deriving their just powers from the consent of the governed; that whenever any form of government becomes destructive of these ends, it is the right of the people to alter or to abolish it, and to institute a new government, laying its foundation upon such principles and organizing its powers in such form as to them shall seem most likely to effect their safety and happiness.

Resolved, That while we claim for ourselves these comprehensive rights of self-government, and also, as a consequence of sovereignty, the right to be exempt from the coercion, control, or interference of others in the management of our internal affairs, we concede to others the same measure of right, the same unqualified independence.

Resolved, That it is upon the sacred principle of independent sovereignty that we recognize, in our intercourse with other nations, governments *de facto*, without inquiring by what means they have been established, or in what manner they exercise their powers.

Resolved, That this Government has solemnly adopted, and will perseveringly adhere to, as a principle of international action, the advice given by Washington in his Farewell Address: "Observe good faith and justice toward all nations; cultivate peace and harmony with all." "Give to mankind the magnanimous and too novel an example of a people always guided by an exalted justice and benevolence." "Sympathy for a favorite nation betrays itself into a participation in the quarrels and wars of another, without adequate inducement or justification." "Against the insidious wiles of foreign influence the jealousy of a free people ought to be constantly awake; for foreign influence is the most baneful foe of republican governments." "The true rule of conduct for us in regard to foreign nations is, in extending our commercial relations, to have with them as little political connection as possible." "Why quit our own to stand upon foreign ground? Why, by interweaving our destiny with that of any part of Europe, entangle our peace and prosperity in the toils of European ambition, rivalship, interest, humor, or caprice?"

Resolved, That, while we cherish the liveliest sympathy toward all who strive for freedom of opinion and for free institutions, yet we recognize our true policy in the great fundamental principles given to us by Jefferson: "Equal and exact justice to all men, of whatever state or persuasion, religious or political; peace, commerce, and honest friendship, with all nations, entangling alliances with none."

Resolved, That, although we adhere to these essential principles of non-intervention, as forming the true and lasting foundation of our prosperity and happiness, yet whenever a provident foresight shall warn us that our own liberties and institutions are threatened, then a just regard to our own safety will require us to advance to the conflict rather than await the approach of the foes of our constitutional freedom and of human liberty.

To these resolutions William H. Seward [N. Y.] offered the following amendment:

Strike out all after the second resolution and insert the following:

Resolved, That while the United States, in consideration of the exigencies of society, habitually recognize governments *de facto* in other states, yet that they are, nevertheless, by no means indifferent when such a government is established against the consent of any people by usurpation or by armed intervention of foreign states or nations.

Resolved, That, considering that the people of Hungary, in the exercise of the right secured to them by the laws of nations, in a solemn and legitimate manner asserted their national independence, and established a government by their own voluntary act, and successfully maintained it against all opposition by parties lawfully interested in the question; and that the Emperor of Russia, without just or lawful right, invaded Hungary and, by fraud and armed force, subverted the national independence and political constitution thus established, and thereby reduced that country to the condition of a province ruled by a foreign and absolute power: the United States, in defence of their own interests, and of the common interests of mankind, do solemnly protest against the conduct of Russia on that occasion as a wanton and tyrannical infraction of the laws of nations; and the United States do further declare that they will not hereafter be indifferent to similar acts of national injustice, oppression, and usurpation, whenever or wherever they may occur.

Lewis Cass [Mich.] also offered the following substitute for Senator Clarke's resolutions:

Resolved, That while the people of the United States sympathize with all nations who are striving to establish free governments, yet they recognize the great principle of the law of nations which assures to each of them the right to manage its own internal affairs in its own way, and to establish, alter, or abolish its government at pleasure, without the interference of any other Power; and they have not seen, nor could they again see, without deep concern, the violation of this principle of national independence.

On February 9 Senator Clarke spoke upon his resolutions and Senator Cass's substitute. Reply was made on February 10 by Senator Cass, and on March 9 by Senator Seward.

NON-INTERVENTION

SENATE, FEBRUARY 9-MARCH 9, 1852

SENATOR CLARKE.—These resolutions affirm the true doctrines of self-government, as set forth in the Declaration of our

Independence. They take the farewell advice of the great and good Washington for our political chart, and they reiterate the wise declarations of Jefferson, whose precepts are oftener upon the lips than in the hearts of those who claim to be his peculiar disciples. His conservative principles, by no means extreme, are cast aside as the dogmas of a bygone age. Sir, it is time that we recurred to our ancient political landmarks. As the mariner consults his chart, and takes by day the altitude of the sun, and at night his observations are directed to the stars, so, sir, it is healthful for us to go back to the principles and the policy of our Government—break upon the altar of our faith the sacramental bread, and renew our fidelity to the maxims which our fathers established, and which have borne them and us from feeble infancy to a high and vigorous and unsullied manhood.

Senator Clarke then recounted the events which had led up to Washington's Proclamation of Neutrality in the French-British War of 1793 [see Chapter I], and read the proclamation.

John Marshall, in his "Life of Washington," speaking of this proclamation, says:

"This measure derives importance from the consideration that it was the commencement of that system to which the American Government afterward inflexibly adhered, and to which much of the national prosperity is to be ascribed."

Mr. President, the policy of our Government, thus settled by Washington, has been confirmed and reaffirmed by succeeding statesmen from that to the present day, and can hardly be obliterated from the faith of either of the great parties of the country.

The Senator from Michigan has offered a substitute for the resolution which I propose—repudiating the Farewell Address of Washington.

Gently and tenderly he tells us that the interference of one nation in the affairs of another cannot be seen without "deep concern." But he proposes no definite action.

The substitute assumes "that the people of the United States sympathize with all nations who are striving to establish free governments," which is palpable, and to its utmost extent true. But the Senator from New York, in the amendment offered by him, goes more boldly to his purpose. In the first place, he would "protest" against national intervention, and afterward "would not be indifferent to similar acts of national injustice."

In a quarrel between the retainers of the rival houses of Montague and Capulet we have a fair example of this mode of warfare by protest. "Deep concern" and not being "indifferent to national injustice" (preceded by an avowal that no force is contemplated) is here well illustrated in the quarrel between the retainers of the houses.

> "*Abram.* Do you bite your thumb at us, sir?
> "*Sampson.* Is the law on our side if I say aye?
> "*Gregory.* No.
> "*Sampson.* I do not bite my thumb at you, sir; but I bite my thumb, sir.
> "*Gregory.* Do you quarrel, sir?
> "*Abram.* Quarrel, sir? No, sir."

The doctrine of non-intervention in the internal affairs of other nations has been the settled and reiterated policy of our country. A departure from these established truths can lead only to a resort to the strong arm, and put at hazard the rich inheritance of freedom which we enjoy, and the rich fruits which a benign Providence has mercifully bestowed upon us.

Far more are we doing for the liberation of man by our quiet and peaceful example than could possibly be effected by wasting our energies in a conflict of opinion with the despots of the world, and in favor of a people unsuited, by intelligence and education, to appreciate blessings prematurely forced upon them by even a Christian charity, which would waste itself and do them no good.

The liberty and happiness of our country, now and forever, may be in our keeping, and the solemn trust should be executed with judgment, with caution, and with prudence. The vast and incomprehensible influence of such a people will silently but surely work its way among the nations of the earth, and our institutions will shed a mild and gentle light upon degraded and oppressed humanity. It is our solemn duty carefully to cherish and preserve the rich blessings we enjoy, and which have never before been given to man, and not to venture them upon the sea of every nation's disquietude. And as that duty is performed, so will God and our own right arm protect us.

SENATOR CASS.—My objections to the original proposition are not to the great truths it enunciates—truths drawn from our own State papers, of the best days of the Republic, for to their eternal justice I yield a cheerful acquiescence—but to the narrow application it is designed to make of them. They met, and were intended to meet, the circumstances of the country, connected with our right to the new position we had assumed as a member of the family of nations, and with occurrences which took place not long afterward, but they went no further. The obligations which subsequent events might impose upon us in relation to ambitious pretensions, incompatible with the public law and the independence of nations, they neither foresaw nor defined. And thus is it that we must push our inquiry beyond these limits before we reach the great question of our true duty and policy now in face of us.

In the brief examination I propose to give to the subject before us, with a view to practical results rather than to profitless speculations, I have no intention of entering into the vexed question of the origin of international law, nor into the true grounds of the obligations by which civilized communities are required to submit to it. I assume at once the duty of all Christian people to recognize its binding force, and to aid its operations so far as they can properly do it. Certainly we cannot trace back this code to a universal legislative origin as we can trace back a municipal statute to its local source. It grew out of the necessity of regulating the intercourse between independent countries, in peace and in war; and traces of its existence may be found in the earliest recorded annals of nations. It began by assuaging the horrors of war, and by restraining the cruelties of barbarous conquerors; and by degrees, from a few simple maxims, it has become an elaborate system, coextensive with civilization, and appealing not less to the sense of interest than to that of morality by substituting fixed and just principles for those wayward passions which, without such an arbiter, would make the world one vast theater of carnage.

The elementary commentaries of wise and learned men, the decisions of enlightened jurists, and the discussions of able statesmen have built up the system, and it is a beautiful monument of the progress and improved condition of society. For it has not been a fixed and immutable code, but has accommodated itself to the advancing opinions and necessities of the world. Few and meager were at first its provisions, like the wants it was designed to meet; but, as these increased, it increased with them, till it has become one of the most useful, if not one of the proudest, works of the human intellect.

And let no one reproach it with inutility or imbecility, because it is not always a barrier against interest and ambition;

but rather let us be thankful that it is so often appealed to and so often effectual in restraining the turbulent passions of our nature. And such is the force of public opinion, in this the days of its strength, that, even when the provisions of international law are evaded or neglected, its obligations are rarely, never indeed, denied, but constructions for selfish purposes are put upon it, forced and false it is true, but a tribute to its worth, even while its injunctions are practically disregarded.

It well becomes us and the principles of our institutions to profess our fealty to this great code of public morality; and not merely to profess it, but prove it, by our acts and declarations, and labor to enforce its obligations and its observance. It is a curious subject to trace the changes it has undergone, even in very late years, almost all marked by the progress of just opinions and by meliorations honorable to the spirit of the age. It is a great engine for good, but powerless for evil—a barrier against injustice and oppression, asserting the empire of reason over that of force.

The time has come when we have as much right and as much power to speak authoritatively on this subject as any other nation on the face of the globe. All we want, while professing the duty of obedience, is that other nations should equally obey it. There is none so high as to be above its obligations; none so low as to be beneath its protection.

We believe in the right and in the capacity of man for self-government—not that he is everywhere prepared for institutions like ours. We know, while we regret, that he is not. But we believe that he is everywhere fitted even now for taking some part in the administration of political affairs, greater or less, in proportion to his experience and condition; and that everywhere, with time and practice, he may improve himself and his government till both become as free as the state of society will permit. And certainly the expression of the warm hope that this time will come and come speedily is consistent with every respect for other powers.

We claim no right to interfere in their internal concerns. While we are firm believers in our own political faith, we enter into no crusade to establish it elsewhere. Propagandism is no part of our creed, unless it be that propagandism which works its own way by the force of example, thus inviting the oppressed nations of the earth to do as we have done, and to be as free and happy as we are. But we cannot be indifferent to the condition of the human race, however widely scattered. A desire for its improvement, morally and materially, is a sentiment natural to man. And an American can hardly shut himself up in his own selfish egotism, thanking God, in the spirit of the Pharisee, that his country is better off than any other, and indifferent to the oppression, and degradation, and misery which centuries of bad government have entailed upon so large a portion of the earth. Unless the many were made for the few, the governed for the governors, our sympathies should be excited, as were those of Washington, for every people unfurling the banner of freedom, and a God-speed them be uttered, not only in the effort to improve their political system, but in the greater effort to maintain it by improving the condition of the great body of those for whom governments are instituted. And may we not say, as an English parliamentary orator said very recently for his country, "that the spirit of our people is for freedom everywhere?" And may we not echo his sentiment and declare "that they would not rest satisfied with seeing the *ultima ratio* of European policy lodged in the bayonet of the barbarian?"

Now, sir, what we want is that freedom should have a fair battlefield. That whenever a struggle is commenced to overthrow an arbitrary government, other despotic powers should not be permitted to take part in the contest and with foreign bayonets decide the issue.

Such is our desire, and this principle of non-interference is well established in the code of public law. It lies at the very foundation of national independence. I need not multiply proofs or illustrations of the truth of this doctrine. It was well laid down by Mr. Roebuck in the English House of Commons, when he said: "The important principle with which we have to deal was that in the internal affairs of any country there should be no external force or pressure." Its recognition goes back to the time of the Romans, for we are told that, when certain Carthaginians preferred charges against Hannibal, Scipio declared that the Roman senate would not be justified in intermeddling in the affairs of Carthage.

There is one highly respectable authority—and I know of no other—Vattel, who holds that, in a state of civil war, any other power may assist the party which it believes to be just. But it is obvious that such a principle would open every case to direct armed intervention at the will of any foreign government; which has only to say, such a party has justice on its side and I will aid it. Now, sir, this doctrine is contradicted as well by reason as by the whole current of authorities. Wildman, one of the most recent as well as one of the most able commentators on the law of nations, condemns the position of Vattel, into which he says he was led by "a misconstruction of a passage of Grotius," and "that it is as little reconcilable with reason as it is with precedent." He examines the cases fully and shows how erroneous is this doctrine, and announces the result thus:

"But this restriction of interference in favor of the cause of justice is an absolute prohibition of interference on the part of those who have no jurisdiction to determine the justice of the cause. Hence it follows that no foreign power has any right to interfere in the internal affairs of an independent state."

Establish this doctrine of Vattel, and the Emperor Nicholas, who no doubt believes every despotic cause a just one, would have a right to send his armies everywhere to repress the efforts of freedom.

The system of international law would not be worth the paper on which it is written if such examples of contempt for the feelings and rights of mankind as Russia has exhibited in the case of Hungary admitted neither resistance nor remonstrance. "Concession," says Bentham, in his forcible language, "Concession to notorious injustice invites fresh injustice"; and this is nowhere more true than in the career and conduct of nations. And we find that the right of independent powers to express their opinions upon grave questions of public law, when that law has been violated, has been so often and so openly exercised that no doubt can exist of the right and indeed of the duty of thus acting, when the nature and the gravity of the circumstances require such a measure.

It is the interest of each nation that the rights of all should be respected, because the spectator of injustice to-day may be its victim to-morrow; and none of the barriers against ambition and tyranny can be broken down without danger to the civilized world. Every power must judge for itself how far its own interests may be touched by the pretensions advanced, and what course true policy requires it should take. It is not necessary that the evil day should be upon it before it makes known its disapprobation, for, in that case, aggressions would be eternal, or war the only remedy to resist them.

We have a direct interest, a material interest, if you disclaim every principle of action but the utilitarian principle, in the benefits of commercial intercourse, and in the prosperity and stability and independence of nations, by which the resources and commerce of a country are increased, and in the maintenance of those great principles which protect these rights.

But I agree with one of the most independent of the public men of England, Mr. Roebuck, that higher considerations may justly influence our actions, and that "we should not bind up all our feelings in the interchange of commodities, or the sordid question of profit or loss. He believed there was something more in the souls of the people than that." And the sentiment, advanced by Lord Palmerston, that a great country should not "be a passive and mute spectator of everything that goes on around" deserves our commendation and concurrence.

There is not a page of modern diplomatic history in which may not be read the outlines I have already referred to of national conduct. But a strange error seems to prevail respecting one branch of this subject which it is necessary to examine, not from the support it derives from reason or authority, but from the confidence with which it is urged, and because, if not corrected, it may paralyze the national action in all time to come.

This erroneous doctrine has been widely and confidently spread and seeks to deter us from expressing any opinion upon the law of nations by an apprehension of the consequences. It is maintained that in all cases where a nation makes such a declaration it is bound to support its views by war if these are not acquiesced in, or it will lose its own self-respect and subject itself to the contumely of the world. There is not the least foundation in reason or authority or precedent, for such an assumption. It is gratuitous as it is untenable.

Mr. President, the particular form in which a nation makes known its views, from the most common diplomatic note to the most solemn protests, neither adds to nor takes from its responsibility or obligation. It appears to be assumed that there is some peculiar pugnacious quality attached to a protest which necessarily leads to armed action. This is not so. A public declaration in that form no more imposes on the nation making it the duty of vindicating it by arms than the every day representations which the usual diplomatic intercourse renders necessary. To be sure, the proceeding is more solemn, as the subjects generally are more grave; and it goes forth to the world under circumstances of deliberation which give to such declarations more than usual importance. But that they are necessarily followed by war whenever they fail in the result is contradicted by all the diplomatic experience of modern times.

"Manifestoes," says Bentham, and such declarations are a kind of protest, "are in common usage. A manifesto is designed to be read either by the subjects of the state complained of or by other states or by both. It is an appeal to them. It calls for their opinion.'' A new school of expounders has arisen which denounces them as appeals to force.

Our own history presents a memorable example of the exercise of this right to declare a principle of national law. Mr. Monroe's views on a similar question, solemnly announced to Congress and the world, form a well-known part of our political history. And, though his doctrine has not been wholly efficacious, it has, no doubt, contributed, with other causes, to the stability of the independence of the American States, and to check the spirit of colonization.

Certainly solemn public declarations of this nature should not, would not indeed, often be made, for their frequent occurrence would impair, if not destroy, their moral effect. They should be reserved for those extraordinary events, affecting the honor and stability of all nations, which stand prominently forward in the history of the world; characteristics, indeed, of the age in which they occur. Let no man, therefore, object that such a *conservative* remedy, for once the epithet is a just one, will lead to abuse or will destroy itself by too frequent application.

We ought neither to mistake our position nor neglect the obligations it brings with it. We have at length reached the condition of one of the great powers of the earth, and yet we are but in the infancy of our career. The man is now living who will live to see one hundred and fifty millions of people, free, prosperous, and intelligent, swaying the destinies of this country, and exerting a mighty influence upon those of the world. And why not, Mr. President? Is it not likely to be more beneficially exerted than the influence now exercised by the despotic powers of the earth? No one can doubt this. Why, sir, even Vattel, enlightened as he was, tells us that ''the law of nations is the law of sovereigns. It is principally for them and for their ministers, that it ought to be written,'' etc. The age has got far beyond this degrading doctrine. That law was made for the great civilized community of the world, and its obligations and their violations will be judged by this high tribunal, and its voice will become, from day to day, louder and more efficacious. Let us aid it by the expression of our views, whenever questions arise interesting to all the members of the great commonwealth of nations. There are no considerations of right or expediency to restrain us from such a course; for, as I have shown, we are just as free to act or forbear, after such a declaration, as before. But, it has been asked, why proclaim your opinion unless you mean to maintain it by the strong hand? For the same reason that countless representations and remonstrances have been made by independent powers when they had reason to apprehend the adoption of measures hostile to the just principles of national intercommunication. To mark their disapprobation of the act and of the doctrine, that their silence might not be construed into acquiescence, and that, when, in the mutation of political affairs, the proper time should come they might interpose effectually, if they should desire it, not concluded by the success of violence nor by the lapse of time; that the power itself, contemplating the step, might pause and review its position and its pretensions and the consequences to which it might be led; not knowing, of course, what measures might follow these appeals to its sense of right should they fail to be effectual; and, above all, that the public opinion of the world should be rightly instructed and brought to aid these peaceful efforts to preserve the rights of mankind.

It has been said, in condemnation or in reproach of this effort, that there are many other suffering people and violated principles calling equally for the assertion of this right, and why, it is asked sneeringly, if not triumphantly, why do you not extend your regards and your action to all such cases? And as that is impossible with any useful result, as every one knows, we are, therefore, to sit still and do nothing because we cannot do everything. Such is no dictate of wisdom or duty, either in political or ethical philosophy. The prudent statesman looks to what is practicable, as well as what is right.

Many objections, more or less plausible, have been presented to deter us from any action in this matter, but not one of them with more confidence of pertinacity, nor with less regard to the true circumstances of our position, than that which warns us that by such a proceeding we should violate alike the traditions of our policy and the advice of our wisest statesmen, and especially the injunctions of Washington and Jefferson. Never were just recommendations more inappropriately applied than in this attempt to apply the views of those great men to the circumstances in which we are placed.

Non-intervention, it is said, was the policy they maintained and the legacy they bequeathed to us; but is it possible that a single American can be found who believes that either of those patriots would condemn the declaration of his country's opinion upon a great question of public law because they condemned its interference with the affairs of other nations? Why, this is our affair, sir; an affair as interesting to us as to any other community on the face of the globe; one which involves the safety of independent states, and the true intent and obligation of the code that regulates their intercourse.

What did Washington say on this subject? These are his words:

"It is our true policy to steer clear of permanent alliances with any portion of the foreign world."

"Hence, therefore, it must be unwise in us to implicate ourselves by artificial ties in the ordinary vicissitudes of her [European] politics, or the ordinary circumstances or collisions of her friendships and enmities."

These sentiments speak for themselves and are commended no less by the authority that uttered them than by their own justice to the American people. Ingenuity itself cannot torture them into the service of the opposition to the present proposition, one which seeks no "alliances" and asks for no "artificial ties." It limits itself to a simple declaration of opinion.

And the authority of Mr. Jefferson has been invoked with as little reason in condemnation of this measure. "Peace," said that Patriarch of the Democratic faith, "Peace, commerce, and honest friendship with all nations; entangling alliances with none." Why, sir, there is no room for argument between the man who gives to this language of Mr. Jefferson its true and natural import and him who applies it to the assertion of a great national right. They have no common ground to stand upon. When the declaration of an important principle, common to all nations and made in connection with none, is shown to be an entangling alliance with one of them, then may this sentiment be appealed to and the people warned against its violation.

Mr. President, the wonderful advance of skill and science has brought Europe nearer to us now than was Savannah to Philadelphia at the adoption of the Constitution. And similar causes are probably destined yet more to diminish the distance; and the increase of the moral and material interchange consequent upon the progress of the age has not been less remarkable than the increase in the facilities of intercourse. We cannot be insensible to the onward march of events in the old hemisphere, nor indifferent to their operation upon the great mass of the people. Undoubtedly Europe, to some extent, has peculiar interests and a peculiar policy, with which we have no concern. Dynastic laws, the balance of power, the influence claimed by five great states—these and other maxims of policy give rise to questions with which we have no desire to intermeddle. But, besides these, there are great principles of the laws of national intercommunication often coming up for discussion and decision in Europe, and which affect the interest and the safety of all the independent states of the world. The former we may regard merely with the natural interest which is felt in passing events; but the latter we should watch with sleepless vigilance, taking care that no innovation be established in the public laws without our consent, to which we should be called upon to submit hereafter on the ground of its having been sanctioned by time and acquiescence; as the right to search our vessels would have been established had we not resisted the claim at its very inception.

Mr. President, it has often been said that we have a mission to fulfill, and so, indeed, has every nation; and the first mission of each is to conduct its own affairs honestly and fairly, for its own benefit; but after that its position and institutions may give to it peculiar influence in the prevailing moral and political controversies of the world which it is bound to exert for the welfare of all. While we disclaim any crusading spirit against the political institutions of other countries, we may well regard with deep interest the struggling efforts of the oppressed through the world, and deplore their defeat, and rejoice in their success. And can any one doubt that the evidences of sympathy which are borne to Europe from this great Republic will cheer the hearts, even when they do not aid the purposes, of the downtrodden masses to raise themselves, if not to power, at least to protection? Whatever duties may be ultimately imposed on us by that dark future which overshadows Europe, and which we cannot foresee, and ought not to undertake to define, circumstances point out our present policy, while at the same time they call upon us to exert our moral influence in support of the existing principles of public law, placed in danger not merely by the ambition but still more by the fear of powerful monarchs—the fear lest the contagion of liberty should spread over their dominions, carrying destruction to the established systems of oppression.

Our present duty and policy are to place our views upon record, thus avoiding conclusions against us and reserving all our rights and all our remedies, whatever these may be, for future consideration, when the proper exigency may arise.

SENATOR SEWARD.—If war is to follow this protest, then it must come in some way, and by the act of either ourselves or our enemy. But the protest is not a declaration, nor a menace, nor even a pledge of war in any contingency. War, then, will not come in that way, nor by or in consequence of our act. If war is nevertheless to come, it must come in retaliation of the protest, and by the act of Russia, or of Austria, or of both. Assume, now, that it shall so come, will it be just? The protest is a remonstrance addressed to the conscience of Russia, and, passing beyond her, carries an appeal to the reason and justice of mankind. As by the municipal law no remonstrance or complaint justifies a blow, so by the law of nations no remonstrance or complaint justifies war. The war then would be unjust, and so the protest would be not a cause, but a pretext. But a nation that will declare war on a pretext will either fabricate one or declare war without any.

And now, honorable Senators, I ask, if we are to shrink from this duty through fear of unjust retaliation, what duty shall we not shrink from under the same motive? And what will be the principle of our policy when thus shrinking from obligations but fear instead of duty?

And who are we, and who are Austria and Russia, that *we* should fear *them* when on the defence against an unjust war? I admit, and I hope all my countrymen will learn it without a trial, that we are not constituted for maintaining long, distant wars of conquest or of aggression. But, in a defensive war levied against us on such a pretext, the reason and the sympathies of mankind would be on our side, coöperating with our own instincts of patriotism and self-preservation. Our enemies would be powerless to harm us, and we should be unconquerable.

Why, then, I ask, shall we refrain from the protest? The answer comes up on all sides: Since, then, the measure is pacific, Russia will disregard it, and so it will be useless. Well, what if it should? It will at least be harmless. But Russia will not disregard it. It is true that we once interpleaded between the belligerents of Europe twenty-five years by protests and remonstrances in defence of our neutral rights, and vindicated them at last by resistance against one party, and open, direct war against the other. But all that is changed now. Our flag was then a stranger on the seas; our principles were then unknown. Now, both are regarded with respect and affection by the people of Europe. And that people, too, are changed. They are no longer debased and hopeless of freedom, but, on the contrary, are waiting impatiently for it, and ready to second our expressions of interest in their cause. The British nation is not without jealousy of us. Let us only speak out. Do you think that they would be silent? No, sir. And when the United States and Great Britain should once speak, the ever-fraternizing bayonets of the army of France, if need were, would open a mouth for the voice of that impulsive and generous nation. Who believes that Russia, despotic as she is, would brave the remonstrances of these three great powers, sustained as they would be by the voice of Christendom? Sir, I do not know that this protest will do Hungary or European democracy any good. It is enough for me that, like our first of orators (Mr. Webster) in a similar case, I can say, "I hope it may."

And now, sir, why must we go to war to sustain our protest? You may say, because we should be dishonored by abandoning an interest so solemnly asserted. Sir, those who oppose the protest are willing to forsake the cause of Hungary now. Will it be more dishonorable to relinquish it after an earnest effort than to abandon it without any effort at all in its behalf? Sir, if it be mere honor that is then to prick us on, let the timid give over their fears. A really great, enlightened, and Christian nation has just as much need to make war on a false point of honor as a really great, enlightened, and Christian man has need to engage in a personal contest in the same case; and that is no necessity at all. Nor shall we be reduced to the alternative of war. If Hungary shall never rise, there will be no *casus belli*. If she shall rise, we shall have right to choose the time when to recognize her as a nation. That recognition, with its political influence and commercial benefits, will be adequate to prevent or counterbalance Russian intervention. But I am answered that we shall unnecessarily offend powers whom it is unwise to provoke. I reply that it is not enough for a nation that it has no enemies. Japan and China are in that happy condition. It is necessary that a state should have some friends. To us, exemption from hatred obtained by insensibility to crime is of no value; still less is the security obtained by selfishness and isolation. Only generosity ever makes friends, and those that it does bring are grateful and enduring.

There remains the objection that flows so readily from all conservative pens and tongues on this side of the Atlantic, and still more freely from the stipendiary presses of Paris and Vienna, that a protest would be a departure from the traditional policy of our country and from the precepts of Washington. It is passing strange, sir, that Louis Napoleon and Francis Joseph should take so deep an interest in our adherence to our principles, and in our reverence of the memory of him who inculcated them, not for the immunity of tyrants, but for the security of our own welfare.

Sir, granting for a moment that Washington inculcated just such a policy as is claimed by my opponents, is it so entirely certain that it ought always and under all circumstances to be pursued? Here is a message of his in 1792 that illustrates the policy be adopted toward, not one only, but all the Barbary Powers, and it received, I think, the unanimous and favorable response of the Senate of the United States.

Here the Senator read Washington's proposition to ransom American captives in Algiers, and pay tribute to the Berber Government.

Sir, you and I and all of us would have answered in the affirmative to these questions, had we lived and occupied these places in the last century. I desire to ascertain how many votes such a treaty would receive here now? And I address myself to the honorable Senator from Rhode Island [Mr. Clarke], who moved resolutions against any departure from the policy of Washington. Would you, sir, pay a Barbary pirate $40,000 to ransom thirteen captives, and $25,000 bonus, and $25,000 annually, for exemption from his depredations. He looks dissentingly. I demand from the honorable Senator from New Jersey [Mr. Stockton], who in the triple character of Senator, Commodore, and General, presided at the Birthday Congressional Banquet in honor of Washington, and dishonor of his Hungarian disciple, Kossuth, would you, sir? No, not he. All who are in favor of such a treaty, let them say aye. What, sir, not one vote in the Senate of the United States for the continuance of what was in its time a wise and prudent as well as humane policy of Washington? No, not one. And why, sir? The answer is easy: The times have changed, and we have changed with them.

I will not venture on such a question as whether humanity and justice may not in some contingencies require that we should afford substantial aid to nations as weak as we were in our revolutionary contest.

It is clear enough, however, that we distrust our strength seldom except when such diffidence will serve as a plea for the non-performance of some obligation of justice or of humanity. But it is not necessary to press such inquiries. What is demanded here is not any part of our fifty millions of annual revenue, nor any use of our credit, nor any employment of our Army or of our Navy, but simply the exercise of our free right of speech. If we are not strong enough now to speak, when shall we be stronger? If we are never to speak out, for what were national lungs given us?

Senators and Representatives of America, if I may borrow

the tone of that sturdy republican, John Milton, I would have you consider what nation it is of which you are governors—a nation quick and vigorous of thought, free and bold in speech, prompt and resolute in action, and just and generous in purpose—a nation existing for something, and designed for something more than indifference and inertness in times of universal speculation and activity. Why else was this nation chosen, that "out of her, as out of Sinai, should be proclaimed and sounded forth the first tidings and trumpet" of political reformation to all nations? I would have you remember that the love of liberty is a public affection which this nation has deeply imbibed and has effectually diffused throughout the world; and that she cannot now suppress it, nor smother her desires to promote that glorious cause, for it is her own cause.

Let others employ themselves in devising new ligaments to bind these States together. For myself, I am content with the old ones just as I find them. I believe that the Union is founded in physical, moral, and political necessities, which demand one Government and would endure no divided States. I believe, also, that it is righteousness, not greatness, that exalteth a nation, and that it is liberty, not repose, that renders national existence worth possessing.

It has already come to this, that whenever in any country an advocate of freedom, by the changes of fortune, is driven into exile, he hastens to seek an asylum here; that whenever a hero falls in the cause of freedom on any of her battlefields, his eyes involuntarily turn toward us, and he commits that cause with a confiding trust to our sympathy and our care. Never, sir, as we value the security of our own freedom, or the welfare and happiness of mankind, or the favor of Heaven that has enabled us to protect both, let that exile be inhospitably repulsed. Never let the prayer of that dying hero fall on ears unused to hear, or spend itself upon hearts that refuse to be moved.

CHAPTER XI

"FIFTY-FOUR FORTY OR FIGHT"

[THE OREGON BOUNDARY]

Lewis F. Linn [Mo.] Introduces in Senate Bill to Assert Claims to the Territory of Oregon Against Great Britain—Debate: in Favor, Thomas H. Benton [Mo.], Levi Woodbury [N. H.]; Opposed, John C. Calhoun [S. C.], George McDuffie [S. C.]; Carried—Bill Is Reported Adversely in the House—Abortive Negotiations with the British Minister—President James K. Polk Asserts "Our Title to the Whole of Oregon" (54° 40′)—Resolutions to This Effect Are Introduced in the Senate by Edward A. Hannegan [Ind.]—Debate: in Favor, Hannegan, William Allen [O.], Lewis Cass [Mich.], Sydney Breese [Ill.]; Opposed, John C. Calhoun [S. C.], Thomas H. Benton [Mo.], John J. Crittenden [Ky.], Daniel Webster [Mass.], William L. Dayton [N. J.], William H. Haywood [N. C.]—Charles J. Ingersoll [Pa.] Introduces Resolutions in the House to Give Notice to Great Britain Terminating Joint Occupancy of Oregon—Debate: in Favor, Henry W. Hilliard [Ala.], Howell Cobb [Ga.], Stephen A. Douglas [Ill.]; Opposed, William L. Yancey [Ala.], Robert M. T. Hunter [Va.], Jefferson Davis [Miss.]—New Resolutions Are Passed Authorizing the President to Continue Negotiations—Treaty Is Signed Fixing the Boundary at 49° N. L.

WHILE a treaty, completed with Great Britain in August, 1842 (the Webster-Ashburton Treaty), had fixed the northeastern boundary of the United States, the northwestern boundary remained in dispute. Several thousand Americans had permanently settled in the Oregon region, entering chiefly into the fur trade, and there arose a strong patriotic sentiment in the Northern and Western States to secure the entire Pacific region northward to the Russian occupation (54 degrees and forty minutes north latitude).[1] They viewed with anxiety the subsequent encroachments of the Hudson Bay Company in introducing British immi-

[1] Senator William Allen [O.] coined the phrase, "Fifty-four Forty or Fight," as the slogan of those who made this demand.

grants into the region, shepherds and farmers, and erecting forts there, pushing southward as far as California, and eastward to the Rocky Mountains, as well as the decree of Parliament which extended the criminal laws of Great Britain to the very confines of Arkansas and Missouri.

As early as December 29, 1839, Lewis F. Linn (Missouri) had introduced in the Senate resolutions declaring that the title of the United States to the Territory of Oregon was indisputable and would never be abandoned; that the laws of the United States should be extended over the Territory; that regular troops should be sent there for the protection of the settlers against the Indians and any foreign force which might seize the country, and that land be freely offered to settlers. He did not press the resolutions, being dissuaded by other Congressmen who feared that the negotiations with Great Britain over the northeastern boundary would thereby be embarrassed. Therefore they did not come up for discussion until January 9, 1843.

The bill was passed on February 3 by a vote of 24 to 22. The chief speakers in its behalf were Thomas H. Benton (Missouri) and Levi Woodbury (New Hampshire). Its leading opponents were John C. Calhoun (South Carolina) and George McDuffie (South Carolina).

THE OREGON BILL

SENATE, JANUARY 9-FEBRUARY 3, 1843

SENATOR BENTON.—British interests have grown up on the Columbia; and the British Government owes protection to these interests, and will give it! This is now the language of British ministers; and this is what we have got for forty years' forbearance to assert our title! The nest-egg laid by British diplomacy has undergone incubation, and has hatched, and has produced a full-grown bird—a game cock—which has clapped his wings and crowed defiance in the face of the American eagle! and this poor eagle, if a view could be got of him as he stood during the "informal conferences" between Mr. Webster and Lord Ashburton, would be found (no doubt) to have stuck his head under his wing, and hung out the white and craven feather.

British interests have grown up on both sides of the Columbia—to the south as well as to the north of the river—and it is the intention of the British Government to protect the whole. So say Mr. Huskisson and Mr. Addington. But this is diplomacy—modern diplomacy—equivalent to finesse. The south of the Columbia has not been seized to be retained, but to be given up! The north is to be retained, for that is the commanding bank. The south is only seized to be given up as an equivalent, according to the modern system of compromising so successfully introduced in the case of Maine. Seize all! then give back half! call this a compromise! and there will be people (for the minds of men are various)—there will be people to applaud the fine arrangement, and to thank God for such a happy deliverance from war. No, sir; no. This is a joke about holding on to the south bank. The settlements made there are for surrender, not for retention. They are made there to be given up as equivalents for what is taken from us on the north; and thus settle the Columbia question according to the precedent of Maine.

But the settlements on the north bank—there protection is no joke. The British mean to hold on to them, for they command the remainder. And, after the experiment which the British have just made of our peace-loving temper, it is not to be supposed that we shall get out of this scrape without seeing the match applied to the priming, or having the cup of dishonor held to our lips until we drink it to the dregs.

SENATOR WOODBURY.—I am glad to find that there is not a single member of the Senate who seems to entertain the slightest doubt of our just title to the entire territory. All contend that our right to all we claim is indefeasible. Why, then, should there be any hesitation about exercising our ownership over the territory?

Our citizens, who have cast their fortunes in the territory, claim our protection, and it is our duty to grant it. It is the duty of the United States to protect our citizens in their lawful pursuits on every portion of our territory, no matter how remote or inconvenient from the nucleus of Government. It is the duty of Congress to extend its territorial laws for the benefit of those remotely settled citizens.

Senator Calhoun opposed the bill on the ground that in the existing "imbecile condition of the Government" it would be impolitic to risk war with so great a naval power as Great Britain over a region which it would be almost impossible for us to occupy with forces sent overland. It was because he wished to retain the Territory that he advised that events be allowed to take their natural course.

There is only one means by which it can be preserved, but that, fortunately, is the most powerful of all—*time*. *Time* is acting for us; and, if we shall have the wisdom to trust to its operation, it will assert and maintain our right with resistless force, without costing a cent of money, or a drop of blood. There is often, in the affairs of government, more efficiency and wisdom in non-action, than in action. All we want to effect our object in this case, is "a wise and masterly inactivity." Our population is rolling toward the shores of the Pacific, with an impetus greater than we realize. As the region west of Arkansas and the State of Missouri, and south of the Missouri River, is occupied by half-civilized tribes, who have their lands secured to them by treaty, the spread of population is prevented in that direction, causing this great and increasing tide to take the comparatively narrow channel to the north of that river and south of our northern boundary. Some conception may thus be formed of the strength with which the current will run in that direction, and how soon it will reach the eastern gorges of the Rocky Mountains. I say some conception; for I feel assured that the reality will outrun the anticipation.

SENATOR McDUFFIE.—What do we want with this territory? What are we to do with it? What is to be the consequence of our taking possession of it? What is the act we are called on now to do? Why, it is neither more nor less than an act of colonization, for the first time proposed since the foundation of this Government. If this were a question of gradual, and continuous, and progressive settlement—if the territory, to which our citizens are invited, were really to become a part of this Union, it would present a very different question. But, sir, does any man seriously suppose that any State which can be formed at the mouth of the Columbia River, or any of the inhabitable parts of that territory, would ever become one of the States of this Union? I have great faith in the power of the representative principle to extend the sphere of government; but I confess that, even in the most sanguine days of my youth, I never conceived the possibility of embracing within the same government people living five thousand miles apart. But, sir, the worthy Senator from New Hampshire (Mr. Woodbury) seems to have discovered a principle much more potent than the representative principle. He refers you to steam, as far more potent. I should doubt very much whether the elements, or powers, or organization of the principles of government, will ever be changed by steam. Steam! How are we to apply steam in this case? Has the Senator examined the character of the country? What is the character of the country? Why, about seven hundred miles this side of the Rocky Mountains is uninhabitable, where rain scarcely ever falls —a barren sandy soil.[1] On the other side—we have it from a very intelligent gentleman, sent to explore that country by the State Department, that there are three successive ridges of mountains extending toward the Pacific, and running nearly parallel; which mountains are totally impassable, except in certain parts, where there are gaps or depressions, to be reached only by going some hundred of miles out of the direct course. Well, now, what are we to do in such a case as this? How are you going to apply steam? Have you made anything like an estimate of the cost of a railroad running from here to the mouth of the Columbia? Why, the wealth of the Indies would be insufficient. You would have to tunnel through mountains five or six hundred miles in extent.[2] It is true, they have constructed a tunnel beneath the Thames; but at a vast expenditure of capital. With a bankrupt treasury, and a depressed and suffering people, to talk about constructing a railroad to the western shore of this continent manifests a wild spirit of adventure which I never expected to hear broached in the Senate of the United States. And is the Senate of the United States to be the last intrenchment where we are to find this wild spirit of adventure which has involved this country in ruin? I believe that the farmers, the honest cultivators of the soil, look now only to God, in His mercy, and their own labor to relieve them from the wretchedness in which the wild and visionary schemes of adventure have involved them.

The bill went to the House, where it was referred to the Committee on Foreign Relations. The committee on February 16, 1843, reported against its adoption and no action upon it was taken during the session.

[1] This region was known at the time and for many years afterward as "The Great American Desert." It was so designated in the school geographies.

[2] The Senator evidently thought that the tunneling would be lengthwise under the ridges!

DECLARATION OF PRESIDENT POLK

Early in 1844 Senator Calhoun was appointed Secretary of State by President Tyler. From July, 1844, until January, 1845, he conducted negotiations in the Oregon Territory with the British minister, Richard Pakenham, but these proved abortive, Pakenham demanding as the boundary the line of 49 degrees north latitude as far westward as the crossing of the Columbia river, and, from this point onward, the river, but agreeing to have the question arbitrated, and Calhoun, while receding from the contention that 54 degrees and 40 minutes north latitude was the proper boundary, insisting on the line of 49 degrees westward from its crossing with the Columbia river to the Pacific Ocean, and refusing to consider arbitration.

This refusal, followed, as it shortly was, by the bold declaration, in his inaugural address, of President Polk, that ''our title to the whole of Oregon'' was indisputable, and must be maintained, raised a strong feeling in Great Britain and Canada for war with the United States.

It was clearly seen that assertion of the claim of the Territory as far north as the line of Russian occupation—54 degrees and 40 minutes north latitude—would precipitate hostilities with the greatest naval power in the world, the outcome of which would probably be the loss of the territory between the mouth of the Columbia River and 49 degrees north latitude, if not of all the American possessions on the Pacific coast.

Accordingly, after consultation with Senator Thomas H. Benton, the Secretary of State, James Buchanan, proposed to the British Government that the boundary be fixed at 49 degrees. This was refused. The knowledge of the offer leaked out, and the extremists in the Democratic party were greatly incensed at this recession from the claim in the Democratic platform upon which the President had been elected, and from the declaration of his inaugural address. To appease them, Secretary Buchanan formally withdrew his offer, and in his annual message on December 2, 1845, the President again as-

serted "our title to the whole of Oregon," and also
advised that notice be given to Great Britain that the
United States would terminate the joint occupancy of
the territory agreed upon in 1827.

In the Senate on December 18 William Allen (Ohio)
introduced a resolution authorizing the President to give
such notice, and on December 30 Edward A. Hannegan
(Indiana) introduced resolutions that "the whole" of
Oregon belonged to the United States; that there was
no power in the Government to alienate any part of
the national domain, nor to transfer to another government the allegiance of its citizens, and that the surrender of Oregon in particular would be an "abandonment of the honor, character, and the best interests of
the American people." To these latter resolutions John
C. Calhoun (South Carolina) opposed others, declaring
that the President and Senate had the constitutional
power to make treaties, which included the adjustment
of contested boundaries, and accordingly that the President, in proposing the line of 49 degrees north latitude,
did not exceed his power, nor "abandon the honor, the
character, or the best interests of the American people."
In the interest of peace, Calhoun proposed resumption
of negotiations with Great Britain, and therefore a continuance of the joint occupancy of Oregon. Senators
Allen and Hannegan then urged a resolution directing
the President to give Great Britain the twelve months'
notice designated in the convention for terminating this
occupancy.

In the debate which ensued leading speakers who
demanded that there be no recession from the claim of
the whole of the territory in dispute, and who therefore
opposed Senator Calhoun's motion were Hannegan,
Allen, Lewis Cass (Michigan) and Sydney Breese
(Illinois); the speakers who were willing to compromise
on the line of 49 degrees north latitude were Calhoun,
Thomas H. Benton (Missouri), John J. Crittenden
(Kentucky), Daniel Webster (Massachusetts), William
L. Dayton (New Jersey) and William H. Haywood
(North Carolina).

THE OREGON COMPROMISE

SENATE, DECEMBER 30, 1845-MARCH 31, 1846

SENATOR HANNEGAN.—The Senator from South Carolina [Mr. Calhoun] will not deny that the whole aspect of the question has been changed since the proposition of the President, by the peremptory and almost contemptuous refusal of the British minister. If it were not so, I am a freeman as well as the President of the United States; and although I have ever been his political friend, and ever expect to be so, yet, if the President on any occasion or occasions assume a position which I can not endorse, I have the right, and will maintain it—as well here as at home—to express my sentiments without intending, desiring, or wishing to convey any censure. I represent the same people that the President does, and, as such representative, I have a right to express my views on all questions pertaining to the Government. If the adoption of my resolutions, which contain the immutable principles of truth, shall bring war on us, let war come! What American is there who, through fear of war, would hesitate to declare the truth in this Chamber?

There has been a singular course pursued on this Oregon question contrasting strangely with a precisely similar question —the annexation of Texas. Texas and Oregon were born the same instant, nursed and cradled in the same cradle—the Baltimore Convention—and they were at the same instant adopted by the democracy throughout the land. There was not a moment's hesitation, until Texas was admitted, but, the moment she was admitted, the peculiar friends of Texas turned, and were doing all they could to strangle Oregon! But the country were not blind or deaf. The people see, they comprehend, and I trust they will speak. It is a most singular state of things. We were told that we must be careful not to involve ourselves in a war with England on a question of disputed boundary. There was a question of disputed boundary between us and Mexico; but did we hear, from the same quarter, any warnings against a collision with Mexico when we were about to consummate the annexation of Texas?

Senator Hannegan closed by saying that he never would consent to a surrender of any portion of the country north of 49 degrees, nor one foot by treaty or otherwise under the line of 54 degrees 40 minutes north latitude.

SENATOR CALHOUN.—The Senator from Indiana [Mr. Hannegan] has endeavored to draw a contrast between my course upon the Texas question and his course upon this. The views which governed me upon that question govern me also upon this. I pursued in reference to Texas what I conceived to be the best course. If I acted boldly and promptly on that occasion, it was because boldness and promptness were necessary to success. It was the golden opportunity; and one year's delay would have lost Texas to us forever. If I am for more deliberate measures on this occasion, it is not because I am not a friend to Oregon. I believe that precipitancy will lose you Oregon forever—no, not forever; but it will lose you Oregon in the first struggle, and then it will require another struggle hereafter, when we become stronger, to regain it.

If you institute a comparison between Oregon and Texas, I would say that the former is as valuable to us as the latter, and I would as manfully defend it. If the Senator and myself disagree, we disagree only as to the means of securing Oregon and not as to its importance. I do not suppose that the Senator intends to reflect upon the President; but there can be no difference, as far as the principle involved in this question is concerned, between the circumstances when the proposition for a division at the forty-ninth parallel was made and now. It was as sensible then to make the offer as it would be now.

SENATOR ALLEN.—In the assertion of her claims, Great Britain has not been influenced so much by her actual right to what she claims as by her own imaginary superiority over us in strength. And this view has entered into the arguments of those among ourselves who are opposed to a proper vindication of our rights; who maintain that we ought to surrender them because we are not in a condition to resist the power of Great Britain, and because, owing to her vast superiority, she will obtain what she claims at the point of the sword. We are therefore not only compelled to receive the tone of our thoughts and feelings from her but also her mandates. All this was made well understood in England; and, in all the Parliamentary speeches, we never heard of any one who asserted that she is not able to carry her purposes through, or that her power is even likely to be weakened in a contest with our Democracy. No one there urged timid counsels in order to paralyze her arm. She tells us that she has rights in Oregon which she will cause to be respected; and that if we adopt certain measures she will consider the act as cause of war. There is no crouching there, by declarations that she is not prepared. Had it been with

Mexico instead of Great Britain that we had had to deal, we should have given this notice and been in possession of the territory fifteen years ago.

Great Britain will calculate the effect of the measure on her own interests, and, if she finds they are not likely to be benefited, she will find a way to evade a contest. She has colonies which she cannot afford to lose, while our possessions lie contiguous, and are confined to our soil. And even could she obtain Oregon, she would not be able to retain it twenty-five years before it would be reached and occupied by an advancing population which is doubling every few years. The first act of our Government, in case of war, would be to expel the British power from all her possessions on this continent. Knowing this, she will count the cost before she goes into a war. Before she could assail us, she would have to cross three thousand miles of the Atlantic. All the armed navies she could collect could not subjugate this country.

Of all the five allied Powers of Europe, England is the weakest. A single defeat ensures her fall.

During the wars of the close of the last century she was compelled to incur her heavy debt in order to pay the foreign navies which she subsidized, taxing her people to the amount of sixty-five millions of pounds annually for twelve years. And nothwithstanding she has enjoyed thirty years of peace, this enormous debt still remains unreduced, and her taxes amount now to fifty-two millions of pounds per annum—little less than when she had all the navies of Europe in her pay. She is at this moment a pauper; for in one year, when her taxes amounted to fifty-two millions, the total value of her exports reached only fifty-one millions. Yet in this condition of weakness and poverty she is held up to us as a power from which we are to turn and run. Our Government is strong enough for all the purposes of our destiny, and nothing is required but to expel the delusion which has been thrown about the public mind as to the power of Great Britain. All we have to do is, to do as her statesmen do—not to depreciate our own power while we exaggerate hers.

We have existed more than half a century, unstained by the blood of a single individual for political offences. With twenty millions of people, powerful enough to do wrong, and five thousand prisons, there is not one of these twenty millions incarcerated in one of these prisons on any political charge. A short time since there was one imprisoned for a political offence,[1] but so strong was the force of public sympathy in his

[1] William Lloyd Garrison.

favor that even they who imprisoned him opened the prison
doors and invited and urged and coaxed him to accept of his
liberty. Throughout the remoter sections of our country, a
magistrate is mounted on his horse, travels to a distant court-
house, holds his court, pronounces judgment, and secures the
execution without the aid of a sword or even a cudgel. And
this because the hearts of the people vindicate the supremacy of
the laws. It is thus that we possess all the elements of the
strongest government by which mankind was ever banded together. We then can have no fears of Great Britain.

All this arises from the fact that, instead of being in the
rear of our institutions, the people are always in advance of
those who are in power. The people have no fears of Great
Britain; and if in our national councils is to be found something like timidity, it is owing to the fact that delegated power
is always more fearful of responsibility than that which is primitive. It is the policy of Great Britain boldly to assert a claim,
and then, by giving us the alternative of yielding or fighting,
to obtain the surrender of a part of it. It is our duty to exhibit
no symptoms of quailing to Great Britain, but to treat her as
she has treated us. When she talks of power, let us talk back to
her of power. When she strips for a fight, let us strip. With
the bravest people in the world, what cause have we for fear?
Let this resolution pass—and I know this body well enough to
be sure that it will pass easily, and that all the other measures
to which it will lead will also pass—and we shall hear no more
of war.

Senator Benton spoke against the continuance of the
joint-use convention.

Abram and Lot, although they were brethren, and sent to
the chosen spot by the Deity himself, could not live together
in the wilderness without strife. They had to separate to
avoid contention. It must be so with the British and Americans on the Columbia, and worse. The two people can neither
live together without law and government nor with double
law and government. The condition is impossible. Collisions,
violence, bloodshed must ensue if we leave the people as they
are. It is our duty to prevent these mischiefs, and we become
responsible for all that may happen if we do not prevent them.

The first step is to terminate the joint convention, and to
recover our right to the complete possession of the Columbia
under the Ghent treaty. We have a right to the possession

of that river and its valley under the treaty of Ghent. We hold a treaty with the British for our right of possession, and we have the amplest admission of a British minister, Lord Castlereagh, of our right to be the party in possession while treating of the title, and until the title is decided. Let us resume these great rights, so improvidently lost for thirty years by the delusive convention of 1818. The notice is necessary to this resumption, and I rejoice that the moment is at hand for giving it.

The notice is a peace measure, and can operate no way but beneficially. It will give us the immediate and exclusive possession of one-half the contested country, with the right of possession until the title to the whole is decided. This will separate the people, and keep peace among them, and will bring to conclusion this aged and barren negotiation which has produced no fruit in thirty years. It will change the condition of parties and make the British themselves desire negotiation. As long as things remain as they are, they are content. They have the exclusive possession of three-fourths of the country, and the joint use of the remaining fourth: this is all they ask, and more than they ask, in the way of territory. They have the free use of the river and its harbor, for the export of their furs and the importation of goods from Europe and Asia, without paying of duties: this is all they could ask in the way of navigation. They have law for the government of their people: we have none. And, more than all, they have an excuse for not complying with the Ghent treaty—an excuse which must fail them as soon as the notice takes effect, and leave them under the necessity of evacuating the country or violating a treaty for the execution of which we hold their order. As things are, the British are content. They want no change. The joint convention, while it stands, gives them all they ask, and more too. They fear its termination: they fear the notice! But they are not going to make war for the notice. It will make them treat, not fight.

SENATOR CRITTENDEN.—They who should involve this country in a needless war will bear responsibility heavy enough to sink a navy, sir. Let them be warned. To defend the rights of their country is one great duty. To protect the interests of their country is their duty; and of those interests peace is the greatest and mightiest of all. These duties are not inconsistent. It is no vaunting spirit that is to be acted on here. No fanaticism in politics must be suffered to guide the counsels of a great nation upon so solemn and serious a question. Considerations of a much more profound, of a higher and nobler character should influence those who are intrusted with a nation's destiny. No hasty conclusions between individual negotiators; no little pouting and fretting, or strutting upon the stage, can be any justification to the American people, or before the world at large, that out of these cabinet squabbles or diplomatic quarrels two nations and the world shall be set to war and to cut each other's throats. A great majority of the Senate is anxious —we are all anxious for peace. A majority is decidedly in favor of preserving the peace of the country honorably, and of settling this question peaceably and honorably, by compromise, negotiation, arbitration, or by some other mode known and recognized among nations as a suitable and proper and honorable mode of settling national questions.

SENATOR WEBSTER.—The President can expect nothing but a continuance of this dispute or its settlement by negotiation. I am bound to suppose that he expects its settlement by negotiation. What terms of negotiation? What basis of negotiation? What grounds of negotiation? Every thing that we hear from the Executive department is "the whole or none"; and yet negotiation! Sir, it is in vain to conceal from ourselves, from the country, or from the world, the gross inconsistency of this course of conduct. I say I do not understand the position in which the Executive Government has placed itself: in favor of negotiation all the time; but all the time refusing to take any thing less than the whole! What consideration—what compromise—what basis—what grounds, therefore, for negotiation? If the Government of the United States has made up its mind—I speak of the Executive Government—that, so far as it is concerned, it will not treat for anything less than the whole of Oregon, then it should say so, and throw itself on the two Houses of Congress, and on the country.

If we will not recede, and England will not give up the whole of her claims, what is more natural than that war is likely to happen?

I am desirous of expressing my judgment on this subject, whenever I can do so without embarrassing the Administration. If negotiations be pending, I wish to hold my tongue. It shall be blistered before I would say anything derogatory to the title of the United States while the Government of the United States was engaged in negotiating for that territory on the strength of our title. Gentlemen see the embarrassment in which we stand. I will aid the Administration in all honorable efforts to obtain all that belongs to us, and all that we can rightfully and honorably acquire with all my heart—with all my heart. But, then, as a citizen of the country, I claim a right to know something of the views, purposes, expectations, and objects of the Administration. I cannot reconcile myself to be much longer kept in a posture of things in which no preparations are made to defend the country—in which negotiation is held out every day as that course of proceeding which is expected to bring the question to a settlement, and to settle the question by England giving up the whole matter in dispute. In my opinion, it is not the judgment of this country that, at the hazard of a war, we shall now reject as no longer proper for our consideration propositions made and repeated twenty years ago. Compromise I can understand—arbitration I can comprehend—but negotiation, with a resolution to take and not to give—negotiation, with a resolution not to settle unless we obtain the whole of our demands, is what I do not comprehend in diplomacy or matters of government.

Senator Cass opposed reopening negotiations with Great Britain.

Mr. President, what right have you to suppose that the British government, under any circumstances, will be influenced in their conduct by your offer to compromise? I do not say they will not; but, without retracing their steps before the world, without gainsaying much they have said, without relinquishing much that they have claimed, without abandoning much that they have demanded, without retracing their steps before the world, and doing what a proud nation does with great reluctance, I cannot see how the difficulty is to be avoided.

Senator Breese belittled the power of Great Britain and prophesied that in the event of war with her our damage would be limited to the loss of a few merchant ships.

The Senator from New Jersey replied to him:

SENATOR DAYTON.—The Senator from Illinois [Mr. Breese] takes no account of the oceans of blood to be spilled in case of a war in this controversy; he takes no account of the wretchedness in every form which is to tread in the track of this war; he makes no account of the taxes that will harass the people; he forgets the fact that war has retrograded the position of the world; that it would stop at one blow all our internal improvements; diminish the wealth and cripple the resources of the country; he forgets that it is peace that makes our railroads, peoples our hill-sides, and plows our prairies. He takes no account of all this. He thinks, upon a point like this, when all are united and so very desirous for 54° 40', if we only wake up we will astonish ourselves! Why, if such language as this were to come from some persons who stood backside of the Allegheny mountains, I should think it was irony—the very bitterness of irony; but coming from my friend from Illinois, distinguished for his courtesy, I know that it is nothing but—54° 40'.[1]

I cannot but feel that all this argument in reference to the relative power of our adversary, rating or berating her, is in very questionable taste in existing circumstances. If we are forced to touch her shield with the point of the lance, let us do it with the chivalrous feeling and dignity of a high-toned nation. Then let each wheel into position, and God defend the right. I am willing to go to the American people on principles of compromise. I am persuaded that the people will sustain the man and the Administration that settle this question on that basis. It is a common notion that the war party of this country must be the popular party of the country. I do not believe it. It is an error; and it is an error which tends to produce the very mischief that would have no existence without it. There is always to be found a class of men who prefer arranging themselves with that party which is supposed to be a popular party in the country. Now it would be a great public benefit to explode the error that a war party would be popular in all circumstances. Heretofore our wars have been popular because they have been wars for great principles, and not wars for mere property. The Revolutionary War, I need not say, was not a war about three cents on a pound of tea. It involved the rights of man—the great principles of free government. The late war was not a war about property; it was about principles all over—the freedom of the seas—the honor of our flag. Like causes will produce like effects; and, in the same, or like, circumstances, war would be popular again. But think you that a war about the pine logs of Maine would have been a popular war? Think you that a war about Oregon, or rather a part of Oregon above 49°, would be a popular war? It might be so at the beginning with certain classes; but the brunt of the war —the taxes to carry it on—would fall upon a different class of men altogether—on honorable, prudent, thinking men; on your merchants and mechanics. These are the men who would be nec-

---

[1] In other words, *buncombe!*

essarily compelled to bear the brunt of the war. As long as your war is a war of principles these men will stand by you; as soon as it becomes simply a war of property they will count the cost.

The intelligence, the prudence, the thought of this country must govern the country at last. Unless it be so, your institutions, which place the power in the hands of the people are an empty name. Public men are sometimes too apt to distrust the capacity of the people to govern themselves; they are too apt to draw back from the control of public opinion. But we need never despair of the people, when a man can stand on this floor and speak in a voice that shall reach every hamlet beyond the mountains—never, never. Let the public men of this country, of both sides of this Chamber, stand up to their responsibilities and the people will stand by them. Popular sentiment is not always right. The needle itself is not forever constant to the pole. But the hidden influence is there. Remove extraneous and disturbing causes—give the public mind fair play; it may vibrate for a time, but at last it settles—tremulously perhaps, but faithfully—to the north. Let the public men of this country who believe that a war for 54° 40′ would be wrong but do their duty, neither the present Administration nor any other Administration dare involve the country in such a war. If they do, whatever may be their purity, their patriotism, a political blunder of that magnitude would inevitably bring any Administration, and all its aiders and abettors, to the block.

SENATOR HAYWOOD.—This question of Oregon had been turned into a party question, for the purpose of president-making. I repudiate any submission to the commands of factious meetings, got up by demagogues, for the purpose of dictating to the Senate how to make a treaty. I do not regard such proceedings as indicative of that true Democracy, which, like a potato, grew at the root, and did not, like the spurious Democracy, show itself from the blossom. The creed of the Baltimore convention directs the party to reannex Texas and to reoccupy Oregon. Texas has been reannexed, and now we are to go for the reoccupation of Oregon. Now, Old Oregon, embracing all the territory on which American foot ever trod, comprised merely the valley of Willamette, which did not extend above 49°; and, consequently, this portion was all which could be contemplated in the expression "reoccupation," as it would involve an absurdity to speak of reoccupying what we had never occupied.

Senator Hannegan denied that the resolution of the Baltimore convention referred merely to "Old Oregon," and asserted that, by the expression "the whole of Oregon," they claimed the entire territory in dispute.

The Democratic party is thus bound to the whole of Oregon —every foot of it; and let the Senator rise in his place who will tell me in what quarter of this Union—in what assembly of Democrats in this Union, pending the Presidential election, the names of Texas and Oregon did not fly together, side by side, on the Democratic banners. Everywhere they were twins— everywhere they were united. "Texas and Oregon" cannot be divided; they dwell together in the American heart. Even in Texas I have been told the flag of the lone star has inscribed on it the name of Oregon. Then it was all Oregon. Now when you have got Texas, it means just so much of Oregon as you, in your kindness and condescension, think proper to give us. You little know us if you think the mighty West will be trodden on in this way. Let gentlemen look at their own recorded votes in favor of taking up the Oregon bill at the close of the last session, and then let them look at the language of that bill and see if it did not propose to take possession of Oregon up to 54° 40', after giving unqualified notice to Great Britain that the convention must cease.

The Senator from North Carolina [Mr. Haywood], in his defence of the President, put language into his mouth which I undertake to say the President will repudiate, and I am not the President's champion. I would not be the champion of power. I defend the right, and the right only. But, for the President, I deny the intentions which the Senator from North Carolina attributes to him—intentions which, if really entertained by him, would make him an infamous man—aye, an infamous man. He (Mr. Haywood) told the Senate yesterday— unless I grossly misunderstood him, along with several friends around me—"that the President had occasionally stickings-in, parenthetically, to gratify—what?—the ultraisms of the country and of party; while he reposed in the White House with no intentions of carrying out these parenthetical stickings-in." In plain words, he represents the President as parenthetically sticking in a few hollow and false words to cajole the "ultraisms of the country." What is this, need I ask, but charging upon the President conduct the most vile and infamous? If this allegation be true, these intentions of the President must sooner or later come to light, and when brought to light, what must follow but irretrievable disgrace? So long as one human eye remains, to linger on the page of history, the story of his abasement will be read, sending him and his name together to an infamy so profound, a damnation so deep, that the hand of resurrection will never be able to drag him forth. He who is the traitor to his country can never have forgiveness of God, and cannot ask mercy of man.

The last steamer from Europe, it is said, puts this question in such a position that for Oregon we can get free trade. Free trade I love dearly; but never will it be bought by me by the territory of my country. He who would entertain such an idea is a traitor to his country. I speak for myself, and my own section of the country. Free trade for a surrender of the ports and harbors on the Pacific? Never, sir; never. Whence this movement for free trade on the part of England? Does not everyone know that she has been driven into this course by the outcries of starving millions? that she has been forced into this policy by the land owners, to save their lives from the knife of the midnight assassin, and their palaces from the torch of the prowling incendiary? But the West is to be provided for; it is to have a new and most profitable market. Some of us know that from the Baltic England would get her wheat long before we could send a ton into her market. I advert to this simply because I do not know that I shall have another opportunity to do so. I have only to add that, so far as the whole tone, spirit, and meaning of the remarks of the Senator from North Carolina are concerned, if they speak the language of James K. Polk, James K. Polk has spoken words of falsehood, and with the tongue of a serpent.

SENATOR CALHOUN.—Peace is preëminently our policy. There are nations in the world who may resort to war for the settlement of their differences, and still grow great; but that nation is not ours. Providence has cast our happy inheritance where its frontier extends for twenty-three degrees of latitude along the Atlantic coast. It has given us a land which in natural advantages is perhaps unequaled by any other. Abundant in all resources; excellent in climate; fertile and exuberant in soil; capable of sustaining, in the plentiful enjoyment of all the necessaries of life, a population of two hundred millions of souls. Our great mission as a people is to occupy this vast domain—there to fulfil the primeval command to increase and multiply, and replenish the land with an industrious and virtuous population; to level the forests, and let in upon their solitude the light of day; to clear the swamps and morasses and redeem them to the plow and sickle; to spread over hill and dale the echoes of human labor and human happiness and contentment; to fill the land with cities, and towns, and villages; to unite its opposite extremities by turnpikes and railroads, to scoop out canals for the transmission of its products, and open rivers for its internal trade. War can only impede the fulfillment of this high mission of Heaven; it absorbs the wealth and diverts the energy which might be so much better devoted to the improvement of our country. All we want is peace—established peace; and then time, under the guidance of a wise and cautious policy, will soon effect for us all the rest.

I say time will do it, under the influence of a wise and masterly inactivity—a phrase than which none other has been less understood or more grossly misrepresented. By some who should have known better it has been construed to mean inaction. But mere inertness and what is meant by a wise inactivity are things wide apart as the poles. The one is the offspring of ignorance and of indolence; the other is the result of the profoundest wisdom—a wisdom which looks into the nature and bearing of things; which sees how conspiring causes work out their effects, and shape and change the condition of man. Where we find that natural causes will of themselves work out our good, our wisdom is to let them work; and all our task is to remove impediments. In the present case, one of the greatest of these impediments is found in our impatience.

He who cannot understand the difference between an inactivity like this and mere stupid inaction and the doing of nothing is as yet but in the horn book of political science. Yes, time—ever-laboring time—will effect everything for us. Our population is now increasing at the annual average of six hundred thousand. Let the next twenty-five years elapse, and our average increase will have reached a million a year, and, before many of the younger Senators here shall have become as gray-headed as I am, we shall count a population of forty-five millions. Before that day, it will have spread from ocean to ocean. The coasts of the Pacific will then be as densely populated and as thickly settled with villages and towns as the coast of the Atlantic is now. In another generation we shall have reached eighty millions of people, and, if we can preserve peace, who shall set bounds to our prosperity, or our success? With one foot planted on the Atlantic and the other on the Pacific, we shall occupy a position between the two old continents of the world—a position eminently calculated to secure to us the commerce and the influence of both. If we abide by the counsels of common sense—if we succeed in preserving our constitutional liberty, we shall then exhibit a spectacle such as the world never saw. I know that this one great mission is encompassed with difficulties; but such is the inherent energy of our political system and such its expansive capability that it may be made to govern the widest space. If by war we become great, we cannot be free; if we will be both great and free, our policy is peace.

PRESIDENT (C)ASS BEGINNING OPERATIONS, LOSING NO TIME
[General Taylor on left and General Scott on right.]
From the collection of the New York Historical Society

SENATOR CASS.—I am a firm believer in the sure and mighty efficacy of the great agent Time, but I believe that Great Britain will not herself permit this state of things to continue. ''Whoever has Oregon will command the North Pacific'' is the language which has been used in England; and is it to be expected that she will quietly witness the occupation of that country by a dense population of American citizens? If she will ever abandon the country, she will do it now, when there can be no dishonor in giving it up; not when there has grown up there a great power capable of resisting her.

The evils of war have, in my opinion, been too gloomily represented by the Senator from South Carolina. Admitting that a war of ten—of five—years will be disastrous to us; it cannot exist without bringing into collision the great questions of our day—the right to govern and to obey. But, if it were to be

even more disastrous than he represented, was it right for the
Senator to make the prediction that such a war would produce
the overthrow of this Government? In that view, a war would
at once be a signal of destruction, and we have nothing left but,
when smitten on the one cheek, to turn the other. I believe
that, although we should suffer severely, we should come out
from another conflict with many glorious wreaths on our brows.

Many a raven has croaked in the last war. Many a Cas-
sandra has foretold the ruin of the country. But nothing has
come of their forebodings. I regard our country as the strongest for good, and the weakest for evil, in the world. Resting on
public opinion, it is the only Government in which there can be
no revolution.

Similar resolutions to those of Senator Allen were
introduced in the House by Charles J. Ingersoll (Pennsylvania) on January 5, 1846, who on February 9 also
introduced a joint resolution of the House and Senate
to give Great Britain notice of the termination of the
convention. The joint resolution passed on the same
day by a vote of 163 to 54. It passed the Senate on
March 31 by a vote of 40 to 14.

THE OREGON COMPROMISE

HOUSE OF REPRESENTATIVES, JANUARY 5-FEBRUARY 9, 1846

Speakers in the House in favor of insisting on "the
whole of Oregon" were Henry W. Hilliard (Alabama),
Howell Cobb (Georgia), Stephen A. Douglas (Illinois);
those opposed to it were William L. Yancey (Alabama),
Robert M. T. Hunter (Virginia) and Jefferson Davis
(Mississippi).

MR. HILLIARD.—England and the United States are the only
competitors for the trade of Southern China. England imports
every year four hundred and fifty thousand chests of tea, while
we import two hundred thousand, besides muslins and silks and
other commodities of great value. In this gainful traffic, England regards us as a rival power, and she is by no means disposed to give it up. The coast of Oregon fronts that of China,
and presents great facilities for carrying on this important
branch of our commerce. Fully to avail ourselves, however, of
these advantages, we ought to connect Oregon with the State

of Missouri by the construction of a railroad. This is not so wild and visionary a scheme as at the first view some gentlemen might be disposed to consider it. Let them reflect that it is but fifteen years since Mr. Huskisson lost his life between Liverpool and Manchester, in an experimental trip over the first railroad ever constructed in England. And what was she doing in that system now? And then look on the Continent, and see one continuous line of railroad, extending twenty-seven hundred miles, entirely across Europe, from Odessa to Bremen, while another line extends from the Adriatic for near a thousand miles. And yet gentlemen stand here and look aghast when anyone speaks of a railroad across our continent, as if it were something wondrous and altogether unheard of before.

Should such a road be constructed, it will become the great highway of the world; we shall before long monopolize the trade of the eastern coasts of Asia. At present the shortest possible voyage from London to Canton occupies seventy days; but by such a railroad a traveler might pass from London to Canton in forty days. There is no wildness, no extravagance in the idea; but it is a matter of sober sense and plain calculation. What a magnificent idea does it present to the mind, and who could calculate the results to which it would lead? With a route so short and so direct as this, may we not reasonably hope, in a great measure, to command both the trade and the travel of the world? Engrafted on this plan, and as its natural adjunct is the extension of a magnetic telegraph, which should follow the course of the road; unite the two, and where is the imagination which can grasp the consequences?

When Oregon shall be fully in our possession, when we shall have established a profitable trade with China through her ports, when our sails traverse the Pacific as they now cross the Atlantic, and all the countless consequences of such a state of things begin to flow in upon us, then will be fulfilled that vision which wrapt and filled the mind of Nuñez as he gazed over the placid waves of the Pacific.

MR. YANCEY.—We are now on the very portals of success in carrying out those noble principles of government which our fathers bequeathed to us, and which, if once wholly in operation, will do more than anything else to advance the cause of liberty and happiness. We have just purged the old Republican party of that system of bastard Republicanism which the war of 1812 bequeathed to the country, and have infused into it a new life and energy. We are on the point, too, of purchasing the magnificent territory of California, which, with Oregon, would.

give us a breadth of Pacific coast suited to the grandeur and commercial importance of our Republic.

All this would be blighted by war. California would be lost to us; Oregon would be lost to us. A debt of five hundred millions would be imposed upon the country. The paper system, in its worst form, will necessarily have been imposed upon us. The pension list—that spring of life and immortality to patriotic valor—would be almost indefinitely increased. The Government will have become centralized; its checks weakened; its administration federalized in all its tendencies. The fabric of State rights will have been swept away, and remain only as a glorious dream; and a strong military bias will have been given to the future career of our country, which, while it may be splendid in appearance, will bear within itself the certain elements of destruction.

I have endeavored, Mr. Chairman, to demonstrate that giving to England notice that we design to take exclusive possession of Oregon will produce a war; that war will either terminate in the loss of Oregon or in effecting nothing toward perfecting possession in us; that England will not give the notice, and that neither the honor nor the wants of the country require us to do so.

I now propose to show, sir, that a system of peaceful measures will tend much more effectually to give us "all of Oregon" than warlike movements will.

I am willing to raise mounted regiments sufficient to protect emigration to Oregon over our vast Western plains.

I am ready to build such a station at the South Pass as will enable the emigrants, as they reach a point from which they can look upon the vast Atlantic slope on the one hand, and that of the Pacific on the other, to recruit and refit there.

I am ready to cover our people there with the ægis of our laws to the extent that England has protected her subjects.

I am ready to offer such other and more tempting inducements to its settlement as gentlemen may devise, in order that, in five years' time, one hundred thousand men may be thrown in the vales and amidst the hills of this disputed land.

It would then be a part and parcel of our Union. As such, it never could be conquered. I sincerely believe what was the wish at the time of Lord Castlereagh, expressed twenty years ago to our minister—"Why are you Americans so anxious to push this negotiation? In a short time you would conquer Oregon in your bed-chambers." And most assuredly this will not be deemed treason in me, if I say that such a mode of perfecting possession of that disputed land is far preferable to any more bloody issue.

I would go a step further than the notice, and extend the protection of our laws over our citizens in Oregon. If we do not, we shall fall short of our duty. After doing this, I would go still further, and create those bands of iron which were to bind indissolubly together in one union the people of the Atlantic and the people of the Pacific. I would go for a railroad across the Rocky Mountains—for annihilating time and space between us and the inhabitants of the Pacific coast. In a military point of view, this railroad will be necessary. We shall be obliged, for the protection and defence of the country, to establish this mode of communication. While it will afford military protection for the defence of the country, it will be the means of creating a vast trade between the Eastern and Western portions of the continent. The immediate consequence of such a trade will be to open a traffic in our manufactures with the people of the East Indies; next, we shall be able to drive out all competition on the part of the British fabrics in that lucrative and important trade. We will, by means of this overland communication, be soon able to create immense commercial depots on the coast of the Pacific. We can make voyages to the East Indies in half the time that Great Britain can. Our manufactures will thus compete in that important and increasing market with those of Great Britain, and, indeed, drive out all competition; and thus they will become established on a firm foundation, without the aid of a black tariff to maintain them. I have always opposed internal improvements by the general Government; but I would adopt this improvement as a military work—one necessary for the public defence, though it would be used for civil and commercial purposes.

MR. DOUGLAS (chairman of the Committee on Territories). —We propose, on the part of the United States, to give notice for the termination of that treaty of 1827 which continued in force the convention of 1818; and we are met by the declaration that this notice is a hostile movement—that it is a war measure—that it is equivalent to a declaration of war by this country against Great Britain; and hence we are called upon to pause and reflect before we make this movement, which may bring the thunders of the British fleet and of the British army to our shores; and appeals are made to our fears in order to deter us from adopting this measure. Sir, I know not whether the giving this notice and the annulment of the treaty may lead to war or not; I know not whether war will be the result. But, sir, there is one thing which I do know—and a thing which is far more important in the decision of this question than the other—and that one thing is this: that the giving of this notice will afford no just cause of war. It is immaterial with reference to influencing our decision of this question whether war is to be the consequence or not; but it *is* important for us to inquire whether the act we are about to perform will give good ground of offence—just cause of war. If it will, we ought to pause and consider well before we proceed. But if it give no just cause of war, it is no argument that Great Britain will choose to *make* it a cause of war.

If gentlemen will reflect a moment on the history of this question, they will find that, at the breaking out of the late war, the valley of the Columbia river was in the possession of citizens of the United States; that, during that war, it was captured by Great Britain; and that by the treaty of peace it was provided that all countries captured by Great Britain should be restored to us. I hold in my hand the first article of the treaty of Ghent. In it, it was agreed that "all territory, places, and possessions, whatsoever, taken by either party from the other during the war, or which may be taken after the signing the treaty, excepting only the islands hereinafter mentioned [in the Bay of Fundy], shall be restored without delay."

The treaty of peace then provided for the restoration of all places, possessions, or territories captured by either party. Sir, as quick as that treaty was ratified and published to the world, the American Government demanded of Great Britain the restoration of the valley of the Columbia river in pursuance of the treaty. What did Great Britain do? She objected; she set up a claim to that country; she said it was a part of the British empire. But, sir, you find by examining the negotiation at that time that, notwithstanding all her objections, when Mr. Rush replied to them, that by the treaty we were entitled to the full possession, or repossession (in his own language), she admitted that right, and she acknowledged that the United States under the treaty of Ghent were entitled to the actual, the full repossession of the valley of the Columbia, and that we had the right to remain in possession while negotiating of the title.

Then, Great Britain, in pursuance of that treaty, did surrender the settlement of Fort George in the Columbia valley. That settlement was not merely a fort; not merely a fort was surrendered, but the settlement comprising Astoria and several other posts, and that settlement commanding the whole valley of the Columbia river. It was, then, the valley of the Columbia that was surrendered by the British Government, which government then acknowledged the right of the American Government "to be reinstated, and to be the party in possession while treating on the question of title."

That was the relative position of the two parties prior to entering into the treaty of joint occupation—the United States in possession, Great Britain setting up a claim, but acknowledging our right to the possession while adjudicating the claims of the respective parties. That would have been our right had it not been for that treaty. That treaty suspends that right; but it provides that nothing in it shall be construed to impair or affect the rights of either party. Hence, if you terminate the treaty, if you annul the treaty, the right of the United States to exclusive possession under the treaty of Ghent is revived, and Great Britain cannot—dare not—resist the restitution of the Columbia valley. It is no cause of war—no war movement. It is carrying into effect our treaty stipulations; and the effect of giving this notice will be to suspend the joint occupancy, to restore possession to us; and, when in possession, we will be ready to treat upon the title, and not till then. Is it, then, a matter of no consequence which party is in possession while treating upon the title? Carry on the negotiation now, leave the treaty of joint occupation in force, and Great Britain is the party in possession; but give this notice, terminate the treaty, and the United States will be the party in possession. But gentlemen may say that Great Britain will never acknowledge this exclusive right of the United States to the possession of the valley of the Columbia before the question is settled. In reply to this, I say that Great Britain has acknowledged that right; and that she has not only acknowledged it in words, but by a solemn act that must stand prominent in the history of that government; so long as that history shall exist, she has estopped herself from denying our right to the possession. She has once acknowledged it, and has once restored possession under that acknowledgment. Can she refuse again to make a similar restoration when the parties in respect of their rights are similarly situated? If she does refuse to make that restoration when the notice shall have been given and shall have expired, she will have to violate her solemn treaty stipulations; she will become the aggressor; she will be violating her plighted faith in the eyes of the civilized world; and she dare not take the responsibility of such an act of perfidy and bad faith after she herself has once acknowledged her obligations by performing the same act of surrender.

Gentlemen who oppose giving the notice say that they are

for getting possession. But how getting possession? Why, they are for continuing the treaty of joint occupation in force, and then for stealing possession in violation of that treaty of joint occupation. Yes; they are for adopting the high, the chivalrous course of stealing into that country under a treaty of joint occupation, and then seizing it in violation of the treaty itself. Will that not lead to war? Is that the peaceful remedy? Will not that wound the pride of the British Government? Sir, I aver that the attempt to carry that policy out leads inevitably to war; and not only to war, but it puts us on the wrong side. It convicts our Government of an act of duplicity and perfidy. It arrays the whole civilized world against us, and renders us subject to the charge that we are faithless and dishonorable. But if we rely on the treaty stipulations of the country—if we stand high on our undeniable rights, and give the notice according to the treaty, and demand possession under the treaty of Ghent, and insist upon it—if we require the surrender, as we have done once before—then, sir, we get peaceful possession of that country; and, when in peaceful possession, we can then stand on high ground and say to Great Britain: "Certainly we deprecate war; we are ready to negotiate, and are willing you should take your own time to bring that negotiation to a determination. You may do it with all the care, with all the deliberation you may desire; and you can take your own time to terminate it." But, in the mean time, we are in possession, with the acknowledged right of possession, until we arrive at an amicable adjustment.

For one, I never will be satisfied with the valley of the Columbia, nor with 49°, nor with 54° 40'; nor will I be, while Great Britain shall hold possession of one acre on the northwest coast of America. And, sir, I will never agree to any arrangement that shall recognize her right to one inch of soil upon the northwest coast; and for this simple reason: Great Britain never did own, she never did have a valid title to, one inch of that country. The question was only one of dispute between Russia, Spain, and the United States. England never had a title to any part of the country. Our Government has always held that England had no title to it. In 1826 Mr. Clay, in his dispatches to Mr. Gallatin, said: "It is not conceived that the British Government can make out even a colorable title to any part of the northwest coast."

Mr. Cobb.—Mr. Chairman, I am not prepared to go to the full extent with some who declare that the inevitable result of the passage of this notice will be to involve this country in a bloody and destructive war. Nor am I prepared, on the other hand, to go with those who fearlessly assert that there is no danger to result from our action in reference to Oregon. I plant myself on this ground that the prosecution of the just rights of my Government is the course called for by the national faith and honor of my country. If peace be the result, I shall gladly welcome it. If war be the consequence, we must meet it. It is a crisis not to be avoided, not to be evaded, but to be met with boldness, firmness, and decision. When we have discharged our duties, then, sir, it will be for another department of our Government, and for the government with whom we are in collision upon this subject, to do what they may conceive to be their duty. That we should suffer from a war I do not pretend to deny; that we shall lose the Oregon Territory by resorting to war, I utterly but respectfully repudiate the idea. Whenever this Government shall be engaged in a conflict of this kind with the British Government or with any other government on earth, peace will never be declared upon terms leaving one foot of territory which has ever been consecrated to American freedom and American principles afterward to be profaned by monarchical or despotic principles. No; Canada may be acquired; I do not dispute that position of gentlemen who have argued this proposition before the House; but that Oregon will ever be abandoned peacefully, or in the struggle of war, my mind has never been brought to that conclusion, nor will it be. Sir, upon this day, this memorable, glorious 8th of January,[1] let it not be said by American statesmen, in an American Congress, that this Government can be injured, can be deprived, can be weakened in her just and unquestionable rights by a conflict with Great Britain, or with any other government. If war come, I venture the prediction that when it terminates we will have the consolation of knowing that not a British flag floats on an American breeze; that not a British subject treads on American soil. There is where war ought to terminate, if come it must; there is where I believe and trust in Heaven it will terminate.

MR. HUNTER.—Mr. Chairman, I appeal to all candid and reflecting men from the West—to those who go for Oregon and the whole of Oregon—to those who might desire war for Oregon, but who do not desire Oregon for war—I appeal to these men to let this controversy remain as it is. Let us not renew the negotiation; make no more offers to Great Britain; but let us trust to the process of colonization now so rapidly in prog-

[1] The anniversary of the Battle of New Orleans.

ress, and we shall quietly, peaceably, and certainly obtain the whole of what we claim. I care not how glorious the war may be, it would be better to avoid it; for it is in this way alone that we may reasonably hope to obtain what gentlemen so ardently desire—"the whole of Oregon."

Sir, the making of any treaty fixing a boundary would be a palpable violation of the very principle the President has put forth in his message. Bearing this point in mind, gentlemen will easily understand the meaning of the President in all his recommendations—when he said that no compromise of this question could be made which the United States ought to accept —when he said that he reasserted our claim to the whole continent, and maintained it by irrefragable facts and arguments— when he said that the notice must be given and the exclusive possession regained—when he said our laws must be extended there—when he said that at the end of the year the time would have arrived when we must either maintain our claim or abandon the whole of it.

But gentlemen say we must not assert this broad doctrine— this principle of American independence of all European crowns —because they say it will lead to war. Well, sir, I know not nor care whether it will produce war or not; although I am not for war, I prefer war to the abandonment of duty and honor. Did our forefathers abandon their resistance to the Stamp Act because it would lead to war? There was a panic party in the country then as now—a peace party; but the patriots did not abandon their resistance. They stopped only to inquire as to the question of right: "Does our duty to ourselves and to our country require us to do it? and, if so, we will do it at the hazard of life, property, and sacred honor." That was the principle that animated them.

Sir, at a later period the States of this country did not abandon the embargo because it would lead to war. They did not relinquish their opposition to the impressment of American seamen because it would lead to war. At a later date they did not falter on the French indemnity because it would lead to war; nor upon the right of search, nor at a still later day on the Texas annexation. Sir, the war argument, the war panic— that stereotyped argument of all men that predicate their action upon the timidity of the people—their war argument was used then as it is now. The only question, then, for us to determine is, as our forefathers did, Is this policy right, Have we the right to maintain it? If we have the right, it is our duty to maintain it at the hazard of war: First, sir, in demanding and obtaining exclusive possession of the valley of the Columbia river, as a peace measure under the treaty of Ghent; second, in refraining from all and any negotiation about title until our possession shall be restored; and, thirdly, in maintaining this position of undying, unyielding opposition to any future European colonization on the American continent. Do this firmly, boldly, unitedly, and let the consequences, sir, take care of themselves.

MR. DAVIS.—It is as the representative of a high-spirited and patriotic people that I am called on to resist this war clamor. My constituents need no such excitements to prepare their hearts for all that patriotism demands. Whenever the honor of the country demands redress, whenever its territory is invaded, if then it shall be sought to intimidate by the fiery cross of St. George—if then we are threatened with the unfolding of English banners if we resent or resist, from the gulf shore to the banks of that great river throughout the length and breadth, Mississippi will come down to the foe like a stream from the rock. And whether the question be one of Northern or Southern, of Eastern or Western aggression, we will not stop to count the cost, but act as becomes the descendants of those who, in the war of the Revolution, engaged in unequal strife to aid our brethren of the North in redressing their injuries.

Sir, when ignorance and fanatic hatred assail our domestic institutions, we try to forgive them for the sake of the righteous among the wicked—our natural allies, the Democracy of the North. We turn from present hostility to former friendship— from recent defection to the time when Massachusetts and Virginia, the stronger brothers of our family, stood foremost and united to defend our common rights. From sire to son has descended the love of our Union in our hearts, as in our history are mingled the names of Concord and Camden, of Yorktown and Saratoga, of Moultrie and Plattsburg, of Chippewa and Erie, of Bowyer and Guilford, and New Orleans and Bunker Hill. Grouped together, they form a monument to the common glory of our common country. And where is the Southern man who would wish that monument were less by one of the Northern names that constitute the mass? Who, standing on the ground made sacred by the blood of Warren, could allow sectional feeling to curb his enthusiasm as he looked upon that obelisk,[1] which rises a monument to freedom's and his country's triumph, and stands a type of the time, the men, and the event

---

[1] The Bunker Hill Monument.

that it commemorates, built of material that mocks the waves of time, without niche or molding for parasite or creeping thing to rest on, and pointing like a finger to the sky to raise man's thoughts to philanthropic and noble deeds.

On April 23, 1846, both Houses agreed to a new resolution (which was inspired by the Executive Department) authorizing the President, while giving the notice, *to continue negotiations*. The reason for this amendment transpired on June 6, 1846, when the British Ambassador, Richard Pakenham, offered to accept the line of 49 degrees north latitude clear to salt water. The President, desirous of accepting this offer, but unwilling to take the responsibility for receding from his demand of 54 degrees 40 minutes as the boundary, left the decision to the Senate, the majority in which was Whig. To the credit of the opposition it must be said that, while realizing the purpose of the President, they acted as patriots rather than partisans, and advised acceptance. The treaty was ratified accordingly at London on July 17, 1846.

CHAPTER XII

The Mexican War

William C. Preston [S. C.] Introduces in the Senate a Resolution for the
Annexation of Texas; It Is Tabled—John C. Calhoun, Secretary of
State, Concludes Annexation Treaty with Texas—It Is Rejected by the
Senate—Slavery and Texas as Issues in the Polk-Clay Presidential Cam-
paign—Annexation Bill Introduced in the Senate by Thomas H. Benton
[Mo.]; and in the House by Charles J. Ingersoll [Pa.]—Tilt in the
Senate Between George McDuffie [S. C.] and John J. Crittenden [Ky.]
on Power of Congress to Make War or Peace—Debate in the House on
the Ingersoll Bill: in Favor, Mr. Ingersoll, Stephen A. Douglas [Ill.];
Opposed, Robert C. Winthrop [Mass.], John Quincy Adams [Mass.];
Bill Is Passed by Both Houses and Approved by the President—Out-
break of Hostilities—President James K. Polk's War Message—Bill Is
Introduced in the Senate Providing for the Prosecution of the Existing
War—Debate: in Favor, General Samuel Houston [Tex.], Lewis Cass
[Mich.]; Opposed, John C. Calhoun [S. C.], John M. Berrien [Ga.],
James D. Westcott [Fla.], Senator Crittenden—Mr. Douglas Introduces
Bill in the House to Admit Texas into the Union; in Favor, Mr.
Douglas; Opposed, Julius Rockwell [Mass.]; Carried; Debate in the
Senate: in Favor, Senator Berrien; Opposed, Daniel Webster [Mass.];
Carried—Bill Is Introduced in the House Making Appropriations for
Soldiers at the Front—Debate: Advocates of the War, Mr. Douglas,
J. H. Lumpkin [Ga.]; Opponents, Joshua R. Giddings [O.], Columbus
Delano [O.], John W. Houston [Del.], John Quincy Adams [Mass.],
Robert Toombs [Ga.]—Treaty of Peace—Speech of Senator Thomas
Corwin [O.] Against the War—Tilt Between Senators Thomas H. Ben-
ton [Mo.] and John C. Calhoun [S. C.] on "Who Is Responsible for the
War?"—Abraham Lincoln [Ill.] Introduces in the House His "Spot
Resolutions": His Arraignment of President Polk—Treaty of Peace.

EVER since the treaty with Spain, whereby the
United States had acquired ownership of Florida
at the cost, among other considerations, of foregoing all disputed claims to Texas arising from the
Louisiana Purchase, this country had looked with
covetous eyes upon the relinquished territory. In 1827
and 1829 the Secretaries of State, Henry Clay and

Martin Van Buren respectively, had made cash offers for
it to Mexico, $1,000,000 in the former case, and $5,000,-
000 in the latter, but these were refused. All the while
the province was being settled by Americans who were
desirous of its annexation to this country. Owing to
their agitation, Texas, on March 4, 1836, declared its
independence from Mexico, and virtually achieved it in
a brief war ending with the battle of San Jacinto, April
10, in which General Samuel Houston, leader of the
revolutionists, defeated and captured Santa Anna, the
Mexican general, who obtained his freedom by signing
a treaty acknowledging the independence—a convention,
however, which the Mexican Government repudiated.
The United States recognized the new republic in
March, 1837, thus giving Mexico a cause of grievance
against this country.

In August, 1837, Texas applied for admission into
the Union, and during the special session beginning in
the following month William C. Preston (South
Carolina) introduced in the Senate a resolution to this
effect which was tabled by a vote of 24 to 14. From
this time until the annexation was accomplished in
December, 1845, the subject became a political issue,
and a disturbing one in that it was connected with the
agitation on the slavery question, since the South desired
the annexation, and the North opposed it because it
would greatly increase the extent of slave territory,
Texas having permitted slavery within its borders, from
which it had been excluded while the country was a
part of Mexico.

An annexation treaty was concluded on April 12, 1844,
by John C. Calhoun, Secretary of State, but it was
rejected by the Senate, 16 ayes to 35 nays. The adoption of this treaty would have precipitated war with
Mexico for the same reason that the subsequent annexation did so, namely, because it fixed the southwestern
boundary of Texas at the Rio Grande del Norte instead
of at the Rio Nueces, Mexico claiming the intervening
region.

While the question was in suspense the Texan authorities, in order to promote an early and favorable

decision, distributed throughout the Southern States a
vast number of land warrants which converted their
recipients into ardent annexationists. The Southern
politicians were appealed to on the ground that a number
of new States could be carved out of the territory, all
of which would naturally enter the Union with slavery,
and so preserve between the sections the balance of

CLEANSING THE AUGEAN STABLE

[1844]

From the collection of the New York Historical Society

power which was in danger of inclining toward the North
in the admission of free States.

During the Presidential campaign of 1844, while the
Democrats minimized in the North the issue of Texan
annexation, and strove to outbid the Whigs in a demand for the assertion of the Oregon claims, in the
South annexation was the sole issue, and the now
familiar threat of "Disunion" if the demands of the
section were not granted was again raised.

The Northern statesmen were afraid of annexation,
fearing that it would bring forward slavery as a paramount issue and cause a new political alignment in which
other men than themselves would make themselves

leaders. Accordingly, when the question was put directly to them, Martin Van Buren and Henry Clay, the leading aspirants of the Democratic and Whig parties respectively, for the nomination for the presidency, declared themselves against the annexation. This rendered certain the nomination of Clay, since a majority of the Whigs were opposed to the admission of more slave States, and it laid the basis for the loss of the nomination to Van Buren, since his Southern opponents, preliminary to the ballot in the Democratic convention held May 17, 1844, secured the passage of the two-thirds rule (which has been maintained ever since in Democratic conventions), and thus, although in the minority, by uniting on a Southern annexationist, James K. Polk of Tennessee, and standing resolutely for him, finally secured his nomination. For Vice-President the Whigs nominated Frederick T. Freylinghuysen (New Jersey), and the Democrats George M. Dallas (Pennsylvania). Both parties declared for asserting the Oregon claims. Polk and Dallas were elected over Clay and Frelinghuysen by a vote of 170 to 105. The Whig candidate would have been victorious had it not been for the increase in strength of the "Liberty Party," an Abolition party which had come into existence in the preceding presidential campaign, casting a negligible vote of 7,059 for James G. Birney of Kentucky and Francis J. Lemoyne of Pennsylvania (both of whom had declined the nomination). It now, however, cast a vote of 62,300 for Birney and Thomas Morris (Ohio), drawn almost wholly from the Whigs, and decided the electoral vote of New York (36) and Michigan (5) in favor of Polk and Dallas, who otherwise would have received 129 to 146 votes cast for Clay and Freylinghuysen. The annexation of Texas, which quickly followed the election, forced the restriction of slavery in front of its abolition as a practical question, and gave rise to a Free Soil party, with which the Abolitionists thereafter wisely coöperated, voting for its tickets in the next two presidential elections.

On June 10, 1844, Thomas H. Benton (Missouri) introduced in the Senate a bill to annex Texas, which provided for a division of the acquired territory with four States, two in the South to enter the Union with slavery, and two in the North without it. It also provided for a conference with Mexico on the subject of the boundary, although, if this could not be amicably adjusted, Congress, and not the President, was empowered to annex Texas without Mexico's assent. By such a course, said Benton, "if the solution of the question brings war, we shall at least have the consolation to know that it comes constitutionally; that it is brought upon us by the authority that has the constitutional right to make war, and not by the unconstitutional act of the President and Senate, or President alone."

This bill had been introduced with no hope of its passage, but for the purpose of providing material in the pending presidential campaign.

Soon after the opening of the next session of Congress, Senator Benton reintroduced his annexation bill in the Senate, and Charles J. Ingersoll (Pennsylvania) introduced in the House a joint resolution of the Senate and House for the annexation of Texas, and its admission into the Union "as soon as may be consistent with the principles of the Federal Constitution."

This superseded the Benton bill in the Senate, and on February 26, 1845, was passed there by a vote of 27 to 25. On February 28 the House passed the joint resolution by a vote of 132 to 76. The President signed the act on March 1.

In December, 1845, Texas was formally admitted into the Union.

PEACE BY NON-RESISTANCE

In the debate in the Senate the discussion hinged largely on the question of the power of Congress to declare war or make peace, since the passage of the joint resolution would almost certainly lead to war with Mexico. George McDuffie (South Carolina) asserted that Congress had this power, and John J. Crittenden (Kentucky) denied that it had, saying that this was a part of the treaty-making power which vested in the

Executive and the Senate jointly. An amusing colloquy
occurred between the two on this point.

SENATOR CRITTENDEN asked: Where was the power of making peace given to Congress by the Constitution? Would the
Senator from South Carolina tell him how Congress could make
peace?

SENATOR McDUFFIE.—Yes, sir: by disbanding the army and
navy. [Laughter.]

SENATOR CRITTENDEN.—That would not stop the war.

SENATOR McDUFFIE.—I do not presume the Executive and
Senate would undertake to carry on the war after Congress disbanded the army and navy.

SENATOR CRITTENDEN.—No, sir; but it would be a very good
time for the enemy to carry on the war. [Great laughter.]

A few days later Senator McDuffie, who, it would
seem, had an overweening sense of personal dignity and
a lamentable lack of the sense of humor, wrote to the
editor of the (Washington) *Globe,* which had reported
the colloquy, a long letter, intended for publication, in
which he attempted to set himself right in the matter.

In the debate in the House the chief speakers in
favor of annexation were Mr. Ingersoll, the mover of
the resolutions, and Stephen A. Douglas (Illinois); and
the chief opponents, Robert C. Winthrop (Massachusetts) and John Quincy Adams (Massachusetts).

THE ANNEXATION OF TEXAS

HOUSE OF REPRESENTATIVES, JANUARY 3-FEBRUARY 28, 1845

MR. INGERSOLL.—Like that of Maine, the Texas question is
national; and national considerations should prevail in the latter as they did in the former, when the Union, south, and west,
and central, sustained the Northeast in its plan of settlement.
It is undeniable, however, that Southern interests, Southern
frontiers, Southern institutions—I mean slavery and all—are
to be primarily regarded in settling the restoration of Texas.
It is a Texas question and a Southern question. If Southern
Secretaries of State—one of whom originated and another is
striving to consummate the affair[1]—betray Southern partialities

---

[1] John Forsyth [Ga.], Secretary of State under Van Buren, inspired the
Preston annexation bill of 1837, and John C. Calhoun [S. C.], the present
Secretary, had made annexation his foremost policy.

which many of us may deem not quite national, that is no reason' why a great national measure should not be effected on great national considerations. So, if our minister to Mexico discuss the matter with the Mexican authorities in a tone or temper which we may not approve, that is no sufficient reason why the affair itself should be frustrated. We must regard the merits and substance of the measure, and negotiation concerning it, without being prejudiced or prevented by the mere manner of dealing with them.

MR. WINTHROP said: One of the greatest complaints made by our fathers of the Revolution against the British Government was that it considered slavery a good and a blessing; that it had refused its assent to acts of the Colonies for its suppression; that it reprimanded the Governor of South Carolina for having given his assent to one of those acts. It seemed to him that arguments on this question more particularly belonged to those who maintained the affirmative of the proposition, and not to those who were opposed to it. It was for those who contemplated so momentous a change in our system—who were for running off for foreign lands and foreign alliances—it was for those who sought to jeopard the peace and union of the country, in order to find a more ample theater for their transcendental patriotism, to furnish arguments to sustain them. It was for them to make out their case. It was for them to show the policy of the act, and to point out the precise terms in which it was to be consummated. For us (said Mr. W.), who desire no change, who are content with the country as it is, and with the Constitution as it is—whose whole policy looked to the aggrandizement of the country by internal developments, and not by foreign acquisitions, we want no arguments. It is only necessary for us to content ourselves by sitting quietly in our seats and answer, as the old barons of England did, *nolumus leges Angliæ mutari*.[1] Sir (said Mr. W.) we have the Constitution. That Constitution is one of limited powers and of specific grants of power. That Constitution contains the clause that the powers therein enumerated shall not be construed to deny or disparage others retained by the people; and it also contained the clause that the powers not thereby granted are reserved to the States or to the people.

Now it was for those who contended for the annexation of a foreign territory to show that the power they attempt to exercise is contained in the grant. He was not at all astonished that the friends of this measure should have desired to throw

[1] "We are unwilling that the laws of England be changed."

off the load of argument from their own shoulders and impose it on their opponents. Having tried all the means in their power of reconciling the difficulties among themselves in regard to the accomplishment of this measure; having tried the *ultima ratio*[1] of a letter from the Hermitage in vain, the old Roman cement having lost its binding force, their last hopes were that the blows of their enemies might, more successfully than the love pats of their friends, knock their project into some shape that would render it acceptable to all. It seemed to be supposed by them that some anti-slavery feeling would manifest itself in the course of the debate, in such sudden and violent outbursts as to compel certain Southern members to give their votes for this measure, or their States to send other members here in their places next session who would be more complaisant. For himself, he was not disposed to minister to this feeling. Though he had no hesitation in saying that one of the grounds of his opposition to the annexation of Texas was that it would result in the extension of slavery, and, if his hour held out, he should treat it in connection with the question of slavery, yet he would do it in entire deference to the Constitution of the United States, which he was sworn to support. He should do it with the entire admission, which no Northern statesman has ever withheld, that so far as slavery exists in the States of the Union, this Government had no right whatever to interfere.

It was impossible for him to realize the fact that this subject was actually before the House for discussion. The introduction of a vast foreign nation into our boundaries—the naturalization of some thousands of Texans, as well as Mexicans—the introduction of 25,000 slaves into the Union in defiance of the Constitution, which prohibits it—the admission of a territory not only of a size sufficient to create two or three new States, but of a capacity to disturb the orbits of all the other stars and drive them into a new center toward other suns, and all this, too, by one simple act of legislation, was a thing so monstrous as almost to exceed belief. What was it? It was a measure devised by a Chief Magistrate[2] who was not the choice of the people, but who was the Chief Magistrate by accident, for his own ambitious views. It was rejected by the Senate, after mature deliberation and a thorough discussion; and it was now brought forward, after an hour's consultation in the Committee on Foreign Affairs, and was to be passed with as

[1] "Last resort"; the reference to ex-President Jackson.
[2] President Tyler.

little consideration as was ordinarily bestowed on an act to grant a salary or create an office.

The whole of the scheme was unconstitutional in substance and in form; it was contrary to the law of nations, and was a violation of the good faith of our own country; and, in his judgment, it was eminently calculated to involve this country in an unjust and dishonorable war. He also objected to it on account of its relation with domestic slavery. He was one of those who utterly denied the authority of this Government to annex a foreign State to this Government by any process short of an appeal to the people in the form which the Constitution prescribed for its amendment.

MR. DOUGLAS.—The gentleman from Massachusetts had been pleased to tell them that it had been devised by a President of the United States not elected by the people. Mr. D. denied that the accidental President of the United States had the credit of originating the project of the annexation of Texas to the Union. The honorable gentleman from Massachusetts [Mr. Adams] could assert a claim to that honor, founded on the fact that when President of the United States, in 1825, he and his secretary [Mr. Clay] proposed to annex Texas to this Union, and offered millions of dollars in order to secure this valuable acquisition. It was possible, inasmuch as the gentleman from Massachusetts [Mr. Adams] did originate the measure, that his colleague [Mr. Winthrop] had referred to him [laughter] when he had said that the scheme was originated by a President not elected by the people. [Renewed laughter.][1] Those who were opposed to the annexation of Texas seemed to have adopted the plan of raising up objections, of suggesting difficulties, and of keeping the friends of the measure employed in removing them, so that they would be prevented from going into the main question. They had found that the people were against them on that subject and that they had expressed their will more unequivocally in favor of the annexation of Texas than on any of the issues that were presented for their consideration. They therefore were reluctant to argue the question on its merits, and preferred a discussion on collateral issues.

He agreed with the gentleman from Massachusetts that, if we annexed Texas to the Union, it must be done consistently with the Constitution, and he was satisfied that Congress had the constitutional power to do it. In regard to the power to

---

[1] Adams had been elected by Congress, although Jackson had received more electoral votes.

annex foreign territory to the Union, he had only to call the attention of gentlemen to the fact that, in the articles of the old confederation, there was a proviso that Canada might be admitted into the Union as a matter of right, whenever she asked it, and that any other colony might be admitted with the consent of nine States. What other colonies were alluded to? The old thirteen States were included in the confederacy, and therefore none of them could have been alluded to. But gentlemen said that the colonies of Nova Scotia and New Brunswick were alluded to, but he would ask if Florida could not have been admitted under that article. It certainly was the intention of the framers of the confederacy to admit foreign states into the Union if they could get nine States to vote for it. Mr. Douglas went on to show that, after the confederacy, the power of admitting foreign states into the Union was not restricted by the Constitution, but enlarged by it. Propositions to restrict the admission of foreign states into the Union were made in the convention which framed the Constitution, and were rejected; after which the convention adopted the clause giving Congress the power of admitting new States into the Union. What else did they do? They struck out the proviso requiring the assent of nine States for the admission of new states, and inserted the proviso that Congress might do it. They also voted down the proviso requiring two-thirds, and provided that Congress might do it by the votes of a majority. Mr. D. then referred to the treaties of Louisiana and Florida to show the power of Congress to acquire foreign territory, and to the admission of Louisiana, Missouri, etc., into the Union, to show the power of Congress to admit territory so acquired into the Union as States. Mr. D. then went into an explanation of the powers of Congress to pass such laws as are necessary to carry the powers given by the Constitution into effect, drawing a distinction between the grounds of indispensable necessity, as held by the Democratic party, and the latitudinarian doctrine of convenience and expediency, as held by their opponents. It was on the former grounds, he said, that he contended for the constitutionality of the admission of Texas.

Mr. Adams referred to the argument that Texas was comprehended in the territory ceded by the Louisiana treaty, and therefore the United States were bound by the terms of that treaty to admit them into the Union, contending that Texas was not included in that territory. He also referred to the assertion that he was the first who originated the idea of annexing Texas to the United States, for that in 1825, during his presidency, he made overtures to Mexico for the acquisition of that territory. He admitted this to be true. He did make overtures to Mexico for the acquisition of Texas; but there was a slight difference between his action on that subject and that now contemplated, which the gentleman from Illinois had overlooked. He had proposed to purchase Texas with the consent of its owner; but the gentleman and his friends proposed now to take it without the owner's consent. There was the same difference between his action and that now contemplated as there was between purchase and burglary. Further, when he proposed to purchase Texas of Mexico, slavery did not exist there, and he proposed to take it without slavery, which he was willing to do now, with the consent of Mexico.

In all the treaties for the acquisition of territory it was not the acquisition of territory which constituted the power not within the Constitution, it was the bearing on the people of the territory acquired. We could acquire territory; territory was inanimate—it was matter. Man was an immortal soul; man had rights peculiar to himself; and they could not, without his consent, transfer man from one country to another. There was no such power; it could not be conferred. That was his opinion, and he expressed it in the case of the Louisiana treaty. He maintained it then; he conversed particularly with Mr. Madison on the subject. He [Mr. M.] agreed with him on that point. He [Mr. A.] showed Mr. Madison a proposition of amendment of the Constitution of the United States, and a paper in order to take the vote of the people of Louisiana on that treaty. When they annexed foreign territory to this country they dissolved our Union; the Union was dissolved. We might form another; but the people of a nation, the immortal mind, could not form a political union with another people without their own consent. This was his doctrine then; it was his doctrine now; and nothing on earth but the precedent which was settled against him could be adduced against it. If a man had rights, what were they? Were they not to live under the government of his own choice, and to refuse or consent to the terms by which he was made a part of a community to which he did not belong? In the acquisition of territory was included the disposal of human rights. It was not a subject of treaty; or, if it was a subject of treaty, it was between the sovereign powers who were the first principals, viz., between the people; and that was what he had proposed in the case of Louisiana.

OUTBREAK OF HOSTILITIES

President Polk, in his first message to Congress (December, 1845), had announced that the "accession (of Texas) to our territory has been a bloodless achievement." But it was not to remain so long. On March 12, 1846, General Zachary Taylor, in command of reg-

THE MEXICAN RULERS
Migrating from Matamoras with their Treasures
From the collection of the New York Historical Society

ular troops stationed on the border of the territory between the Rio Nueces and Rio Grande del Norte, advanced under orders into this disputed region. On April 25 a reconnoitering squadron of American dragoons was surrounded and captured by a superior force of Mexican cavalry, one officer and eight men of the Americans being killed. On May 8 General Taylor, with his entire force (2,300), met the Mexican General, Arista, with 6,000 men and defeated him at Palo Alto; following after the retreating foe on the next day Taylor completely routed him at Resaca de la Palma, and drove him across the Rio Grande.

On May 11 President Polk sent to Congress a war message in which he enumerated various wrongs committed by Mexico against the United States and its citizens during the period of differences between Mexico and Texas and, ignoring Mexico's reasonable claim to the territory invaded by General Taylor, asserted that "Mexico had passed the boundary of the United States and shed American blood on American soil." On the following day the Senate passed an act "providing for the prosecution of the *existing* war between the United States and Mexico," the preamble of which asserted, as the title assumed, that a state of war obtained between the two countries. On the question of whether this was in accordance with fact, and the proper attitude for the United States Government to assume, or the situation required that a formal declaration of war be made, a spirited debate took place in the Senate in which the supporters of the resolution were General Samuel Houston (Texas) and Lewis Cass (Michigan), and its opponents were John C. Calhoun (South Carolina), John M. Berrien (Georgia), James D. Wescott (Florida), and John J. Crittenden (Kentucky).

THE ACT OF WAR

SENATE, MAY 12. 1846

SENATOR CALHOUN said that he was prepared to vote the supplies on the spot and without an hour's delay; but it was just as impossible for him to vote for that preamble as it was for him to plunge a dagger into his own heart, and more so. He could not; he was not prepared to affirm that war existed between the United States and Mexico, and that it existed by the act of that government.

As to what might be said on such a course, and all that was called popularity, he did not care the snap of his fingers. If he could not stand and brave so small a danger, he should be but little worthy of what small amount of reputation he might have earned. He could not agree to make war on Mexico by making war on the Constitution; and the Senate would make war on the Constitution by declaring war to exist between the two governments when no war had been declared, and nothing had occurred but a slight military conflict between a portion of two armies. Yet he was asked to affirm, in the very face of the Constitution, that a local recontre, not authorized by the act of either government, constituted a state of war between the Government of Mexico and the Government of the United States— to say that, by a certain military movement of General Taylor and General Arista, every citizen of the United States was made the enemy of every man in Mexico. It was monstrous. It stripped Congress of the power of making war; and, what was more and worse, it gave that power to every officer, nay, to every subaltern commanding a corporal's guard. He therefore moved that the bill be referred to the Committee on Military Affairs.

The Senate, by a vote of 20 yeas to 26 nays, refused the reference.

GENERAL HOUSTON.—Was not the crossing of the Rio Grande by the Mexican forces of itself an act of war? Was not the entering our territory by an armed force an act of war? However the decision might hereafter be in regard to the precise extent of our territory, the Mexicans knew full well that the river had been assumed as the boundary. Up to the time of annexation it had been so considered, and, more than that, the Mexicans had never once established a military encampment on the east side of the river; it had never been held, even by themselves, to be within the limits of Mexico, otherwise than upon the ridiculous ground of claiming the whole of Texas to be theirs.

They had marched across the river in military array—they had entered upon American soil with hostile design. Was this not war? And now were Senators prepared to temporize and to predicate the action of this Government upon that of the Mexican Government, as if the latter was a systematic, regular, and orderly government? He, for one, was not prepared to do so. How many revolutions had that government undergone within the last three years? Not less than three, with another now in embryo. Perhaps the next arrival might bring us news of another change, and that the American army on the Rio del Norte had been destroyed while awaiting the action of the Mexican Government, in the supposition that it was a regularly constituted government, instead of being a government of brigands and despots, ruling with a rod of iron, and keeping faith with no other nation, and heaping indignities upon the American flag. A state of war now existed as perfect as it could be after a formal declaration or recognition of a state of war by the Congress of the United States. Their action had been continually indicative of a state of war, and the question now was, whether the Government of the United States would respond to that action and visit the aggressors with punishment.

CARICATURE OF LEWIS CASS

[1848]

From the collection of the New York Historical Society

SENATOR CASS.—It is true, sir, that there may be accidental or unauthorized recontres which do not therefore constitute war. But the nature and circumstances of an aggression sufficiently indicate its true character and consequences. A Mexican army invades our territory. How far may the invaders march before we are satisfied that we are at war with Mexico? Why, sir, such a state of things must be judged by moral evidence, by the circumstances attending it. It might be enough to say that the invasion itself throws the responsibility upon the Mexican Government, and is a sufficient justification for us in holding that government accountable. The negative proof is not upon us. The moral presumption is sufficient for our action.

A hostile army is in our country; our frontier has been penetrated; a foreign banner floats over the soil of the Republic; our citizens have been killed while defending their country; a great blow has been aimed at us; and, while we are talking and asking for evidence, it may have been struck and our army been annihilated. And what then? The triumphant Mexicans will march onward till they reach the frontiers of Louisiana, or till we receive such a formal certificate of the intentions of the Mexican Government as will unite us in a determination to recognize the existence of the war, and to take the necessary measures to prosecute it with vigor.

I have no doubt the boundary of Texas goes to the Rio del Norte. But I do not place the justification of our Government upon any question of title. Granting that the Mexicans have a claim to that country as well as we, still the nature of the aggression is not changed. We were in the possession of the country—a possession obtained without conflict. And we could not be divested of this possession but by our own consent or by an act of war. The ultimate claim to the country was a question for diplomatic adjustment. Till that took place the possessive right was in us; and any attempt to dislodge us was a clear act of war.

We have but one safe course before us. Let us put forth our whole strength. Let us organize a force that will leave no doubt as to the result. Let us enter the Mexican territory and conquer a peace at the point of the bayonet. Let us move on till we meet reasonable proposals from the Mexican Government; and if these are not met this side of the capital, let us take possession of the city of Montezuma and dictate our own conditions.

Senator Berrien.—The proposition of the Senator is that war exists. How does he prove it? Why, by the presence of a Mexican army around the United States army. Does he not thus decide the question of boundary? No. I beg to ask how that possession was acquired, and by whom? It was by the march of the United States army into the territory. If conceding that it was a disputed territory, the right of Mexico was equal with that of the United States to enter the territory. If our possession was derived from marching our army there, cannot Mexico exercise the same right? Does priority in an act of hostility vest a national right? The argument of the Senator is that the march of the Mexican army was an act of hostility. If so, I have demonstrated that the march of the United States army was an equal act of hostility. War does not, then, exist by any act of the constituted authorities, in whose hands alone is the power to create war.

SENATOR WESTCOTT.—Without a formal declaration of war and without the express authority of Congress, the President cannot issue commissions to privateers—issue letters of marque and reprisal—cannot authorize the blockade of the Mexican ports—cannot authorize the capture of Mexican vessels on the high seas as prizes of war. Without such declaration, Mexicans taken in arms, after defeat in attacking our citizens or soldiers, cannot be held by the Executive authority as prisoners of war —treason in aiding her troops may even go unpunished; and, above all, without it the observance of the duties of other nations toward us, the duty of neutrality, so likely to be violated, could not be properly enforced. Without such declaration, Mexico may be supplied with arms, ammunition, and munitions of war by other nations; and, if captured, they would not be liable to forfeiture as *"contraband of war."* The declaration of war will in every way strengthen the Executive arm in this contest —at home, abroad, on the field of contest, and in these halls. It will increase the efficiency of the supplies of men and money we propose to give threefold. It will convince the world we are in earnest in this matter.

SENATOR CRITTENDEN.—He saw no reason for the advance of the troops to the Rio Grande—for the hazarding of those consequences which every sensible man must have foreseen. It was not for a moment to be imagined that the angry armies of two angry and quarreling nations should, day after day, face each other with cannons pointed at each other, and only a fordable river between them, and conflict not result. It was conceded that this was disputed territory. What right had the United States to take possession of it? Had not the other disputing claimant an equal right? But he would not prosecute that view of the subject at present. He was willing to consider the exigency as urgent as they pleased, and to make adequate preparation. As it was the wish of some Senators to rest with that in the meantime, he should be entirely content with that course, but he did not know that he would be willing to limit the Government to repelling invasion. Perhaps he would be satisfied with an expression of what he meant by repelling invasion. He meant by that, pursuing, beating down, till the borders were freed from danger of a repetition of the invasion.

A SENATOR.—"That would be war."

MR. CRITTENDEN.—No; there was a shade of difference—a very perceptible one. He would be willing to give the means

to the President for the purpose of repelling invasion and otherwise prosecuting hostilities till the peace of the country be
secured from the danger of further invasion. He would move
to strike out the preamble, of which he saw no necessity—there
was none in the declaration of war in 1812.

Senator Crittenden's motion was negatived, 20 yeas,
25 nays. The question "Shall the bill pass?" was then
put and resulted 40 yeas to 2 nays, Senators Berrien
and Calhoun not voting, and Senator Crittenden voting
"aye, except the preamble."

On December 10, 1845, Stephen A. Douglas (Illinois),
chairman of the Committee on Territories, introduced in
the House of Representatives joint resolutions of the
House and Senate to admit Texas into the Union. Remonstrances were presented from various Northern
State legislatures and other bodies against admission of
the State with slavery. After some debate the resolutions came to a vote on December 16 and were adopted
by 141 yeas to 56 nays. While they omitted all direct
allusions to slavery, permission to introduce it into the
State was implicit in the statement of the resolutions that
Texas should be "admitted into the Union on an equal
footing with the original States *in all respects whatever.*"

Julius Rockwell (Massachusetts) was the chief
speaker in opposition to the resolutions.

This Texas slavery question was a new question now for the
first time presented to the consciences of men. As one called
to represent in part the people of his own ancient Commonwealth he must enter his solemn protest against the extension of
slavery as an evil directed against the truest interests of his
country; as militating directly against its prosperity and freedom, and darkening that national character which she ought
to hold up to all nations and ages of the world; as being in opposition to the Constitution which had preserved us hitherto in
concord; as against the principles of the fathers of the Republic, who lived themselves in slaveholding States, who would have
saved us, if they could, from so great an evil, and who openly
confessed that they trembled for their country when they remembered that God is just.

The joint resolution for admitting Texas into the

Union with slavery was presented in the Senate on December 22, 1845, and was thoroughly debated, John M. Berrien (Georgia) speaking in the affirmative, and Daniel Webster (Massachusetts) in the negative. It passed by a vote of 31 to 14.

ADMISSION OF TEXAS INTO THE UNION

SENATE, DECEMBER 22, 1845

SENATOR WEBSTER.—While I hold, with as much integrity, I trust, and faithfulness as any citizen of this country to all the original arrangements and compromises in which the Constitution under which we now live was adopted, I never could and never can persuade myself to be in favor of the admission of other States into the Union as slave States, with the inequalities which were allowed and accorded to the slaveholding States then in existence by the Constitution. I do not think that the free States ever expected, or could expect, that they would be called on to admit further slave States having the advantages, the unequal advantages, arising to them from the mode of apportioning representation under the existing Constitution.

On looking at the proposition I find that it imposes restraints upon the legislature of the State as to the manner in which it shall proceed (in case there is a desire to proceed at all) in order to abolish slavery. I have perused that part of the constitution of Texas, and, if I understand it, the legislature is restrained from abolishing slavery at any time, except on two conditions: one, the consent of every master; and, the other, the payment of compensation. Now, I think that a constitution thus formed does tie up the hands of the legislature effectually against any movement under any state of circumstances, with a view to abolish slavery; because if anything is to be done it must be done within the State by general law, and such a thing as the consent of every master cannot be obtained.

Mr. President, I was not in the councils of the United States at the last session of Congress, and of course I had no opportunity to take part in the debates upon this question; nor have I before been called upon to discharge a public trust in regard to it. I certainly did, as a private citizen, entertain a strong feeling that if Texas were to be brought into the Union at all she was to be brought in by diplomatic arrangement, sanctioned by treaty; but it has been decided otherwise by both Houses of

Congress: and, whatever my own opinions may be, I know that many who coincided with me feel themselves, nevertheless, bound by the decision of all branches of the Government.

I discharge my own duty and fulfil the expectations of those who placed me here by giving this expression of their most decided, unequivocal, and entirely unanimous dissent and protest; and stating, as I have now stated, the reasons which have impelled me to withhold my vote.

I agree with the unanimous opinion of the legislature of Massachusetts; I agree with the great mass of her people; I reaffirm what I have said and written in the last eight years, at various times, against this annexation. I here record my own dissent and opposition; and I here express and place on record, also, the dissent and protest of the State of Massachusetts.

SENATOR BERRIEN.—The pledge of this Government has been given, and it must be redeemed. The only question, therefore, is whether the people of Texas have complied with the conditions specified in the joint resolution? Now, sir, I have given a somewhat attentive consideration to the constitution which they have adopted, and am of opinion that these conditions have been complied with. I see nothing in the provisions of that constitution on the subject of slavery which ought to prohibit the consummation of the measure as promised in the resolutions of the last Congress. Much to which the Senator from Massachusetts refers, the inhibition to the legislature, except on certain conditions, to pass laws of emancipation, it seems to me is somewhat beyond the province of Congress to entertain. It is perfectly open, as I have before said, to any Senator to question the propriety of the admission of Texas on the ground of its tendency to disturb the political balances between the States contemplated by the Constitution; but the question of emancipation, when, how, and under what circumstances to be allowed, it would appear to me should be left with her own Legislature, as a subject for domestic regulation, belonging exclusively to the State, and with which the Congress of the United States has no authority, either directly or indirectly, to interfere.

During the progress of the war a spirited debate took place in the House on the occasion of making appropriations for the support of the army. The speakers who defended the war as just were Stephen A. Douglas (Illinois) and J. H. Lumpkin (Georgia), and those who denounced it as unjust, though with the exception of Joshua R. Giddings (Ohio) they were willing to support the army now that hostilities had begun, were Giddings, Columbus Delano (Ohio), John W. Houston (Delaware), John Quincy Adams (Massachusetts) and Robert Toombs (Georgia).

"My Country, Right or Wrong"

Debate on the Mexican War, House of Representatives, May 13-19, 1846

Mr. Giddings.—The President in his message, as a pretext for sending our army to invade and conquer the country upon the Rio Grande, says:

"Texas, by its act of December 19, 1836, had declared the Rio del Norte to be the boundary of that republic."

This mere declaration on paper by the legislature of Texas could not change or alter the *facts*. *They* were entered upon the page of history, as well as upon the records of eternal truth; and no flagrant falsehood by that body, indorsed by a dignitary of this Government, can change or alter them. The truth is that Texas had agreed upon the Nueces as her boundary.

Were Mexico to declare, by a legislative act, that her eastern boundary is the "Hudson River," and, on paper, attach the whole of our States south and west of that stream to her congressional districts, and then, on paper, divide our seaboard into collection districts, without being able to enforce her laws in any way whatever, her president may, at the next meeting of her congress, adopt this portion of President Polk's message, and urge, with equal propriety, that Pennsylvania and Ohio are Mexican territory. But if Mexico possessed the power and disposition to enforce such views, we should regard the carrying them out to be an outrage unparalleled among civilized and Christian nations; and were a Mexican army to invade our country, in order to compel us to unite with their government, we should meet them sword in hand and would yield our country only with our lives.

I apprehend that much blood and much treasure will be expended before the people of New Mexico will be compelled to unite with slave-holding Texas. Those Mexicans love freedom. They have abolished slavery, for which they entertain an unconquerable detestation. If I had time, I should like to inquire of gentlemen from New England and from our free States what benefit our nation or the world are to receive from a conquest of that country and the extension of slavery over it?

But the President says this Mexican country "is now included in one of our congressional districts." These thirty thousand people who, so soon as the bill which passed this House yesterday shall receive the sanction of the Senate, and shall be approved by the President, will be in a state of war with this nation, are to be represented on this floor because Texas has *on paper* attached them to one of her congressional districts. If this act of the Texan legislature has any binding force whatever, it will render every Mexican who opposes our army a *traitor against this Government,* and will subject him to the punishment of death.

Yes, the men who burned their dwellings at Point Isabel and with their wives and little ones fled before our invading army are to be represented in this body. Should their representative, according to the democratic doctrine, carry out the views of his constituents, the President himself may, in an unguarded moment, find a "lasso" about his own neck, and the members of our body be assassinated agreeably to the hearty wishes of the people of that district.

I regard the message as having been put forth to divert public attention from the outrage committed by the President upon our own Constitution, and the exercise of usurped powers, of which he has been guilty in ordering our army to invade a country with which we are at peace, and of provoking and bringing on this war. I am led to this inevitable conclusion from the fact that he dare not rest his justification upon *truth.* He reminds us of the grievous wrongs perpetrated (as he says) by Mexico upon our people in former years, and alludes to the delay of that government in the payment of debts due our people, and mourns over the loss of our commerce with Mexico; all for the purpose of justifying himself in sending the army to the Rio Grande, and commencing the work of human butchery!

If the country be *ours,* why does he seek to justify the taking possession of it by reference to the fact that Mexico is indebted to some of our people? If it be not ours, and he has taken possession of it in order to compel Mexico to pay those debts, why not say so? The fact that Mexico has not paid the debts due to our citizens can have no legitimate connection with taking possession of our own soil. But the writer of the message was obviously conscious that this invasion of the Mexican territory could not be justified; and he endeavored to extenuate the act by assuring us that "the movement of the troops to the Del Norte was made under positive instructions to abstain from all aggressive acts toward Mexico or Mexican citizens unless she should declare war."

What aggressive acts toward a foreign power could our army commit while on our own territory? While the army was within the United States they could not commit violence upon Mexico. The order was also to abstain from all aggressive acts toward "Mexican citizens." It seems that the President expected General Taylor to find Mexican citizens located within the United States. And this sentence evidently alludes to the order of the Secretary of War, in which General Taylor was directed to take possession of the whole country "except that which was in the actual occupation of Mexican troops or Mexican settlements." Here is a distinct admission that this country, claimed by the President as a portion of the United States, was in the actual possession of Mexican troops and Mexican settlements. The idea that our army could *peaceably* surround those military posts occupied by Mexican troops could be entertained by no reflecting mind. The President must have known, and we all know, that those military posts were established for the sole purpose of protecting the country, and the sending of our army there must have been done with the moral certainty that war would ensue. The truth is most obvious to the casual reader. The President obviously intended to involve us in war with Mexico. No sophistry can disguise that fact. That truth will stand on the page of history in all coming time, to the disgrace of this nation and of the age in which we live.

Sir, I regard this war as but one scene in the drama now being enacted by this Administration. Our Government is undergoing a revolution no less marked than was that of France in 1792. As yet, it has not been characterized by that amount of bloodshed and cruelty which distinguished the change of government in France. When the Executive and Congress openly and avowedly took upon themselves the responsibility of extending and perpetuating slavery by the annexation of Texas, and by the total overthrow and subversion of the Constitution, and that, too, by the aid of Northern votes, my confidence in the stability of our institutions was shaken, destroyed. I had hoped that the free States might be aroused in time to save our Union from final overthrow; but that hope has been torn from me. The great charter of our political liberties has

been tamely surrendered by our free States to purchase perpetual slavery for the South. Our Union continues, but our
Constitution is gone. The rights of the several States and of
the people now depend upon the arbitrary will of an irresponsible majority, who are themselves controlled by a weak but
ambitious Executive.

Sir, no man regards this war as *just. We know,* the country knows, and the civilized world are conscious, that it has
resulted from a desire to extend and sustain an institution on
which the curse of the Almighty most visibly rests. Mexico
has long since abolished slavery. She has purified herself from
its crimes and its guilt. That institution is now circumscribed
on the southwest by Mexico, where the slaves of Texas find an
asylum. A gentleman from Matamoras lately assured me that
there were in and about that city at least five hundred fugi-
tives from Texan bondage. Experience has shown that they
cannot be held in servitude in the vicinity of a free government. It has therefore become necessary to extend our dominions into Mexico in order to render slavery secure in Texas.
Without this, the great objects of annexation will not be attained. We sought to extend and perpetuate slavery in a
peaceful manner by the annexation of Texas. Now we are
about to effect that object by war and conquest. Can we invoke the blessing of Deity to rest on such motives? Has the
Almighty any attribute that will permit Him to take sides
with us in this contest?

I know it is said that a large army and heavy appropriations
will make a short war. God grant that the prediction may
prove true. I apprehend that Mexico has maturely considered
the subject, and enters upon the war with a solemn conviction
that her existence as a nation depends upon her resistance to
our aggressions. The devotion of her people at Point Isabel
conclusively shows it. Why, sir, look at General Taylor's report, and you will see a devotion manifested by the officers and
peasantry of Mexico that speaks in thunder tones to those who
regard the conquest of that people as a trifling matter. See
the females and children, at the approach of our troops, leave
their homes, consecrated by all the ties of domestic life, and,
while they are fleeing to the Mexican army for protection, see
their husbands and fathers apply the torch to their own dwellings, and then fly to arms in defence of their institutions. I
confess I was struck with deep solemnity when that communication was read at your table; and, in imitation of William Pitt,
I was ready to swear that, if I were a Mexican, as I am an

American, I would never sheathe my sword while an enemy remained upon my native soil.

Yesterday I was asked to declare to the world that "Mexico had made war upon us." That assertion I knew would be untrue, as I have already shown. I felt most deeply the impotence of this body, in thus attempting to change or alter great and important facts already entered upon the records of eternal truth, where they will remain while a God of truth shall exist. Sir, when we were about to assume upon ourselves the awful responsibility of involving our country in a serious and bloody war, with all its consequences; when about to appeal to a God of justice and of truth for his aid in maintaining our national rights, I dared not do so with an impious falsehood upon my lips.

But I hear it said that "we must go for our country, right or wrong." If this maxim be understood to require us to go with our country, or with the majority of our country, to commit a wrong upon other nations or people, either in time of peace or in time of war, I deny its morality; but if it be understood as imposing upon us, at all times and under all circumstances, the obligation of using all our influence and efforts to set our country in the right when we find her wrong, or to keep her right when we find her in the path of duty, then, sir, I yield my assent to its correctness. We are not to abandon our country because our Government is badly administered; but, in such case, we should use our efforts to correct the evil and place the Government in just and able hands.

Again it is said, "we must stand by our country." The man who would do otherwise would be unworthy of any country. He only is a true friend of his country who maintains her virtue and her justice; and he is not a true friend to his country who will knowingly support her in doing wrong. To-morrow this nation will probably be in a state of war with Mexico. It will be an aggressive, unholy, and unjust war. It will then be my duty to use my efforts to restore peace at the earliest practicable moment that it can be done on just and honorable principles. But while the war continues efforts will probably be made to conquer Mexico, and we shall be called on to appropriate money and raise troops to go there and slay her people and rob her of territory. But the crime of murdering her inhabitants and of taking possession of her territory will be as great to-morrow, after war shall have been declared, as it would have been yesterday.

Justice is as unchangeable as its Author. The line of moral

rectitude will never bend to our selfish passions. In the murder of Mexicans upon their own soil, or in robbing them of their
country, I can take no part, either now or hereafter. The guilt
of these crimes must rest on others; I will not participate in
them; but if Mexicans or any other people should dare invade
our country, I would meet them with the sword in one hand and
a torch in the other; and, if compelled to retreat, like the Mexicans at Point Isabel, I would lay our dwellings in ashes, rather
than see them occupied by a conquering army.

We may always justify ourselves for defending our country, but never for waging a war upon an unoffending people
for the purpose of conquest. There is an immutable, an eternal principle of justice pervading the moral universe. No nation, or people, or individual ever did or ever will violate that
law with impunity.

Suppose we send an army into Mexico and kill hundreds
and thousands of her people, burn her cities, and lay waste
her country; do you think we shall escape the dread penalty
of retributive justice? I tell you, we shall not. As sure as
our destiny is swayed by a righteous God, our troops will fall
by the sword and by pestilence; our widows will mourn; and
our orphans, rendered such by this unholy war, will be thrown
upon our public charity.[1]

But it is said that war is always popular. I deny this assertion. I believe that nine-tenths of our people regarded the
Florida war with contempt.[2] Their disgust arose from the fact
that it was unjust and cruel, and arose from an effort to sustain slavery. This war is equally unjust, and arises from the
same cause, and must be viewed in the same light by the people.
It is impossible, in the nature of things, for it to be otherwise.
Our people feel no hostility to those of Mexico. The Mexicans
have remained at home, "under their own vines and fig-trees";
they have not molested us or encroached upon our rights. It is
true that their population is less intelligent than that of our
free States; and it is equally true that they are more rapidly
improving their condition than are those of our slave States.
They are surely in advance of them in the diffusion of universal liberty among their people. The means of intelligence and
enjoyment are open to all.

Indeed, taking the whole population of our slave States and
of Mexico into consideration, I think we shall find the Mexicans

---

[1] It is estimated that the number of victims who fell in this war, by
pestilence and the sword, were eighty thousand. Of these, thirty thousand
were Americans, and fifty thousand Mexicans.

[2] The Seminole War. See Volume VIII, Chapter VI.

the best informed, most intelligent, and most virtuous. Our people of the North have sympathized with them in their efforts to render their free government permanent and respectable. Can the lovers of liberty now desire to see a sister republic wantonly subverted while just coming into existence and struggling for the permanent establishment of civil freedom? It cannot be. You may declare war; display your banners, your glittering arms, your blazing uniforms; you may raise the battle-cry and sound your trumpets; but you cannot induce the intelligent men of the North to march to Mexico for the purpose of bathing their hands in Mexican blood for the extension of slavery. You may for the moment excite the young, the giddy and thoughtless; but their "sober second thoughts" will lead them to inquire for the *cause* of the war in which they are asked to engage. The true answer to that inquiry must overwhelm its authors with disgrace.

. There is, however, one cheering circumstance in the distant future. All history informs us that for ages no nation or people, once having adopted the system of universal freedom, was ever afterward brought to the maintenance of slavery. There are now probably eight or nine millions of people in Mexico who hate slavery as sincerely as do those of our free States. You may murder or drive from their country that whole population, but you can never force slavery upon them. This war is waged against an unoffending people, without just or adequate cause, for the purposes of conquest; with the design to extend slavery; in violation of the Constitution, against the dictates of justice, of humanity, the sentiments of the age in which we live, and the precepts of the religion we profess. I will lend it no aid, no support whatever. I will not bathe my hands in the blood of the people of Mexico, nor will I participate in the guilt of those murders which have been and which will hereafter be committed by our army there. For these reasons I shall vote against the bill under consideration and all others calculated to support this war.

MR. DELANO said: We were in the midst of a war which we had engaged in without authority of law and without being in the right, yet, now that war had begun, on the principle of "my country, may she be always right, but, right or wrong, my country," he was ready to adopt purely defensive measures. Where this war would end he could not predict. But we had not yet settled the Oregon question. He never had any confidence in the sincerity of the President's declarations of a purpose to maintain our rights in Oregon. He believed that he would give away all Oregon to prosecute this war for a territory not belonging to us.

We had declared war without notice. It came upon the country like a clap of thunder in a clear sky. The pirates were ready to be let loose upon our unprotected commerce. We had everything to lose—nothing to gain. Send your armies, in the prosecution of this illegal, unrighteous, and damnable war, to the mountains of Mexico, and disease and the foe will sweep them off in thousands. The passes and mountains of Mexico would become a charnel-house for our people, and their bones would be scattered all over its vast territory before this peace would be conquered.

Mr. Douglas said: What reliance shall we place on the sincerity of gentlemen's professions that they are for the country, right or wrong, when they exert all their power and influence to put their country in the wrong in the eyes of Christendom, and invoke the wrath of Heaven upon us for our manifold crimes and aggressions? With professions of patriotism on their lips, do they not show that their hearts are against their own country? They appeal to the consciences and religious feelings of our countrymen to unite in execration of our Government, army, citizen soldiers, and country, for prosecuting what they denounce as an unholy, unrighteous, and damnable cause. They predict that the judgment of God will rest upon us; that sickness, and carnage, and death will be our portion; that defeat and disgrace will attend our arms. Is there not treason in the heart that can feel and poison in the breath that can utter such sentiments against their own country, when forced to take up arms in self-defence, to repel invasion by a brutal and perfidious enemy? They for their country, right or wrong, who tell our people, if they rally under their country's standard, their bones will bleach on the plains of Mexico, and the enemy will look down from the mountain top to behold the destruction of our armies by disease and malarias, and all those mysterious elements of death which Divine Providence employs to punish a wicked people for prosecuting an unholy and unjust war! Sir, I tell these gentlemen that it requires more charity than falls to the lot of frail man to believe that these sentiments are consistent with the sincerity of their professions —with patriotism, honor, and duty to their country. Patriotism emanates from the heart, fills the soul, infuses itself into the whole man, and speaks and acts the same language. A friend of his country in war will feel, speak, and act for his country; will revere his country's cause and hate his country's enemies. America wants no friends, acknowledges the fidelity of no citizen who, after war is declared, condemns the justice of her cause or sympathizes with the enemy. All such are traitors in their hearts; and would to God that they would commit such overt act for which they could be dealt with according to their deserts.

I will not proceed to examine the arguments by which the gentleman from Ohio [Mr. Delano] and those with whom he acts pretend to justify their foreign sympathies. They assume that the Rio del Norte was not the boundary line between Texas and Mexico; that the Republic of Texas never extended beyond the Nueces—and consequently our Government was under no obligation, and had no right, to protect the lives and property of American citizens beyond the last-mentioned river. In support of this assumption, the gentleman has referred to the dispute which he says arose between the provinces of Coahuila and Texas, and the decisions of Almonte and some other Mexican general thereon prior to the Texan revolution, and while those provinces constituted a state of the Mexican Confederacy. I will direct the gentleman's attention to the various maps, records, histories, and authorities—Spanish, English, and French —by which it is shown that the Rio del Norte was the boundary line between the French province of Louisiana and the Spanish provinces of Mexico. The gentleman can also satisfy himself on that point if he will take the pains to read a dispatch (I might with propriety say a book, from its very great length) written by the American Secretary of State, John Q. Adams, to the Spanish minister [Don Onis] in 1819. He will there find the authorities all collected and reviewed with a clearness and ability which defy refutation and demonstrate the validity of the American title under the treaty of 1803 to the country in dispute, together with the expression of his opinion, by the venerable gentleman from Massachusetts [Mr. Adams] that our title to the Del Norte was as clear as to the island of New Orleans. This was the opinion of Mr. Adams in 1819. It was the opinion of Messrs. Monroe and Pinckney in 1805. It was the opinion of Jefferson and Madison—of all our Presidents, and all Administrations, from the day of the purchase of Louisiana in 1803 to the fatal treaty of relinquishment to Spain in 1819. I give the gentleman the opinion of these men in opposition to the opinion of Almonte and his brother Mexican general, and then leave the question of boundary prior to the Texan revolution. Will he tell us and his constituents that those distinguished statesmen, including his friend from Massachusetts [Mr. Adams], as well as Mr. Polk and the American Congress, were engaged in an unholy, an unrighteous, and damnable cause in claiming title to the Rio del Norte?

But, sir, I have already said that I do not deem it necessary to rely upon these old authorities for the full and complete justification of our Government in defending possession of the country on the left bank of the Rio del Norte. There is better and higher evidence than this. The Republic of Texas held the country by a more glorious title than can be traced through the old maps and musty records of Spanish and French courts. She held the country by the same title that our forefathers of the Revolution acquired our territory and achieved the independence of this Republic. She held it by virtue of her Declaration of Independence, setting forth the inalienable rights of man, by men who had hearts to feel and minds to comprehend the blessings of freedom; by principles successfully maintained by the irresistible power of her arms, and consecrated by the precious blood of her glorious heroes. These are her muniments of title to the empire which she has voluntarily annexed to our Union, and which we have plighted our faith to protect and defend against invasion or dismemberment. We have received the Republic of Texas, with her entire territory, into this Union, as an independent and sovereign State, and have no right to alienate or surrender any portion of it.

Immediately after the battle of San Jacinto, Santa Anna made a proposition to the commander of the Texan army to make a treaty of peace, by which Mexico would recognize the independence of Texas, with the Rio del Norte as the boundary. In May, 1836, such a treaty was made between the government of Texas and Santa Anna, in which the independence of the republic of Texas was acknowledged, and the Rio del Norte recognized as the boundary. In pursuance of this treaty, the remnant of the Mexican army were ordered by Santa Anna to retire beyond the confines of the Republic of Texas, and take their position on the west side of the Rio del Norte, which they did in conformity with the treaty of peace.

Mr. J. W. HOUSTON.—I wish to ask of the gentleman from Illinois was that treaty ever ratified by the Government of Mexico?

Mr. DOUGLAS.—I will answer the gentleman's question with great pleasure. That treaty was never ratified on the part of Mexico by anybody except Santa Anna, for the very good reason that, in the year previous, Santa Anna had usurped the Government of Mexico, had abolished the constitution and the regularly established government, and taken all the powers of government into his own hands. This treaty was entered into by the Government of Mexico *de facto*, Santa Anna combining in his own person at the time all the powers of the government, and as such was binding on the Mexican nation.

MR. ADAMS.—I desire to inquire of the gentleman from Illinois if Santa Anna was not a prisoner of war at the time, and in duress, when he executed that treaty?

MR. DOUGLAS, in reply.—Santa Anna was a prisoner of war at the time, and so was the entire Government of Mexico, he being the government *de facto*, and clothed with all the powers of government, civil and military. The government was a prisoner at the time, and in duress. Will the gentleman from Massachusetts contend that a treaty made with us under those circumstances would not be binding, because, forsooth, the government was a prisoner at the time? How is a conquered nation ever to make peace if the gentleman's doctrine is to prevail? They refuse to make peace before they are conquered, because they hope for victory. They are incompetent to do so afterward, because they are in duress! I fear that, if this doctrine shall prevail, these gentlemen will soon find their Mexican friends in a most pitiable condition. Perhaps, if that government should be reduced to captivity, these gentlemen would require that our armies should retire within our own territory, and set the government at liberty, before negotiations for peace could be opened. This may be their view of the subject, but I doubt whether it is the view which the American Government or the American people will deem it their duty to act upon. Our crude notions of things may teach us that the city of Mexico would be the most suitable place to form a treaty of peace.

MR. ADAMS.—Has not that treaty with Santa Anna been discarded by the Mexican Government since?

MR. DOUGLAS.—I presume it has; for I am not aware of any treaty or compact which that government ever entered into that has not either been violated or repudiated by them afterward. It is sufficient for my purpose that the treaty was entered into and sanctioned by the government *de facto* for the time being. The acts of a government *de facto* are binding on the nation as against foreign nations, without reference to the mode in which that government was established, whether by revolution, usurpation, or rightful and constitutional means.

MR. LUMPKIN.—The people of this country were, to some extent, divided as to the policy of admitting Texas as a State into this Union. This, I admit, was an honest difference of opinion; and the measure was one about which the most patriotic might with propriety at that time disagree. But, sir, the question now assumes another aspect. Texas has been admitted into the Union, the people of both countries have been consulted, and they have solemnly determined to unite their destiny under the broad and ample folds of the American banner. The deed has been consummated and ratified by the action of both governments; and Texas has as much claim upon our protection as any other State in this Confederacy. The boundary of the United States is now extended to the western limit of Texas; her soil is our soil, her people our people; and her resources contribute to our greatness in peace and to our defence in war. We have done all this, and it is now too late to urge objections to the policy of this measure; and at a time like this, when our country has been invaded by hostile troops—when our soldiers have been captured, wounded, and killed in unequal and desperate conflict, and our army is exposed to peril from the overpowering numbers of the enemy, it is treasonable to withhold the supplies necessary for their relief; and no good but much evil must result from a prolonged discussion upon the policy of annexing Texas to the United States, and the propriety or impropriety of the conduct of the President in directing the occupation by the army of the country between the Nueces and the Rio Grande.

It is enough for us to know that our soil has been desecrated; that our country has been invaded; that a hostile band of armed soldiers have killed and wounded our citizens; and that the American army, under General Taylor, is in a hazardous situation and in need of assistance. At a time like this shall we be struggling for a mere party triumph? Can no circumstances or conditions of the country, no perils, however great, induce gentlemen in the opposition to cease their cavilling against the Administration or postpone their hostility to the President? Is not this an occasion when, for a time, all party distinctions and differences shall be forgotten, and, with one voice, with one heart, and with one hand, we all shall march forward in defence of the soil, the rights, and the honor of the country? Does patriotism require at your hands, as the faithful representatives of the people, that you should now, in your elevated position, denounce the President for a violation of the Constitution, by making an unauthorized and unholy invasion on the soil and territory of Mexico? Does your regard for the Constitution of the country require you to denounce this war with Mexico as unauthorized, unjust, and damnable? Will you promote the success of our arms by destroying, if such a thing were possible, the influence of the President? Are you encouraging enlistments for the service of the country by proclaiming to your countrymen that your Government is the aggressor?— that the President has, in violation of the Constitution, without authority of Congress, made an aggressive, unjust, and damnable war against an unoffending sister republic? I beg such gentlemen to pause and reflect before they give utterance to such sentiments in this place at a time like this. Retrace your steps, and withdraw, for a time, these charges, perhaps inconsiderately and too hastily made, and come forward with the same ability you have displayed against the Executive in support of all the measures necessary to the efficient and successful prosecution of the war against Mexico, and, my word for it, the result will be such as to rejoice the patriots of all parties. If these charges are to be investigated, and if gentlemen will insist that they are made in good faith, and that they are prepared to sustain them before the greatest of all human tribunals—the enlightened public opinion of the civilized world—I call upon them, in the name of my countrymen of all parties, to postpone these bickerings and discussions until the rainbow of peace shall again span our country's horizon.

MR. TOOMBS remarked that it was a little remarkable, when the country was represented by the friends of the Administration to be suffering from foreign invasion, and that the blood of American citizens, shed, as was contended, on American soil, was calling aloud for immediate vengeance, instead of responding to those appeals to patriotism which had been made, even this occasion must be consecrated to party, and a preamble placed before the bill to cover the usurpations of the Executive —a preamble declaring what no man could rise in his place and say he knew, that war had been made by Mexico. They could have voted supplies to defend Texas as well without this preamble; but it was too precious an opportunity to be lost to appeal to the people to sanction the wrongs and the usurpations of the Executive. And all those who were unwilling to subscribe to this declaration, the truth of which they could not know, and which he believed to be false, were to be branded as enemies to their country—as destitute of patriotism. If this were patriotism, he hoped there were but few patriots in the country.

The true question was not whether we should vote supplies for our army or protect our citizens in Texas. These questions were extraneous to that which was the subject of discussion,

viz.: the defence of the Executive. It was not a question of
dividing the country, but a question, where is the boundary
of the country? And it was a fact that should be borne in mind,
that, out of fifteen or sixteen propositions for the annexation
of Texas, there was but one that did not define its limits; and
that one was passed by the House of Representatives and the
Senate, and became a law. That left the question of boundary
an open question, expressly declaring that "*so much* of the
territory as *rightfully belongs* to Texas should be annexed to
the United States." Congress could not untie the Gordian knot
at that time, or define precisely what the boundary was; it was
left for the Executive to do this, and Congress was called upon
to sanction that act.

He proclaimed in the face of this House and the country that
the marching our army to the Rio Grande was contrary to the
laws of this country, a usurpation on the rights of this House,
and an aggression on the rights of Mexico. Gentlemen were
invited to make the most of this declaration.

Early in the second year of the war (1847) it was
seen that the march to the city of Mexico to dictate
terms of peace in the halls of Montezuma was not going
to be the easy, quick, and inexpensive progress that
had been prophesied by the Administration party, and
a popular reaction occurred against the war. A number
of Senators and Representatives found courage enough
to vote against further appropriations for what they
termed the "conquest" of a sister republic. Among
these was Senator Thomas Corwin (Ohio), who, on
February 11, 1847, justified his vote by a long and able
speech of which the following was the peroration:

AGAINST THE MEXICAN WAR

SENATOR CORWIN

What is the territory, Mr. President, which you propose to
wrest from Mexico? It is consecrated to the heart of the Mexican by many a well-fought battle with his old Castilian master.
His Bunker Hills, and Saratogas, and Yorktowns are there.
The Mexican can say, "There I bled for liberty! and shall I surrender that consecrated home of my affections to the Anglo-
Saxon invaders? What do they want with it? They have

Texas already. They have possessed themselves of the territory between the Nueces and the Rio Grande. What else do they want? To what shall I point my children as memorials of that independence which I bequeath to them, when those battlefields shall have passed from my possession?"

Sir, had one come and demanded Bunker Hill of the people of Massachusetts, had England's lion ever showed herself there, is there a man over thirteen and under ninety who would not have been ready to meet him—is there a river on this continent that would not have run red with blood—is there a field but would have been piled high with the unburied bones of slaughtered Americans before these consecrated battlefields of liberty should have been wrested from us? But this same American goes into a sister republic, and says to poor, weak Mexico, "Give up your territory—you are unworthy to possess it—I have got one-half already—all I ask of you is to give up the other!" England might as well, in the circumstances I have described, have come and demanded of us, "Give up the Atlantic slope—give up this trifling territory from the Allegheny mountains to the sea; it is only from Maine to St. Mary's—only about one-third of your republic, and the least interesting portion of it." What would be the response? They would say, we must give this up to John Bull. Why? "He wants room." The Senator from Michigan says he must have this. Why, my worthy Christian brother, on what principle of justice? "I want room!"

Sir, look at this pretence of want of room. With twenty millions of people you have about one thousand millions of acres of land inviting settlement by every conceivable argument. But the Senator from Michigan [Mr. Cass] says we will be two hundred millions in a few years, and we want room. If I were a Mexican I would tell you, "Have you not room in your own country to bury your dead men? If you come into mine we will greet you with bloody hands, and welcome you to hospitable graves."

The demand for "room," said Senator Corwin, had been "the plea of every robber-chief from Nimrod to the present hour." The Senator called the roll of the great conquerors, with significant remarks about the fitting retribution which had been meted out to them for their rapacity.

Ammon's son (so was Alexander named), after all his victories, died drunk in Babylon! The vast empire he conquered to "get room" became the prey of the generals he had trained; it was disparted, torn to pieces, and so ended.

I was somewhat amazed, the other day, to hear the Senator

THE LAND OF LIBERTY

Cartoon by Richard Doyle in "Punch," 1847

from Michigan [Lewis Cass] declare that Europe had quite forgotten us till these battles waked them up. I suppose the Senator feels grateful to the President for "waking up" Europe. Does the President, who is, I hope, read in civic as well as military lore, remember the saying of one who had pondered upon history long—long, too, upon man, his nature and true destiny?

Montesquieu did not think highly of this way of "waking up." "Happy," says he, "is that nation whose annals are tiresome."

The Senator from Michigan has a different view of this. He thinks that a nation is not distinguished until it is distinguished in war; he fears that the slumbering faculties of Europe have not been able to ascertain that there are twenty millions of Anglo-Saxons here, making railroads and canals, and speeding all the arts of peace to the utmost accomplishment of the most refined civilization. They do not know it! And what is the wonderful expedient which this democratic method of making history would adopt in order to make us known? Storming cities, desolating peaceful, happy homes, shooting men—ay, sir, such is war—and shooting women, too!

This—this is the way we are to be made known to Europe. This—*this* is to be the undying renown of free, republican America! "She has stormed a city—killed many of its inhabitants of both sexes—she has room!" *So* it will read. Sir, if this were our only history, then may God of his mercy grant that its volume may speedily come to a close.

Mr. President, this uneasy desire to augment our territory has depraved the moral sense, and blunted the otherwise keen sagacity of our people. What has been the fate of all nations who have acted upon the idea that they must advance? Our young orators cherish this notion with a fervid, but fatally mistaken zeal. They call it by the mysterious name of "destiny." "Our destiny," they say, is "onward," and hence they argue, with ready sophistry, the propriety of seizing upon any territory and any people that may lie in the way of our "fated" advance.

Rome thought, as you now think, that it was her destiny to conquer provinces and nations, and no doubt she sometimes said as you say, "I will conquer a peace." And where now is she, the Mistress of the World? The spider weaves his web in her palaces, the owl sings his watch-song in her towers. Teutonic power now lords it over the servile remnant, the miserable memento of old and once omnipotent Rome. Sad, very sad, are the lessons which time has written for us. Through and in them all I see nothing but the inflexible execution of that old law, which ordains as eternal that cardinal rule, "Thou shalt not covet thy neighbor's goods, nor *anything* which is his."

Since I have lately heard so much about the dismemberment of Mexico, I have looked back to see how, in the course of events, which some call "Providence," it has fared with other nations who engaged in this work of dismemberment. I see that in the latter half of the eighteenth century three powerful nations, Russia, Austria, and Prussia, united in the dismemberment of Poland. They said, too, as you say, "it is our destiny." They "wanted room." Doubtless each of these thought, with his share of Poland, his power was too strong ever to fear invasion or even insult. One had his California, another his New Mexico, and the third his Vera Cruz. Did they remain untouched and incapable of harm? Alas! No—far, very far, from it. Retributive justice must fulfill its destiny, too. A very few years pass off, and we hear of a new man, a Corsican lieutenant, the self-named "armed soldier of Democracy," Napoleon. He ravages Austria, covers her land with blood, drives the Northern Cæsar from his capital, and sleeps in his palace. Austria may now remember how her power trampled upon Poland. Did she not pay dear, very dear, for her California?

But has Prussia no atonement to make? You see this same Napoleon, the blind instrument of Providence, at work there. The thunders of his cannon at Jena proclaim the work of retribution for Poland's wrongs; and the successors of the Great Frederick, the drill-sergeant of Europe, are seen flying across the sandy plain that surrounds their capital, right glad if they may escape captivity or death. But how fares it with the Autocrat of Russia? Is he secure in his share of the spoils of Poland? No. Suddenly we see, sir, six hundred thousand armed men marching to Moscow. Does his Vera Cruz protect him now? Far from it. Blood, slaughter, desolation spread abroad over the land, and finally the conflagration of the old commercial metropolis of Russia closes the retribution she must pay for her share in the dismemberment of her weak and impotent neighbor. Mr. President, a mind more prone to look for the judgments of Heaven in the doings of men than mine cannot fail in this to see the providence of God. When Moscow burned it seemed as if the earth was lighted up, that the nations might behold the scene. As that mighty sea of fire gathered and heaved and rolled upward, and yet higher, till its flames licked the stars, and fired the whole heavens, it did seem as though the God of the nations was writing in characters of flame on the front of his throne that doom that shall fall upon the strong nation which tramples in scorn upon the weak.

And what fortune awaits him, the appointed executor of this work, when it was all done? He, too, conceived the notion that his destiny pointed onward to universal dominion. France was too small—Europe, he thought, should bow down before him. But as soon as this idea took possession of his soul he, too, becomes powerless. Right there, while he witnessed the humiliation, and doubtless meditated the subjugation of Russia, He who holds the winds in his fist gathered the snows of the north and blew them upon his six hundred thousand men; they fled—they froze—they perished. And now the mighty Napoleon, who had resolved on universal dominion, *he*, too, is summoned to answer for the violation of that ancient law, "thou shalt not covet anything which is thy neighbor's." How is the mighty fallen? He, beneath whose proud footstep Europe trembled, he is now an exile at Elba, and now finally a prisoner on the rock of St. Helena, and there, on a barren island, in an unfrequented sea, in the crater of an extinguished volcano, *there* is the deathbed of the mighty conqueror. All his *annexations* have come to that! His last hour is now come, and he, the man of *destiny*, he who had rocked the world as with the throes of an earthquake, is now powerless, still—even as a beggar, so he died. On the wings of a tempest that raged with unwonted fury, up to the throne of the only Power that controlled him while he lived, went the fiery soul of that wonderful warrior, another witness to the existence of that eternal decree, that they who do not rule in righteousness shall perish from the earth. He has found "room" at last.

And France, *she*, too, has found "room." Her "eagles" now no longer scream along the banks of the Danube, the Po, and the Borysthenes. They have returned home to their old eyrie, between the Alps, the Rhine, and the Pyrenees; so shall it be with yours. You may carry them to the loftiest peaks of the Cordilleras, they may wave with insolent triumph in the Halls of the Montezumas, the armed men of Mexico may quail before them, but the weakest hand in Mexico, uplifted in prayer to the God of Justice, may call down against you a Power, in the presence of which the iron hearts of your warriors shall be turned into ashes.

One hundred millions of dollars will be wasted in this fruitless war. Had this money of the people been expended in making a railroad from your northern lakes to the Pacific, as one of your citizens has begged of you in vain, you would have made a highway for the world between Asia and Europe. Your Capitol then would be within thirty or forty days' travel of any and every point on the map of the civilized world. Through this great artery of trade you would have carried through the heart of your own country the teas of China, and the spices of India, to the markets of England and France. Why, why, Mr. President, did we abandon the enterprises of peace and betake ourselves to the barbarous achievements of war? Why did we "forsake *this* fair and fertile field to batten on that moor"?

There is one topic connected with this subject which I tremble when I approach, and yet I cannot forbear to notice it. It meets you in every step you take. It threatens you which way soever you go in the prosecution of this war. I allude to the question of slavery. Opposition to its further extension, it must be obvious to every one, is a deeply rooted determination with men of all parties in what we call the non-slaveholding States. It is vain now to speculate about the reasons for this. Gentlemen of the South may call it prejudice, passion, hypocrisy, fanaticism. I shall not dispute with them now on that point. The great fact that it is so, and not otherwise, is what it concerns us to know. You nor I cannot alter or change this opinion if we would. These people only say we will not, cannot, consent that you shall carry slavery where it does not already exist. They do not seek to disturb you in that institution, as it exists in your States. Enjoy it if you will, and as you will. This is their language, this their determination.

How is it in the South? Can it be expected that they should expend in common their blood and their treasure in the acquisition of immense territory, and then willingly forego the right to carry thither their slaves, and inhabit the conquered country if they please to do so? Sir, I know the feelings and opinions of the South too well to calculate on this.

If, then, we persist in war, which if it terminate in anything short of a mere wanton waste of blood as well as money, must end (as this bill proposes) in the acquisition of territory, to which at once this controversy must attach—this bill would seem to be nothing less than a bill to produce internal commotion. Should we prosecute this war another moment, or expend one dollar in the purchase or conquest of a single acre of Mexican land, the North and the South are brought into collision on a point where neither will yield.

Oh, Mr. President, it does seem to me, if hell itself could yawn and vomit up the fiends that inhabit its penal abodes, commissioned to disturb the harmony of this world, and dash the fairest prospect of happiness that ever allured the hopes of men, the first step in the consummation of this diabolical purpose would be to light up the fires of internal war and plunge the sister States of this Union into the bottomless gulf of civil strife. We stand this day on the crumbling brink of that gulf —we see its bloody eddies wheeling and boiling before us—shall we not pause before it be too late! How plain again is here the

path, I may add the only way of duty, of prudence, of true
patriotism. Let us abandon all idea of acquiring further territory, and by consequence cease at once to prosecute this war.
Let us call home our armies, and bring them at once within our
own acknowledged limits. Show Mexico that you are sincere
when you say you desire nothing by conquest. She has learned
that she cannot encounter you in war, and if she had not she
is too weak to disturb you here. Tender her peace, and, my life
on it, she will then accept it. But whether she shall or not, you
will have peace without her consent. It is your invasion that
has made war, your retreat will restore peace. Let us then close
forever the approaches of internal feud, and so return to the
ancient concord and the old way of national prosperity and
permanent glory. Let us here, in this temple consecrated to the
Union, perform a solemn lustration; let us wash Mexican blood
from our hands, and on these altars, in the presence of that
image of the Father of his country that looks down upon us,
swear to preserve honorable peace with all the world, and eternal brotherhood with each other.

Other statesmen began to exonerate themselves from
having been parties to the conflict, and to charge each
other with this responsibility. The most notable of these
recriminations occurred in the Senate on February 24
when Thomas H. Benton (Missouri) charged John C.
Calhoun (South Carolina) with being the author of the
war while acting as Secretary of State under President
Tyler,[1] and Senator Calhoun replied acknowledging responsibility for the *annexation* of Texas, and any *defensive* measures which that act involved, but throwing
upon President Polk and his supporters, among whom
Senator Benton might, for certain acts, be numbered,
all the blame for involving the country in a war of invasion, thus putting the Government in the wrong, and
presenting the United States before the world in the
evil light of an aggressor.

LINCOLN'S "SPOT RESOLUTIONS"

On December 22, 1847, Abraham Lincoln (Illinois)
introduced in the House his famous "Spot Resolutions,"
calling on the President for information:

[1] See page 334.

First. Whether the spot on which the blood of our citizens was shed, as in his message declared, was or was not within the territory of Spain, at least after the treaty of 1819 until the Mexican revolution.

Second. Whether that spot is or is not within the territory which was wrested from Spain by the revolutionary government of Mexico.

Third. Whether that spot is or is not within a settlement of people, which settlement has existed ever since long before the Texas revolution, and until its inhabitants fled before the approach of the United States army.

Fourth. Whether that settlement is or is not isolated from any and all other settlements by the Gulf and the Rio Grande on the south and west, and by wide uninhabited regions on the north and east.

Fifth. Whether the people of that settlement, or a majority of them, or any of them, have ever submitted themselves to the government or laws of Texas or of the United States, by consent or by compulsion, either by accepting office, or voting at elections, or paying tax, or serving on juries, or having process served upon them, or in any other way.

Sixth. Whether the people of that settlement did or did not flee from the approach of the United States army, leaving unprotected their homes and their growing crops, *before* the blood was shed, as in the message stated; and whether the first blood, so shed, was or was not shed within the inclosure of one of the people who had thus fled from it.

Seventh. Whether our citizens, whose blood was shed, as in his message declared, were or were not, at that time, armed officers and soldiers, sent into that settlement by the military order of the President, through the Secretary of War.

Eighth. Whether the military force of the United States was or was not so sent into that settlement after General Taylor had more than once intimated to the War Department that, in his opinion, no such movement was necessary to the defence or protection of Texas.[1]

On January 12, 1848, Mr. Lincoln spoke upon his resolutions. His conclusion was as follows:

[1] These resolutions Mr. Lincoln took great pride in at the time, considering them a political *coup de main*, if not, indeed, a *coup d'état*, but they proved to be a *coup de grace* to his immediate political aspirations. His opponents ridiculed them as ''spot'' resolutions, with such effect that Lincoln's constituents turned against him; he did not seek a renomination, and a Democrat was elected to succeed him.—Henry C. Whitney, ''Life of Lincoln,'' vol. I, page 154.

ARRAIGNMENT OF PRESIDENT POLK

ABRAHAM LINCOLN, M. C.

If the President can show that the soil was ours where the first blood of the war was shed then I am with him for his justification. But if he cannot or will not do this then I shall be fully convinced of what I more than suspect already—that he is deeply conscious of being in the wrong; that he feels the blood of this war, like the blood of Abel, is crying to Heaven against him; that originally having some strong motive—what, I will not stop now to give my opinion concerning—to involve the two countries in a war, and trusting to escape scrutiny by fixing the public gaze upon the exceeding brightness of military glory—that attractive rainbow that rises in showers of blood—that serpent's eye that charms to destroy—he plunged into it, and has swept on and on till, disappointed in his calculation of the ease with which Mexico might be subdued, he now finds himself he knows not where. How like the half-insane mumbling of a fever dream is the whole war part of his late message! At one time telling us that Mexico has nothing whatever that we can get but territory; at another showing us how we can support the war by levying contributions on Mexico. At one time urging the national honor, the security of the future, the prevention of foreign interference, and even the good of Mexico herself as among the objects of the war; at another telling us that "to reject indemnity, by refusing to accept a cession of territory, would be to abandon all our just demands, and to wage the war, bearing all its expenses, without a purpose or definite object." So, then, this national honor, security of the future, and everything but territorial indemnity may be considered the no-purposes and indefinite objects of the war!

As to the mode of terminating the war and securing peace the President is equally wandering and indefinite. First, it is to be done by a more vigorous prosecution of the war in the vital parts of the enemy's country; and, after apparently talking himself tired on this point, the President drops down into a half-despairing tone, and tells us that "with a people distracted and divided by contending factions, and a government subject to constant changes by successive revolutions, the continued success of our arms may fail to secure a satisfactory peace." Then he suggests the propriety of wheedling the Mexican people to desert the counsels of their own leaders, and, trusting in our protestations, to set up a government from which we can secure a satisfactory peace; telling us that "this may become the only mode of obtaining such a peace." But soon he falls into doubt of this, too; and then drops back onto the already half-abandoned ground of "more vigorous prosecution." All this shows that the President is in nowise satisfied with his own positions. First he takes up one, and in attempting to argue us into it he argues himself out of it, then seizes another and goes through the same process, and then, confused at being able to think of nothing new, he snatches up the old one again, which he has some time before cast off. His mind, taxed beyond its power, is running hither and thither, like some tortured creature on a burning surface, finding no position on which it can settle down to be at ease.

Again, it is a singular omission in this message that it nowhere intimates when the President expects the war to terminate. At its beginning, General Scott was by this same President driven into disfavor, if not disgrace, for intimating that peace could not be conquered in less than three or four months. But now, at the end of about twenty months, during which time our arms have given us the most splendid successes, every department and every part, land and water, officers and privates, regulars and volunteers, doing all that men could do, and hundreds of things which it had ever before been thought men could not do—after all this, this same President gives a long message, without showing us that as to the end he himself has even an imaginary conception. As I have before said, he knows not where he is. He is a bewildered, confounded, and miserably perplexed man. God grant he may be able to show there is not something about his conscience more painful than all his mental perplexity.

On February 2, 1848, a treaty of peace known from the place where it was made as the "Treaty of Guadalupe Hidalgo," was signed by Mexico and the United States, and on July 4 was proclaimed to be in force. The American negotiator was Nicholas P. Trist of Virginia. By the terms of this treaty the Rio Grande was established as the boundary of the eastern portion of the cession, and in the west the Rivers Gila and Colorado were so followed as to give the United States all the territory then known as New Mexico and Upper California. The United States agreed to pay Mexico $15,000,000, and to assume the payment of all claims

adjudged against Mexico in the conventions of 1839
and 1843.

AN AVAILABLE CANDIDATE

THE ONE QUALIFICATION FOR A WHIG PRESIDENT

[Caricature of General Scott in 1852]

From the collection of the New York Historical Society

CHAPTER XIII

THE TRENT AFFAIR

Captain Charles Wilkes, U. S. N., of the *San Jacinto*, Takes John Slidell and James M. Mason, Confederate Commissioners, to Great Britain, from British steamer *Trent*—Act Is Approved by Gideon Welles, Secretary of the Navy—Negotiations with British Government—William H. Seward, Secretary of State, Delivers Up the Commissioners to Great Britain—Debate in the Senate on This Act: in Favor, Charles Sumner [Mass.]; Opposed, John P. Hale [N. H.].

IN the Civil War the chief hope of the Southern Confederacy lay in securing foreign intervention. In the beginning of the conflict it sent as commissioners to Great Britain ex-United States Senators James M. Mason (Virginia) and John Slidell (Louisiana). On October 12, 1861, they sailed with their families on the blockade-runner *Theodora* from Charleston to Havana, and there took the British mail steamer *Trent* sailing for England *via* St. Thomas, a Danish island in the West Indies. On November 8 Captain Charles Wilkes of the United States war frigate *San Jacinto* compelled the *Trent*, which had not yet arrived at St. Thomas, to stop; entering the British steamer he took the commissioners on board of his own vessel and carried them to Fort Warren in Boston harbor, where they were held as prisoners of war.

This act was approved by Gideon Welles, Secretary of the Navy. In his report to Congress on December 2, he said:

The prompt and decisive action of Captain Wilkes on this occasion merited and received the emphatic approval of the department; and if a too generous forbearance was exhibited by him in not capturing the vessel which had these Rebel enemies on board, it may, in view of the special circumstances, and of its patriotic motives, be excused; but it must by no means be permitted to constitute a precedent hereafter, for the treatment of any case of similar infraction of neutral obligations by foreign vessels engaged in commerce or the carrying trade.

However Lincoln's logical instincts engendered in his mind the opinion that Wilkes' action was technically unauthorized and would be seized upon by England as a pretext to involve the nation in a war. He therefore conferred with the Hon. Thomas Ewing [O.], a retired statesman of the preceding generation, who assured him that Captain Wilkes had been wrong by the law of nations. Accordingly, on November 30 a dispatch was sent to our minister recounting the facts, disavowing any complicity in Captain Wilkes' act, and expressing a desire to treat with England on the subject. On the same day the British minister for foreign affairs sent a note to Lord Lyons, the British minister at Washington, expressing the desire of the British Cabinet that our nation would disavow any authority in the affair, would yield up the prisoners, and make an apology; all of which were impressed with the force and authority of an *ultimatum*.

Long after the war it transpired (in the publication of the letters of Lord Palmerston, Prime Minister of Great Britain at the time of the Trent affair) that the legal advisers of the British Crown on November 11, 1861, two weeks before the seizure of the Confederate commissioners was known in England, had delivered an opinion by which an act such as that of Captain Wilkes was justified. This opinion was based on the uniform practice of Great Britain herself as upheld by no less an authority on maritime law than Sir William Scott, Lord Stowell. It was given in reference to an American war vessel (other than the *San Jacinto*) which was actually in an English port at the time, as to whether she had the right, by international law, to stop and search the West India packet then expected soon to arrive in England.

One of these letters of Lord Palmerston was to the editor of the London *Times*. It said:

It appeared that according to the principles of international law laid down in our courts by Lord Stowell and practiced and enforced by us, a belligerent has a right to stop and search any neutral not being a ship of war and being found on the high seas and being suspected of carrying enemy's dispatches; and that consequently this American cruiser might by our own principles of international law stop the West India packet, search her, and if the Southern men and their dispatches and credentials were found on board either take them out or seize the packet and carry her back to New York for trial.

Two days later Lord Palmerston wrote to the Queen to the same effect.

However, it seemed good to the British Administration directly to reverse their policy in this matter. By acceding to this reversal the United States Government thereby secured the British acknowledgment of its contention, adhered to through war and peace from the beginning of the nation, that the "right of search" was in contravention of the true principles of international law. Secretary Seward therefore seized the opportunity thus afforded him, and on December 26 handed Lord Lyons a dispatch in which he waived the question of Captain Wilkes' right to do as he did, and, ingeniously taking advantage of the officer's infraction of the prize law (in not bringing the prisoners into a prize court for adjudication), he ordered their discharge. The Confederate commissioners were given over to the custody of a British vessel by which they were transported to London. There they made no political impression and remained abroad until they died, expatriated.

THE TRENT AFFAIR

SENATE, DECEMBER 26, 1861-JANUARY 20, 1862

Discussion of the Trent affair came up in the next Congress on December 26, upon a resolution of Senator John P. Hale (New Hampshire) asking the President to transmit to the Senate the correspondence with Great Britain regarding it, which motion, after speaking thereon, he withdrew, indicating that he wished merely to denounce the surrender of the Confederate commissioners. Said Senator Hale:

To my mind a more fatal act could not mark the history of this country—an act that would surrender at once to the arbitrary demand of Great Britain all that was won in the Revolution, reduce us to the position of a second-rate power, and make us the vassal of Great Britain. I would go as far as any reasonable man would go for peace, but no further. I would not be unwilling to submit this subject to the arbitration of any of the great powers of Europe; but I would not submit to the arbitrary, the absolute demand of Great Britain, to surrender these men, and humble our flag even to escape from a war with Great Britain. No man would make more honorable concessions than I would to preserve the peace; but sometimes peace is less honorable and more calamitous than war. The Administration which is now in power ought to know what the feeling of the country is. If my friend from Indiana [Henry S. Lane] will permit me, I will repeat what he said to me this morning at the breakfast table. [Mr. Lane assented.] The honorable Senator said the State of Indiana has now sixty thousand men in the field, and she would double that number in sixty days if a war with Great Britain should be brought about. I have seen many gentlemen, and I have seen none, not a man can be found, who is in favor of this surrender; for it would humiliate us in the eyes of the world, irritate our own people, and subject us to their indignant scorn. If we are to have war with Great Britain it will not be because we refuse to surrender Messrs. Mason and Slidell; that is a mere pretence. If war shall come it will be because Great Britain has determined to force war upon us. They would humiliate us first and fight us afterward. If we are to be humiliated, I prefer to take it after a war, and not before. It is true, war would be a sacrifice to the people. I think I see its horrors, its disasters, its carnage, its blood, and its desolation; but, sir, let war come; let your cities be battered down, your armies be scattered, your fields barren, to preserve untarnished the national honor; a regenerating spirit among your people will restore your armies, and rebuild your cities, and make fruitful your fields. Francis the First of France, at the battle of Pavia, his army overthrown and scattered and himself a prisoner, exclaimed, "All is lost but honor!" That honor preserved then was the germ of the greatness and the glory of France to-day. I pray that this Administration will not surrender our national honor. I tell them that hundreds and thousands and hundreds of thousands will rush to the battlefield, and bare their breasts to its perils rather than submit to degradation.

If this Administration will not listen to the voice of the people they will find themselves engulfed in a fire that will consume them like stubble; they will be helpless before a power that will hurl them from their places. If war comes we shall not, Mr. President, be entirely without consolation and encouragemen. If war shall be forced upon us, as some gentlemen suppose, we shall be fighting in a great cause—the cause of constitutional liberty, whose baptism centuries ago was in the blood which flowed in England from the scaffold, and which animates millions to-day on the face of the earth, even of Englishmen, whatever may be the policy of their administration. If this war is determined upon in England it will be because it is out of the hands of statesmen and in those of pettifoggers, who are called the law officers of the Crown, who, it seems, can rush us into war. If we are, sir, to preserve peace it must be with honor. But if we are to have war—I do not say that we shall—it will not be without its advantages. It will be a war that cannot be carried on without fighting; and if we only understand our true position we can proclaim to every man who speaks the English language on God's footstool the cause for which we are fighting; and this appeal will reach the hearts of millions of Englishmen, Irishmen, and Frenchmen.

We have heard, Mr. President, some fears expressed that Louis Napoleon is taking sides with England, and that we are to contend with the combined energies of both France and England. I do not believe it. I believe if Louis Napoleon harbors one single sentiment, if his action is guided by one single principle, if he has one single feeling that is predominant over all others, it is to have a fair field to retrieve the disastrous issue of Waterloo. And, besides, sir, all over this country, throughout Canada, and in Ireland, there are hundreds and thousands and hundreds of thousands of true-hearted Irishmen who have long prayed for an opportunity to retaliate upon England for the wrongs which for centuries that government has inflicted upon their fatherland. If we know our own position and our own strength—I refer to the strength of principle—there will be nothing to be afraid of in this contest. If war must come, let it come; but I tell you, and I do not pretend to be a prophet, I think the slightest sagacity in public councils will sustain me in the position that if England enters upon this war she will enter upon one of more than doubtful contingency. She will be at war with the spirit of the age, with the irresistible genius of liberty, and with the sympathies of her own best people; she will war with a cause that is dear to the hearts of patriots the world over; she will war with a cause upon which we may invoke with confidence the blessings of the God of Liberty, who will not fail in His own good time and in His own way to vindicate His own cause.

I again say, if this war must come, let it come; and let us thank God that He has made us the chosen instrument in His hand to vindicate His own cause. I withdraw my motion.

Senator Charles Sumner (Massachusetts) replied, renewing the motion in order to speak upon it. He begged the Senate not to judge the Administration on insufficient evidence.

I have myself a firm conviction that this question will be peaceably and honorably adjusted. I do not believe that it is a question to be settled by war; and I hail with gratitude the suggestion of the honorable Senator, that, in making his speech, which may, in a certain sense, be called a war speech, he has expressed a willingness to submit the question to arbitration. Let me not be understood as intimating that that mode is under consideration. I am not authorized to say anything on the question. I content myself with repeating what I have already said, that it is in safe hands, and that it will be better for us to reserve ourselves for the question when it shall be presented in a practical form, and not to speak on hypotheses which the facts may afterward show to have been false. I withdraw the motion.

The President voluntarily transmitted the correspondence on January 6, 1862. Senator Sumner thereupon moved its reference to the Committee on Foreign Relations, and announced that he would speak later on the subject. He contented himself with saying:

There is, Mr. President, an important question of international law discussed in the papers, interesting not only to our own country, but to all foreign countries. As a precedent it will be of great value. If Great Britain has been well sustained in her recent course it is only because she has turned her back upon the practice and precedents of her history, and adopted for the moment the practice and the precedents of American history.

On January 20 Senator Sumner made the promised speech.

Mr. President, every principle of international law, when justly and authoritatively settled, becomes a safeguard of peace and a landmark of civilization. It constitutes a part of that code which is the supreme law, above all municipal laws, binding the whole commonwealth of nations. Such a settlement may be by a general congress of nations, or it may be through the general accord of treaties; or it may be by a precedent established under such conspicuous circumstances, with all nations as assenting witnesses, that it shall at once become in itself a commanding rule of international conduct. Especially is this the case if disturbing pretensions long maintained to the detriment of civilization are practically renounced by the power which has maintained them. Without any congress or treaties such a precedent has been established.

Here the Senator recounted the facts in the case.

While on their way, the embassadors were arrested by Captain Wilkes, of the United States steamer *San Jacinto,* an accomplished officer, already well known by his scientific explorations, who, on this occasion, acted without instructions from his Government. If, in this arrest, he forgot for a moment the fixed policy of the Republic, which has been from the beginning like a frontlet between the eyes, and transcended the law of nations, as the United States have always declared it, his apology must be found in the patriotic impulse by which he was inspired, and the British examples which he could not forget. They were the enemies of his country, embodying in themselves the triple essence of worst enmity—treason, conspiracy, and rebellion; and they wore a pretended embassadorial character which, as he supposed, according to high British authority, rendered them liable to be stopped.

If this transaction be regarded exclusively in the light of British precedents; if we follow the seeming authority of the British admiralty, speaking by its greatest voice; and especially if we accept the oft-repeated example of British cruisers, upheld by the British Government against the oft-repeated protests of the United States, we shall not find it difficult to vindicate it. The act becomes questionable only when brought to the touchstone of these liberal principles which, from the earliest times, the American Government has openly avowed and sought to advance, and which other European nations have accepted with regard to the sea. Indeed, Great Britain cannot complain except by now adopting those identical principles; and, should we undertake to vindicate the act, it can be done only by repudiating those identical principles. Our two cases will be reversed. In the struggle between Laertes and Hamlet the two combatants exchanged rapiers; so that Hamlet was armed with the rapier of Laertes and Laertes was armed with the rapier of Hamlet. And now on this sensitive question a similar exchange has occurred. Great Britain is armed with American principles, while to us are left only those British principles which, throughout our history, have been constantly, deliberately, and solemnly rejected.

An English writer put the case for his government as follows:

"It is not to the right of search that we object, *but to the following seizure without process of law.* What we deny is *the right of a naval officer to stand in place of a prize court* and adjudicate, sword in hand, with a *sic volo sic jubeo* [1] on the very deck which is a part of our territory."

Thus it appears that the present complaint of the British Government is not founded on the assumption by the American war steamer of the belligerent right of search; nor on the ground that this right was exercised on board a neutral vessel between two neutral ports nor that it was exercised on board a mail steamer, sustained by a subvention from the Crown, and officered in part from the royal navy; nor that it was exercised in a case where the penalties of contraband could not attach; but it is founded simply and precisely on the idea that persons other than apparent officers in the military or naval service cannot be taken out of a neutral ship at the mere will of the officer who exercises the right of search, and without any form of trial. Therefore, the law of nations has been violated, and the conduct of Captain Wilkes must be disavowed, while men who are traitors, conspirators, and rebels, all in one, are allowed to go free.

Surely that criminals, though dyed in guilt, should go free is better than that the law of nations should be violated, especially in any rule by which war is restricted and the mood of peace is enlarged; for the law of nations cannot be violated without overturning the protection of the innocent as well as the guilty. On this general principle there can be no question. It is but an illustration of that important maxim, recorded in the Latin of Fortescue, "Better that many guilty should escape

[1] "So I will, so I order."

than one innocent man should suffer,'' with this difference, that in the present case a few guilty escape, while the innocent everywhere on the sea obtain new security. And this security becomes more valuable as a triumph of civilization, when it is considered that it was long refused, even at the cannon's mouth.

Do not forget, sir, that the question involved in this controversy is *strictly a question of law*—precisely like a question of trespass between two neighbors. The British cabinet began proceedings by taking the opinion of their law advisers, precisely as an individual begins proceedings in a suit at law by taking the opinion of his attorney. To make such a question *a case of war,* or to suggest that war is a proper mode of deciding it, is simply to revive, in colossal proportions, the exploded ordeal by battle, and to imitate those dark ages when such proceeding was openly declared to be the best and most honorable mode of deciding even an abstract point of law.

In similar spirit has it been latterly proposed, amid the amazement of the civilized world, to withdraw the point of law, now raised by Great Britain, from peaceful adjudication and submit it to trial by combat. But the irrational anachronism of such a proposition becomes more flagrant from the inconsistency of the party which makes it; for it cannot be forgotten that, in times past, *on this identical point of law,* Great Britain persistently held an opposite ground from that which she now takes.

A question of international law should not be presented on any mere *argumentum ad hominem.* It would be of little value to show that Captain Wilkes was sustained by British authority and practice, if he were condemned by international law as interpreted by his own country. It belongs to us now, nay, let it be our pride, at any cost of individual prepossessions or transitory prejudices, to uphold that law in all its force, as it was often declared by the best men in our history, and illustrated by national acts; and let us seize the present occasion to consecrate its positive and unequivocal recognition. In exchange for the prisoners set free we receive from Great Britain a practical assent, too long deferred, to a principle early propounded by our country, and standing forth on every page of our history. The same voice which asks for their liberation renounces in the same breath an odious pretension, for whole generations the scourge of peaceful commerce.

In municipal questions Great Britain drew inspiration from her own native common law, which was instinct with freedom; but in maritime questions arising under the law of nations this power seems to have acted on that obnoxious principle of the Roman law, positively discarded in municipal questions, *Quod principi placuit legis vigorem habet,*[1] and too often, under this inspiration, to have imposed upon weaker nations her own arbitrary will. The time has been when she pretended to sovereignty over the seas surrounding the British isles, as far as Cape Finisterre to the south, and Vanstaten in Norway to the north. But, driven from this pretension, other pretensions, less local but hardly less offensive, were avowed. The boast of "Rule, Britannia, rule the waves," was practically adopted by British courts of admiralty, and universal maritime rights were subjected to the special exigencies of British interests. In the consciousness of strength, and with a navy that could not be opposed, this power has put chains upon the sea.

The commerce of the United States, as it began to whiten the ocean, was cruelly decimated by these arbitrary pretensions. But the loss of property stung less than the outrage of impressment, by which foreigners, under the protection of the American flag, and also American citizens, without any form of trial, and at the mere mandate of a navy officer, who for the moment acted as a judicial tribunal, were dragged away from the deck which should have been to them a sacred altar. This outrage, which was feebly vindicated by the municipal claim of Great Britain to the services of her own subjects, was enforced arrogantly and perpetually on the high seas, where municipal law is silent and international law alone prevails. The belligerent right of search, derived from international law, was employed for this purpose, and the quarter-deck of every British cruiser was made a floating judgment-seat. The practice began early, and was continued constantly; nor did it discriminate among its victims. It is mentioned by Mr. Jefferson, and repeated by a British writer on international law, that two nephews of Washington, on their way home from Europe, were ravished from the protection of the American flag, without any judicial proceedings, and placed as common seamen under the ordinary discipline of British ships of war. The victims were counted by thousands. At our Department of State six thousand cases were recorded, and it was estimated that at least as many more might have occurred, of which no information had been received. If a pretension so intrinsically lawless could be sanctioned by precedent, Great Britain would have succeeded in interpolating it into the law of nations.

Protest, argument, negotiation, correspondence, and war

[1] "What is pleasing to the prince has the force of law."

itself—unhappily the last reason of republics as of kings—were all employed in vain by the United States to procure a renunciation of this intolerable pretension. The ablest papers in our diplomatic history are devoted to this purpose; and the only serious war in which we have been engaged, until summoned to encounter this rebellion, was to overcome by arms this very pretension which would not yield to reason. Beginning in the last century, the correspondence is at last closed by the recent reply of Mr. Seward to Lord Lyons. The long-continued occasion of conflict is now happily removed, and the pretension disappears forever—to take its place among the curiosities of the past.

But I do not content myself with asserting the persistent opposition of the American Government. It belongs to the argument, that I should exhibit this opposition and the precise ground on which it was placed—being identical with that now adopted by Great Britain. And here the testimony is complete. If you will kindly follow me, you shall see it from the beginning in the public life of our country, and in the authentic records of our Government.

Here the speaker quoted extensively from opinions of various American Secretaries of State: Thomas Jefferson, Timothy Pickering, John Marshall, James Madison, Daniel Webster, and Lewis Cass, and of Presidents John Adams, James Monroe, and John Quincy Adams. He also quoted an expression of the British doctrine made by the Prince Regent (afterwards George IV) on January 9, 1813, in refusing an armistice which had been proposed by President Madison on condition that Great Britain abandon her practice of searching American vessels and impressing seamen thereon on the ground of their being British subjects:

"His Royal Highness can never admit that, in the exercise of *the* UN-DOUBTED *and hitherto undisputed right of searching neutral merchant vessels in time of war, the impressment of British seamen,* when found therein, *can be deemed any violation of a neutral flag.* Neither can he admit that the taking of such seamen from on board such vessels *can be considered by any neutral state as a hostile measure or a justifiable cause of war.*"

The war was closed by the treaty at Ghent; but perversely the British pretension was not renounced.

Such is an authentic history of this British pretension, and of the manner in which it has been met by our Government. If Captain Wilkes is right, then throughout all these international debates, extending over at least two generations, we have been wrong.

But it has been sometimes said the steam packet having on board the rebel emissaries was on this account liable to capture, and therefore the error of Captain Wilkes in taking the emissaries was simply an error of form and not of substance. I do not stop to consider whether an exercise of summary power against which our Government has so constantly protested can be under any circumstances an error merely of form, for the policy of our Government, most positively declared in its diplomacy, and also attested in numerous treaties, leaves no room to doubt that a neutral ship with belligerent passengers—not in the military or naval service—is not liable to capture, and therefore the whole proceeding was wrong, not only because the passengers were taken from the ship, but also because the ship, howsoever guilty morally, was not guilty legally in receiving such passengers on board. If this question were argued on English authorities it might be otherwise; but according to American principles the ship was legally innocent.

Here the speaker cited numerous treaties.

But still another question occurs. Beyond all doubt there were "dispatches" from the rebel belligerents on board the ship —such "dispatches" as rebels can write. Public report, the statement of persons on board the ship, and the boastful declaration of Jefferson Davis in a public document that these emissaries were proceeding under an appointment from him—which appointment would be a "dispatch" of the highest character —seem to place this fact beyond denial. Assuming this fact, the ship was liable to capture and to be carried off for adjudication, according to British authorities—unless the positive judgment of Sir William Scott in the case of the *Atalanta* (6 Robinson R., p. 440), and also the Queen's proclamation at the commencement of this rebellion, where "dispatches" are enumerated among contraband articles, are treated as nullities, or so far modified in their application as to be words, and nothing more. But, however binding and peremptory these authorities may be in Great Britain, they cannot be accepted to reverse the standing policy of the United States, which here again leaves no room for doubt. In order to give precision to the rights which it claimed and at the same time accorded on the ocean, our Government has sought to explain in treaties what it meant by contraband. As early as 1778, in the treaty with France, negotiated by Benjamin Franklin, after specifying contraband articles, without including dispatches, it is declared that

"Free goods are all other merchandise and *things* which are not comprehended and particularly mentioned in the foregoing enumeration of contraband goods."—*Statutes at Large*, Vol. 8, p. 26.

This was before the judgment of Sir William Scott, recognizing dispatches as contraband; but in other treaties subsequent to this judgment, and therefore practically discarding it, after enumerating contraband articles, without specifying "dispatches," the same provision is introduced.

Clearly, then, according to American principles and practice, the ship was not liable to capture on account of dispatches on board.

But there is yet another question which remains. Assuming that dispatches may be contraband, would their presence on board a neutral ship, sailing between two neutral ports, render the voyage illegal? The mail steamer was sailing between Havana, a port of Spain, and St. Thomas, a port of Denmark. Here, again, if we bow to British precedent, the answer will be prompt. The British oracle has spoken. In a well-considered judgment, Sir William Scott declares that dispatches taken on board a neutral ship, sailing from a neutral country and bound for another neutral country, are contraband; but that, where there was reason to believe the master ignorant of their character, "it is not a case in which the property is to be confiscated, although in this, as in every other instance in which the enemy's dispatches are found on board a vessel, he has justly subjected himself to all the inconveniences of seizure and detention, and to all the expenses of those judicial inquiries which they have occasioned." (The *Rapid*, Edwards's Rep., 221.) Such is the law of nations according to Great Britain.

But even if this rule had not been positively repudiated by the United States it is so inconsistent with reason, and, in the present condition of maritime commerce, so utterly impracticable, that it can find little favor. If a neutral voyage between two neutral ports is rendered illegal on this account, then the postal facilities of the world, and the costly enterprises by which they are conducted, will be exposed to interruptions under which they must at times be crushed, to the infinite damage of universal commerce. If the rule is applicable in one sea it is applicable in all seas, and there is no part of the ocean which may not be vexed by its enforcement. It would reach to the Mediterranean and to the distant China seas as easily as to the Bahama Straits, and it would be equally imperative in the chops of the British channel. Not only the stately mail steamers which traverse the ocean would be liable to detention and possible confiscation, but the same penalties must attach to the daily packets between Dover and Calais. The simple statement of such a consequence, following directly from the British rule, throws an instant doubt over it which the eloquent judgment of Lord Stowell cannot remove.

And now, as I conclude what I have to say on contraband in its several divisions, I venture to assert that there are two rules in regard to it, which the traditional policy of our country has constantly declared, and which it has embodied in treaty stipulations with every power which could be persuaded to adopt them: First, that no article shall be contraband unless it be expressly enumerated and specified as such by name. Secondly, that when such articles, so enumerated and specified, shall be found by the belligerent on board a neutral ship, the neutral shall be permitted to deliver them to the belligerent whenever, by reason of their bulk in quantity, such delivery may be possible, and then the neutral shall, without further molestation, proceed with all remaining innocent cargo to his destination, being any port, neutral or hostile, which at the time is not actually blockaded.

Such was the early fixed policy of our country with regard to contraband in neutral bottoms. It is recorded in several of our earlier European treaties. Approximation to it will be found in other European treaties, showing our constant effort in this direction. But this policy was not supported by the British theory and practice of international law, which was especially active during the wars of the French Revolution; and to this fact may, perhaps, be ascribed something of the difficulty which our Government encountered in its efforts to secure for this liberal policy the complete sanction of European states. But in our negotiations with the Spanish-American states the theory and practice of Great Britain were less felt; and so to-day that liberal policy, embracing the two rules already stated touching contraband, is among all American States the public law of contraband, stipulated and fixed in solemn treaties.

Of course this whole discussion proceeds on the assumption that the rebels are to be regarded as belligerents, which is the character already accorded to them by Great Britain. If they are not regarded as belligerents, then the proceeding of Captain Wilkes is indubitably illegal and void. To a political offender, however deep his guilt—though burdened with the undying

execrations of all honest men, and bending beneath the consciousness of the ruin which he has brought upon his country—the
asylum of a foreign jurisdiction is sacred, whether on shore or
on sea; and it is among the proudest boasts of England, at least
in recent days, that the exiles of defeated democracies as well as
of defeated dynasties have found a sure protection beneath her
meteor flag. And yet this power has not always accorded to
other flags what she claimed for her own. One of the objections
diplomatically presented by Great Britain at the beginning of
the present century to any renunciation of the pretension of
impressment was ''that facility would be given, particularly in
the British Channel, by the immunity claimed by American
vessels, *to the escape of traitors*'' (State Papers, Vol. 3, p. 86),
thus assuming that traitors—the companions of Robert Emmett,
in Ireland, or the companions of Horne Took, in England—
ought to be arrested on board a neutral ship; but that the arrest
could be accomplished only through the pretension of impressment. But this flagrant instance cannot be a precedent for the
United States, which has always maintained the right of asylum
as firmly as it has rejected the pretension of impressment.

If I am correct in this review then the conclusion is inevitable. The seizure of the rebel emissaries on board a neutral
ship cannot be justified according to our best American precedents and practice. There seems to be no single point where
the seizure is not questionable, unless we choose to invoke British
precedents and practice, which beyond doubt led Captain Wilkes
into the mistake which he committed.

Mr. President, let the rebels go. Two wicked men, ungrateful to their country, are let loose with the brand of Cain upon
their foreheads. Prison doors are opened; but principles are
established which will help to free other men, and to open the
gates of the sea. Never before in her active history has Great
Britain ranged herself on this side. Such an event is an epoch.
Novus sæclorum nascitur ordo.[1] To the liberties of the sea this
power is now committed. To a certain extent this cause is now
under her tutelary care. If the immunities of passengers, not
in the military or naval service, as well as of sailors, are not
directly recognized, they are at least implied; while the whole
pretension of impressment, so long the pest of neutral commerce,
and operating only through the lawless adjudication of a quarter-deck, is made absolutely impossible. Thus is the freedom of
the seas enlarged, not only by limiting the number of persons
who are exposed to the penalties of war. but by driving from

[1] ''A new order of the ages is born.''

it the most offensive pretension that ever stalked upon its waves. To such conclusion Great Britain is irrevocably pledged. Nor treaty nor bond was needed. It is sufficient that her late appeal can be vindicated only by a renunciation of early, long-continued tyranny. Let her bear the rebels back. The consideration is ample; for the sea became free as this altered power went forth upon it, steering westward with the sun, on an errand of liberation.

In this surrender, if such it may be called, our Government does not even "stoop to conquer." It simply lifts itself to the height of its own original principles. The early efforts of its best negotiators—the patriot trials of its soldiers in an unequal war—have at length prevailed, and Great Britain, usually so haughty, invites us to practice upon those principles which she has so strenuously opposed. There are victories of force. Here is a victory of truth. If Great Britain has gained the custody of two rebels, the United States have secured the triumph of their principles.

If this result be in conformity with our cherished principles it will be superfluous to add other considerations; and yet I venture to suggest that estranged sympathies abroad may be secured again by an open adhesion to those principles, which already have the support of the Continental governments of Europe, smarting for years under British pretensions. The powerful organs of public opinion on the Continent are also with us. Hautefeuille, whose work on the Law of Nations is the arsenal of neutral rights, has entered into this debate with a direct proposition for the release of these emissaries as a testimony to the true interpretation of international law. And a journal, which of itself is an authority, the *Revue des Deux Mondes*, hopes that the United States will let the rebels go, simply because "it would be a triumph of the rights of neutrals to apply them for the advantage of a nation which has ever opposed and violated them."

But this triumph is not enough. The sea-god will in future use his trident less; but the same principles which led to the present renunciation of early pretensions naturally conduct to yet further emancipation of the sea. The work of maritime civilization is not finished. And here the two nations, equally endowed by commerce, and matching each other, while they surpass all other nations, in peaceful ships, may gloriously unite in setting up new pillars, which shall mark new triumphs, rendering the ocean a highway of peace, instead of a field of blood.

The congress of Paris, in 1856, where were assembled the

plenipotentiaries of Great Britain, France, Austria, Prussia, Russia, Sardinia, and Turkey, has already led the way. Adopting the early policy of the United States, often proposed to foreign nations, this congress has authenticated two important changes in restraint of belligerent rights; first, that the neutral flag shall protect enemy's goods except contraband of war, and secondly, that neutral goods, except contraband of war, are not liable to capture under an enemy's flag. This is much. Another proposition, that privateering should be abolished, was defective in two respects: first, because it left nations free to employ private ships under a public commission as ships of the navy, and, therefore, was nugatory; and, secondly, because, if not nugatory, it was too obviously in the special interest of Great Britain, which, through her commanding navy, would thus be left at will to rule the sea. No change can be practicable which is not equal in its advantages to all nations; for the Equality of Nations is not merely a dry dogma of international law, but a vital national sentiment common to all nations. This cannot be forgotten; and every proposition must be brought sincerely to this equitable test.

But there is a way in which privateering can be effectively abolished without any shock to the Equality of Nations. A simple proposition, that private property shall enjoy the same immunity on the ocean which it now enjoys on land, will at once abolish privateering, and relieve the commerce of the ocean from its greatest perils, so that, like commerce on land, it shall be undisturbed except by illegal robbery and theft. Such a proposition will operate equally for the advantage of all nations. On this account, and in the policy of peace, which our Government has always cultivated, it has been already presented to foreign governments by the United States. You have not forgotten the important paper in which Mr. Marcy did this service, or the recent efforts of Mr. Seward in the same direction. In order to complete the efficacy of this proposition, and still further to banish belligerent pretensions, contraband of war should be abolished, so that all ships may freely navigate the ocean without being exposed to any question as to the character of persons or things on board. The Right of Search, which, on the occurrence of war, becomes an omnipresent tyranny, subjecting every neutral ship to the arbitrary invasion of every belligerent cruiser, would then disappear. It would drop, as the chains drop from an emancipated slave; or, rather, it would only exist as an occasional agent, under solemn treaties, in the war waged by civilization against the slave trade; and then it would be proudly recognized as an honorable surrender to the best interests of humanity, glorifying the flag which made it.

With the consummation of these reforms in maritime law, not forgetting blockades under international law, war would be despoiled of its most vexatious prerogatives, while innocent neutrals would be exempt from its torments. The statutes of the sea, thus refined and elevated, will be the agents of peace instead of the agents of war. Ships and cargoes will pass unchallenged from shore to shore; and those terrible belligerent rights, under which the commerce of the world has so long suffered, will cease from troubling. In this work our country began early. It had hardly proclaimed its own independence before it sought to secure a similar independence for the sea. It had hardly made a Constitution for its own Government before it sought to establish a constitution similar in spirit for the government of the sea. If it did not prevail at once, it was because it could not overcome the unyielding opposition of Great Britain. And now the time is come when this champion of belligerent rights "has changed his hand and checked his pride." Welcome to this new alliance. Meanwhile, amid all present excitements, amid all present trials, it only remains for us to uphold the constant policy of the Republic, and to stand fast on the ancient ways.

CHAPTER XIV

THE PURCHASE OF ALASKA

William H. Seward, Secretary of State, Negotiates Treaty with Russia for the Purchase of Alaska—Senate Confirms Treaty, and United States Enters into Possession—Debate in the House on Appropriating $7,200,-000 for the Purchase: in Favor, General Nathaniel P. Banks [Mass.], Rufus P. Spalding [O.], General Robert C. Schenck [O.], Thaddeus Stevens [Pa.], Leonard Myers [Pa.], William Higby [Cal.]; Opposed, Cadwalader C. Washburn [Wis.], Benjamin F. Butler [Mass.], John A. Peters [Me.], Samuel Shellabarger [O.], Hiram Price [Ia.], Dennis McCarthy [N. Y.]—Bill Is Passed with Preamble Implying That Consent of the House Is Essential to a Treaty; Senate Rejects Bill on This Account; Compromise Preamble Is Adopted Which Is a Virtual Victory for the House, and Bill Is Passed by the Senate and Approved by President Johnson.

ON March 30, 1867, William H. Seward, Secretary of State in President Johnson's administration, formed a treaty with Russia (absolute in its terms, not referring to the ratification of the Senate and the appropriation by Congress of the purchase price), whereby the United States purchased Alaska (then known as Russian America) for $7,200,000 in gold (equivalent to more than $10,000,000 in "greenbacks"). The ratification of the Senate was readily granted, there being but two dissenting votes, but there was much opposition in the House to making the required appropriation. Indeed it was not attempted to do this until more than a year after the treaty had been made. With a view to forcing Congress to make the appropriation the astute Secretary of State, immediately after the treaty, took formal possession of the country in the name of the United States.

On May 18, 1868, General Nathaniel P. Banks (Massachusetts) introduced in the House a bill making the necessary appropriation to effect the treaty. It came before the House for discussion on June 30.

PURCHASE OF ALASKA

HOUSE OF REPRESENTATIVES, JUNE 30-JULY 14, 1868

General Banks held that, a treaty being the "supreme law of the land," it was the duty of Congress to give effect to that law by such legislation as was necessary to carry it into effect. He gave a review of the origin of the treaty.

It was suggested by those inquisitive, energetic, enterprising, and powerful men who have made this continent what it is; by men who went from my own section—Massachusetts and Maine —when the trumpet sounded for emigration to California, and who, with a still more adventurous spirit than that which sent them to California, were led to the more northern territory, which was then thought to be a bleak and barren wilderness. They looked upon the broad Pacific Ocean, the innumerable islands and bays that skirt and cluster upon and crown the northern Pacific, and they saw, from their experience in New England and in the British provinces, what they believed to be the germ of an inappreciable wealth and power for themselves and their country. They applied to the Russian Government for the privilege to share in what they might do to increase the prosperity of that country. The Russian Government refused it. Russia had ceded to the citizens of the United States by the convention of 1824 the right of fishery in those waters near the shore and other privileges connected with it. Russia believed that the privileges of that convention had been abused by American citizens; and when, at the end of ten years, the privileges expired by limitation, she declined to renew them, and thus deprived American citizens of the liberty of fishing in those waters.

Russia had always been liberal and friendly toward this Government. The Administration, perceiving the necessity and importance of this privilege, applied for a renewal of the treaty. But, upon a full discussion of that question and with a statement of her interests which we could not resist, she declined to accord it, and we were thus without any other right than that of pursuing our course upon the Pacific as upon the Indian or the other oceans of the globe. The enterprising citizens to whom I have referred, regarding with an experienced eye the importance of this privilege to our citizens on the Pacific coast, endeavored to persuade the Government to obtain for them the privileges which had been lost. The Russian Government declined as before, but it conceded what was better than the right of the extension of fishery; it conceded to this Government the right of purchase, and the territory to which the fisheries were incident was purchased for $7,200,000.

The territory that has been transferred to us by the treaty of 1867 is substantially contiguous territory to the United States. I speak of its contiguity, not as being entirely without interruption, but as contiguous to territory long claimed and unwisely surrendered by us, and as a part of the continent which we could not allow to pass into the hands of any other people on the face of the earth. It is necessary for the defence of this country, for the preservation of its institutions and its power. It cannot in the nature of things remain with perfect certainty, and possibly not for a long time, in the possession of Russia. It is likely to be conceded and transferred to some other power, and it is indispensable to us that in such an event it should in the nature of things be transferred to the United States. It is five hundred and seventy-four thousand square miles in extent, three hundred and ninety-four thousand miles on land and one hundred and twenty-six thousand on the sea, making in land and water jurisdiction between five and six hundred thousand square miles. It commands a most important portion of this continent which we cannot afford to leave to the control of other nations. The peninsula of Alaska, from the central part, extends into Behring's sea. It is continued by a succession of islands—one hundred or more—which carries the jurisdiction of the United States into Behring's sea within five or six hundred miles of the Asiatic coast, and thus offers to the American people a territorial connection and a political jurisdiction which bring us to such a point that the citizens of this country can pass in an open boat, not being at any one time more than two days at sea, from the American coast on the Pacific to the Asiatic countries on the same ocean.

It is said that this territory is worthless, that we do not want it, that the Government had no right to buy it. These are objections that have been urged at every step in the progress of this country from the day when the forefathers from England landed in Virginia or in Massachusetts up to this hour. Whenever and wherever we have extended our possessions we have encountered these identical objections—the country is worthless, we do not want it—the Government has no right to buy it.

Here the speaker reviewed the objections urged against the acquisition of Louisiana, Texas, and California.

It was said at a later day in the Senate that the valley of the Columbia river was useless to us, costing more every year for its government than its entire value. "We are going to war," it was said, "for the navigation of an unnavigable river."

Upon representations like these we surrendered British Columbia to Great Britain. Mr. John Quincy Adams said in this House that she had no title to it whatever. We acquired it by the treaty of Ghent, then unsettled our title by joint occupation, and finally gave it up altogether upon the pretext now urged in regard to Russian America, that it was worth nothing, costing more than its value every year to govern it.

It is but a few years since the whole world regarded the country between the hundredth meridian of longitude and the Oregon cascade as barren and worthless. It was compared by the officers of the Government in 1863 to the Asiatic deserts. This country is now organized into prosperous States and Territories, and in 1870 will contain more than six hundred thousand people; and one of the States of this region has given us in five years an industrial product of more than fifty million dollars.

The Hudson Bay Company's possessions in British America were constantly described in the House of Commons as "sterile, ice-bound, unfit for the support of human beings." It is now called "the fertile belt," which, through the medium of colonization and a Pacific railway, is to bind together the British American colonies, and preserve to the mother country her waning power on the Atlantic and Pacific oceans. During the present month it was declared in the House of Commons that "The British possessions on the Pacific united to the colonies east of the Rocky Mountains would make the finest dominion in the world."

Now, sir, I propose for a few moments to consider what advantages Alaska possesses for the United States. Is it worthless? Do we need it? Has the Government the right to buy it? And, first, I speak of its geographical, commercial, and political importance. No man who looks upon the political condition of Europe can fail to see that it is quite possible it may be thrown at a day not distant into the vortex of a terrible war. There are to be great changes in the future; and it is certain that Russia will be among the first and the greatest of the powers of that future, whatever it may be. Whoever is engaged against her will strike for the conquest of this territory on the Pacific which did belong to her, and which will still belong to her **if** we refuse to execute the treaty for its purchase. This is not mere supposition. During the Crimean war the French and English squadrons in the Chinese sea secretly departed in 1853 for the purpose of taking possession of the Russian possessions in America. The Russian admiral, Futzujelm, illy prepared as he was for their attack, encountered them successfully and they were defeated.

The *British Colonist,* published in Vancouver, speaking in view of these events and on this subject, declared in 1853 that the Russian possessions must be English possessions. The Canadians at the same time echoed the same sentiment. Mr. Roebuck said in the House of Commons ten years ago that it was "the destiny of England to establish British colonies in India, Africa, and the whole of North America." And it is at least probable, if not certain, that if in the war in which we were recently engaged there had been a failure of our Government promptly to maintain its power and position, Russian America might in the end have gone to England, Mexico to France, and the Pacific coast would have been divided between them.

Now, sir, what is this territory? It begins at the parallel of 54° 40', running north to the seventy-second parallel north latitude. The territory has about the same extent in width. The southern portion, commencing at latitude 54° 40', the northern boundary of British Columbia, is the first feature of importance. It is a strip about three hundred miles in length and thirty miles wide, fronting upon British Columbia, and excluding it to this extent from the ocean. Governor Simpson said in reference to this strip of Russian America, which had been leased by the Hudson Bay Company from the Russian Government, that without it the British possessions on the Pacific would be comparatively worthless. It was leased upon that view by the Russian Government out of regard for the English interest on that coast. This reduces the ocean frontage of the English on the Pacific coast to the possession of Vancouver's Island, and a small strip of coast further north, which, however, without Vancouver's Island, would be of comparatively little or no value to them.

In the controversy upon the Oregon question it was the wish of a portion of our people, regarding it as a possession of small importance, to surrender altogether that territory; and in the final settlement, to use the language of Mr. Adams, the Government gave up six degrees of latitude to England without any consideration whatever, and with it Vancouver's Island, which was as clearly ours as any territory we ever possessed. We surrendered it to England with the agreement that Vancouver should belong to her, but that the island of San Juan, between Vancouver and the continent, should be a part of the American possessions. The language of the treaty was that the boundary should be the strait which "separates Vancouver from the continent." But since that time England has interpreted the treaty to mean a strait which "separates the continent from Vancouver's Island," thus establishing a boundary which gives her the island of San Juan as well as that of Vancouver.

Thus the British Government extends her claims—and if the philosophy for which gentlemen now contend here is allowed to prevail she is likely to be successful not only in obtaining possession of San Juan, but of adjacent territory, upon the general plea that it is worthless, that we do not want it, that it will cost more to govern it every year than it is worth, and that the Government has no right to maintain possession of worthless territory held by disputed or doubtful titles. We agreed to a joint occupation of this island with England a few years ago, and having accomplished a joint occupation she is likely to get undisputed and permanent possession without any consideration whatever if the philosophy now urged upon us is allowed to prevail.

Transatlantic communication between England and the Pacific coast was proposed by Sir Edward Bulwer Lytton when at the head of the colonial offices thirty years ago, as necessary to preserve that coast to Great Britain. And, sir, within this month, on the 9th of June, there occurred in the House of Commons an elaborate discussion of this subject. Lord Milton, who has, perhaps, written the best work on the British colonial policy on this continent, declared that "the time had arrived when it was necessary for the English Government to consider whether it wished to keep the Pacific colonies in their present state of loyalty; and that if anything was to be done to establish a through communication from the Atlantic to the Pacific they must look to the Pacific colonies rather than to the Atlantic; for the British Pacific colonies," he said, "derived even their food from the United States. There was every year a great influx of Americans into the colonies, and there was a growing desire on the part of the colonists to join the United States."

And this is while Alaska is in the possession and under the control of the Russian Government, the Russian American Fur Company, and the Hudson Bay Company, and before it has gained any strength from its transfer to the American Government. Napoleon, at the seige of Toulon, pointed out the place to the members of the constituent assembly, and he said to them, "there is Toulon." When we speak of Alaska in view of such declarations in the House of Commons as those I have quoted in regard to the loyalty of the British colonies on the Pacific, we may very well point the House to the territory between the forty-ninth and fifty-fourth parallels north, and say "there is Alaska!" The silent and irresistible influence of the American people will control the Pacific coast from the southern limit of California to Point Barrow on the Arctic Ocean.

A colony thrust in upon us on the Pacific by an arrangement unjust to this country, affecting its society and never satisfactory to its people, and which cannot long exist, a colony which is restrained from coming to us by the active intervention of the parent government, and is maintained upon considerations of foreign interest waiting for a moment when hostile demonstrations may be within its power, such a colony has not a natural existence, and can claim of us no consideration or support. It is not within the rule of international comity to insist upon maintaining and perpetuating its power by exterior aid where it has no self-supporting capacity, which alone gives governments a just claim to the respect of the nations of the world.

Well, sir, let me speak now of the advance of our power upon this continent, and what is likely to be its effect. The government of the world changes once or twice every century, and the theater of human history is transferred to different parts of the globe in the course of one or two centuries. A change of this character is now dawning upon us. Hitherto the Atlantic ocean has been the theater of its power and its triumphs. The control of the world hitherto has been in European hands, because Europe was the sovereign of this great sea. So long as the Atlantic ocean controls the destinies of men, so long the destiny and the idea of that control will be European, and so long as it is European it will stand in the way of the progress of civilization and bar the movements of the people to the acquisition or the resumption of the power that by the laws of nature belongs to them. How can it be changed? By intervention, by war? No, sir. The providence of God arranges other means for the control of the great families of men than such methods of violence. The changes in the theater of operation point out new fields, new pastures, green and beautiful, to which the children of creation may go. They come from the Atlantic, and they take their position upon what is called the great ocean of the world—the Pacific Ocean. That, with the Indian Ocean, which is part of the Pacific, so spoken of by geographers, covers

one hundred million square miles, and rolls between six hundred
million people (Asiatics) on one side, and about three hundred
million (Americans and Europeans) on the other. That ocean
will be the theater of the triumphs of civilization in the future.
It is on that line that are to be fought the great battles of the
hereafter. It is there that the institutions of this world will
be fashioned and its destinies decided. If this transfer is successful it will no longer be an European civilization or an European destiny that controls us. It will be a higher civilization
and a nobler destiny. It may be an American civilization, an
American destiny of six hundred million souls. Across that
great ocean of the future there is not one that is not a friend of
this country, nor a government that is not willing to strike
hands with us in any just movement for any just purpose.
Russia, China, Japan, India—so far as she is left to herself—
even Turkey, the whole of these powers have been and are and
still may be, even to the end, friendly to us. As for ourselves
we have nothing to fear from Europe. In this future and in
the presence of these powers Europe loses, as every nation in
time loses, her prestige and becomes subordinate to the new
powers in the progress of human civilization and the destiny of
nations.

Now, sir, the possession of Alaska is the key of this ocean.
It brings this continent within seventy or eighty miles of the
Asiatic coast on the north. It gives us the control of the Arctic,
whatever it may be, and of that Arctic Ocean we yet know nothing. This Arctic Ocean, too, has a future, it may be a boundless
and glorious future, and it is for us. The possession of Alaska
makes Behring sea substantially an American sea. It throws out
from its peninsula the mysterious chain of Aleutian Islands
almost to the Asiatic coast. Our watermen can communicate
with an open boat by this strange chain of islands between
America and Asia, between the continents of the New and the
Old World, and with the aid of the chain of Kurile Islands, reach
by the same boat China, Japan, or India, never being more than
two or three days at sea, rarely or never out of sight of land,
and exposed to as slight perils of the sea as mariners can ever
expect to encounter. We can thus return, according to Cheva-
lier, the visits which hundreds of years since the Asiatic people
made to America by the same chains of Aleutian and Kurile
Islands, who first settled Alaska, California, Mexico, and Central
America, and gave to this continent its first faint impress of the
coming civilization, traces of which are still seen on the coast
and in the interior, in the language and in the customs of the

people, from the Arctic Ocean to the Gulf of Mexico. But our visits will be for a different purpose, with nobler results. They returned nothing to the distant lands from which they came. In our return visit we take to the other continent civilization, laws, progress, and the ideas of justice between man and man in the government of nations. Before we have time to go, they come to us. A tale of the Arabian nights has nothing so marvelous as the recent movement of the Chinese nation. Abandoning, of their own motion, the policy of isolation, placing themselves first in the great movements of modern nations, they come first to us because we are territorially nearest and most ready to receive them. They take as their representative one of our own citizens, perhaps least likely to have been selected in advance for such a mission, who has by great good sense, as well as great good fortune, impressed upon them his spirit, and to whom they have confided their hopes and their power. There is nothing left that is impossible. Hereafter our civilization may be theirs. It is based upon the same idea. The civilization of Europe rests upon education of masters, the ignorance of the masses. The civilization of America of the present age and of the future rests upon universal education and intelligence. In China every person of mature age can read and write. Intelligence is at the basis of their government and the source of their power. It is the foundation upon which they construct their classes of society and their orders in government. And however their institutions of the family or the state may differ from ours, where intelligence is the common bond of union and the representative of the common power, as it is with us and with them, we shall be led gently but surely to the same objects and the same end. And they come to us at the moment when by a strange coincidence we push our territorial jurisdiction toward them. Both were animated by the same spirit and without the knowledge of each other moving to the same end by different means.

Now, through the advent of this spirit and power by the possession of Alaska on the north, with the Aleutian Islands in the center, and amicable arrangements not for possession—because we do not press upon others, and certainly not upon feeble nations to deprive them of their property—but with amicable relations of commerce and trade with the government of the Sandwich Islands, which cannot be long postponed, we have in our grasp the control of the Pacific Ocean, and may make this great theater of action for the future whatever we may choose it shall be. But it is indispensable that we shall possess these

islands, this intermediate communication between the two continents, this drawbridge between America and Asia, these step-
ping-stones across the Pacific Ocean. If we give them to another
government, if we subject the Pacific Ocean to the control of
Europe and European civilization, the power of the future is
theirs and not ours, and its progress is after their spirit and
idea and not ours. Instead of giving new light and leading to
new thought other nations, we lose our own, and are followers
rather than guides.

General Banks then spoke of the military importance
of the acquisition.

I pass now to a consideration of the character and resources
of the territory itself.

I received only a day or two since a letter from Mark Whiteman, a native of Russian Poland, who has been in this country
twenty-one years, who served the United States in the survey of
New Mexico, who went to California in pursuit of gold, thence
to Australia, thence to Fraser's river, and then with his companions from the sources of the Stikine in a direct line north,
working his way through the whole of Alaska. He says that
we know nothing of the great importance of these new possessions; that in every direction it is rich in minerals, and that the
natives are peaceful and friendly.

But I do not desire to put my statement solely upon human
testimony. There are laws of nature, results of national experience running through many centuries, to which we refer for the
support of our conclusions. Since the sixteenth century, until
a very recent period, it has been the belief of everybody that the
precious metals were confined to the tropics. It was not till
California was acquired and gold discovered that this opinion
ceased to have control of the public mind.

Moving from the tropics northward we found gold in California, even up to the very boundary of British Columbia. It
was then discovered still further northward, at the sources of
the Stikine, and the miners are still following it further northward. It was this law of nature so recently discovered that led
Mark Whiteman and his associates from the sources of the
Stikine river, through Alaska, to the Arctic Ocean, and that
exhibited to them up to the ocean itself its limitless mineral
wealth.

We have from everybody in Alaska—from miners, from
correspondents, from sea-faring men, from lumber-men, from

explorers, from natives, from Russians connected with the government there, and from Americans—confirmation of these deposits they found there. It was exactly the same evidences of the existence of these mineral deposits that were seen fifteen or twenty years ago in California, and later still in British Columbia.

CADWALADER C. WASHBURN [Wis.].—If the gentleman has any authority to show that there are precious metals of any kind in Alaska I beg he will refer me to the document and page where I can find it.

GEN. BANKS.—There is no authority which will convince the gentleman from Wisconsin [Mr. Washburn]. If he could lay his hand on the print in the side he would not believe.

Mark Whiteman found the precious metals himself, and brought them away with him; among others, platina in large quantities, the nature and value of which he did not understand until the specimens which he brought home were analyzed in California.

Many beds of bituminous coal have been discovered on the coast and in the Aleutian Islands. The Russian steamers have long taken coal from the mines of Kodiak, which can furnish it for future commerce for many years yet.

We have received within a few days a carefully prepared and elaborate statement of Professor Davidson, whose opinions cannot be discredited, who says that in this territory is to be found the purest and the best coal upon the Pacific coast.

Pure copper is found in large cubic masses. Copper plates, hammered out by the natives, and with hieroglyphics engraved upon them, the history of their tribes and families, have been found. Silver is also found in many places; also quartz, with sulphate of iron and lead.

There is no doubt whatever about the existence of large quantities of gold on the Stikine river, and also on other streams washing down from the mountains which extend through the whole of this territory.

GEORGE F. MILLER [Pa.].—I desire to ask the gentleman from Massachusetts to explain what quantity of the land embraced in this purchase is susceptible of cultivation.

GEN. BANKS.—The territory between the forty-fifth and sixtieth parallels of north latitude, west of the Rocky Mountains, on the Pacific coast, embraces three hundred thousand square miles of cultivable, arable land, according to the statement of the land commissioner, based upon the authority of Mr. Blodgett, the climatologist, a gentleman of Pennsylvania, whose character is perfectly well known and highly appreciated in this country. There are three hundred thousand square miles of cultivable and arable land between the forty-fifth and sixtieth parallels, the greater portion of which is in Russian America—that part between the forty-fifth and fifty-fourth degrees above Vancouver's Island to the Russian possessions, west of the mountains, being narrow and unimportant—according to Mr. Blodgett's statement. The Commissioner of Public Lands says there are twelve million eight hundred thousand acres—twenty thousand square miles—of land which can be brought into cultivation by actual settlers under the present land system of the United States.

The correspondents of the *Alta Californian* and *Journal* say there are twenty thousand square miles of cultivable and arable lands in the vicinity of Cook's inlet, which they call the garden of Alaska. There is more arable land in Alaska, according to the official statement of the land office, than there was estimated to be in California when we purchased that country from Mexico.

The testimony of newspaper correspondents and of our own officers and scientific men shows that in many portions of this territory herds-grass, of excellent quality, grows wild without care or culture; white and burr clover are found there; cattle are fat, and beef tender and delicate; oats and barley thrive like native grasses; peas grow at Oonalaska in latitude 64°; turnips, potatoes, carrots, beets, cabbages, and other root crops are the main support of the people. Winter gooseberries, blackberries, cranberries, raspberries, huckleberries, and thimbleberries are abundant. The rose, poppy, marigold, astrea, and hollyhock grow in perfection in the gardens of the officers at Sitka. Plants are found in the Arctic regions which belong to a temperate climate. Poisonous plants are few and not virulent, and reptiles, toads, and lizards are never seen.

This is the character of the country in its agricultural aspect. It is covered with gigantic pine forests, with the exception of a strip of land upon the northern coast opposite Behring Strait. Trees measure between three and six feet.

The timber of Alaska consists of white fir, spruce fir, white and yellow pine, cedar and hemlock, alder, some oak, and a few other species of timber of which we know little. The Alaska cedar for ship-building is the best in the world. An imperial commission of the French Government sitting at Toulon in 1860 reported that masts and spars from Vancouver's Island are superior to those from Riga. The timber of Alaska is of the same quality as that of Vancouver's Island. The hemlock will be used for tanning hides, which are abundant in Siberia, and the alder is extensively used in curing fish.

Gentlemen tell us, although this timber may exist in quantities and of the excellent character described, it is of no use, because we have enough elsewhere. They forget that the world changes. Everywhere we see evidences that this continent is being rapidly stripped of its forests, which once covered it as they now cover Alaska.

At any rate, we cannot have too much timber. What is the market for the timber of the Pacific coast? It is, in the first place, Russia, China, Japan, India, Australia, California, Mexico, South America, all the countries that line the coasts of the Pacific Ocean. We send it also to the Atlantic side of South America, and even into the Gulf of Mexico on that side. The unsurpassed masts and spars of the Pacific coast are sent to every port in every part of the world. Who is here to say that we have too much of this property, or that it is a crime to increase our supply?

Let me come now to the matter of the fisheries. When the committee were considering the matter of the fisheries, a statement from the officers of the Coast Survey relating to the quantity of fish found in these bays and rivers was presented, and it was so extravagant that gentlemen of the committee thought it would be better to omit it in the report.

Mr. Chairman, there is in no part of the world, except on a small scale in the fiords of Norway, anything like the arrangement of the bays and rivers and islands on the Alaska coast. Here is an ocean covering a hundred million square miles that has never been fished so far as we know. When we consider the vast multitude of fish that the Pacific Ocean must contain we can very well believe that when storms drive them into these bays they are as numerous as they are represented to be. It is not a matter of fancy, but a matter of fact. The Indians from all portions of Alaska go down to the coast when, from indications which they get from the flight of birds, whose flocks darken the heavens, that the fish are coming in schools upon the coast, and lay in their supply for the year. These waters abound in whale, cod, halibut, salmon, and all the varieties of fish that inhabit the cold waters. The whale has abandoned the seas of the northeast coast and is pursued to seas adjacent to Alaska, twenty thousand miles from whence he is followed into the Arctic Ocean. The superintendent of the Bureau of Statistics informs me that there are sixty thousand men engaged every year in the fisheries of the northwestern coast of North America. Now, here are two hundred and forty thousand square miles of fishing grounds, which will give occupation to at least one hundred and twenty thousand men in the cod and halibut fisheries alone. The fisheries of the United States return every year a product of $34,000,000, four-fifths of which is from the whale and cod fishing. Of that we obtain our share now from the eighty-four thousand square miles of the fisheries of the northeast coast of America, sharing its wealth with England and France, who have by far the best opportunities, to whose fishing grounds we are admitted only upon the payment of onerous tonnage taxes. By this purchase we treble the extent of the fisheries of which we have exclusive possession, and of course we obtain a corresponding increase of employment and product.

I come now to a question of practical importance. What is the value of these things to us? They add to the industrial product of the country, from native industries alone, employment for fishermen, lumbermen, miners, colliers, mariners, shipbuilders, trappers, hunters, farmers, ice-cutters, and traders. From the native industries of this possession, carrying nothing there but men, we will find, when the resources of the territory are fully developed, employment for two hundred and fifty thousand persons. A quarter of a million of people will be engaged in peaceful, honorable, profitable, national, native industries in this territory alone. And, allowing each man to represent a family of four persons, it will furnish a support for a population of a million souls.

Who is interested in this purchase? The Pacific States. Will you say to them that it is worthless; that we do not want it; that the Government has no right to acquire it? They know better. They know that the possession of this territory is hereafter identified with the prosperity of this Government and the development and increase of our industry. California proved herself a fast and important friend of this Government in our hour of trial. She gave the whole Pacific coast to the cause of liberty and union, and to us, through the Providence of God, the victory. She asks now the extension of our interests on the Pacific coast. With what grace can the East deny her request? With what justice can the Mississippi valley, that was acquired by a similar treaty, deny to California a favor which, while it strengthens her interests, enlarges, consolidates, and extends those of the whole country?

At every step from 1780 up to this hour Russia has been our friend. In the darkest hour of our peril, when France and England were contemplating the recognition of the rebel confederacy, the whole world was thrilled by the appearance in San Francisco of a Russian fleet, and nearly at the same time, whether by accident or design, a second Russian fleet appeared in the harbor of New York. Who knew how many more there were on the voyage here? From that hour, France on one hand and England on the other receded, and the American Government regained its position and power.

Now, shall we flout the Russian Government in every court of Europe for her friendship? Having sought from her for twenty-five years the fisheries of the northwest coast, and having received from her not only the incident of the fisheries but the substance of the territorial possession incident to the fisheries, shall we do what never before has been done, refuse to execute the treaty she has made at our solicitation with our own Government, upon the conditions and according to the letter of our own Constitution? I do not believe it. Whoever of the Representatives of the American people in this House on this question turns his back not only upon his duty, but upon the friends of his country, upon the Constitution of his Government, the honor of his generation, cannot long remain in power.

There is one precedent we must dismiss from memory before we can do that. We must erase from our history the glorious incident of Jackson's administration, when he compelled France to pay under a treaty contracted with us, and when France answered, as we are now urged to answer, that the appropriation of money was another matter. Although she was the best friend we had, yet Jackson asserted he would compel the execution of the treaty at the hazard of war. Gentlemen cannot make a distinction between that case and the one now presented. If we do refuse to appropriate this money, when we owe another government under treaty stipulations, it will be a greater dishonor than our country yet has known.

Mr. Washburn replied to General Banks on the following day (July 1).

If gentlemen will come down from the region of the clouds to which they were transported by the honorable gentleman, and from those realms of fancy and imagination in which he reveled, to plain matters of every-day fact, I shall not despair of doing something yet to protect the rights of my constituents and of the people of this country.

Gentlemen could not fail to observe all through the speech

made by the gentleman on yesterday the extreme lack of authorities to sustain his statements, and the great preponderance, instead, of spread-eagle oratory. Sir, I shall enter into no contest with the gentleman in the eagle business; I resign that to him altogether. But I shall ask those members who have not arrived at the sublime position of the gentleman from Massachusetts, who declared "that he did not rely on human testimony, that he was above it"—I shall ask those gentleman who do care for such testimony to listen while I unfold the facts that surround this most extraordinary case.

I shall attempt to demonstrate five propositions, and if I shall succeed in doing so I think I may claim the judgment of this committee and of the House. Those propositions are:

1. That at the time this treaty was negotiated not a soul in the whole United States asked for it.

2. That it was secretly negotiated and in a manner to prevent the representatives of the people from being heard.

3. That by existing treaties we possessed every right that is of any value to us without the responsibility and never-ending expense of governing a nation of savages.

4. That the country is absolutely without value.

5. That it is the right and duty of the House to inquire into the treaty, and vote or not vote the money according to its best judgment.

My first proposition is that on the 30th day of March, 1867, the day on which this treaty was signed, there was not a man in the whole length and breadth of the United States who had ever conceived the idea that this territory of Alaska was a valuable territory for the United States to possess; not even the gentleman from Massachusetts, though he now declares it to be absolutely necessary to the very safety and existence of this nation. Even on the Pacific coast, which is now said to be clamorous for it, no such idea had entered the brain of any man there.

As to the gentleman's point that we are in honor bound to appropriate money to execute treaties, I would say that, although the House has never refused to appropriate money to carry out treaties, it has, nevertheless, asserted its right to do so, and the point has never been yielded; and when money has been voted to execute treaties it has always been on the ground that the House approved them, and not because it was believed that they were under any obligation to do so.

On this point I invite attention to the opinion of Judge John McLean, of the Supreme Court of the United States. The case of Turner *vs.* American Baptist Missionary Union (5 Mc-Lean, 344) decides as follows:

"A treaty is the supreme la.7 of the land only when the treaty-making power can carry it into effect.

"A treaty which stipulates for the payment of money undertakes to do that which the treaty-making power cannot do; therefore the treaty is not the supreme law of the land.

"To give it the effect the action of Congress is necessary. And in this action the Representatives and Senators act on their own judgment and responsibility, and not on the judgment and responsibility of the treaty-making power.

"*A foreign government may be presumed to know the power of appropriating money belongs to Congress.*

"No act of any part of the Government can be held to be a law which has not all the sanctions to make it law."

But it is said that Russia has given us possession, and for that reason we should vote the money. Quite otherwise. Why was possession taken by the Executive of this Government and yielded by Russia before the money was paid or even voted? No interest of this Government was suffering for the want of immediate possession, and it is believed that no benefit could arise to this Government from having possession before the time stipulated for the payment of the money. The same may be said in regard to Russia, unless the country was so worthless that every day she held possession was a positive damage to her, and for that reason she was in haste to be rid of it. It requires no great stretch of imagination to divine the scarcely hidden causes which governed the parties negotiating this treaty in stipulating for immediate possession. They could hardly have failed to foresee that this treaty would be strongly opposed in this House, and that upon its merits it could have no chance for the necessary appropriation. An extraordinary pressure was seen to be necessary, and that pressure was sought for in giving and taking possession.

Will this House allow itself to be coerced by any such performance? To state the question is to answer it. But it is said that Russia, our best friend, will be offended if we fail to appropriate the money. I fully recognize the friendly character of the Russian Government in the past, and the importance of cultivating friendly relations in the future; but, for the reason stated, it is denied that any just ground of offence can exist if this House fails to sanction the treaty. It is maintained that the refusal to appropriate money to carry this treaty into execution would be cause of war on the part of Russia, and the action of President Jackson is cited, in the case of the refusal of France to pay the money stipulated to be paid in the treaty of Paris, negotiated in 1831. But that case is in no sense parallel to the one under consideration. There the claim of this Government existed long before the treaty was negotiated. The treaty merely liquidated the amount which France was to pay. Our right to the money was perfect and complete before the treaty was made, and a refusal to pay it was as much a cause of war before the treaty as afterward; and had there been no treaty liquidating the amount, the right to demand payment would still have existed, and, if need be, to use force to compel it.

Every intelligent man must see that if we had an existing treaty with Russia that gave us the right to trade on that coast, the right to fish on that coast, the right to land and cure fish on the coast, and the right to visit the interior waters and trade with the natives, we had virtually everything that is desirable, and that there could be no excuse for this treaty. Neither the chairman of the committee nor any other gentleman will dispute that if we could have those privileges it would be better for us to have them without the responsibility and never-ending expense of ruling and governing a nation of savages. Now the gentleman from Massachusetts undertakes to say that we had no such treaty rights. As these things are denied, it is made my duty to prove them.

In 1832 a treaty was negotiated with Russia, the negotiators being Hon. James Buchanan on the part of the United States and Count Nesselrode on the part of Russia. That treaty gave us the rights I have mentioned, and was of full force and effect at the time of the negotiation of the late treaty for the purchase of Russian America.

The gentleman says that this treaty was abrogated. I take issue with him. This treaty having been in existence ten years, that provision of it in article four, which allowed our people to go inland into the harbors and bays and rivers to trade with the natives, was abrogated, and the reason assigned was that our people went there not for the purpose of legitimate trade, but for the purpose of selling whiskey and firearms to the Indians; and that provision was therefore abrogated after a long conference and correspondence between the State Department, through Mr. Forsyth, and the Russian Government. Mr. Forsyth maintained always, and never yielded the point, that under the first article of the treaty we had the right of landing on the coast, but not to visit the interior bays, and that right was not and could not be terminated.

This treaty of which I speak—the treaty of 1832—has never

been abrogated, and never can be abrogated until a certain notice has been given, which never has been yet given. It is a good and valid treaty to-day; and under that treaty we are entitled to all the rights which they have granted to Great Britain or to any other country, including the fishing rights granted to Great Britain in 1859.

Gentlemen who have looked into this matter will have discovered that when this treaty was first negotiated the proposition was to pay only $7,000,000; that was the original agreement. But Mr. Seward insisted that it should be free from all incumbrances; and Mr. Stoeckl agreed to that, and then Mr. Seward said very mildly, without inquiring what those incumbrances were: "I will give you a couple of hundred thousand dollars in gold in addition if you will do so." Of course Mr. Stoeckl agreed to take the additional $200,000 in coin.

Now, I will tell you what those incumbrances are, and which are not yet removed, and which cannot be removed. First, the treaty with Great Britain, which cannot be abrogated for ten years from 1859, and which gives them the right to navigate these rivers forever.

GENERAL BANKS.—It is not provided by that treaty that Great Britain shall have the right to navigate the rivers of Russian America forever. It provides that in relation to the rivers rising in British Columbia and passing through this portion of Russian America in front of British Columbia the right of navigation shall be secured to Great Britain. It is a right which covers the Stikine only, and it is a right which this country has claimed from its very foundation; that where a river takes its rise in one country and passes through another country the people of the country where the river took its rise have the right to follow the river to its mouth.

MR. WASHBURN.—This provision does not apply to the Stikine river only. Every river of any importance in Alaska rises in British America, and the British people have the right to navigate those rivers forever. By that same treaty Sitka is guaranteed to Great Britain as a free port for the term of ten years. It is a free port to-day for the Government of Great Britain. Does the gentleman deny it? Yet here he asks us to pay $7,200,000 in gold for this territory before these incumbrances are removed.

GENERAL BANKS.—The ten years will have expired next year.

MR. WASHBURN.—Very well; when the incumbrance is removed it will be time enough to talk about paying this money for it. And how do you propose to remove the incumbrances on the rivers which are made free to Great Britain forever? The sailors, traders, and fishermen of Great Britain have the right to-day to go into all the interior waters of Alaska under this treaty; just the same right that our people have. Great Britain to-day has the same right on the coast of Alaska that we have, except the miserable privilege of governing the fifty, sixty, or seventy thousand wretched savages there. And yet the gentleman comes in here and coolly asks us to vote $7,200,000 in gold for this territory.

Now, sir, this treaty was negotiated in secret. I say it was negotiated in such a manner that the representatives of the people might not know of it, as it was justly feared they would protest against it. The negotiation was carried on here while we were in session in March, 1867. Mr. Stoeckl, on the 25th of March, 1867, said to Mr. Seward that he would accept his proposition. The trade was closed between them, but they kept it a profound secret until our adjournment. Why? This House adjourned on the 30th of March, 1867, at twelve o'clock. On the same day was signed this treaty in Washington. I believe that signatures were withheld until after our adjournment that no remonstrance could be heard from the representatives of the people.

I wish I had time to answer every proposition of the gentleman from Massachusetts at length; but I cannot follow him in his flights of fancy. He pictured Alaska as the finest country upon the face of the earth. He declared solemnly there was no country on the face of God's earth which could support as many industries as Alaska. He said it would support one million people in more industries than any other country. He told us it was a magnificent agricultural country. If gentlemen would like through the eye to have an idea of this territory, of Alaska, they can look upon a photograph of Sitka which I have here, the most favorable place upon the coast. [Here Mr. Washburn held up a large photograph.] They have established themselves on various places, but had finally to give them up and confine themselves to Sitka. We have testimony that there are not a dozen acres of arable land in the neighborhood of Sitka, yet we are told by the Commissioner of the General Land Office that there are twelve million acres of arable land in Alaska. He has no information of his own, and yet he undertakes to instruct us and make statements that have no foundation whatever. He has written a letter containing an "infinite deal of nothing." He has no authority for anything

he says. There is not one grain of wheat in this bushel of chaff.
He talks of deposits of gold. I defy any living man upon the
face of the earth to produce any evidence that an ounce of
gold was ever extracted from the territory of Alaska.

My friend from Massachusetts gets up here and tells us
there are over twelve million acres of arable land in Alaska,
and that it is capable of sustaining a thrifty and happy population of over one million freemen. Now, sir, without resorting
to that kind of testimony that he has brought in, I have official
documents from St. Petersburg of a date no longer ago than
August last. Mr. Seward, dear soul, in his simplicity of heart,
wrote to Cassius M. Clay, Minister to Russia, to ascertain what
system of disposing of lands prevailed in Alaska. Well, Mr.
Clay submitted that letter to the Russian Cabinet, and I think
I see them reading it, and they must have had a very jolly time
of it at the expense of the Secretary of State. Here is the answer they gave:

"The native population of each separate island is so insignificant that
the inhabitants of any one could not meet with the slightest cause of collision of interest in the use of lands; in addition to this, the soil itself being perfectly barren and unfit either for agricultural or grazing purposes,
there was no reason why the natives should endeavor to extend the limits of
their lands." . . .

"There was even less ground for the enactment of any particular regulations in view of immigrant settlers. Who can ever have a mind to settle
in that country, where permanent fogs and dampness of atmosphere and
want of solar heat and light, leaving out of the question anything like agriculture, make it impossible to provide even a sufficient supply of hay for
cattle, and where man, from want of bread, salt, and meat, to escape
scurvy must constantly live upon fish, berries, shell-fish, sea-cabbages, and
other products of the sea, soaking them profusely with the grease of sea
beasts. The Aleutian Islands may attract transient traders, but no permanent settlers; to inhabit them one must be an Aleute; and, if it were not
for the sea surrounding the islands, this country, owing to its unfavorable
climatic conditions and the sterility of its ground, would have never been
inhabited at all."

This is the paradise which we heard depicted in such eloquent terms yesterday, and I was almost led to believe that the
generally received account we have that the Garden of Eden
was on the green banks of the Euphrates was a mistake, and
that the paradise of our first parents was really on "Oonalaska's
shore."

But, sir, I desire to call the attention of the committee to
the influences that have been brought to bear to induce this
House to vote this appropriation. It dates back to the time
when the treaty was first negotiated. I believe I state nothing
more than the fact when I say that the Secretary of State did

not act entirely upon his own judgment when he bought this territory. I believe the fact to be that when he conceived the idea of purchasing it he telegraphed to General Halleck, at San Francisco, to inquire of him how much it would do to pay for Alaska, and General Halleck replied that it would answer to pay from five to ten million dollars. Mr. Seward thought it would not be quite right to offer the smallest sum; so he split the difference and offered $7,000,000.

The treaty having been negotiated, it became necessary to get it through the Senate; and the first piece of machinery is a telegram from General Halleck, as follows:

SAN FRANCISCO, CALIFORNIA, *April 4, 1867.*

HON. EDWIN M. STANTON, *Secretary of War:*

I learn from a gentleman who has recently visited many parts of Russian America that its value is greater than has been supposed. The rejection of the treaty will cause great dissatisfaction on this coast, especially in California.

H. W. HALLECK, *Major General.*

This dispatch was instantly made public here to operate on the Senate. It will be observed that he says that its rejection would cause great dissatisfaction in California. How could he know that? No man in California or Washington not behind the scenes knew that any such scheme was on foot on the 4th day of April, the date of his dispatch. Now, sir, there is no evidence produced that any desire for this acquisition existed on the Pacific coast, either at the time the treaty was negotiated or now. A leading Republican paper of California, one of the ablest, if not the ablest, in the State, the Sacramento *Union,* as late as November last speaks of the treaty in very contemptuous terms, calls Alaska a *terra incognita,* and says:

"That persons well informed as to Alaska are ungrateful enough to hint that we could have bought a much superior elephant in Siam or Bombay for one hundredth part of the money, with not a ten thousandth part of the expense incurred in keeping the animal in proper condition."

After the treaty was negotiated Captain Howard, of the revenue service, was sent up to explore Alaska. He was told to look for fishing banks, for coal, and for precious metals. I have his report here.

In regard to minerals, the geologist of the expedition, Mr. Blake, says that "exaggerated ideas have been formed of the mineral wealth of Alaska." None of these gentleman succeeded in finding mineral wealth of any kind there, although they were constantly in pursuit of it.

Exaggerated reports in regard to this country in reference to its furs have been circulated. Mr. Wilson, in his letter, says that the value of the fur seals alone is over half a million annually.

Now, I assert—and I have the facts and figures to prove it—that the fur trade is becoming rapidly exhausted, and that the total value of all the furs gathered in Alaska is considerably less than two hundred thousand dollars a year, and is diminishing from year to year with great rapidity.

Mr. Bulkley, who says that the seal fisheries alone could be made to pay for Alaska, admits himself that unless the seal fisheries are protected as the Russians protected them they will not last any length of time. And Professor Davidson says that with the utmost care on the part of the Russian authorities the furs and fur-bearing animals have rapidly diminished from year to year. With the transfer to this Government, and the consequent invasion of the country by our people, it can safely be said that the fur trade will soon cease to exist. Under the Russian system they only captured about thirty-three thousand seals a year, which, at three dollars a piece, their highest value, is $99,000; and yet we are told that the seal trade will pay for the whole purchase. Now, if under the Russian system they received less than $100,000 a year for the fur seals captured, how long would it take to pay off this debt of $7,200,000? It is a good deal like the sum that used to be in the arithmetic about the frog at the bottom of the well jumping up two feet and falling back three feet each day, and about the time that the frog would get to the surface you would pay off this debt from the fur seal trade.

In regard to salmon, we read of such immense numbers up those streams that they are driven up on the shores, forming winrows three feet in depth, and that they sell for seven cents a pound in gold, and we are also informed that the bears come down from the mountains to feed upon them, their dainty appetites selecting only the heads, rejecting the other parts of the salmon altogether. This is told in the report of the majority of the committee, and we are gravely asked to believe it, and the gentleman from Massachusetts has stated substantially the same in his speech, and gave us the philosophy of it. Wilson, the philosopher, must look to his laurels.

Now, Mr. Chairman, I have no doubt that there are many salmon in the rivers of Alaska. That is also the case in regard to the rivers of Washington Territory and Oregon. Inexhaustible numbers of salmon annually visit the rivers, sounds, and bays of our western coast, and we have now no occasion, and will have no occasion for a hundred years to come, to visit the rivers of Alaska for salmon.

The gentleman from Massachusetts also quotes the testimony of Captain Bryant, who says that Behring Sea is an immense reservoir for codfish. Yet Colonel Bulkley, of the telegraphic expedition, whom my friend from Massachusetts says is good authority, says there are few or no codfish in Behring Sea, and he, too, gives the "philosophy" why codfish do not exist up in that sea.

There is one other subject that I ought to speak of, and that is the timber of this region. I will only say that it does not exist to any extent on the Aleutian Islands, nor north of Cook's inlet, and that what there is is on the inaccessible mountains that skirt the coast south of Mount St. Elias, and along a strip of country but thirty miles wide.

Now I think, Mr. Chairman, I have pretty clearly demonstrated the utter worthlessness of this Alaska territory. You are not simply asked to appropriate $7,200,000 in gold for a worthless country—if we could get off with that I might, perhaps, be content to submit to it—but with this $7,200,000 come the annual expenses of this territory, in my judgment amounting to several million dollars a year, with no corresponding return.

You will recollect, Mr. Chairman, that I called attention to the agency of a gallant general on the Pacific coast in forcing this purchase upon the country. I will now read from a letter of his of May 22, 1867, to the Adjutant-General of the army, in which he gives his opinion as to how much this country will cost us. After we had acquired it he began to see its true character. He says:

"This country and the adjacent British territory contain a very large Indian population, some of whose tribes are warlike, and of a character far superior to those of Oregon, California, Nevada, and adjacent countries. Should our Indian system, with its treaties, annuities, agents, frauds, and peculations, be introduced there, Indian wars must inevitably follow, and instead of a few companies for its military occupation as many regiments will be called for, with the resulting expenditure of many million dollars every year."

Such are the kind of inhabitants you acquire with Alaska. It is said this is only a little sum; only $7,200,000. Yes, sir; it is only $7,200,000. But let me tell gentlemen that if they pass this appropriation it will be but a few days before you will hear of the ratification by the Senate of the treaty for the purchase of St. Thomas; and if the doctrine of my friend from Massachusetts [Mr. Banks] obtains here, you cannot avoid paying $7,500,000 more for the purchase of St. Thomas. Now, the gentleman will not say that St. Thomas is not as valuable a purchase as Alaska. If we pay for Alaska we shall pay for St. Thomas.

But are we to stop with the purchase of Alaska and St. Thomas? No, sir. I believe a treaty is now being negotiated with Denmark for the purchase of Greenland and Iceland. [Laughter.] Well, gentlemen, laugh at it. I tell gentlemen who go for Alaska that Greenland to-day is a better purchase. And the man who votes for Alaska must vote for Greenland or he will be an inconsistent man. This is not mere loose talk. I have had placed upon my table since I began to speak to-day some pages of a document now printing at the Government Printing Office for the State Department, which shows that the purchase of Greenland is in contemplation.

Men talk about "manifest destiny," and assure us that we are destined to absorb this entire continent, and the idea seems so grand that no one feels inclined to count the cost or inquire into consequences. When that day comes we shall cease to be the "United States," but "States dissevered, discordant, belligerent." Sir, I will be no party to the inauguration of this policy you now propose, of acquiring remote and worthless possessions at the expense of my constituents, and to them I appeal for my justification.

Other speeches upon the Alaska Purchase are thus summarized by Mr. Blaine in his "Twenty Years of Congress":

General Benjamin F. Butler (Massachusetts) sustained Mr. Washburn's position in a characteristic speech, especially answering General Banks' argument that we should pay this amount from a spirit of friendship for Russia.

"If we are to pay this price as usury on the friendship of Russia, we are paying for it very dear indeed. If we are to pay for her friendship, I desire to give her the seven million two hundred thousand dollars in cash, and let her keep Alaska, because I think it may be a small sum to give for the friendship if we could only get rid of the land, or rather the ice, which we are to get by paying for it."

He maintained that it was in evidence before the House officially "that for ten years the entire product of the whole country of Alaska did not exceed three million dollars."

John A. Peters (Maine) pronounced the territory "intrinsically valueless, the conclusive proof of which is found in the fact that Russia is willing to sell it." He criticised the action of the Senate in negotiating the treaty.

"If the treaty-making power can buy, they can sell. If they can buy land with money, they can buy money with land. If they can buy a part of a country, they can buy the whole of a country. If they can sell a part of our country, they can sell the whole of it!"

Rufus P. Spalding (Ohio) on the other hand maintained that "notwithstanding all the sneers that have been cast on Alaska, if it could be sold again, individuals would take it off our hands and pay us two or three millions for the bargain."[1]

General Robert C. Schenck (Ohio) thought the purchase in itself highly objectionable, but was "willing to vote the money because the treaty had been made with a friendly power; one of those that stood by us, almost the only one that stood by us when all the rest of the powers of the world seemed to be turning away from us in our recent troubles."

Thaddeus Stevens (Pennsylvania) supported the measure on the ground that it was a valuable acquisition to the wealth and power of the country. He argued also in favor of the right of the Senate to make the treaty.

Leonard Myers (Pennsylvania) was sure that if we did not acquire Alaska it would be transferred to Great Britain.

"The nation which struggled so hard for Vancouver and her present Pacific boundary, and which still insists on having the little island of San Juan, will never let such an opportunity slip. Canada, as matters now stand, would become ours some

---

[1] Indeed, one proposition to this effect was formally presented to Congress.

day could her people learn to be Americans; but never if England secures Alaska.''

William Higby (California) answered the objections relating to climate.

"I do not know whether the people of the East yet believe what has been so often declared, that our winters on the Pacific are nearly as mild as our summers, and yet such is the fact."

Samuel Shellabarger (Ohio) opposed the purchase. He said those nations which had been compact and solid had been the most enduring, while those which had the most extended territory lasted the least space of time.

Hiram Price (Iowa) thought that it was "far better to expend the $7,200,000 in improving the Mississippi river, in order that bread-stuffs may be transported cheaply from the West to the seaboard." He had no faith in the value of the territory proposed to be purchased.

Dennis McCarthy (New York) rejected the plea that we should purchase Alaska because Russia is a friendly power.

"I ask this House whence this friendship comes. It comes from self-interest. She is the absorbing power of the eastern continent, and she recognizes us as the absorbing power of the western continent; and through friendship for us she desires to override and overbalance the governments of Europe which are between her and us."

General Butler moved a proviso, that:

"The payment of $500,000 of said appropriation be withheld until the imperial government of Russia shall signify its willingness to refer to an impartial tribunal all such claims by American citizens against the imperial government as have been investigated by the State Department of the United States and declared to be just, and the amounts so awarded to be paid from said $500,000 so withheld."

General James A. Garfield, presiding at the time over the Committee of the Whole, ruled it out of order, and on an appeal being taken the decision was sustained by 93 ayes and 27 nays. After dilatory motions and the offer of various amendments which were rejected the bill was passed on July 14 by 113 ayes and 43 nays.

The House prefaced the bill by a preamble, asserting in effect that "the subjects embraced in the treaty are among those which by the Constitution are submitted to the power of Congress, and over which Congress has jurisdiction, and for these reasons it is necessary that the consent of Congress should be given to the said stipulations before the same can have full force and effect." There was no mention of the Senate's ratification, merely a reference to the fact that "the President has entered into a treaty with the Emperor of Russia, and has agreed to pay him the sum of seven million, two hundred thousand dollars in coin." The House by this preamble evidently claimed that its consent to the treaty was just as essential as the consent of the Senate—that it was, in short, a subject for the consideration of Congress.

The Senate was unwilling to admit such a pretension, especially when put forth by the House in this bald form, and therefore rejected the bill unanimously. The matter was sent to conference, and by changing the preamble a compromise was promptly effected, which preserved the rank and dignity of both branches. It declared that "whereas the President had entered into a treaty with the Emperor of Russia, and *the Senate thereafter gave its advice and consent to said treaty, . . . and whereas said stipulations cannot be carried into full force and effect, except by legislation to which the consent of both Houses of Congress is necessary;* therefore be it enacted that there be appropriated the sum of $7,200,000" for the purpose named. With this compromise the bill was readily passed and became a law by the President's approval July 27, 1868.

The preamble finally agreed upon, says Mr. Blaine, though falling far short of the one first adopted by the House, was yet regarded as a victory for that branch. The issue between the Senate and the House, now adjusted by a compromise, was an old one, agitated at different periods ever since the controversy over the Jay treaty in 1794-95. It is simply whether the House is bound to vote for an appropriation to carry out a treaty constitutionally made by the President and the Senate without judging for itself whether, on the merits of the treaty, the appropriation should be made.

CHAPTER XV

The Alabama Claims

Depredations by the *Alabama* and Other Confederate Privateers on Northern Commerce—Great Britain's Complicity in the Matter—Her Early Refusal to Grant Redress—Johnson-Clarendon Treaty: Senator Charles Sumner [Mass.] Opposes Its Confirmation; It Is Rejected—Negotiations Reopened by Great Britain—Treaty of Washington Submits the *Alabama* and Other Disputes with Great Britain to Arbitration—*Alabama* Arbitrators Find in Favor of the United States—Minor British Claims Allowed—Canadian Boundary Dispute Settled in Favor of the United States.

THE Declaration of Paris, adopted by the chief European nations, including Great Britain, in 1856, abolished privateering. The Confederate Government, however, adopted the practice as one of its first acts, and a number of privateers set out from Southern ports to harass the commerce of the North. Meanwhile Queen Victoria had issued a proclamation of neutrality in the American war, according belligerent rights to both contestants, and forbidding her subjects to equip or aid vessels of either party. Notwithstanding this, harbors such as Nassau in the British West Indies became the refuge of Confederate cruisers—privateers no less than blockade runners.

Against this practice Charles Francis Adams, the American minister to Great Britain, made firm and frequent protests which were not heeded.

The Confederate privateer *Alabama* was the most notorious offender against the Declaration of Paris. She was built at Birkenhead, England, ostensibly for the use of British subjects, but under circumstances which indicated that this purpose was a subterfuge, and that, so soon as she was on the high seas, she would be turned over to Confederates for privateering purpose. While

she was building Minister Adams repeatedly protested
to the British Government that this was the purpose,
and, after delaying until she was ready to sail, the
Government took feeble measures to detain her. These
were evaded by the vessel, known simply as "No. 290,"
sailing without registry or clearance on July 29, 1862.
She took on her equipment from two English vessels
in the Azores, assumed the name *Alabama*, and, under
command of Raphael Semmes, began her career of depredation on United States commerce. She had destroyed
seventy United States vessels, before her own destruction on June 19, 1864, near Cherbourg, France, by the
United States war vessel, the *Kearsarge,* John A. Wins-
low, commander. Captain Semmes escaped on a private
English yacht.

In similar manner other Confederate privateers such
as the *Florida, Georgia* and *Shenandoah* were aided by
British subjects, and in this escaped the attention of
British officials. These, too, committed many depredations on United States commerce, the total direct damage
of all the cruisers being enormous. The secondary
damage arising from the decrease of American shipping
for fear of loss and from high insurance rates was
incalculable. These losses greatly increased the strength
of the contention of the Peace party in the North that
the war should be stopped before the commerce and
industry of the country were irreparably injured.
Thereby Mr. Lincoln's Government was greatly impeded
in the prosecution of the war.

At the close of the war in 1865 Minister Adams
proposed to Lord John Russell, the British foreign secretary under Lord Palmerston, premier (whom Russell
succeeded in the same year as premier), that the matter
be submitted to friendly arbitration. This proposal was
flatly refused. Thereupon William H. Seward, the
United States Secretary of State, notified the British
Government that no further efforts for arbitration would
be made. In August, 1866, he submitted to the British
Government a list of individual claims for damages inflicted by the *Alabama.* Mr. Stanley, who had succeeded
to the office of British foreign secretary under the ad-

ministration of his father, the Earl of Derby, who had followed Russell, decisively declined to receive the claims. The Earl of Derby died in 1868 and was succeeded by Benjamin Disraeli, later Earl of Beaconsfield.

In May, 1868, Minister Adams retired from his mission, and in June, 1868, Reverdy Johnson succeeded him. Before he could reopen negotiations on the Alabama claims Disraeli was succeeded by William E. Gladstone, and Lord Stanley, in the Foreign Office, by the Earl of Clarendon.

With Lord Clarendon, Minister Johnson, with the approval of Secretary Seward, promptly agreed upon a treaty in the matter, which reached the United States in February, 1869. It was presented to the Senate, which acted upon it in executive (secret) session. Charles Sumner (Massachusetts), chairman of the Committee on Foreign Relations, opposed confirmation of the treaty in a speech in executive session on April 13, 1869. Later, after confirmation had been refused, the injunction of secrecy was removed by order of the Senate, and the speech was published in the *Congressional Globe*.

OUR CLAIMS ON ENGLAND

SENATOR SUMNER

I do not disguise the importance of this act; but I believe that, in the interest of peace, which every one should have at heart, the treaty must be rejected. A treaty which, instead of removing an existing grievance, leaves it for heart-burning and rancor, cannot be considered a settlement of pending questions between two nations. It may seem to settle them, but does not. It is nothing but a snare. And such is the character of the treaty now before us. The massive grievance under which our country suffered for years is left untouched; the painful sense of wrong planted in the national heart is allowed to remain. For all this there is not one word of regret or even of recognition; nor is there any semblance of compensation. It cannot be for the interest of either party that such a treaty should be ratified. It cannot promote the interest of the United States, for we naturally seek justice as the foundation of a good understanding with Great Britain; nor can it promote the in-

terest of Great Britain, which must also seek a real settlement
of all pending questions.

If we look at the negotiation, which immediately preceded
the treaty, we find little to commend. You have it on your table.
I think I am not mistaken when I say that it shows a haste
which finds few precedents in diplomacy, but which is explained by the anxiety to reach a conclusion before the advent
of a new Administration. Mr. Seward and Mr. Reverdy Johnson both unite in this unprecedented activity, using the Atlantic
cable freely. I should not object to haste or to the freest use
of the cable if the result were such as could be approved; but,
considering the character of the transaction, and how completely
the treaty conceals the main cause of offence, it seems as if the
honorable negotiators were engaged in huddling something out
of sight.

The treaty has for its model the Claims Convention of 1853.
To take such a convention as a model was a strange mistake.
This convention was for the settlement of outstanding claims
of American citizens on Great Britain, and of British subjects
on the United States, which had arisen since the treaty of
Ghent in 1815. It concerned individuals only and not the
nation. It was not in any respect political; nor was it to remove any sense of national wrong. To take such a convention
as the model for a treaty, which was to determine a national
grievance of transcendant importance in the relations of two
countries, marked on the threshold an insensibility to the true
nature of the difference to be settled. At once it belittled the
work to be done.

An inspection of the treaty shows how from beginning to
end it is merely for the settlement of individual claims on
both sides, putting both batches on an equality—so that the
sufferers by the misconduct of England may be counterbalanced
by British blockade-runners.

The provisions of the treaty are for the trial of these cases.
A commission is constituted, which is empowered to choose an
arbitrator; but in the event of a failure to agree, the arbitrator
shall be determined "by lot" out of two persons named by
each side. Even if this aleatory proceeding were a proper
device in the umpirage of private claims, it is strangely inconsistent with the solemnity which belongs to the present question. The moral sense is disturbed by such a process at any
stage of the trial; nor is it satisfied by the subsequent provision
for the selection of a sovereign or head of a friendly state as
arbitrator.

The treaty not merely makes no provision for the determination of the great question, but it seems to provide expressly that it shall never hereafter be presented. The petty provision for individual claims, subject to a set-off from the individual claims of England, so that in the end our country may possibly receive nothing, is the consideration for this strange surrender. I borrow a term from an English statesman on another occasion, if I call it a "capitulation." For the settlement of a few individual claims we condone the original, far-reaching, and destructive wrong.

Whatever the treaty may say in terms, there is no settlement in fact, and, until this is made, there will be a constant menace of discord. Nor can it be forgotten that there is no recognition of the rule of international duty applicable to such cases. This, too, is left unsettled.

While doing so little for us the treaty makes ample provision for all known claims on the British side. As these are exclusively "individual" they are completely covered by the text, which has no limitations or exceptions. Already it is announced in England that even those of "confederate bondholders" are included. I have before me an English journal which describes the latter claims as founded on "immense quantities of cotton, worth at the time of their seizure nearly two shillings a pound, which were then in the legal possession of those bondholders"; and the same authority adds, "these claims will be brought, indifferently with others, before the designed joint commission whenever it shall sit." From another quarter I learn that these bondholders are "very sanguine of success *under the treaty as it is worded,* and certain it is that the loan went up from 0 to 10 as soon as it was ascertained that the treaty was signed." I doubt if the American people are ready just now to provide for any such claims. That they have risen in the markets is an argument against the treaty.

Passing from the treaty, I come now to consider briefly, but with proper precision, the true ground of complaint; and here again we shall see the constant inadequacy of the remedy now applied.

Here the speaker recalled British recognition of Confederate belligerency on the sea as well as on the land.

Ocean belligerency being a "fact," and not a "principle," can be recognized only on evidence showing its *actual existence,* according to the rule, first stated by Mr. Canning and afterward recognized by Earl Russell. But no such evidence was adduced; for it did not exist and never has existed.

Too much stress cannot be laid upon the rule that belligerency is a "fact" and not a "principle." It is, perhaps, the most important contribution to this discussion, and its original statement, on the occasion of the Greek revolution, does honor to its author, unquestionably the brightest genius ever directed to this subject. According to this rule, belligerency must be proved to exist, it must be shown. It cannot be imagined or divined or invented; it must exist as a "fact" within the knowledge of the world, or at least as a "fact" susceptible of proof. Nor can it be inferred on the ocean merely from its existence on the land. From the beginning, when God called the dry land earth and the gathering of the waters called He seas, the two have been separate, and the power over one has not necessarily implied power over the other. There is a dominion of the land and a dominion of the ocean. But, whatever power the rebels possessed on the land, they were always without power on the ocean. Admitting that they were belligerents on the land, they were never belligerents on the ocean:

> The oak leviathans, whose huge ribs make
> Their clay creator the vain title take
> Of Lord of thee, *and arbiter of war;*

these they never possessed. Such was the "fact" that must govern the present question. The rule, so simple, plain, and intelligible, as stated by Mr. Canning, is a decisive touch-stone of the British concession, which, when brought to it, is found to be without support.

Unfriendly in the precipitancy with which it was launched, this concession was more unfriendly in substance. It was the first stage in the depredations on our commerce. Had it not been made no rebel ship could have been built in England. Every step in her building would have been piracy. Nor could any munitions of war have been furnished. The direct consequence of this concession was to place the rebels on an equality with ourselves in all British markets, whether of ships or munitions of war. As these were open to the national Government, so were they open to the rebels. The asserted neutrality between the two began by this tremendous concession when rebels, at one stroke, were transformed not only into belligerents, but into customers.

In attributing to that bad proclamation this peculiar influence I follow the authority of the law lords of England, who, according to authentic report, announced that, without it, the fitting out of a ship in England to cruise against the United States would have been an act of piracy. That England became an "arsenal" for the rebels we know, but this could not have been unless the proclamation had prepared the way.

The only justification that I have heard for this extraordinary concession, which unleashed upon our country the furies of foreign war to commingle with the furies of rebellion at home, is that President Lincoln undertook to proclaim *a blockade* of the rebel ports. By the use of this word "blockade" the concession is vindicated. Had President Lincoln proclaimed *a closing* of the rebel ports, there could have been no such concession. This is a mere technicality. Lawyers might call it an *apex juris;* and yet on this sharp point England hangs her defence. It is sufficient that in a great case like the present, where the correlative duties of a friendly power are in question, an act fraught with such portentous evil cannot be vindicated on a technicality. In this debate there is no room for technicality on either side. We must look at the substance and find a reason in nothing short of overruling necessity. War cannot be justified merely on a technicality; nor can the concession of ocean belligerency to rebels without a port or prize court. Such a concession, like war itself, must be at the peril of the nation making it.

The British assumption, besides being offensive from mere technicality, is inconsistent with the proclamation of the President, taken as a whole, which, while appointing a blockade, is careful to reserve the rights of sovereignty, thus putting foreign powers on their guard against any premature concession. After declaring an existing insurrection in certain States, and the obstruction of the laws for the collection of the revenue, as the motive for action, the President invokes not only the law of nations but the "laws of the United States," and, in further assertion of the national sovereignty, declares rebel cruisers to be pirates. Clearly the proclamation must be taken as a whole and its different provisions so interpreted as to harmonize with each other. If they cannot stand together, then it is the "blockade" which must be modified by the national sovereignty and not the national sovereignty by the blockade. Such should have been the interpretation of a friendly power, especially when it is considered that there are numerous precedents of what the great German authority, Heffter, calls "pacific blockade," or blockade without concession of ocean belligerency, as, in the case of France, England and Russia against Turkey,

1827; France against Mexico, 1837-39; France and Great Britain against the Argentine Republic, 1838-48; Russia against the Circassians, 1831-36, illustrated by the seizure of the *Vixen* so famous in diplomatic history (Hautefeuille, *Des Droits et des Devoirs des Neutres*). Cases like these led Heffter to lay down the rule that *"blockade"* does not necessarily constitute *a state of regular war* (*Droit International*, Secs. 112, 121), as was assumed by the British proclamation—even in the face of positive words by President Lincoln asserting the national sovereignty and appealing to the "laws of the United States." The existence of such cases was like a notice to the British government against the concession so rashly made. It was an all-sufficient warning, which this power disregarded.

So far as is now known, the whole case for England is made to stand on the use of the word "blockade" by President Lincoln. Had he used any other word the concession of belligerency would have been without justification, even such as is now imagined. It was this word which, with magical might, opened the gates to all those bountiful supplies by which hostile expeditions were equipped against the United States. It opened the gates of war. Most appalling is it to think that one little word, unconsciously used by a trusting President, could be caught up by a friendly power and made to play such a part.

I may add that there is one other word often invoked for apology. It is "neutrality," which, it is said, was proclaimed between two belligerents. Nothing could be fairer, always provided that the "neutrality" proclaimed did not begin with a concession to one party, without which this party would be powerless. Between two established nations, both independent, as between Russia and France, there may be neutrality; for the two are already equal in rights, and the proclamation would be precisely equal in its operation. But where one party is an established nation and the other is nothing but an odious combination of rebels, the proclamation is most unequal in operation; for it begins by a solemn investiture of rebels with all the rights of war, saying to them, as was once said to the youthful knight, "Rise; here is a sword; use it." To call such an investiture a proclamation of neutrality is a misnomer. It was a proclamation of equality between the national Government on the one side and rebels on the other, and no plausible word can obscure this distinctive character.

Here the speaker recounted the building and escape of the "pirate" ships.

Here beyond all question was negligence, or, according to the language of Lord Brougham on another occasion, "crass negligence," making England justly responsible for all that ensued.

Lord Russell, while trying to vindicate his government and repelling the complaints of the United States, more than once admitted that the escape of the *Alabama* was a "scandal and a reproach," which, to my mind, is very like a confession. Language could not be stronger. Surely such an act cannot be blameless. If damages are ever awarded to a friendly power for injuries received it is difficult to see where they could be more strenuously claimed than in a case, which the First Minister of the offending power did not hesitate to characterize so strongly.

Here the speaker presented evidence showing the enlistment of a crew, many of the "royal navy reserve," with the express understanding that they were to engage in privateering against United States commerce.

The dedication of the ship to the rebel service, from the very laying of the keel and the organization of her voyage with England as her *naval base,* from which she drew munitions of war and men, made her departure as much a *hostile expedition* as if she had sailed forth from Her Majesty's dockyard. At a moment of profound peace between the United States and England there was a hostile expedition against the United States. It was in no just sense a commercial transaction, but an act of war.

The case is not yet complete. The *Alabama,* whose building was in defiance of law, international and municipal, whose escape was "a scandal and reproach," and whose enlistment of her crew was a fit sequel to the rest, after being supplied with an armament and with a rebel commander, entered upon her career of piracy. Mark, now, a new stage of complicity. Constantly the pirate ship was within reach of British cruisers, and, from time to time, within the shelter of British ports. For six days unmolested she enjoyed the pleasant hospitality of Kingston, in Jamaica, obtaining freely the coal and other supplies so necessary to her vocation. But no British cruiser, no British magistrate ever arrested the offending ship, whose voyage was a continuing "scandal and reproach" to the British government.

The excuse for this strange license is a curious technicality, as if a technicality could avail in this case at any stage. Borrowing a phrase from that master of admiralty jurisprudence, Sir William Scott, it is said that the ship "deposited" her original sin at the conclusion of her voyage, so that afterward she was blameless. But the *Alabama* never concluded her voyage until she sank under the guns of the *Kearsarge*, because she never had a port of her own. She was no better than the *Flying Dutchman*, and so long as she sailed was liable for that original sin which had impregnated every plank with an indelible dye. No British cruiser could allow her to proceed, no British port could give her shelter without renewing the complicity of England.

Thus her depredations and burnings, making the ocean blaze, all proceeded from England, which, by three different acts, lighted the torch. To England must be traced also all the widespread consequences which ensued.

I take the case of the *Alabama* because it is the best known, and because the building, equipment, and escape of this ship were under circumstances most obnoxious to judgment; but it will not be forgotten that there were consort ships, built under the shelter of that fatal proclamation, issued in such an eclipse of just principles, and, like the ships it unloosed, "rigged with curses dark." One after the other ships were built; one after the other, they escaped on their errand; and, one after the other, they enjoyed the immunities of British ports. Audacity reached its height when iron-clad rams were built, and the perversity of the British government became still more conspicuous by its long refusal to arrest these destructive engines of war, destined to be employed against the United States. This protracted hesitation, where the consequences were so menacing, is a part of the case.

It is plain that the ships which were built under the safeguard of this ill-omened proclamation; which stole forth from the British shores and afterward enjoyed the immunities of British ports, were not only British in origin, but British in equipment, British in armament, and British in crews. They were British in every respect, except in their commanders, who were rebel, and one of these, as his ship was sinking, owed his safety to a British yacht, symbolizing the omnipresent support of England. British sympathies were active in their behalf. The cheers of a British passenger ship crossing the path of the *Alabama* encouraged the work of piracy, and the cheers of the House of Commons encouraged the builder of the *Alabama*, while he defended what he had done and exclaimed, in taunt to him who is now an illustrious member of the British Cabinet,

John Bright, that he "would rather be handed down to posterity as the builder of a dozen *Alabamas*" than be the author of the speeches of that gentleman "crying up" the institutions of the United States, which the builder of the *Alabama,* rising with his theme, denounced "as of no value whatever and as reducing the very name of liberty to an utter absurdity," while the cheers of the House of Commons echoed back his words.

There are two circumstances by which the whole case is aggravated. One is found in the date of the proclamation, which lifted the rebels to an equality with the national Government; opening to them everything that was open to us, whether shipyard, foundries, or manufactories; and giving to them a flag on the ocean coequal with the flag of the Union. This extraordinary manifesto was issued on the day before the arrival of our minister in England. The British government knew of his coming. But in hottest haste they did this thing.

The other aggravation is found in its flagrant, unnatural departure from that anti-slavery rule, which, by manifold declarations, legislative, political, and diplomatic, was the avowed creed of England. Often was this rule proclaimed, but, if we except the great act of emancipation, never more pointedly than in the famous circular of Lord Palmerston, while Minister of Foreign Affairs, announcing to all nations that England was pledged to the universal abolition of slavery. And now, when slaveholders, in the very madness of barbarism, broke away from the national Government and attempted to found a new empire with slavery as its declared cornerstone, anti-slavery England, without a day's delay, without even waiting the arrival of our minister, who was known to be on his way, made haste to decree that this shameful and impossible pretension should enjoy equal rights with the national Government in her shipyards, foundries, and manufactories, and equal rights on the ocean. Such was the decree. Rebel slaveholders, occupied in a hideous attempt, were taken by the hand, and thus, with the official protection and the God-speed of anti-slavery England, commenced their accursed work.

I close this part of the argument by the testimony of Mr. Bright, who, in a speech at Rochdale, among his neighbors, February 3, 1863, thus exhibits the criminal complicity of England:

"I regret more than I have words to express this painful fact, that, of all the countries in Europe, this country is the only one which has men in it who are willing to take steps in favor of this intended slave government. We supply the ships;

we supply the arms, the munitions of war; *we give aid and comfort to the foulest of crimes. Englishmen only do it.''*—*Bright's Speeches,* Vol. I, p. 239.

At last the rebellion succumbed. British ships and British supplies had done their work, but they failed. And now the day of reckoning has come; but with little apparent sense of what is due on the part of England. Without one soothing word for a friendly power deeply aggrieved, without a single regret for what Mr. Cobden, in the House of Commons, called "the cruel losses" inflicted upon us, or for what Mr. Bright called "aid and comfort to the foulest of crimes," or for what a generous voice from Oxford University denounced as a "flagrant and maddening wrong," England simply proposes to submit the question of liability for "individual losses" to an anomalous tribunal where chance plays its part. This is all. Nothing is admitted even on this question; no rule for the future is established; while nothing is said of the indignity to the nation, nor of the damages to the nation. On an earlier occasion it was otherwise.

Here the speaker referred to the *Chesapeake* affair (see page 129).

The brilliant Mr. Canning, British Minister of Foreign Affairs, promptly volunteered overtures for an accommodation, by declaring His Majesty's readiness to take the whole of the circumstances of the case into consideration and "to make reparation for *any alleged injury to the sovereignty of the United States,* whenever it should be clearly shown that such injury has been actually sustained and that such reparation is really due." After years of painful negotiation the British minister at Washington, under date of November 1, 1811, offered to the United States three propositions: first, the disavowal of the unauthorized act; secondly, the immediate restoration, so far as circumstances would permit, of the men forcibly taken from the *Chesapeake;* and, thirdly, a suitable pecuniary provision for the sufferers in consequence of the attack on the *Chesapeake.*

I adduce this historic instance to illustrate partly the different forms of reparation. Here, of course, was reparation to individuals; but there was also reparation to the nation, whose sovereignty had been outraged.

The speaker then referred to the burning by Canadians of the American vessel *Carolina* in 1837.

Mr. Webster, in his negotiation with Lord Ashburton, characterized this act as "of itself a wrong and offence to the sovereignty and the dignity of the United States, for which to this day no atonement, or even apology, has been made by Her Majesty's government"; all these words being strictly applicable to the present case. Lord Ashburton, in reply, after recapitulating some mitigating circumstances and expressing a regret "that some explanation and apology for this occurrence was not immediately made," proceeds to make these. Here again was reparation for a wrong done to the nation.

Looking at what is due to us on the present occasion, we are brought again to the conclusion that the satisfaction of individuals whose ships have been burned or sunk is only a small part of what we may justly expect. As in the earlier cases where the national sovereignty was insulted, there should be an acknowledgment of wrong, or at least of liability, leaving to the commissioners the assessment of damages only. The blow inflicted by that fatal proclamation, which insulted our national sovereignty and struck at our unity as a nation, followed by broadside upon broadside, driving our commerce from the ocean, was kindred in character to those earlier blows, and, when we consider that it was in aid of slavery, it was a blow at civilization itself. Besides degrading us and ruining our commerce, its direct and constant influence was to encourage the rebellion, and to prolong the war waged by slave masters at such cost of treasure and blood. It was a terrible mistake, which I cannot doubt that good Englishmen must regret. And now, in the interest of peace, it is the duty of both sides to find a remedy, complete, just, and conciliatory, so that the deep sense of wrong and the detriment to the republic may be forgotten in that proper satisfaction which a nation loving justice cannot hesitate to offer.

Individual losses may be estimated with reasonable accuracy. Ships burned or sunk with their cargoes may be counted and their value determined; but this leaves without recognition the vaster damage to commerce driven from the ocean, and that other damage, immense and infinite, caused by the prolongation of the war, all of which may be called *national* in contradistinction to *individual*.

Our *national losses* have been frankly conceded by eminent Englishmen. I have already quoted Mr. Cobden, who did not hesitate to call them "cruel losses." During the same debate in which he let drop this testimony, he used other words, which show how justly he comprehended the case. *"You have been,"*

said he, "*carrying on war from these shores with the United
States,* and have been inflicting an amount of damage on that
country greater than would be produced by many ordinary
wars. It is estimated that the loss sustained by the capture
and burning of American vessels has been about $15,000,000, or
nearly £3,000,000 sterling. *But this is a small part of the injury which has been inflicted on the American marine.* We
have rendered the rest of her vast mercantile property useless."
After confessing his fears with regard to "the heaping up of a
gigantic material grievance such as was then rearing," he adds,
in memorable words:

"You have already done your worst toward the American
mercantile marine. What, with the high rate of insurance, what
with these captures, and what with the amount of damage you
have done to that which is left, you have virtually made valueless that vast property. Why, if you had gone and helped the
Confederates by bombarding all the accessible seaport towns
of America a few lives might have been lost which, as it is,
have not been sacrificed, but you could hardly have done more
injury in the way of destroying property than you have done
by these cruisers. [Hear, hear.]"

In the same debate William E. Forster said that so entirely
was our commerce driven from the ocean that for six weeks
not an American vessel was seen by the *Georgia* on her second
cruise.

Mr. Forster announced that "the carrying trade of the
United States was transferred to British merchants"; and Mr.
Cobden declared this circumstance to be "the *gravest part* of
the question of our relations with America." But this "gravest
part" is left untouched by the pending treaty.

Such is the candid and explicit testimony of Englishmen,
pointing the way to the proper rule of damages.

I refer to the interesting report of Mr. Morse, our consul at
London, made during the last year and published by the Secretary of State. After a minute inquiry the report shows that,
on the breaking out of the rebellion in 1861, the entire tonnage
of the United States, coasting and registered, was 5,539,813
tons, of which 2,642,625 tons were registered and employed in
foreign trade, and that, at the close of the rebellion in 1865,
notwithstanding an increase in coasting tonnage, our registered
tonnage had fallen to 1,602,528 tons, being a loss during the
four years of more than a million tons, amounting to about
forty per cent. of our foreign commerce. During the same four
years the total tonnage of the British empire rose from 5,895,-

369 tons to 7,322,604 tons, the increase being especially in the foreign trade. The report proceeds to say that, as to the cause of the decrease in America and the corresponding increase in the British empire, "there can be no room for question or doubt."

Beyond the actual loss in the national tonnage there was a further loss in the arrest of our natural increase in this branch of industry, which an intelligent statistician puts at five per cent. annually, making, in 1866, a total loss on this account of 1,384,958 tons, which must be added to 1,229,035 tons actually lost. The same statistician, after estimating the value of a ton at forty dollars gold, and making allowance for old and new ships, puts the sum total of national loss on this account at $110,000,000.

To these authorities I add that of the National Board of Trade, which, in a recent report on American shipping, after setting forth the diminution of our sailing tonnage, says that it is all to be traced to the war on the ocean, and the result is summed up in the words, that, "while the tonnage of the nation was rapidly disappearing by *the ravages of the rebel cruisers* and by sales abroad, there was no construction of new vessels going forward to counteract the decline even in part." Such is the various testimony, all tending to one conclusion.

This is what I have to say for the present on *national losses* through the destruction of commerce. These are large enough; but there is another chapter where they are larger far. I refer, of course, to the national losses caused by the prolongation of the war and traceable directly to England. No candid person, who studies this eventual period, can doubt that the rebellion was originally encouraged by hope of support from England; that it was strengthened at once by the concession of belligerent rights on the ocean; that it was fed to the end by British supplies; that it was quickened into renewed life with every report from the British pirates, flaming anew with every burning ship; nor can it be doubted that without British intervention the rebellion would have soon succumbed under the well-directed efforts of the national Government. Not weeks or months, but years were added in this way to our war, so full of the most costly sacrifice. The subsidies which, in other times, England contributed to Continental wars were less effective than the aid and comfort which she contributed to the rebellion. It cannot be said too often that the *naval base* of the rebellion was not in America, but in England. Mr. Cobden boldly said in the House of Commons that England made war from her shores on the United States "with an amount of damage to that country greater than in many ordinary wars.'' According to this testimony, the conduct of England was war; but it must not be forgotten that this war was carried on at our sole cost. The United States paid for a war waged by England upon the national unity.

The sacrifice of precious life is beyond human compensation; but there may be an approximate estimate of the national loss in money. The rebellion was suppressed at a cost of more than four thousand million dollars, a considerable portion of which has been already paid, leaving twenty-five hundred millions as a national debt to burden the people. If, through British intervention, the war was doubled in duration, or in any way extended, as cannot be doubted, then is England justly responsible for the additional expenditure to which our country was doomed; and, whatever may be the final settlement of these great accounts, such must be the judgment in any chancery which consults the simple equity of the case.

This plain statement, without one word of exaggeration or aggravation, is enough to exhibit the magnitude of the national losses, whether from the destruction of our commerce or the prolongation of the war. They stand before us mountain-high, with a base broad as the nation, and a mass stupendous as the rebellion itself. It will be for a wise statesmanship to determine how this fearful accumulation, like Pelion upon Ossa, shall be removed out of sight, so that it shall no longer overshadow the two countries.

Perhaps I ought to anticipate an objection from the other side to the effect that these national losses, whether from the destruction of our commerce or the prolongation of the war, are indirect and remote, so as not to be a just cause of claim. This is expressed at the common law by the rule that ''damages must be for the natural and proximate consequence of an act.'' (2 *Greenleaf, Ev.*, p. 210.) To this excuse the answer is explicit. The damages suffered by the United States are twofold, individual and national, being in each case direct and proximate, although in the one case individuals suffered and in the other case the nation. It is easy to see that there may be occasions, where, overtopping all individual damages, are damages suffered by the nation, so that reparation to individuals would be insufficient; nor can the claim of the nation be questioned simply because it is large, or because the evidence with regard to it is different from that in the case of an individual. In each case the damage must be proved by the best possible evidence, and this is all that law or reason can require. In the case of the nation the evidence is historic; and this is enough. Impartial history will record the national losses from British intervention, and it is only reasonable that the evidence of these losses should not be excluded from judgment. Because the case is without precedent, because no nation ever before received such injury from a friendly power, this can be no reason why the case should not be considered on the evidence.

Even the rule of the common law furnishes no impediment; for our damages are the natural consequence of what was done. But the rule of the Roman law, which is the rule of international law, is broader than that of the common law. The measure of damages, according to the Digest, is, "whatever may have been lost or might have been gained": *quantum mihi abest, quantumque lucrari potui.* This rule opens the door to ample reparation for all damages, whether individual or national.

There is another rule of the common law, in harmony with strict justice, which is applicable to the case. I find it in the law relating to *nuisances,* which provides that there may. be two distinct proceedings, first, in behalf of individuals, and, secondly, in behalf of the community. Obviously reparation to individuals does not supersede reparation to the community. The proceeding in the one case is by action at law, and, in the other, by indictment. The reason assigned by Blackstone for the latter is "because the damages being common to all the king's subjects, no one can assign his particular proportion of it." (3 *Black. Com.,* p. 219.) But this is the very case with regard to damages sustained by the nation.

A familiar authority furnishes an additional illustration, which is precisely in point:

"No person, natural or corporate, can have an action for a *public nuisance,* or punish it; but only the king in his public capacity of supreme governor and *pater familias* of the kingdom. Yet this rule admits of one exception; where a private person suffers some extraordinary damage beyond the rest of the king's subjects."—*Tomlins' Law Dict.,* Art. Nuisance.

Applying this rule to the present case, the way is clear. Every British pirate was a *public nuisance,* involving the British government, which must respond in damages, not only to the individuals who have suffered but also to the national Government, acting as *pater familias* for the common good of all the people.

Thus by an analogy of the common law, in the case of a public nuisance, also by the strict rule of the Roman law, which enters so largely into international law, and even by the rule of the common law relating to damages, all losses, whether individual or national, are the just subject of claim. It is not I who say this; it is the law.

Here the speaker recounted the sharp refusals by Great Britain on our repeated early presentations of the claims.[1]

Had the early overtures of our Government been promptly accepted, or had there been at any time a just recognition of the wrong done, I doubt not that this great question would have been settled; but the rejection of our very moderate propositions and the protracted delay, which afforded an opportunity to review the case in its different bearings, have awakened the people to the magnitude of the interests involved. If our demands are larger now than at our first call it is not the only time in history where such a rise has occurred. The story of the Sibyl is repeated, and England is the Roman king.

Shall these claims be liquidated and canceled promptly, or allowed to slumber until called into activity by some future exigency? There are many among us who, taking counsel of a sense of national wrong, would leave them to rest without settlement, so as to furnish a precedent for retaliation in kind, should England find herself at war. There are many in England who, taking counsel of a perverse political bigotry, have spurned them absolutely; and there are others who, invoking the point of honor, assert that England cannot entertain them without compromising her honor. Thus there is peril from both sides. It is not difficult to imagine one of our countrymen saying with Shakespeare's Jew, "The villainy you teach me I will execute, and it shall go hard, but I will better the instruction"; nor is it difficult to imagine an Englishman firm in his conceit, that no apology can be made and nothing paid. I cannot sympathize with either side. Be the claims more or less, they are honestly presented, with the conviction that they are just, and they should be considered candidly, so that they shall no longer lower, like a cloud ready to burst, upon two nations, which, according to their inclinations, can do each other such infinite injury or such infinite good. I know it is sometimes said that war between us must come sooner or later. I do not believe it. But if it must come, let it be later, and then I am sure it will never come. Meanwhile, good men must unite to make it impossible.

[1] See Chapter VII.

The Senate promptly rejected the Johnson-Clarendon Treaty with the approval of President Grant. The rejection was announced to the British Government by John Lothrop Motley, who had succeeded Mr. Johnson as our minister to Great Britain. Hamilton Fish, our Secretary of State, suggested to Mr. Motley that negotiations be temporarily suspended, though with maintenance of the justice of our claims.

In his second annual message (December, 1870) President Grant inaugurated a reopening of the claims by his recommendation that Congress should authorize a commission to fix the amounts, ownership, etc., of the private claims, notifying the British minister at Washington (Sir Edward Thornton) of the fact, and should give the United States Government power to prosecute these, as well as its own claim for general damages.

This declaration of the President made a profound impression on Great Britain. The Franco-American war was then in progress, and Great Britain was apprehensive that she might become involved in a European conflict. Therefore she was apprehensive that in event of this the United States would use the precedent of the *Alabama* and other cases to engage in privateering against British commerce. Accordingly, early in January, 1871, she sent to the United States Sir John Rose, an English banker, on a secret mission upon the matter. As a result of his prompt and adroit action, an understanding was reached between the two countries which resulted in a proposal, on January 26, from the British Government, presented by its minister at Washington, to reopen the settlement of the *fishery question and all other matters affecting the relations of the United States to British America* by establishing a *Joint High Commission* to meet at Washington.

Secretary Fish suggested to Minister Thornton that the *Alabama* claims should also be settled by this commission. Under instructions cabled by the Earl of Granville, British Secretary of Foreign Affairs, Minister Thornton accepted the suggestion. On February 22 the British commissioners arrived in this country, having been so hurried by their Government, it was said. that they came with hand luggage only, leaving their trunks to follow with their servants.

The British commissioners were Earl de Grey; Lord Ripon, President of the Queen's Counsel; Sir Stafford Northcote, late Secretary of the Exchequer; Minister Thornton; Sir John MacDonald, Canadian Premier; and Montague Bernard, Oxford Professor of International Law.

The American commissioners were Secretary Fish; Robert C. Schenck, who had just been appointed Minister to Great Britain; Samuel Nelson, Associate-Justice of the Supreme Court; E. Rockwood Hoar, late Attorney-General; and George H. Williams, late Senator from Oregon. The American commissioners were appointed by the President with confirmation by the Senate.

The Joint High Commission concluded the Treaty of Washington on May 8, 1871. By this the *Alabama* claims were to be adjusted by five arbitrators, one to be named by Queen Victoria, one by President Grant, one by the King of Italy, one by the President of Switzerland, and one by the Emperor of Brazil. The question was to be settled according to the principles of International Law as prevailing at the time, the British Government, to save its face, not conceding that it recognized these principles at the time the claims originated, when it had refused to admit the principles.

Other claims for damages between citizens of the two countries arising during the war were to be adjusted by a commission meeting in Washington; and the boundary dispute (San Juan) with Canada was to be referred to the Emperor of Germany.

On the Geneva Commission Great Britain appointed Sir Alexander Cockburn; the United States, Charles Francis Adams; Italy, Count Frederick Sclopis; Switzerland, Jacob Staempfli; Brazil, Baron d'Itajubà. The commission met in December, 1871, and sat until September 14, 1872, when it gave judgment that Great Britain should settle the claims in full by paying $15,500,000 in gold. Sir Alexander Cockburn was the only arbitrator who dissented from the award.

The American case before the arbitrators was prepared by J. C. Bancroft Davis and argued by William
M. Evarts, Caleb Cushing, and Morrison R. Waite. The
chief counsel for Great Britain was Sir Roundell Palmer.
The chief contention was over the American claims for

SETTLING THE ALABAMA CLAIMS

indirect damages (see preceding speech of Senator
Sumner). Several times dissolution of the commission
was threatened on this issue, and finally these claims
were disallowed.

The award was paid by Great Britain in 1872. On
June 23 of this year Congress created a Court of Claims
to distribute the award among the individual claimants.
This court rendered judgments aggregating $9,315,753.
A second and similar court was established on June
5, 1882. Much of the remainder of the award remains
undistributed. At various times it has been proposed,
but without result, to return the balance to Great
Britain.

The commission to adjust other war claims between

British and American citizens was constituted of three appointees by President Grant, Queen Victoria, and by these two appointees. It met at Washington on September 26, 1871, and after several adjournments made its final award at Newport, Rhode Island, on September 25, 1873. All American claims were rejected and British claims to the amount of $1,929,819 were allowed. This was subsequently paid.

In the Treaty of Washington an attempt was made to settle definitely the fishery dispute, by allowing citizens of the United States to take fish of any kind except shellfish, in all Canadian waters, and British subjects to do the same in all waters of the United States north of 39° north latitude. But as it was asserted by Great Britain that the privilege of fishing in American waters was worthless, the subject was referred to a commission, to be composed of one appointee from the United States, one from Great Britain, and a third to be named by the Emperor of Austria. The commission met in Halifax, Nova Scotia, on June 5, 1877. It awarded Great Britain $5,500,000 for the use of her fisheries for twelve years, the period of the treaty. The money was appropriated by Congress in 1878 with the proviso that the fishery articles in the Treaty of Washington "ought to be terminated at the earliest period consistent with the provisions of the treaty." The articles were therefore discontinued on July 1, 1885. In 1888 a new treaty was negotiated, but was rejected by the Senate. Not until 1910 was the vexatious fishery dispute finally settled. On June 1 of that year Great Britain and the United States submitted the question to the International Court of Arbitration at The Hague. The decision of the Court was announced on September 7. The Court decided:

1. Great Britain has the right to make regulations for the preservation of her fisheries without the consent of the United States.

2. Inhabitants of the United States have the right to employ as members of their fishing crews persons not inhabitants of the United States.

3. The requirement that American fishing vessels

report at Canadian custom-houses is not unreasonable. But American fishermen must not be subjected to light, harbor or other dues not imposed upon Canadian fishermen.

4. Americans are entitled to fish in the bays, creeks and harbors of the treaty coasts of Newfoundland and the Magdalen Islands.

The Canadian boundary dispute which was referred to the Emperor of Germany, who in turn referred it to experts, was settled purely on the legal construction of the treaty of June 15, 1846, and on geographical facts. The decision (rendered October 21, 1872) was in favor of the United States, which thereby acquired possession of the island of San Juan in Pacific waters. This was largely due to the fact that the American case was presented by George Bancroft, minister at Berlin, who had been minister to Great Britain when the treaty of 1846 was made, and was therefore thoroughly conversant with the subject. The decision was the last of the various boundary disputes which had been a source of irritation between the United States and Great Britain (including Canada) since the close of the Revolution.